Acknowledgments

This volume is published under the auspices of the Center of International Studies of Princeton University. The Center sponsored a two-year-long project on privatization and public sector reform culminating in this collection of studies.

The entire enterprise was made possible by the generosity of the J. Howard Pew Freedom Trust. The Pew Charitable Trusts perceived the importance of the study and supported it in all its phases.

The Mellon Foundation provided funds to Princeton University to bring visiting scholars and practitioners to Princeton to discuss the issues analyzed here. A seminar of these visitors and the contributors to this volume met regularly over the lifetime of the project and contributed directly to its success.

Finally, a special debt is owed to Jerri Kavanagh, who administered the project with efficiency and goodwill, and to Hangqiu Yang, who carried out much of the production of final drafts with unfailing energy and patience.

We wish to thank the Boeing Company for its support of the Center's work on privatization and for its contributions to Ezra Suleiman's and John Waterbury's research on public sector reform and privatization.

Henry Bienen
Director, The Center of International Studies
Princeton University

The Political Economy of
Public Sector Reform
and Privatization

The Political Economy of
Public Sector Reform
and Privatization

EDITED BY

Ezra N. Suleiman
and
John Waterbury

Westview Press
BOULDER • SAN FRANCISCO • OXFORD

RECEIVED

AUG 1 2 1991

Kennedy School
Library

Copyright © 1990 by Westview Press, Inc.

Published in 1990 in the United States of America by Westview Press, Inc., 5500 Central Avenue, Boulder, Colorado 80301, and in the United Kingdom by Westview Press, 36 Lonsdale Road, Summertown, Oxford OX2 7EW

Library of Congress Cataloging-in-Publication Data
The political economy of public sector reform and privatization / edited
    by Ezra N. Suleiman and John Waterbury.
        p.   cm.
ISBN 0-8133-7996-2
    1. Government ownership.   2. Government business enterprises—Case
studies.   3. Privatization.   4. Privatization—Case studies.
I. Suleiman, Ezra N., 1941–   .   II. Waterbury, John.
HD3850.P62   1990
338.9—dc20   90-44537
                                                                                          CIP

Printed and bound in the United States of America

The paper used in this publication meets the requirements
of the American National Standard for Permanence of Paper
for Printed Library Materials Z39.48-1984.

10   9   8   7   6   5   4   3   2   1

Contents

Note on Contributors

DAVID BACHMAN is Assistant Professor of Politics at Princeton University. He is the author of *Chen Yun and the Chinese Political System* (1985) and *To Leap Forward: Bureaucracy, Economy and Leadership in China, 1956–1957* (forthcoming 1991); and co-editor and co-translator of *Yan Jiaqi and China's Struggle for Democracy* (forthcoming, 1991). His essays have appeared in *World Politics, Pacific Affairs, Asian Survey,* and other journals and edited collections.

NANCY BERMEO is Associate Professor of Politics at Princeton University. She writes on Iberian and Greek politics and is the author of *The Revolution Within the Revolution: Workers' Control in Rural Portugal* (1986). Her current research focuses on the causes and consequences of regime change in Southern Europe and Latin America.

KENT E. CALDER is currently Associate Professor of Politics and International Affairs at the Woodrow Wilson School of Public and International Affairs, Princeton University, and Director of Princeton's Program on U.S.-Japan Relations. He is the author of *Crisis and Compensation: Public Policy and Political Stability in Japan* (1988), and co-author of *The Eastasia Edge* (1982).

FORREST D. COLBURN is Assistant Professor of Politics at Princeton University. He is the author of *Post-Revolutionary Nicaragua: State, Class, and the Dilemmas of Agrarian Policy* and *Managing the Commanding Heights: Nicaragua's State Enterprises,* and he is the editor of *Everyday Forms of Peasant Resistance.* His articles have appeared in *World Politics, Comparative Politics,* and *Latin American Research Review.* He is currently writing a book on revolutions.

JEFFREY HERBST is Assistant Professor of Politics and International Affairs at Princeton University's Woodrow Wilson School. He is the author of *State Politics in Zimbabwe* (1990) and several articles on political change and political economy in Africa. For 1989–1990, he has received a Robert S. McNamara Fellowship from the World Bank to study structural adjustment in Ghana.

G. JOHN IKENBERRY is Assistant Professor of Politics and International Affairs at Princeton University. He is the author of *Reasons of State: Oil Politics and the Capacities of American Government*, co-author of *The State* (with John A. Hall) and co-editor of *The State and American Foreign Policy*. His articles have appeared in *International Organization, World Politics, International Studies Quarterly, Comparative Politics*, and *Political Science Quarterly*. He is currently writing a book about the spread of policy ideas in the international system.

ATUL KOHLI is Associate Professor of Politics and International Affairs at Princeton University. He is the author of *The State and Poverty in India: The Politics of Reform* and *Democracy and Disorder: India's Growing Crisis of Governability*.

PETER M. LEWIS is a doctoral candidate in the Department of Politics at Princeton University and an Instructor at James Madison College at Michigan State University.

BEN ROSS SCHNEIDER is Assistant Professor of Politics at Princeton University. He has published several articles on the process of political transition and economic reform in Brazil and Mexico, and is currently completing a manuscript on bureaucratic elites and industrial policy in authoritarian Brazil.

CARL SHAPIRO is Professor of Economics and Business Administration at the University of California at Berkeley. He has published articles on consumer protection and product quality, the economics of innovation, product standardization and compatibility, antitrust and oligopoly theory, and business strategy. His publications include "Premiums for High Quality Products as Returns to Reputation" (1983) "Equilibrium Unemployment as a Worker Discipline Device" (with Joseph E. Stiglitz, 1984), "Network Externalities, Competition and Compatibility" (with Michael L. Katz, 1985), "Theories of Oligopoly Behavior" (1989), and "Horizontal Mergers: An Equilibrium Analysis" (with Joseph Farrell, 1990).

PAUL E. SIGMUND is Professor of Politics and former Director of the Program in Latin American Studies at Princeton University. He is the author of fourteen books on political theory and Latin American politics, including *The Overthrow of Allende and the Politics of Chile, 1964–1976* (1977); *Multinationals in Latin America: The Politics of Nationalization* (1980); and *Liberation Theology at the Crossroads: Democracy or Revolution?* (1990).

PAUL STARR is Professor of Sociology, Princeton University, and founder and co-editor of *The American Prospect*, a new public policy journal. He is the author of *The Social Transformation of American Medicine* (winner of the Pulitzer Prize for Nonfiction and the Bancroft Prize in American History). Among his other books are *The Discarded Army* and *The Politics of Numbers* (co-edited with William Alonso).

EZRA N. SULEIMAN is IBM Professor of International Studies and Director of the Council on Regional Studies at Princeton University. He is the author of *Politics, Power and Bureaucracy in France* (1974), *Elites in French Society* (1978), and *Private Power and Centralization in France* (1988).

ROBERT L. TIGNOR is Professor of History at Princeton University and the author of many works on modern Egypt and Kenya, including *Modernization and British Colonial Rule in Egypt, 1882–1914* (1966), *The Colonial Transformation of Kenya* (1976), and *State, Private Enterprise and Economic Change in Egypt, 1918–1952* (1984).

JOHN WATERBURY is William Stewart Tod Professor of Politics and International Affairs at the Woodrow Wilson School of Public and International Affairs, Princeton University. A specialist in the political economy of the contemporary Middle East, he is author of *The Egypt of Nasser and Sadat* and co-author (with Alan Richards) of *The Political Economy of the Middle East*. He is currently at work on a comparative study of public enterprise in Egypt, India, Turkey, and Mexico.

ROBERT D. WILLIG is Professor of Economics and Public Affairs at Princeton University and author of *Welfare Analysis of Policies Affecting Prices and Products* and *Theory of Industry Structure* (with W. Baumol and J. Panzar), and co-editor of *The Handbook of Industrial Organization*. He has written numerous articles, including "Consumer's Surplus Without Apology" and "Free Entry and the Sustainability of Natural Monopoly."

PART ONE

General Context

1

Introduction:
Analyzing Privatization in
Industrial and Developing Countries

Ezra N. Suleiman and John Waterbury

Public sector reform and privatization are public policy issues that are always embedded in other issues pertaining to structural adjustment, degrees of state economic intervention, and the regulation of markets. They are organically linked to the quintessentially political issues of public resource allocation, the provision of collective goods, and the distribution of wealth in society. It is an artificial exercise to separate out these issues, especially privatization, from the larger policy context. Public sector reform and privatization never take place in isolation from broader efforts at macro-economic and political adjustment.

This collection of essays seeks to probe and explicate these interlinkages, both through case studies and through more general conceptual analyses. Our evidence is drawn from experiences that, in terms of process, range from the restructuring of public sectors, to initiatives to deregulate markets, to the sale or transfer of publicly owned assets to private interests. In some instances all three processes have been pursued. What cuts across the variables of policy priorities and processes is the level of development of specific countries. The collection contains a good mix of cases in that respect, and here we shall suggest some of the ways in which levels of development shape reform and privatization.

At the heart of the changes under scrutiny is a concern for economic efficiency. At a minimum, states throughout the world are trying to promote greater degrees of market allocation through deregulation and decontrol while evaluating the performance of public assets more on the

1

basis of economic returns than has been the case heretofore. For some—
Chile and Britain, for example—the commitment to such change has been
nearly religious (Sigmund and Suleiman in this volume); for others, it has
been a matter of expediency (Wilson 1988: 28). In both developed and
developing countries (LDCs) these reforms have been part of structural
adjustment efforts to promote switching of factors of production from the
nontraded to the traded sector and to reduce public outlays and commitments to public welfare.

The process is by nature painful and politically dangerous. It is begun
and sustained in response to crisis: outsized public deficits, high inflation,
deteriorating trade balances, the inability to meet external debt obligations, and ultimatums from public and private creditors. In some developing countries *all* of these elements of crisis are present simultaneously. In
taxonomic form, one can list the policy variables that are likely to shape
the processes of public sector reform and privatization in any country.
Macroeconomic responses include defict reduction, revenue generation, and
increased allocational efficiency. *Responses to external pressures* will involve debt servicing and the maintenance of credit flows and foreign investment flows. *Political responses* may focus on efforts to generate electoral support through popular capitalism, reconstitute political coalitions
and clineteles, undermine organized labor, and unburden the state of
major responsibility for social welfare and equity. It is the task of empirical investigation to attribute weights to *each of these variables* in a given
situation.

But lists are of little use if dynamic interrelationships cannot be specified. There is, however, precious little consensus among economists and
political scientists as to what drives what. For example, there are five important analytic questions upon which we hope to shed some light. First,
does property in the juridical sense (that is, public versus private ownership) make much difference in how the assets perform, or is the structure
of market competition the crucial variable? Second, is there a kind of
structural logic to the expansion and contraction of public sectors, or does
ideology have a significant, independent impact on the process? Third,
do the origins and ages of public sectors shape the way in which they
are restructured or liquidated? Fourth, is the reform process driven essentially in response to domestic considerations, by pressure from creditors, or by international example? Finally, once under way, are market-
promoting policies irreversible?

We do not pretend to have definitive answers to these questions, and in
some instances we have contradictory evidence and conclusions. Indeed,
these questions are particularly important precisely because there is so
much variance across the cases we examine.

Reducing the State and Encouraging the Market

The 1980s will no doubt come to be associated with the selling by states of public assets, much as the 1970s has come to be associated with the impact of the petrol shocks caused by the OPEC cartel. "The movement toward privatization is international, just as the movement toward *état-isme* was international after the War," notes Edouard Balladur (1987: 64), the French minister of finance responsible for the privatization of French industries and financial institutions. As *The Economist* noted much earlier than 1987, "Everybody's doing it" (Dec. 25, 1987, p. 71). According to an estimate by the investment bank Salomon Brothers, between 1980 and mid-1987, fifty-five enterprises had been privatized worldwide, raising proceeds of $48 billion, while two thousand more enterprises, with an approximate value of $130 billion, had been designated for privatization by 1990 (*Financial Times*, Sept. 16, 1987).

Any popular movement with an international sweep is justified not by its international character but by reference to national exigencies. After all, countries often respond differently when confronted with the same economic crisis. Yet, the voyages of ideas and ideologies across countries lead to demonstration effects. This is a little-studied phenomenon but one that needs greater attention in view of the fact that the internationalization of economies has restricted the choices that political parties in democratic societies can adopt. A measure adopted elsewhere can be imported more easily because it arrives wrapped in a certain legitimacy. It also helps the innovative image of a particular party in search of "new" solutions. That the French center-right government that put into effect the privatization program was heavily influenced by the perceived success of President Ronald Reagan's attempt to curtail the role of the U.S. federal government and by Prime Minister Margaret Thatcher's privatization program cannot be doubted. There is, in other words, what John Ikenberry refers to as a "policy bandwagoning" (Ikenberry, this volume).

Reform and privatization measures are rarely justified on economic grounds alone; indeed, the reasons that drive the process are always explicitly political (for example, the reduction of trade union power, political and social stability through widespread shareholding) but rarely overtly avowed. It is clear that motivations vary among societies and that, consequently, no single factor determines the sale of assets by the state. In general, however, governments may seek to restructure the public sector or to privatize for a variety of reasons that we can summarize as follows. (1) The growing size of the public sector is judged to have reached an excessive level that leads only to inefficiency. (2) Privatized companies will be better managed and better financed through the capital markets than through the state budget. (3) Privatization contributes to the development of financial markets and hence can finance new and growing enterprises. It leads to increased availability of funds for industry. (4) Privatization leads to a substantial increase in the state's revenue from the sales of equity. (5) Increase in the state's revenue can lead to the lowering of taxes and to the use of the available funds for specific political purposes. (6) Privatization can promote broad-based sharing-holding in society and so be a bulwark against social disorder. (7) The state in the "new participatory capitalist system" may help to detach workers from trade unions; and a weakened trade union movement may help dampen demand, increase investment, and facilitate adjustment.

The grounds on which public sector reform and privatization policy are implemented are always economic, whether they involve something as specific as reducing a state's budget deficit or whether they rely on the belief that the policy will make enterprises more efficient. But they can have consequences that may be unintended or reveal advantages that were not foreseen. Hence, it is necessary to separate the factors that give the original impetus to these policies from those that lead to their continuation, or even acceleration.

An important leitmotif of the essays in this volume is the belief that the breadth of the phenomenon reveals that we are witnessing a fundamental shift in industrial and financial ownership and in the management of economies. Although the process in a specific context may be slowed down as a result of a government change, by and large it represents a reaction to an earlier trend that is judged to have long since passed its heyday. Just as the welfare state represented an "international policy culture," so too does privatization today represent such a "culture." By the same token, just as several policies associated with the welfare state have fallen from favor, so too may the drive to reduce the size and extent of state assets. It may be that in advanced industrial economies the market-reinforcing momentum cannot be reversed (see Calder in this volume), but we anticipate that in the LDCs reassertions of state intervention are well within the realm of possibility. The experience of Japan in the first half of this century, Turkey after 1960, and Chile in 1983 provide good examples of the conditions under which cyclical movements of state expansion and contraction may take place.

Public Sector Reform and Privatization in Industrial Economies

The move toward privatization—the transfer of assets from public to private ownership—is important because it substantially alters the means by which the state intervenes in the economy. It should be noted that we see deregulation and trade liberalization as complementary to but distinct from privatization. In the advanced industrial countries, privatization has not come about as a result of the need for structural adjustment. Nor has it come about because of external pressures (for example, from the International Monetary Fund). Nor, finally, is it a result of purely domestic forces and pressures. All of these factors played a role and were strengthened by what had become an international "phenomenon."

In a number of LDCs, as several of the essays in this volume show, privatization virtually became a policy of last resort; that is, it was imposed on countries whose deficits and debts had grown beyond control and could not be reversed by a continuation of the policy of state ownership. But alongside the beleaguered states of Africa and countries such as Peru, Egypt, and Turkey, a number of developing countries have undertaken extensive market-supporting reforms in the absence of significant external arm-twisting: India and Algeria are significant cases in point. Even in those LDCs where direct donor and creditor pressure has been most obvious (Egypt, Tanzania, Mexico, and others), there is good evidence of an internal recognition among policymakers and technocrats that the state has been neither a good planner nor a good manager of the economy.

In the advanced industrial countries, the policy of privatization has been guided much more by social and political considerations and has been legitimized by economic considerations. In both sets of countries, advanced and developing, the policy of privatization was part and parcel of the reform of the public sector. In both sets, in fact, there was frequently a sequence of reforms, first focused on improving public sector performance (one thinks of the experiments begun in France in the mid-1960s to draw up detailed contracts between ministries and subsidiary public enterprises), and then, sometimes out of frustration, moving on to the liquidation or sale of publicly owned assets. In either case, the reforms have been designed to bring about a fundamental transformation of state economic activity.

It is probable that a new consensus has been formed on the need to reduce the role of the state in the economy of industrial countries. But there is no consensus on how much this role should be reduced or on the likely outcomes of this reduction. Policymakers know little about how the policy of privatization affects people's attitudes, what they judge to be acceptable changes, what the consequences are for a firm's profitability or for its capacity to compete internationally. In the social sphere—mostly where mentalities and attitudes of employees are concerned—the Left and the Right have vastly different hopes and considerations.

In the economic sphere, the question of efficiency remains open, since there is no definitive proof that publicly owned firms are, by definition, less competitive and less efficient than those privately owned. The debate here is of great theoretical and empirical importance. What is referred to as the property rights school argues that ownership matters greatly for the performance of the firm and that privately owned assets used to maximize financial returns to their owners are, all things otherwise equal, more economically efficient than those publicly owned. Steve Hanke puts the case succinctly:

> The consequences of public ownership are thus predictable. Public managers and employees allocate resources (assets) that do not belong to them. Hence they do not bear the costs of their decisions; nor do they gain from efficient behavior. Since the nominal owners of public enterprise, the taxpayers, do not have strong incentives to monitor the performance of public employees, the costs of shirking are relatively low. Public employees therefore commonly seek job-related perquisites which increase production costs and divert attention from serving consumer demands. (1987: 49)

Other economists would counter that the structure of markets and the structure of ownership are far more important than the legal designation of the property. Sappington and Stiglitz (1987) point out that the risks of ownership may be as widely diffused among shareholders as among taxpayers, with as little incentive for any shareholder to monitor the performance of the firm. Moreover, in large private corporations, the separation of management and ownership may attenuate the concern managers have for productivity and profits. Finally, if firms, whether public or private, enjoy monopolistic or oligopolistic market positions, the legal form of ownership will probably have little to do with the performance of the enterprise.[1]

We make only two observations on this issue. First, although in theory public enterprises can and sometimes do operate as efficiently as private enterprises, empirically such performance is rare. Second, taxpayers and shareholders are not even remotely alike. Taxpayers are given no legal choice in the amount of risk they must bear, nor can they divest themselves of that risk. Shareholders can choose to invest or not and to sell or shift holdings. If enough do so, the affected enterprise will receive a very direct and compelling signal that should lead to altered performance. By contrast, where the government is the shareholder, it is stuck with its investment. In important ways, to sell or liquidate its shares is an avowal of its own poor judgment some time in the past, and such avowals are both embarrassing and politically costly. It may require a new government or even a new regime to reform and divest.

If, as we have argued, the search for greater economic efficiency is common to virtually all reform and privatization experience, then the question of the impact of legal ownership upon economic performance becomes far more than academic. Elf-Aquitaine, the French oil company, and the Renault automobile company have operated within markets, both domestic and international, that are extremely competitive. On the other hand, privatized companies (such as British Telecom and British Gas) are able to operate in a monopolistic context. In Britain, public oligopolies were transferred to the private sphere. By contrast, in the People's Republic of China there has been no legal change in the ownership of productive assets, but the unit of management, such as the family in rural production, has been changed, as has the structure of market incentives (see Bachman in this volume). The publicly owned hotel sector in Egypt has been put out to private interests on long-term leases with the goal of enhanced economic performance, while Spain has sold some public enterprises to foreign corporate interests. In nearly all instances, the process of reform and privatization is too recent to yield firm answers as to what strategies work, but the mix of approaches to the redefinition of state economic activity is so great that we should in the not-too-distant future have the empirical evidence we need.

Policymakers do not always heed what passes for objective fact, but they do learn. We find time and again in our case studies that ideological preferences do count in initiating a process of state expansion, as well as in curtailing it. Nehru, Nasser, Papandreou, and Mitterand all had ideological justifications for nationalizations, just as Thatcher, Pinochet, Jayawardene, and Chirac had ideological grounds for the opposite. Leaders and policymakers monitor the performance of what they create, and they respond to, as well as shape, public opinion. In many instances the reduction of state economic activity is the result of observed poor performance and of palpable public disillusionment with state intervention.

In France, the Socialists embarked on a massive program of nationalization of banks and major industries after they came to power in 1981. The Spanish Socialists refused to follow this course in the early 1980s, believing that to burden the state in an open economy was the wrong course. Instead, they came to adopt a privatization policy. When the French Socialists returned to power in 1988, they neither reverted to nationalization nor extended the privatization program begun under their predecessors.

In view of the differences that distinguish the origins of the policy of reform and privatization from the process itself, we need to understand the factors that have made this policy sufficiently common to the advanced industrial countries. These factors, which can be grouped into negative (a reaction to a prevailing state of affairs) and positive (an expectation of likely outcomes) categories, can also allow us to differentiate the process in the advanced industrial countries from that in the LDCs.

The Question of the Welfare State

Chief among the "negative" factors that inspired the process in the advanced industrial countries was a reaction to the social and economic role of the state, a phenomenon that is often (wrongly) referred to as the "welfare state." From the end of the World War II to the late 1970s, the commitment of industrial societies to the welfare state was not questioned. Along with the consensus concerning the welfare state went a commitment to the direct intervention of the state in the economy. Intervention took different forms and followed standard phases, the successes of which were widely accepted: "indicative" planning, industrial policies, public ownership of industrial and credit institutions, support and subventions of small and medium-sized firms as well as internationally competitive ones. The state saw itself as responsible for increasing social programs and for guiding the economy. The increase in the state's role in the economy in Western and Southern European countries was not tied to a particular regime. The essays in this volume show clearly that conservative as well as socialist governments (in France, Britain, Greece, Spain, Portugal, and Japan) were equally committed to increasing the state's guiding role in the economy and to restraining the forces of markets.

The reasons for the consensus that obtained across the industrial countries on the substitution of the state for the market resulted from a mixture of socialist ideology and from economic and social conditions predating and buttressed by the experience of World War II. The fear of private monopolies and trusts, the search for profits that would leave socially necessary sectors unattended, the need for long-term investments and the ability to forgo profits in the short-run, the protection of industries judged to be of national importance, the need to assure social and political stability and hence to assume full employment and protect workers' economic conditions and rights—all these factors contributed to strengthening the role of the state and to enlarging the public sector, developments that went unquestioned in the industrial countries until the end of the 1970s.

The growth in the public sector in advanced industrial societies, measured by public employment and by the proportion of the state's share of the gross domestic product (GDP), continued to climb uninterruptedly after World War II (Rose 1988). Gradually, starting in the late 1970s, the critics of the welfare state started to be heard. Government came to be seen as "overloaded" and as ultimately unable to meet its commitments. The state was, many argued, in danger of "delegitimation." In most analyses, the state's role in the economy was confused with that of the welfare state. Consequently, it was the welfare state in its totality that came under attack. As Anthony King noted, people who attack, or defend, the welfare state are apt to "lump together under the heading 'welfare state' just about everything that modern governments do in every field of domestic policy" (1983: 11). This is both an analytic and an empirical error:

> Bismarck, Lloyd George and others were right, Herbert Hoover and those who agreed with him were wrong. The welfare state has contributed to require stability and to stemming the advance of extreme left-wing political parties. . . . The welfare state, in the sense of the maintenance by governments of certain minimum standards of well-being, has been, and is likely to continue to be, a bulwark of political stability. If it did not exist, political conservatives would have to invent it. (King 1983: 22)

In the 1980s, European countries have distinguished between the welfare state and the state's role in the economy. In October 1988, for example, the French parliament approved a law (known as the *revenu minimum d'insertion*, or RMI) guaranteeing a minimum income, in other words, a floor beyond which no citizen can fall. No party voted against it. Unlike the United States, European countries have been much more careful about cutting social programs as part of their deficit-reduction aims.

The welfare state is not in danger in any country in Western Europe, and only in Thatcher's Britain have aspects of it been questioned. Nonetheless, the spectacular development of the welfare state and the increased burden it placed on the state's financial capacity led in the end to the questioning of state's role in the economy. The "overloading" and "overburdening" of the state's resources, described by Rose and Peters (1978), led ultimately to a questioning of the consensus on the proper role of the state in society.

It was not just the *expansion* in the responsibilities of the government that led to fissures in the postwar consensus. This expansion posed few problems when it was accompanied, as was the case from 1950 to the mid-1970s, by rapid economic growth. But once the rate of economic growth slowed considerably, states could not meet their obligations from existing revenues and began funding large deficits. The petrol shocks of the 1970s not only made clear the vulnerability of the industrial countries but also put into question the level of burdens that the state should assume in the industrialized nations.

What occurred in the industrial countries in the mid-1970s was "ideological exhaustion" (Rose 1988: 10), a disenchantment with the consensus and the policies that this consensus inspired. It was time to replace the heavy hand of the state—which, to be sure, had served so well in rehabilitating the postwar devastated economies—with something else.[2]

The Role of Public Enterprises

Disenchantment with the welfare state and the slump in the economies of the industrial countries following the petrol shock led to the questioning of the role of the state in the managing of economies. This attack, not surprisingly, focused on the role of public enterprises, since these represented the clearest manifestation of the operation of nonmarket forces in the economy. As Rose notes,

> In broad terms, *privatization* is the process of increasing the scope of the market—that is, the private actions of producers and consumers—in the production and allocation of good and services. Its opposite is *nationalization*, increasing the scope of government directly or through state-owned corporations producing and allocating goods and services. Privatization is consistent with a liberal political and economic philosophy. Nationalization can reflect a legacy of mercantilist and *dirigiste* values, and also socialist influences. (1988: 3)

Nationalization may indeed reflect socialist values. Clause 4 of the constitution of the British Labor Party calls for the public ownership of the means of production. The French Socialist party also called for nationalization, which "is first of all a made collective ownership, that is, the national collectivity becoming the owner of a number of the means of production and exchange which it transforms into public services" (Dunois 1936: 27). Nonetheless, nationalization as a policy has transcended leftist parties, so that the strengthening of the role of the state in the economy has also been carried out by nonleftist or antileftist parties. De Gaulle was responsible for a major nationalization program after World War II. In Spain, Franco created the major public enterprises. As Nancy Bermeo explains in her essay, one of the reasons that Spain's socialists have undertaken a privatization program under Felipe Gonzales is that the creation of the large public sector was associated with the Franco regime. Similarly, in Japan, as Kent Calder shows, the Meiji era (1868–1880) was responsible for the creation of a number of public enterprises.

It was not difficult to make public enterprises the scapegoats for the economic ills confronting the industrial countries in the mid-1970s. They accounted for a sizable proportion of public employment, and many came to constitute a severe drain on the budget. A number of public enterprises were able to function only with massive injections of subsidies from the state budget. These enterprises came to be regarded as the symbols of the postwar control of the economy by the state. They represented the substitution of the state for the market. Hence, they came to be considered as the prime example of inefficiency. The most radical—and logical—means of reforming the public sector was to make it less public, that is, transfer assets and control to private ownership. As one analyst of the British privatization experience has observed:

> The original impetus for privatization came from a desire to discipline the nationalized industries by subjecting them to market forces. This in turn derived from a realization that the administrative methods of controlling and monitoring the performance of the nationalized industries had largely failed and in its existing institutional form would continue to do so. What was missing was the fear of bankruptcy, and the constant political interference by government ministers in the management of state enterprises had undermined their ability to operate effectively and efficiently. (Veljanovski 1987: 8)

Overregulated Societies

Together with attacks on the welfare state and its inefficiency went an attack on the methods by which the state sought to regulate the economy even when it did not own assets outright. This situation was taken as an example of the pervasive means by which the market was not permitted to express itself.

We noted above that insufficient distinctions were drawn between the welfare functions of the state and the substitution of the state for market mechanisms in the economy. Similarly, "rolling the state back" came to mean both a withdrawal of the state from the economy (through the sale of its assets) and a withdrawal from those areas it did not own through deregulation. Criticisms of the regulatory and control mechanisms of the state were common to all the industrial societies, especially those that had highly developed welfare functions and a well-developed *dirigiste* tradition.

Again, ideological precepts may not always lend themselves to logical, concrete mechanisms. Just as privatization does not necessarily lead to competition, so it does not necessarily reduce regulation. In fact, the recent experience of privatization suggests that the opposite may be closer to reality. The greater the degree of privatization, the more the need for regulation of one form or another (Shapiro and Willig in this volume).

When the state sells its assets, it does not abandon its regulatory or arbitrator function. It comes to have an even greater responsibility for establishing the rules of the game, for ensuring that the rules are obeyed, and for sanctioning transgressions of the rules. It may be necessary to regulate in order to ensure competition. The privatization of British Telecom and British Gas necessitated the creation of two regulatory agencies. The enlarged activity of the Paris *bourse* led to abuses for which the existing controlling mechanism (the Commission des Opérations de Bourse, or C.O.B, the equivalent of the Securities and Exchange Commission) proved vastly inadequate. Hence, a much stronger policing mechanism is now being set up. Although these inconsistencies have become evident after a short experience with privatization, it nonetheless remains the case that deregulating societies and economies was an original impetus to the privatization process.

Privatization is not merely "antinationalization." It also has an avowed social objective: the expansion of what has come to be called popular capitalism through the spread of shareholding by workers, either in their own enterprises or in other privatized firms. There is no doubt that stock ownership has increased considerably in those societies (Portugal, France, and Britain, but also in other industrial societies) where public enterprises have been privatized and where particular incentives for share ownership were made available.

Popular capitalism refers to the spread of ownership of the means of production, as opposed to the concentration of ownership in a few hands, which leaves workers with ownership of their own labor only. Capitalism of the popular type aims to break down the traditional barriers that put workers and owners in opposition in the past. Since the ownership of enterprises by the state made everyone (and hence no one) an owner, popular capitalism is intended to give tangible forms of ownership (even if this represents only a couple of shares) to workers.

Is popular capitalism a reason for privatizing? It is generally regarded as an impetus for privatization, though it may in fact be a consequence of this process. In other words, the original push for privatization scarcely included the development of popular capitalism as an objective. Yet, once the process got under way, popular capitalism tended to become an objective in its own right. This is certainly what occurred in Britain and in France. It is interesting to note that in some LDCs, where capital markets are extremely thin and there is fear that foreign multinationals may be the only available purchasers of public equity, employee stock option programs (ESOPs) are being advocated as a kind of "third way" to privatization.

It is too early to assess the consequences of privatization for popular capitalism. Can such a thing develop? Does the ownership of a few shares actually serve to inspire loyalty to an enterprise, let alone a political party, on the part of a worker? How long does the worker have to hold these few shares in order to justify his loyalty? Might not these shares be looked upon in the way most investments are, namely, with an eye to realizing a profit?

Political Objectives

What are the political objectives of reform and privatization, and how can one decipher them? The objective of popular capitalism represents the political objective of reducing trade union power. In Japan, privatization was made possible because of the declining power of trade unions, whereas in Britain and France it was intended to lead to the decline of union power.

The importance of trade unions in the advanced industrial countries, particularly public sector unions and particularly in the 1960s and 1970s, gave rise to the belief that the state had nurtured and encouraged a force that was destroying the competitive position of the country. Although the level of unionization has declined sharply in all industrial countries in the 1980s, the preceding postwar decades saw the labor movement in a strong position vis-à-vis the state.

This was particularly the case where unions were well organized, as in Britain. The reduction of trade union power was a major goal of Margaret Thatcher upon coming to power (Jenkins 1988). At first, standing tough on labor disputes and a number of legislative changes were tried. As the privatization process got under way it was realized that trade union power might also be effectively reduced done through giving workers a share in their enterprises. This explains why the goal of popular capitalism became more important as the privatization program advanced in Britain (Vickers and Yarrow 1988). This goal also assumed greater importance in France as the privatization program picked up speed. It is too early to assess the social impact of privatization in the industrial countries, but it is unlikely that trade union power will depend solely on whether enterprises are private or public.

International Influences

In none of the industrial countries was there a large, powerful, identifiable group that sought the privatization of public enterprises. In Britain, France, Spain, Japan, and Portugal, the idea of privatization was launched by a political party, and it subsequently acquired supporters. As noted earlier, it was in part the international spread of the "culture of privatization" that made it an acceptable idea even in countries with strong *dirigiste* traditions.

Similarly, in countries with mass social democratic or labor parties one looks in vain for a program that seeks to counter the liberalization of the economy. Criticism and opposition to the policy have centered, rather, on the mechanisms and process of privatization: the price at which the government sold public assets, the privileging of certain investors by giving them a large share of the privatized companies, the haphazard nature of the choice of companies privatized. None of these criticisms have led to a program that seeks to reverse what is now considered an international trend.

Structural Adjustment and Privatization in the LDCs

Dividing nations into two pools, the advanced industrial and the developing, as we have done here is a heuristic simplification. There is as much or more diversity among the structures of developing countries as there is between those of advanced industrial and developing nations. By and large, the major differences in the reform process between the two sets of countries are political more than economic. In many instances the legitimacy of the regime and the system in which it functions are not well established, the rules of the political game are poorly understood, and the writ of the government is frequently challenged. The governmental and political mechanisms for mobilizing support for and implementing reform programs may be relatively untried.

The long-term economic goal may be to promote economic efficiency, but the short-term impetus toward reform in LDCs is deficit reduction, and it is often undertaken under duress. This does not mean that solutions are imposed by external agents, although in some instances that may be the case; rather, they are a result of external pressure and internal assessment of economic realities. However the *prise de conscience* comes about, it usually arrives in an atmosphere of intense crisis. More so than in the developed countries, leaders are aware of the magnitude of immediate costs rather than of the long-term benefits.

Deficit Reduction

Over the decade 1975–1985, central government deficits of both developing and advanced industrial nations varied within a range of 3 to 5.6 percent of GDP. According to Calder (in this volume), Japan's privatization program was spurred by a rise in the deficit to 6.1 percent of GNP in 1979. Only toward the end of the period, when the U.S. deficit was significantly reduced, did developing country deficits exceed those of the industrialized nations (*IMF Survey*, Jan. 25, 1988). The overall deficits of public sector enterprises are much higher in the LDCs, however, some 4 percent of GDP in the late 1970s, than in the industrialized nations, where they averaged 1.7 percent and were declining (Floyd et al. 1984: 144–145).[3]

The LDCs also typically have large external debts relative to GDP, with heavy servicing requirements. It is crucial that they maintain their creditworthiness and access to external capital. Budget deficit reduction may be the quickest and most direct route to improving public finances and reducing inflation. Inflation reduction will protect efforts to expand exports through currency devaluation, and export expansion may be the measure of international creditworthiness. Peru under Alain Garcia failed this test, while Turkey under Turgut Özal has so far passed it. Public enterprise deficits thus take on a peculiar significance in the adjustment process in the LDCs, and they can be tackled either by improving public enterprise performance or through liquidation and privatization.

The relative size of the middle-income strata varies significantly between the advanced industrial and the developing economies. The narrowness of these strata in most LDCs makes difficult privatization based on the small shareholder and popular capitalism. The same narrowness contributes to the "thinness" of capital markets in LDCs. There is also a preference among established entrepreneurs to raise their capital through banks rather than through the sale of equity. Large conglomerates are reluctant to undergo the financial disclosure that issuing shares on the national exchange would require.[4] With the partial exceptions of India, Brazil, Mexico, and the newly industrializing countries (NICs) of East Asia, privatization in the LDCs may entail forfeit sales to a combination of indigenous oligopolists and foreign multinationals.

Coalitions

The "Keynesian entente" that prevailed in many developed countries until the oil shocks of the 1970s, took the form of explicit or implicit social pacts in many LDCs. In particular, under various strategies of import-substituting industrialization, civil servants, top-level management, organized labor, the military, and public and private sector industrialists constituted the basic coalitions upon which many regimes relied. Policies of liberalization, devaluation, lowered producer and consumer subsidies, deregulation, public sector reform, and privatization threaten all or significant parts of such coalitions. Pacts among urban wage earners, organized labor, and public sector enterprise, on the one hand, and the government, on the other, were broken or put at risk.

There is one school of thought that argues that neither the reforms nor the consequent remaking of dominant coalitions can be carried out in a democratic framework. Rajiv Gandhi's erratic pursuit of economic liberalization in India would seem to confirm this view (Kohli in this volume). Yet Spain, Sri Lanka, Jamaica, and Venezuela appear to offer evidence that reform can be democratically administered.

The issue may be as much one of regime continuity and discontinuity as of democracy and authoritarianism. Even military authoritarians build coalitions with vested interests in the status quo, and there is considerable political peril for them in tampering with existing arrangements. By contrast, new governments, and above all new regimes, whether elected or not, will probably have a strong incentive to undo the economic arrangements that helped to sustain the previous government or regime. Thus, as noted above, Felipe Gonzalez began to demolish Franco's statist edifice, as did Corazon Aquino that of Ferdinand Marcos, while the military undertook the housecleaning in Turkey after 1980. The unusual cases are those in which there is no break in continuity and incumbent leaders begin to promote reforms that damage their own coalitions. Rajiv Gandhi tried but did not go very far; Chedli BenJadid of Algeria has gone quite far and reaped massive rioting in the country's main cities in the fall of 1988; Carlos Salinas of Mexico, in the wake of a partial electoral setback, has given signs of shaking the old coalition of the Partido Revolucionario Institucionál to its foundations. Husni Mubarrak of Egypt, by contrast to the above, has, like his predecessor Anwar Sadat, remained faithful to a coalition that took shape in the mid-1960s.

Unburdening the State of the Social Agenda

The state in many developing countries took upon itself the charge of providing basic health, education, and shelter for its citizens and of redistributing income in a more equitable fashion. Frequently public sector enterprise was called upon to shoulder this charge by providing employment, setting wage levels, promoting the development of backward regions, selling goods and services below market prices, and financing a certain amount of infrastructural development out of enterprise budgets. As long as growth was steady and inflation manageable, this charge could be paid for through deficit financing and foreign borrowing. In the late 1970s, however, as in the advanced industrial economies, developing countries had to shift to policies of financial retrenchment and eventually of structural adjustment.

At that point it became a liability to have the state as the focal point of all distributional issues, and policymakers came to see the advantages of allowing some of those issues (for example, wage levels or levels of employment) to be solved through the market rather than through the political process (Schneider in this volume). In some ways privatization and private sector encouragement can be seen as an attempt by state leaders to force the private sector to absorb some of the costs of welfare provision. Some worsening of income distribution seems an inherent part of the adjustment process; and as the private sector is given new economic opportunities, it is also obliged to share with the state the blame for worsening conditions.

Who Wants Privatization and Public Sector Reform?

The groups that are prepared to support public sector reform and privatization from the outset are small and narrowly based. They must include the top leadership in the country and the senior technocrats in the central bank, ministries of finance, planning, trade, commerce, and so on. Contrary to a widely held assumption (see Jones and Mason 1982: 19), the senior managers of public enterprise may support privatization or reform so long as they survive the process, as they are likely to do (see Waterbury in this volume; Kay and Thompson 1986: 29). Foreign technocrats from private and multilateral creditors are usually part of the mix. There is in the LDCs, as in the advanced industrial nations, the international diffusion factor through which a specific leadership can justify its reform efforts in terms of what is being done elsewhere.

Beyond those groups, it is hard to find visible support for the process. Organized labor generally opposes it because privatization signals the state's gradual relinquishing of its welfare functions. Large supervisory bureaucracies may impede it, as the realm they supervise will be reduced. The military may oppose it if "strategic" sectors of the economy are to be removed from the state domain or the economy as a whole opened up to foreign capital. Finally, the private sector may not welcome it, because privatization will entail the removal of many of the risk-absorbing functions in the provision of credit, cheap inputs, and tariff protection that the state had traditionally supplied.

Is the State Retreating or Retrenching?

When we see the public sector subjected to mounting criticism, sometimes by those who created it, and when we hear policymakers openly admit that the state has tried to overregulate economic life, are we witnessing a crisis of confidence on the part of state elites, soon to be followed by a precipitous retreat of the state from the economic realm? The only developing country in which that has taken place on a broad scale is Chile, and there the driving force was ideology and not a crisis of confidence.

It may be that liberalization, deregulation, and privatization should be seen as efforts to strengthen the state. Deepak Lal (1987) has argued that deregulation may be an attempt to legalize a range of economic activities that had been driven into black or parallel markets, where they could be neither measured nor taxed. Once legalized, however, these activities can add to state revenues through various forms of taxation. In unburdening itself of some of the social welfare agenda, the state can be more selective in its interventions and is less politically exposed when equity issues are debated. Privatization should lead to the financial strengthening of the state.[5]

Public enterprises were intended to be the instruments by which certain fundamental goals could be achieved: strengthen economic sovereignty; promote industrial catching up; promote income redistribution and equity; contribute to national strength. As instruments, they were often deficient and in some ways became obsolete. But if the goals remain relevant, and in most LDCs they do, then the case for the state as an intervener in markets, as the absorber of risk, and as the source of protection for non-state enterprises remains as well. The private sector can contribute in a meaningful fashion only to industrial catching up. In other words, in the LDCs privatization and liberalization may be the harbingers not of the triumph of markets but rather of a new phase in which the state redefines the instruments and scope of its intervention.

Control versus Efficiency

We should expect in the LDCs that political leadership will be torn between the alternatives of long-run economic efficiency (and possibly the strengthening of the state) and short-term political survival (Ames 1987). The latter may seem to or may in fact depend upon the control that the leadership can exert over strategic sectors of the adult population through the resources, jobs, and patronage that the state can distribute. It may be, as noted above, that leaders of democracies will have a harder time making choices than those of authoritarian regimes, but both are likely to hesitate and behave inconsistently. The trade-offs they face can be presented schematically:

Enhance Political Control through Concentration of Resources in the State Sector

- control organized workforce
- control financial resources and sectoral investment
- control of strategic professional groups through public employment
- maintenance of a relative monopoly of discretionary resources
- maintenance of dependent functional groups through administered prices and subsidies

Enhance Macroeconomic Efficiency and the Fiscal Reach of the State

- external and internal trade liberalization
- partial deregulation of private sector activity
- public enterprise reform
- liberalization of financial markets
- privatization of public enterprises
- improved revenue gathering, increased tax revenues

In general, the use of distributional levers of the state to maintain social pacts and corporatist solidarity	*Remove some major distributional issues from the state agenda; increase fiscal reach of the state*

Conclusion

The sweep of market-oriented reforms worldwide has been rapid and, at least in its rhetoric, astounding. The redefinition of the economic role of the state emerged out of crises of varying degrees of severity in which certain structural impediments to improved economic efficiency had to be removed.

But it was, after all, crisis that drove advanced industrial states into highly interventionist policies in the first place, and it was structural impediments to growth that drove states in developing countries to take direct control of their economies. Although the changes brought about in the advanced industrial economies are most likely, for the foreseeable future, irreversible (see Ayub and Hegsted 1986: 38), it is not inconceivable that a worldwide economic slump would provoke a new expansion of the state. It is not clear whether the increasing internationalization of capital will act to spread risk and thus mitigate any emerging global crisis or, as in October 1987, contribute to it.

In the LDCs, the process of state retrenchment has not gone very far; and where it has, it can be easily reversed. Ernest Wilson has suggested in one of three possible scenarios that privatization in the LDCs will be inversely related to the business cycle: when the economy is contracting, privatization will increase; when the economy is expanding the state will expand its sphere along with it (Wilson 1988: 27). The 1970s, a period of upswing for many LDCs, tend to confirm this prospect.

There is another scenario, again crisis-driven, that appears plausible for many LDCs in the next few decades. The adjustment and privatization process has often been accompanied by an effort to promote exports or even to move to an export-led growth strategy. Such efforts generally are highly leveraged, with a handful of private producers learning how to prosper in international markets while riding on a cushion of publicly provided credit and export subsidies. Shifts in international markets, failure to protect or expand one's niche, and changes in interest rates can lead in one or more countries to widespread bankruptcy. In that event, as the Chilean case revealed in 1983, governments may be obliged to step in to pick up the pieces, taking over assets and trying to set them on their feet. Chile has done so successfully, but we already know that once assets come under public ownership it is very hard to dislodge them.

In sum, we should expect cyclical patterns in the expansion and contraction of state intervention in the economy and in the extent of state ownership. The cycles may be smaller and stretched over longer periods of time in the developed than in the developing countries, but severe crisis in either group will likely elicit a strong state response.

Notes

1. There is an extensive literature on all these issues. See, inter alia Kay and Thompson, 1986; Killick and Commander, 1988; Millward, 1988; Nellis and Kikeri, 1988; Van de Walle, 1988; Hemming and Mansour, 1987.

2. On the Thatcher attack on this post-war consensus, see Jenkins 1988.

3. Dani Rodrik has examined thirty LDCs that have undertaken stabilization and structural adjustment programs and has found that most have not improved their deficits; those that have, have done so at the expense of domestic investment (Rodrik 1988: 2).

4. Some big firms do go public. In September 1988 Reliance Petrochemicals of India made a public offering of convertible bonds worth $390 million. They were sold in ten days (*South*, April 1989: 34).

5. Financial strengthening may not take place if the asset is sold at a price below the present discounted value of its (anticipated) future earnings. Such below market sales appear fairly common. Future earnings, however, may be a purely theoretic question if, while in the public sector, the state does not have resources to invest in the asset. The sale of the asset brings an immediate, once-and-for-all resource transfer to the state.

References

Ames, Barry. 1987. *Political Survival: Politicians and Public Policy in Latin America*. Berkeley and Los Angeles: University of California Press.

Ayub, Mahmood Ali, and Hegstad, Sven Olaf. 1986. *Public Industrial Enterprises, Determinants of Performance*. World Bank, Industry and Finance Series, 17. Washington, D.C.

Balladur, Edouard. 1987. *Je crois en l'homme plus qu'en l'état*. Paris: Flammarion.

Bienen, Henry, and Waterbury, John. 1989. "The Political Economy of Privatization in Developing Countries." *World Development*. Forthcoming.

Dunois, Amédée. 1936. *De la concentration capitaliste aux nationalisations*. Paris: Librarie Populaire, 1936.

Floyd, R. H., Gray, C., and Short, R. P. 1984. *Public Enterprise in Mixed Economies*. Washington, D.C.: International Monetary Fund.

Haggard, S. 1988. "The Philippines: Picking Up after Marcos." In *The Promise of Privatization*, ed. R. Vernon. New York: Council on Foreign Relations.

Haggard, S., and Kaufman, R. 1988. *The Politics of Stabilization and Structural Adjustment.* Prepared for the NBER Project on Developing Country Debt.

Hanke, Steve H., ed. 1987. *Privatization and Development.* San Francisco: Institute for Contemporary Studies.

Hemming, R., and Mansoor, A. M. 1988. *Privatization and Public Enterprises.* Occassional Paper 56. Washington, D.C.: International Monetary Fund.

Jenkins, Peter. 1988. *Mrs. Thatcher's Revolution: The Ending of the Socialist Era.* Cambridge, Mass.: Harvard University Press.

Jones, L. P., and Mason, E. S. 1982. "Why Public Enterprise?" In *Public Enterprise in Less-Developed Countries,* ed. L. P. Jones and E. S. Mason, pp. 17–66. New York: Cambridge University Press.

Kay, J. A., and Thompson, D. J. 1986. "Privatisation: A Policy in Search of a Rationale." *The Economic Journal* 96 (March), 18–36.

King, Anthony. 1983. "The Political Consequences of the Welfare State." In *Evaluating the Welfare State: Social and Political Perspectives,* ed. Shimon E. Spiro and Ephraim Yuchtman-Yaar, p. 11. New York: Academic Press.

Lal, Deepak. 1987. "The Political Economy of Economic Liberalization." *World Bank Economic Review* 1, no. 2: 273–299

Nellis, John, and Kikeri, Sunita. 1988. "The Privatization of Public Enterprises." Unpublished.

Rodrik, Dani. 1988. "Liberalization, Sustainability, and the Design of Structural Adjustment Programs." Unpublished.

Rose, Richard. 1988. "Privatization: A Question of Quantities and Qualities." Paper presented at a conference on "A Supply-Side Agenda for Germany?" Cologne, Germany, June 29–30.

Rose, Richard, and Peters, Guy. 1978. *Can Government Go Bankrupt?* New York: Basic Books.

Sappington, E. M., and Stiglitz, Joseph. 1987. "Privatization, Information and Incentives." *NBER Working Paper Series,* Working Paper 2196. Cambridge, Mass.: National Bureau of Economic Research.

Van de Walle, Nicolas. 1988. "Privatization in Developing Countries: A Review of the Issues." *World Development.* Forthcoming

Veljanovski, Cento. 1987. *Selling the State: Privatization in Britain.* London: Weidenfeld and Nicolson.

Vernon, R. 1988. *The Promise of Privatization: A Challenge for U.S. Policy.* New York: Council on Foreign Relations.

Vickers, John, and Yarrow, George. 1988. *Privatization: An Economic Analysis.* Cambridge, Mass.: MIT Press.

Wilson, Ernest. 1988. "Privatization in Africa: Domestic Origins, Current Status and Future Scenarios." *Issue: A Journal of Opinion* 16, no. 2: 24–29.

2

The New Life of the Liberal State: Privatization and the Restructuring of State-Society Relations

Paul Starr

Whether or not the current turn toward privatization discloses a general failure of government, it certainly discloses a general failure of social theory. From the 1950s through the 1970s, theorists of the most diverse persuasions assumed that growing welfare and regulatory states in the West and entrenched communist states in the East were accomplished facts, unlikely to be reversed or undone. And while disagreeing on the exact causes, political economists and other social scientists identified powerful forces behind the growth of government. Similarly, a broad consensus of informed political opinion held that the modern administrative state was unlikely to give up ground it had occupied. As a common metaphor had it, the clock would not be turned back.

Among social scientists, this consensus embraced most of those who regretted an enlarged state as well as those who welcomed it. "Public choice" economists sought to show that public spending and public bureaucracies grow to excessive and inefficient scale (Niskanen 1971; Buchanan 1977, Borcherding 1977; Meltzer and Richard 1978). But if they were correct that systematic biases in the interests of politicians, bureaucrats, and voter coalitions favor government growth, the most reasonable—indeed, the most rational—expectation was that government expansion would continue. Similarly, students of government regulation identified interest group regimes that instigate and preserve inefficient regulatory practices (Bernstein 1955; Lowi 1969; Stigler 1971). If their models had represented the full picture, the direct stakeholders—principally the industries benefiting from regulation—should have continued to thwart the interests of the unorganized public in regulatory reform. Deregulation should never have taken place.

If one turned to the left for illumination in the 1960s and 1970s, the same expectations would have been reinforced. Radicals and Marxists agreed that capitalist societies require increased state intervention to control their internal contradictions and crises (Baran and Sweezy 1966; Miliband 1969). One variant of this position, the theory of "corporate liberalism" popular among the New Left, suggested that higher social expenditures and other liberal policies are merely a means of rationalizing the capitalist order and controlling the oppressed (Weinstein 1968; Piven and Cloward 1971). Programs that seemed to represent concessions to the poor or to protesting groups were really enacted at the behest of far-sighted corporate leaders. Some Marxists regarded such "instrumental" theories as too simpleminded; for them the sources of state intervention lay in the "structural" demands of the system (Poulantzas 1969). For example, in one neo-Marxist account, *The Fiscal Crisis of the State* (1973), James O'Connor suggested that the capitalist state faces two imperatives—capital accumulation and legitimation—that lead it into difficulty. In the interests of accumulation and legitimacy, the state socializes various costs of production, but it leaves capitalists to appropriate the profits—hence, allegedly, the fiscal crisis. But rather than suggest that the state might cut back its commitments, O'Connor thought a likely response would be a further extension of government with the rise of a new "social-industrial" complex. If O'Connor and other Marxists had been right in their understanding of the roots of state intervention, the corporate capitalists and structural constraints of the system should have blocked any misguided efforts to reduce the role of government (for a review, see Block 1987).

Several theories pointed to gradual evolutionary tendencies at work enlarging goverment. An old argument, dating from the nineteenth century and identified with Adolph Wagner, held that the externality problems created by economic growth, among other causes, produce a demand for more public services and higher public spending (Wagner 1877; Bird 1971). A more recent thesis, put forward by William Baumol (1967), contended that a shift in the public-private balance inevitably results from slower productivity growth in services than in manufacturing. Since government primarily produces services, its productivity lags behind the private sector, and it has to draw a growing share of national income to pay wage levels that match manufacturing. From yet another quarter—the theory of post-industrial society—came a related set of reasons to anticipate further growth of government in the advanced Western societies: government would grow because its "businesses," such as education, research, and health care, are growth sectors in post-industrial societies. Post-industrial societies depend on high levels of investment in intellectual and human capital, which only government can adequately provide. Furthermore, consumers with rising discretionary incomes demand more from government. A rising level of public services and public spending was to be expected (Bell 1973).

In addition, there grew up an extensive empirical literature testing these and other hypotheses about rising public expenditures (see Wilensky 1975; Cameron 1978; Taylor 1983). Although these studies avoid making predictions, their disagreements are generally about the sources or rate of government growth, not the secular nature of the trend.

Other branches of social analysis saw a larger role for the state in managing endemic crises of authority and coordination. In the 1970s, some saw a trend toward "neocorporatist" arrangements, with closer state supervision and integration of interest group organizations and a heightened level of economic management, including concerted incomes policies. The economic problems of the 1970s, in this view, were leading toward greater interpenetration of state and society, not any withdrawal by the state (Schmitter and Lehmbruch 1979). The omnipresence of the state in structuring society suggested to yet another school—"critical legal studies"—that the distinction between public and private had become meaningless (Kennedy 1982). Therefore, no aspect of society was really beyond state intervention or should be considered off-limits.

At the same time, most Western theorists viewed the communist world as highly unlikely to experience any significant reduction in state control. The postwar Western theory of totalitarianism taught that the totalitarian state maintains control by totally penetrating society. In an influential book, Carl Friedrich and Zbigniew Brzezinski (1956) argued that twentieth-century totalitarian domination—exercised through a single mass party, a monopoly of mass communications, a monopoly of weapons, the inculcation of an official ideology, terror, and central control of the economy—represents a "novel form of government" (see also Arendt 1951; and, for a review, Schapiro 1972). In the four decades after the close of World War II, many others in the West have argued that it is dangerously naive to suppose that the totalitarian countries would peacefully reform themselves and evolve into liberal democracies. In an influential essay that propelled her to political prominence, Jeane Kirkpatrick (1982) claimed that the difference between totalitarian and authoritarian states is precisely that authoritarian regimes may become more democratic and pluralistic because they leave civil society intact. Totalitarian regimes, in contrast, cannot be expected to relax control and evolve into freer societies. On the one hand, Kirkpatrick assailed liberal theorists of modernization for taking a determinist view of authoritarian regimes; she criticized them for thinking that reform is inevitable and therefore deserting dictators friendly to the United States whenever they come under political challenge. But Kirkpatrick herself took a determinist view of communism as a congealed system of domination: communist societies could not work, but neither could they change.

From all these perspectives, therefore, the movement toward privatization and economic liberalization in both the Western and the Eastern bloc, as well as in the Third World, comes as something of a surprise—gratifying in all respects to some, unwelcome at least in some respects to others, but an unexpected turn from virtually every perspective. To be sure, the picture is not uniform. There is no worldwide trend toward lower rates of government spending; in that fundamental sense, there has been no reversal in the growth of the public economy. Even in Great Britain, Margaret Thatcher has not succeeded in reducing public spending as a proportion of gross domestic product (GDP). Also, in some countries there is more talk about privatization than there is actual change. And in the Soviet Union and China, it remains uncertain, as of this writing, whether the reforms, or even the reformers, will survive.

Nonetheless, the changes already accomplished by the beginning of 1990 are remarkable. The British Conservatives have carried out a massive program of privatization, most of which the Labour party no longer threatens to reverse if it gains power. Privatization in Britain is not an event of merely local importance. British institutions and thinking about economic policy—from Adam Smith to the Fabians, Keynes, and Beveridge—have exercised global influence. When the sun finally set on the outposts of the British empire, it was still shining on the far-flung graduates of the London School of Economics. In the twentieth century, British influence has favored an acceptance of the welfare state and mixed economy. The British public corporation was the specific model for the organization of public enterprises in the United States and other countries, and much of the literature on public enterprise economics and management is British in origin. Moreover, London remains a center of international finance, and its investment banking firms have turned their homegrown expertise in privatization into a service for export (Letwin 1988). So the privatization of Britain's nationalized industries is an event at once laden with symbolism and of wide international consequence (unlike, for example, the earlier radical program of privatization in Pinochet's Chile, which could be dismissed as a marginal and aberrant case, feasible only in a dictatorship).

Similarly, the deregulation of financial markets, broadcasting, telecommunications, and transportation in the United States holds wide implications. The established regulatory regimes seemed impregnable, yet they were overcome (Noll and Owen 1983; Derthick and Quirk 1985). Moreover, some deregulatory measures have proved contagious; other countries have moved in the same direction, particularly in opening up their financial markets and communications media. The trend is by no means uniform: the world is not a free market, whatever that might mean. But the rapid movements of capital and information across national boundaries tend to undermine the regulatory capacities of individual states.

The trend toward privatization and deregulation might be explained in straightforward political and ideological terms if these developments had been limited to Britain under Margaret Thatcher and the United States under Ronald Reagan and George Bush. However, some forms of privatization have been adopted by Labour governments in New Zealand and Australia, by Socialists in Spain, and by a variety of countries with more mixed and pragmatic regimes as different as those of Japan and Mexico. Countries that not long ago were nationalizing multinationals have been inviting new foreign investment, swapping debt for equity, and selling off pieces of the public sector. In the developed countries, old enthusiasms for nationalization have virtually disappeared from public view. The nationalizations undertaken by the French Socialists soon after they took power in 1981 now seem more like a parenthesis or even a flashback, rather than a new chapter, in the evolving relation of states and economies. Many of the companies that the Socialists nationalized were privatized by Chirac half a decade later; and perhaps more important, the French Socialists on their return to power did not seek to renationalize the firms the conservatives sold. Socialists throughout Western Europe now seem more keen on liberalizing markets than on seizing control of the means of production.

Undoubtedly, the most striking turns toward privatization have taken place in the East. Some communist governments had made halting movements toward more liberalized economies even before the revolutions that began in late 1989. Among the Eastern European Soviet bloc countries, Hungary had been most receptive to private ownership in the 1960s and 1970s. In the 1980s China undertook a historic decollectivization of agriculture, introduced new incentives for profit making in industrial firms, and created special economic zones where private investment, some of it from Taiwan, spurred rapid expansion of the private sector. Under perestroika the Soviet Union in the late 1980s began opening up new opportunities for private business cooperatives and independent decision making by industrial enterprises. One communist regime after another abandoned autarchy, invited capital investment from the West, and provided greater rights to foreign investors. These changes testified to an increasing recognition of the positive value of markets, individual incentives, and property rights.

But with the rise of a Solidarity government in Poland, the triumph of reformers in Hungary, the overthrow of the communist government in Czechoslovakia, the overthrow of Stalinism in East Germany, and the revolution in Romania, the tentative moves away from communism turned into a stampede. In January 1990 Poland introduced a radical program of economic liberalization, designed to create a full-fledged capitalist economy. The Czechs adopted a similar program, rejecting the idea that there might be some "third way" between communism and capitalism. The unification of Germany, if fully carried out, seems destined to bring about the same transformation. The draft platform adopted by the Soviet Communist party in February 1990 calls for legalization of private hiring of labor as well as the abolition of the party's monopoly of political power.

How to interpret these various developments East and West? One view with obvious political overtones is already gaining favor. It might be called "the theory of a post-socialist era," and it is being energetically promoted by conservative intellectuals and politicians, including Margaret Thatcher, who see a common thread of vindication for free markets running through contemporary developments (Jenkins 1988). In this view, the old consensus that "the clock cannot be turned back" was simply wrong; history is now writing an epitaph for socialism, whether in the form of Soviet central planning or the British welfare state. Even an economist as sympathetic to socialism as Robert Heilbroner (1989) writes that the contest between capitalism and socialism is over—and capitalism has won. In the United States, conservatives extend that judgment to American liberalism, which is now "obsolete," according to Milton Friedman on the cover of *Forbes*. Marxists long claimed to be running with the tide of history; today it is free-market conservatives who claim the future is theirs and who consign their opponents to history's trash heap.

The idea of a post-socialist era has a plausible ring. Something is afoot—and moving ubiquitously on distant continents. The turn toward privatization, however, is so diverse in its forms and so varied in its settings that its causes and implications are unlikely to be everywhere the same. That, at least, is what I shall argue here. To understand the current turn toward privatization and liberalization, we need to begin, as always, by making some necessary distinctions and discriminations.

Privatization Policies, Programs, and Processes

Privatization has acquired both a general and a specific use in public policy discussion. The general sense refers to any reduction in the scale or scope of government. In this sense, lower taxes, lower spending, and deregulation are all aspects of privatization. The more specific sense of privatization is the transfer of the ownership of assets and production of goods and services from the governmental to the private sector. What is transferred may be ownership and management, management alone, or any of several other functions involved in producing a service. A privatization policy is simply any governmental measure that brings about such a transfer. The chief examples are the sale of state-owned assets and enterprises and the contracting out of public services to private firms. (For further discussion, see P. Starr 1988a; for other definitions, see Glade 1986 and Savas 1987.)

In the more specific and restricted sense (which I will use in the following discussion), privatization policies are distinct from spending reductions, tax cuts, and deregulation, except insofar as those policies shift the locus of production. A reduction in military spending is not a privatization measure; no private group or firm is likely to make up the difference by providing additional defense services. On the other hand, spending reductions in services to consumers, such as health care and education, may well cause a shift of production to the private sector, particularly if the government ceases to provide the service at all. For example, a government that abolishes public family planning programs may be properly said to be privatizing birth control even if it sells no assets.

Most forms of deregulation do not shift production from public to private firms and hence do not constitute privatization in the restricted sense. On the other hand, when governments deregulate entry into industries previously protected as public monopolies, some production will likely shift to private firms. In that case, deregulation is a form of privatization even in the restricted sense.

In general, then, there are four kinds of policies used to bring about privatization of production. Two of these are explicit and direct forms of privatization: (1) disposing of state-owned assets, including land, infrastructure, and state-owned enterprises, through sales, leases, or liquidation; and (2) substituting state-financed but privately produced services for state-produced services, as in contracting out, the distribution of vouchers, and other forms of payment for private provision. The two other general forms of privatization policy are implicit and indirect: (3) the disengagement of government from a sphere of service provision; and (4) the deregulation of entry into state-owned monopolies. Government disengagement may involve simply terminating programs and thereby throwing recipients back on the market or private charity; or it may be a slow process, as a government gradually reduces access to services or their quality so as to bring about a shift by consumers to private alternatives ("privatization by attrition").

Another way to look at these policies is to divide them according to their effects on the role of the state. Both asset sales and governmental disengagement are sometimes described as "load shedding," which implies that the assets and programs unloaded are, indeed, burdensome as sources of deficits and, perhaps, political conflict. On the other hand, contracting out public services and deregulating public monopolies may not involve shedding any governmental assets or fiscal burdens. Selling land, enterprises, and infrastructure involves privatizing some of the means of production, while the various methods of paying private firms for providing public services primarily involve privatizing means of policy implementation. Where governments disengage themselves entirely from some functional responsibility or dispose of all ownership and control, it seems appropriate to speak of total privatization. Much privatization is only partial, however, as when governments pay for but do not operate services, own but do not manage productive assets, or sell off some ownership but retain a controlling interest.

It is critical here to distinguish among the operational, fiscal, and regulatory spheres of government action. If governments pay private providers, they reduce their operational responsibilities, but they still must raise taxes and negotiate contracts with private firms or rules for the use of vouchers. Public officials may not be immediately accountable for service provision, but they will be held ultimately accountable for how private organizations perform with public funds. If governments sell off telecommunications, water supply, or other industries with monopolistic features, they may substitute new systems of regulation for the old system of public ownership. Again, such sales may reduce the immediate operational responsibilities of the public sector, but public officials will be held ultimately accountable for services under the new regulatory rules. In other words, while privatization policies are commonly thought of as a contraction of the state, they also represent a *restructuring* of its role. Indeed, privatization of production may even lead to an increase in public spending (paying private health care providers may well be more expensive than operating public facilities) or to an increase in government regulation (a new regulatory system for private utilities may have more elaborate, formal, and rigid rules than those that previously guided the utilities under public ownership).

Nor does privatization of production guarantee greater competition. A public monopoly can simply be converted into a private one. In such cases, privatization is distinct from economic liberalization (that is, an increase in competition). Governments can privatize without liberalizing, as Great Britain did when it sold British Telecom; they can liberalize without privatizing, as in the American deregulation of telecommunications; or they can privatize and liberalize together by both selling state enterprises and deregulating entry into their markets.

Nearly all discussion of privatization focuses on governmentally adopted privatization policies. But shifts from publicly to privately produced services often take place because of socially generated processes that governments cannot control. In particular, governments may be unable to meet demands for many services, such as education, because of budgetary constraints or because dissenting groups in the society are opposed to the dominant values that state-run services represent and convey. In such cases, private schools and other private institutions may grow up to meet demands that the state is unable or unwilling to satisfy (Levy 1986).

Another important example of a *demand*-driven (as opposed to *policy*-driven) privatization process is the development of the informal or second economy in communist societies and other countries with dominant public sectors. Informal firms and illegal markets are the economic counterparts of underground publications and associations that represent the stirrings of civil society in repressive regimes. Measures that legalize or even encourage the informal economy and voluntary organizations are a kind of lagging or passive privatization policy, which may serve to co-opt submerged and potentially subversive economic and political forces. The rise of a dynamic informal sector has, in fact, been a key source of pressure in some states to adopt privatization as official policy.

In the language I am using here, privatization policies are the ingredients of privatization *programs*. What is new about privatization is not any of the individual policies I have mentioned. Governments have sold assets, contracted out services, disengaged themselves from certain functions, and reduced barriers to entry into public monopolies before. What is new is the adoption of privatization programs—that is, packages of policies pursued by governments with the explicit objective of significantly recasting the role and relations of state, market, and civil society.

Worldwide, three general programs incorporating privatization stand out. I will call them the *institution-building* program, the *balance-shifting* program, and the *boundary-blurring* program. By the institution-building program I mean the attempt to create an enabling framework for civil society and private markets in parts of the Eastern bloc and some developing countries. By the balance-shifting program I mean the divestiture of state-owned enterprises and other efforts to redraw the public-private balance in capitalist societies with relatively large public sectors. And by the boundary-blurring program, I mean the effort particularly in the United States to use private providers for public services and to create public-private partnerships in carrying out public policies.

The distinctions among these privatization programs are not hard and fast, but they typically involve different tasks, arise for disparate reasons, and do not necessarily lead to the same results. I turn now to an outline of the programs and to a general discussion of their origins, their effects on the role and capacities of the state, their relations to political parties, and their prospects for success as economic and political strategies.

Institution Building

Before privatization can take place in countries that have lacked a framework for private markets and civil society, the basic foundations of a private sector need to be constructed. This process is not to be understood as a mere relaxation of state controls. On the contrary, it requires an active effort by the state to design new laws and institutions, to assure security of property rights and rights of voluntary association. In the communist world, private ownership and association need to be given legal status. But legality is not enough. In some countries whose laws formally permit private institutions, government control has in practice been stifling. If these countries are to develop their private economies, they need to reform their regulatory bureaucracies and tax systems to reduce what may be excessively high costs of acquiring and retaining private legal status. In yet other instances, privatization requires governments to construct markets, such as capital markets, where none yet exist. Again, rather than disengaging itself, the state must first design a framework of rules, backed by its own policing powers, to create the necessary public trust for the market to function.

In all these cases, privatization does not simply involve a transfer of ownership from public to private hands, nor can privatization be understood merely as a reduction of state capacities. Privatization may ultimately result in less state control, but it first requires states to develop capacities they may not previously have had, such as the capacity to maintain the rule of law, instill confidence among investors, supervise contracts, and provide expedient administration of official rules and regulations. Privatization, in other words, is an institution-building program in two senses: it requires the design of basic private institutions and the development of public institutions that private firms and associations can depend upon for protection of their legitimate rights and interests.

The design of private institutions involves a complex set of issues involving ownership of property, rights of association, and the structure of markets. Property rights do not take a single form; the package of rights subsumed under the conception of property may be variously constructed. The state must define, first, what counts as property (even in the West today there are severe disagreements about the status of things as various as mathematical algorithms, "designer genes," bodily organs, and the radiomagnetic spectrum). Property rights include the right to use property, to derive income from it, and to sell it; but these rights are divisible and can be limited in countless ways through laws of liability, contracts, eminent domain, rent and other price controls, and, perhaps the most important of all, taxation. States generally retain the authority to endow associations and corporations with a legal personality and to assign rights and powers to the various parties involved. In so doing, they define the constitution of private sector institutions and shape the workings of markets and civil society.

These "constitutive" tasks have been central to the reform programs of communist states and formerly communist states in the last decade. The reform programs did not initially envision a full-fledged system of private property, private corporations, and private markets. They were more concerned with decentralizing authority to firms (and to local party organizations) than with transferring the firms to private ownership. Privatization began in the agricultural and service sectors. Private property rights in land were expanded first in Eastern Europe, particularly in Hungary (Bauer 1988), and they were granted de facto through long-term leases in China (Cheung 1989). With the revolutionary developments of late 1989, more fundamental programs for constituting markets and shaping laws appropriate to a market economy began to get under way.

It would be a mistake, however, to focus entirely on legal formalities, as if privatization were merely being handed down by the state. The turn toward privatization lies not simply in the passage of new laws but in the collapse of old ones. Even before the revolutions of 1989, communist states had lost much of their control over private communication, movement, and exchange. In the 1970s and 1980s, many of the communist societies underwent a process that Brzezinski (1989) aptly describes as "self-emancipation." Underground organizations and the informal economy showed the way, but the phenomenon spread much further even before Gorbachev. According to S. Frederick Starr (1988), it was actually during the Brezhnev era that Soviet society, independent of the state, moved in the direction of "individuation, decentralization of initiative, and privatization." The selection of career, employer, and residence, for example, increasingly became a personal choice rather than one dictated by the state. With the spread of telephones, cassette tape recorders, videocassette recorders, and other personal communication equipment, the Soviet state lost its monopoly of information. New groups began to take shape: "Whether model-airplane enthusiasts, rock music fans, Hare Krishnas, Afghanistan war veterans, or ecologists, interest groups of like-minded people form with relative ease and establish regular channels of communication among their devotees" (S. F. Starr 1988). Pluralism became a fact of Soviet society long before it received any official encouragement.

To see official moves toward pluralism and privatization as responses to a socially generated process puts them in a different perspective from the once-common view of Soviet reform as a top-down initiative controlled by a dynamic national leader. Legalizing the second economy means bringing it within the sphere of taxes and regulations. In this way, what looks like an expansion of the private sphere may simultaneously serve to recoup political control.

But if taxes and official regulations impose too high a cost, much of the private sector may remain informal and underground. In Peru, like much of the developing world, a massive informal sector has developed in housing and the economy. According to Hernando de Soto (1989), more than 400,000 people in Lima alone depend for their livelihood on street vending and illegal markets; and many entire neighborhoods, representing half the housing in Lima, have been built on land illegally seized in massive land invasions. Similarly, private minibuses and vans have invaded the routes of the inadequate public bus system; 90 percent of public transit in Lima is now provided privately in violation of law. De Soto argues that Peruvians have been obliged to defy the law because of the high costs that the Peruvian bureacracy places on the legitimate acquisition of property and business opportunities (for a contrasting analysis, see Portes, Castells, and Benton 1989). De Soto's research institute found that it required almost ten months to get the necessary permits to start a new business; to make a legal purchase of state wasteland to build a house took more than six years. The costs of retaining legal status for a business, chiefly administrative overhead rather than taxes, were equally forbidding. Informality comes at a high price, however. Those who invest their capital in extralegal businesses or informal housing do not enjoy secure property rights. They cannot call upon the state for defense of their property when others threaten it, and they are unable to buy insurance. As a result, they are discouraged from investing in their homes or enlarging their businesses to what might be a more efficient scale. At the root of these problems in Peru, de Soto argues, is a failure of law to provide secure property rights, particularly for many of the poor, often Indians who have migrated to the cities in recent decades and whose arrival was never welcomed by the elites in the first place. Periodically, regimes in power have sought to accommodate the informal sector and have validated land seizures and illegal markets after the fact. But they have been unable to break down the system of bureaucratic controls that prevents a vital private economy from flourishing. In such cases, whether in the Eastern bloc or the developing world, the institution-building problem remains unsolved.

Whereas the informal economy represents a kind of privatization process bubbling up from below, privatization in the Eastern bloc and developing world has also received an impetus from outside. Taiwan, South Korea, and the other East Asian newly industrializing countries have served as both examples and goads to the Chinese leadership. The regime accepted foreign investments and the creation of special economic zones in the hope of turning China into a major commercial power in the world (Bachman, in this volume). The economy's rapid growth in the decade after 1979, at least until the May 1989 uprising in Beijing, seemed to confirm that such a strategy could work. The Soviet Union, far less successful economically in the same period, now faces severe problems and the prospect that, without the capacity to keep up with the West economically and technologically, it cannot ultimately hope to keep up militarily. So international pressures, as well as domestic ones, have pushed it on a path toward liberalization, privatization, and accommodation with the West.

In China, opening the economy and society to the capitalist world while keeping political life closed proved dangerous, though the explosive forces were (at least temporarily) suppressed. It is unclear whether Gorbachev can keep the Soviet political opening under control while pursuing economic reform. Marx was right that property, class formation, and political power are connected; he just failed to anticipate the transformation of ruling communist parties into property-controlling political classes. Privatization of small-scale agriculture and services may be feasible in a communist system only because the classes it generates are weak; further privatization seems to require more thoroughgoing political change.

Private firms in planned economies face an environment controlled by the state, including administratively set prices for the factors of production. Since access to key resources, particularly capital, continues to depend on political decisions, the firms depend on favors from those in power. In addition, the coexistence of plan and market prices creates opportunities to profit from the disparities between them. Under the circumstances, corruption is inevitable. Moreover, the release of market forces engenders large new social and regional inequalities, as well as greater insecurities among workers and managers. The corruption, inequalities, and insecurity are fertile ground for popular as well as party opposition to reform. In short, the "internal contradictions" of market socialism may create unpalatable choices between economic stagnation and political upheaval. As the revolutions of 1989 seemed to confirm, the only route out of stagnation was likely to involve a fundamental political reconstitution, as well as an economic one.

Balance Shifting

In capitalist countries with relatively large public sectors, privatization does not require an entirely new legal framework for public and private institutions. The societies are already differentiated into public and private sectors; the question is primarily the balance between them. Unlike the Eastern bloc, where the organization of agriculture was a leading is-

sue, privatization in the West, particularly in the more advanced economies, has focused chiefly on industrial enterprise. In many countries (as
discussed in much of this volume) privatization is synonymous with the
sale of state-owned companies.

The archetypal image of privatization in the West is Margaret Thatcher
selling off the industries that Labour nationalized after World War II. But
although now identified with parties of the left, state enterprises in Western and developing countries have widely varied origins. The typical
"portfolio" of enterprises in state ownership represents not the realization of some consciously adopted socialist theory but rather a collection of
inheritances from each nation's past. Some government enterprises are
legacies of state and nation building, inherited from distant absolutist regimes that used state monopolies as important sources of revenue or from
more recent regimes that may have seized the enterprises from foreign
owners or ethnic minorities in bursts of nationalism or racial suspicion.
Extensive state ownership of communications media (postal services, telecommunications, radio and television) arose from conceptions of state
and national interests that historically had nothing to do with socialism.
Some enterprises are specifically the legacies of war or war making, taken
over by the state because their prior owners collaborated with foreign
powers or because they were thought to have important strategic value,
or built up by the military as part of its own empire. Still other enterprises
came into the state sector as a result of efforts at economic stabilization. In
a typical scenario, a regime took over banks on the verge of collapse and
then acquired, almost by accident, a series of firms that the collapsing
banks controlled. And not a few enterprises, particularly in public transportation, have fallen into state hands as a result of bankruptcies brought
on by restrictive price regulation.

If public ownership has had diverse origins in capitalist countries, we
might reasonably expect that privatization would have diverse origins,
too. Of course, to some advocates of privatization, explaining the adoption of privatization policies may not be a problem. Privatization, in their
view, promotes faster growth, higher efficiency, and greater freedom;
public opinion has simply awakened to these possibilities after long and
grim experience. However, the record of public enterprise is sufficiently
disputed to make that view of the historical causes of privatization seem
too simple. If there are self-interested reasons for political leaders, bureaucrats, and voter coalitions to favor expanded government, we need to
understand how privatization ever arrived on the political agenda at all.

In an inventory of explanations given for the growth of public expenditures, Daniel Tarchys (1975) points out that, whereas market transactions
depend on two factors, supply and demand, public expenditures depend
on three: demand, supply, and finance. In other words, because individu-

als do not pay directly for the specific government services they receive, the scale of government activity depends on factors affecting not only the demands of voter-consumers or the interests of political and bureaucratic suppliers of services but also the state's fiscal condition and capacities. Finance necessarily comes first in any account of the growing political interest in privatization in the 1980s. In developing countries, debt has been the chief proximate cause of pressure putting privatization on the agenda (Vernon 1988). Privatization promises not only the elimination of subsidies to loss-making state enterprises but also an immediate short-term budgetary boost from the sale of assets. The same fiscal interests tempt goverments in the more advanced industrialized nations. When budgetary pressure stimulates a search for cuts, it focuses attention on budget items that have recently increased. Since many state enterprises in the 1970s began receiving much larger subsidies than in the past, they were a natural target of retrenchment initiatives.

Behind these immediate financial pressures lie the effects of inflation and slow growth in the 1970s and after. The slowdown had an objective impact on the performance of state-owned enterprises and, perhaps more important, caused a variety of political actors to reassess their interests and beliefs. In the early postwar period, the public sector in the West appeared to be doing quite well. French indicative planning, Italy's state investment companies, and even the British nationalized industries drew favorable evaluations (Shonfield 1965; Pryke 1971). Even when Britain's nationalized sector later faltered, the evident success of the Italian "IRI model" was widely imitated in Europe and elsewhere (Holland 1972; Hindley 1983; Kramer 1988). Nonetheless, in the 1970s the performance of state-owned enterprises deteriorated severely in Western Europe and much of the developing world (Redwood 1980; Pryke 1981; Vernon 1988). Political leaders placed increasing demands on the state sector to restrict price increases to control inflation and to rescue foundering firms and maintain excess capacity to preserve employment (Hall 1986). Productivity suffered, labor disputes intensified, and subsidies burgeoned. In short, the slow growth and deeper politicization of the 1970s transformed state-owned enterprises from political assets into political liabilities.

These developments affected various political actors' understanding of their interests. The tax revolts and welfare backlash of the period were early signs of shifts in public opinion that helped conservative parties to power. But equally important were the changes that took place within conservative parties. Ascendant groups on the right became convinced that the postwar consensus accepting a larger public sector had been a mistake. The shifts from Heath to Thatcher in Britain, from Nixon to Reagan in the United States, and from de Gaulle to Chirac in France were representative of these internal party reversals in the attitude toward the role of the state. The adoption of new market-minded policies like privatization served party interests in distancing themselves from earlier policies now widely viewed as failures. In some countries, the internal party shifts were also aided by generational change, with the coming to power of younger "technocrats" professionally trained in economics and contemptuous of older and more paternalistic conservative traditions.

But if the new conditions of the 1970s and 1980s affected the conservative parties, they also had an impact on the nationalized and regulated industries. For example, in Britain the controls on the public sector borrowing requirements (PSBR) applied to the nationalized industries and distorted their investment plans (Curwen 1986). Public enterprise managers now had more reason to take a positive view of any measure, like privatization, that got them out from under the PSBR limits. In the United States, the airlines discovered that the system of price regulation benefited them during periods of price stability but crimped their ability to keep pace with inflation. The industry's growing divisions, as some companies defected from support of regulation, helped to bring down the old regulatory regime (Derthick and Quirk 1985). In France, the volatile economic environment of the 1970s and early 1980s made a mockery of planning and turned it into little more than a ritual even after the Socialists took power (Hall 1986). Of course, neither the parties of the left nor labor unions abandoned belief in the welfare state, industrial policy, and other forms of intervention. The new circumstances of the time, however, produced ambivalence among many old supporters of planning and public ownership and resulted in weaker commitments to the state as micromanager of the economy.

These effects on state finance and changing conceptions of party and group interests were the proximate causes that put privatization on the agenda, but long-term processes at work also helped to destabilize the foundations of many public sector institutions. In the advanced economies, these processes may be described under two related headings: the post-industrial transition and the recapture of flexibility.

The post-industrial transition has brought more than just a shift of investment and employment from manufacturing to services. It is also generating new alternatives for the provision of services and altering patterns of economic organization. New information and communication technology has been a midwife of change. In radio and television, public ownership in Europe and public regulation in America were premised on assumptions of a scarcity of broadcasting channels. With the development of cable, however, and the prospect of other media like fiber optics, channels are no longer scarce. Not only is more competition feasible; in the case of satellite broadcasting, goverments would have to act to stop competition. Telephone systems were premised on assumptions about natural monopoly that are also being eroded by technological innovation. More generally, what the late Ithiel de Sola Pool (1983) called a "convergence of modes"—the growing interpenetration and overlap of computers, telecommunications, broadcasting, publishing, and other information businesses—has generated a multiplicity of alternatives for producing the same services. Technologies and industries now compete with one another across lines that used to divide one market from another. To be sure, new technology does not absolutely require governments to allow or promote competition, but it has made the case for privatization and liberalization more persuasive. As in the case of the informal economy in the Eastern bloc, a privatization process generated independently of the state is encouraging states to adopt privatization as official policy.

The new technology has had particularly notable effects on financial markets. New financial instruments have appeared; the pace and volume of transactions have increased; and the world's financial markets have been integrated in "real" time. In this new context, national governments hoping to impose or maintain controls over financial markets face a higher political and economic cost: more rapid capital flight, lower investment, slower growth. At the very least, the new communications technology at the command of investors and corporations makes the threat of capital flight more credible than ever.

The impact of new technology has not been restricted to the industries most directly involved in producing and distributing information. In other industries, many firms have an increased capacity to respond quickly to changes in demand and to coordinate production globally with independent suppliers. Instead of rewarding large-scale mass production, the new economic environment often favors flexibility of production and responsiveness to market changes and enables many smaller-scale enterprises to compete successfully even on the world market (Piore and Sabel 1984; Hirst and Zeitlin 1989). These developments run contrary to the premises on which many of the state-owned enterprises were built. Some were initially nationalized because they were supposed to be the "commanding heights" of industry; many no longer look so commanding. Committed to a mass production model, they are finding it difficult to compete against mass producers in lower-wage countries and against smaller, more specialized, higher-quality firms nibbling niches in their own countries. Privatization is not merely a way for governments to shed these loads; it has become a way of shaking up rigid organizations and prompting them to reorganize and recapture flexibility. Again, I am not suggesting that technological change dictated deregulation or privatization, but it has helped to make obsolete older forms of organization. These organizations might conceivably have been reorganized under public control and others started with public sponsorship—indeed, that is exactly what some on the left were advocating—but in the prevailing political context of the 1980s, privatization has been the instrument of adaptation and adjustment.

Privatization of enterprises reduces the scale of the public sector, but whether it reduces the capacities of the state is another matter. The simplistic view is that a larger state is a stronger state, but this is not necessarily so. Public enterprises that operate at a loss and involve political leaders in labor strife scarcely enhance the capacities of the state. Moreover, the concept of "state capacity" begs the question: Whose capacity is it, anyway? Political leaders often cannot control the bureaucracies they nominally command; strong administrative capacities may mean weaker governments, not stronger ones. If privatization removes enterprises that are independent power centers, the state reduces its internal "friction" and may operate that much more smoothly.

The political effects of privatization—and therefore the motivations for it—depend on the prior relation of state bureaucracies and political parties. Where one party has become entrenched in the bureaucracy, another party new to power may see privatization as a method of fortifying its position. Thatcher's interest in privatizing industries nationalized by Labour is not so different from the Spanish Socialists' willingness to privatize public enterprises developed by Franco (Bermeo, in this volume). The observation that party turnover promotes privatization undoubtedly reflects the basic politics of friends and enemies.

The theorists who have seen political leaders as inevitably favoring expanded public sectors have underestimated the varied political gains to be achieved through privatization. Awarding patronage jobs in state-owned enterprises may yield some political advantage (if, indeed, it can be done), but privatizing enterprises enables those in power to transfer wealth to their supporters. The potential value of political influence is far greater. In the most crude cases, privatization is a means of magnificently enriching family and political allies. It can also serve to distribute ownership more broadly. By selling shares below their market value, governments can shower gains across a wide portion of the population and hope to harvest the returns at future elections (Mayer and Meadowcroft 1987). Even without underpricing, wider share ownership (or "popular capitalism") may encourage more voters to adopt views congenial to conservative leaders. So Margaret Thatcher believes, and in the case of housing some evidence indicates a conservatizing influence of ownership on voter preferences (Butler and Stokes 1969). Whether wider share ownership adds political supporters to the right is not yet clear.

Shifting the public-private balance involves shifting several balances simultaneously. When governments sell off enterprises, they change not only the ownership of capital but also the employment of labor. Throughout the West since the 1960s, public employee unions have been the most rapidly growing and among the most aggressive in the labor movement. Privatization serves as a method of labor discipline as well as a means of extracting political leaders from labor conflicts. In general, privatization diverts claims away from the state. Just as employment is privatized, so too are consumer dissatisfactions privatized. In this way, privatization is a response to the growing concern about the "ungovernability" of the Western democracies that first appeared in the 1970s.

Economists, reflecting their own professional interests, treat privatization as a matter of efficiency, but it is not evident that efficiency is the uppermost political interest. Thatcher's decision to put privatization ahead of liberalization in the sale of British Telecom is indicative of her stronger interest in spreading share ownership and privatizing labor relations than in the potential efficiency gains from greater competition (Kay, Mayer, and Thompson 1987). The privatization of Britain's ten water authorities is yet another example where ideological concerns seem to be stronger than strictly economic ones (*The Economist*, Feb. 11, 1989). Chilean privatization efforts have even stronger political overtones (Sigmund, in this volume).

That privatization of state-owned enterprise has been a political success in Britain, no one need doubt. Many of the nationalized industries had, in fact, been unpopular for some time. And the success of some companies after privatization seems to confirm the view that many companies would do better under private ownership (Lohr 1987). It is too early, however, for a verdict on the effects of privatization on British economic performance (see Lohr 1989). The rebound in the 1980s may have depended, far more than advocates of privatization would like to believe, on improving conditions in the advanced economies. (The performance of many enterprises still in state ownership in France and Italy, as well as in Britain, also improved significantly in the 1980s.)

Furthermore, as a balance-shifting program, privatization extends beyond the sphere of industrial enterprise to the provision of social welfare. In Britain and elsewhere, the politics of privatizing the welfare state are altogether different from those of privatizing industry. Although the nationalized industries were long unpopular in Britain, the National Health Service (NHS) is not. Thatcher's plans for the development of an "internal market" in the NHS, which might well be preliminary to privatizing many of the hospitals, are widely considered a drag on Conservative party electoral support (*New York Times*, June 26, 1989). In fact, while economists and other analysts have put forward a variety of schemes for privatizing social welfare, few governments anywhere in the world have acted upon them. The one major exception is the Chilean privatization of social security. The usual privatization proposals for health, welfare, and education call for the state to maintain its financial and policy-setting roles and to involve private firms in the delivery of services. That, however, is a matter not just of balance shifting but also of what I prefer to call boundary blurring.

Boundary Blurring

Some privatization policies, like contracting out, vouchers, and other means of paying private firms for providing public services, shrink the state in the sense of reducing public employment. Yet in two different ways they also blur the public-private boundary. In theory, government still sets policy even when private firms provide services; but as partners in implementation, private providers inevitably assume some policy-making power, too. On the other hand, once private firms become recipients of public funds, they are typically subject to more government control and become less distinctively private. Ironically, in both ways, privatization policies of this kind attenuate the distinction between public and private organizations.

Boundary-blurring partial privatization policies have been promoted by ideological conservatives and more pragmatic, managerial reformers. The ideological proponents see the privatization of public provision as a method of breaking up "public spending coalitions" and of introducing free choice into public monopolies (Butler 1985). Some conservatives, including Milton and Rose Friedman (1980), have advocated such steps as a second-best alternative to eliminating public spending for many services altogether. In contrast, the more pragmatic exponents of partial privatization are not necessarily interested in cutting back the domain of public responsibility. They see competition as a healthy check on the public sector, encouraging it to become more efficient and customer-oriented. Consequently, the managerial advocates of market-oriented reform are often indifferent whether the stimulus to better performance comes in the form of internal competition among government agencies or between government agencies and private firms.

Although proposals for greater competition and more private participation in delivering public services have been advanced in many countries, including the developing world (Roth 1987), they occupy an especially prominent place in the American debate. In the United States, where there is little nationalized industry to sell, privatization has almost inevitably meant greater private sector involvement in providing public services and carrying out governmental functions. Of the several forms this involvement can take, contracting out is the most widely discussed.

Contracting with private firms, however, is scarcely a new or radical idea; all levels of American government have long experience with it. The leading American advocates of privatization have gone much further, however, advancing radical proposals to shed public assets and governmental functions long assumed to be proper responsibilities of the liberal state. Among these proposals are plans to privatize national forests and parks (Smith 1982), city streets, prisons, and courts (Fitzgerald 1988), schools (U.S. President's Commission on Privatization 1988), social security (Ferrara 1985), and even money (Rahn 1986). The result is that the privatization movement in America is a mixture of the familiar (contracting out cafeterias for public employees) and the radical (privatizing money).

Both kinds of proposals have raised a boundary-*setting* question: Where do policy makers draw the line? In particular, what functions are "essentially governmental" and, consequently, ought not to be subject to privatization? In the federal government a series of disputes has erupted over the limits of contracting out. The Defense Department, for example, has balked at various privatization efforts on the grounds that they would jeopardize security, although it does contract out the advanced radar detection systems on the Distant Early Warning (DEW) line. The Federal Bureau of Investigation is currently resisting an effort by the Office of Management and Budget to privatize the computerized information system that the FBI maintains on criminals, including their fingerprints. Data from the system are available only to police, not to private citizens or firms. Would they remain so in the hands of a private company? The dispute exemplifies the more general problem of defining what is irreducibly governmental at a time of boundary-challenging and boundary-blurring reform.

Several other examples—private prisons, privatization of infrastructure, school vouchers, and social welfare privatization—also illustrate how privatization blurs public-private boundaries by involving private firms in the performance of functions that government cannot entirely surrender. The management of prisons, like the administration of justice, involves the use of the state's distinctive coercive powers. Private individuals are not ordinarily permitted to confine others against their will. In privatizing prison management, the state delegates a power normally reserved to the sovereign. While contracts may specify the conditions for the use of force, no contract can possibly anticipate all contingencies in the control of unruly inmates; private prison managers necessarily become partners in the discretionary use of force (diIulio 1988). More generally, the idea of privatizing management but not policy making suffers from the old illusion that it is possible to separate policy from administration. Since the two are intertwined, privatization turns private firms into policy makers. The grim history of private prisons in the United States and other countries illustrates the potential hazards of delegating coercive powers to private companies; but even if private prisons were to achieve all that their advocates promise, they blur what diIulio (1988) calls "the moral writ of the community" in carrying out punishment (see also P. Starr 1987).

The use of private firms to own and operate infrastructure, such as highways, bridges, and sewerage and water systems, represents another kind of boundary blurring. The provision of these facilities is typically a state function, not only for historical state-building reasons, but also because they are classic cases of market failure. Advocates of privatization suggest, however, that the facilities can be provided more efficiently by private firms without drawing on state budgets. Private road builders, for example, can recover their investment directly through tolls. Even where advocates of privatization recognize there are natural monopolies, as in water supply, they argue that competitive bidding for long-term franchises produces a more efficient solution (see Hanke and Walters 1987). Yet anticipating long-term developments affecting costs and required investment, such as changes in population and patterns of residence, is extraordinarily difficult. When the original contract or franchise terms prove inadequate, the private firm may threaten a "capital strike" by refusing to make needed investments (see Jacobson 1989 for a history of the rise and fall of private water supply in San Francisco). In effect, rather than being in the choice situation of an open market, the governmental unit finds itself in a litigious tug-of-war with a single supplier.

Short-term fiscal interests have helped generate support for infrastructure privatization. The development of infrastructure under private ownership has an appeal to fiscally strapped governments, which then need not raise the capital themselves. Even if private financing may ultimately be more expensive because the private firms pay higher interest rates, politicians can claim a keen concern for thrift by keeping the debt and interest payments off the public budget (and even off-off-budget). But the community may pay the price partly in diminished public control. Ensuring proper maintenance may be a particular problem, especially if the privatization is for some fixed period of time.

Educational vouchers provide yet another example of the boundary-blurring phenomenon. By turning education budgets into vouchers, privatization reformers hope to enable students and their parents to choose freely among all schools, public and private, and to make the schools more efficient and responsive. The extent of free choice depends, first of all, on the requirements the state sets for schools eligible to receive vouchers. The more detailed the standards, the more private schools become subject to governmental control. The extent of choice also depends on whether the voucher plan permits schools to set tuition above voucher levels and to exercise discretion in admissions and expulsions. In this case, more discretion for schools reduces the choices available to many families; the state may well intervene to ensure choice by prescribing tuition limits and due process standards for schools. Furthermore, once receiving extensive public funds, the schools would be sure to draw increased political and judicial scrutiny. As a result, private schools would likely become less distinguishable from public institutions. When boundaries blur, private institutions can be turned, unintentionally, into public ones.

Blurred boundaries and increased regulation of private providers are commonplace in the sphere of social welfare. As Lester Salamon (1986) has argued, much of the expansion of social welfare in the United States has come in the form of financial support for services delivered by private, often nonprofit organizations. Conservatives have advocated this use of "mediating structures" as a means of diversifying and privatizing social provision (Berger and Neuhaus 1977). But once the private organizations take on these roles, they are inevitably subject to greater public supervision. Scandal is typically the mother of control: every incident of exposed corruption produces a wave of regulation and threatens to undo the very advantages of private organization that such programs aimed to exploit.

Thus privatization often has a feedback effect on state structures. The governmental use of private suppliers under contracts, voucher systems, or other reimbursement arrangements creates a demand for control capacities different from those of conventional bureaucratic administration. Public officials require skills in negotiation, bargaining, and contract supervision and enforcement. Ironically, reliance on contracts puts a premium on planning, since public officials need to envision in advance the service needs and diverse contingencies that might arise over the course of the contract. "Mid-course corrections" are less feasible than when officials directly administer services (National Academy of Public Administration 1989).

Once again, privatization ought to be understood not merely as reducing the state but as restructuring it. In regard to public employees, the threat of contracting out may give political leaders enhanced power. Competition in many services is limited, however, and it may diminish over time as contractors acquire insider advantages. In that event, public officials may become captives of their own contractors. Indeed, with weak political parties, contractors become key sources of campaign finance, and the bargaining capacities of political leaders are frequently limited, if not entirely compromised. Corruption of this kind is an old story. Two new factors seem to be affecting the rate of public sector contracting. One is the impact on governmental organization of new information and communications technology. In the private sector, the new technology has changed the economics of "make-buy" decisions, enabling companies to scan a broader array of supply alternatives and to substitute external suppliers for internal production of parts or services. The new technology thus alters the logic of organizational boundaries. Although governments are not as free to roam the world in search of suppliers, the same logic favors hiving off parts of the state bureaucracy and relying on more contractors. The extreme case in municipal government is the "contract city," which relies on contracts for virtually all municipal operations (Fitzgerald 1988).

But there is another reason for the growth of contracting. The growth of public sector unions in the postwar period produced rising wages and benefits. In the same period, American government at all levels adopted a variety of internal procedural requirements for freedom of information, due process, and checks on conflict of interest. Some of these requirements apply to contractors, but the burden of decades of reform rests more heavily on the public sector. The combined effect of civil service requirements dating from the Progressive Era, collective bargaining agreements of more recent vintage, and the due process revolution have imposed sharply higher costs on public sector agencies than are faced by their non-union, unregulated private counterparts. With one stroke, privatization undoes much of the reform effort. Probably more than anything else, privatization in the United States is being driven by this incentive to escape regulation imposed on the public sector.

Privatization, Civil Society, and the Liberal State

I have been arguing that in different contexts privatization amounts to three different programs for restructuring of the state. In the former Eastern bloc and parts of the developing world, privatization involves the creation of an enabling framework for markets and civil society. In the capitalist countries with large public sectors, privatization aims at shifting the public-private balance. And in a country like the United States, with little nationalized industry, privatization has chiefly meant involving private enterprise in carrying out public policy.

The differences among these programs are fundamental. At stake in the institution-building program is the constitution of society. The developments in the East are of historic proportions whether they succeed or fail. The stakes in the West are not nearly so great. To be sure, some programs to privatize state-owned enterprise, such as Margaret Thatcher's, have significantly reduced the public sector; but the question of extensive nationalization had already been put to rest in Great Britain and other Western democracies. The third program of boundary-blurring reform is a mixture of managerial and radical right-wing ideas for recasting the operation of the state. Its long-run significance, I believe, is likely to be modest: the managerial ideas are easily assimilated, the radical ideas easily dismissed (as George Bush dismissed Pete duPont, standard bearer for the privatization movement during the 1988 Republican primary debates).

But if the programs vary in historical significance, they also vary in their political substance. Depending on the program and the context, privatization may either stimulate or sap the vitality of civil society and public life. Privatization enlivens civil society where the state has had a stranglehold on personal choice and the forms of human involvement. That has been the case not only in the communist regimes but also in some excessively centralized Western and developing societies. But a vital civil society requires more than a rich variety of voluntary associations and independent centers of power; it also needs a rich sphere of public discussion that engages society's diverse classes and groups. The radical right's program of privatization threatens to reduce that public sphere by turning citizens into consumers wherever possible (P. Starr 1987).

The various privatization programs also differ sharply in their immediate political objectives. Some governments in the East, such as the Soviet Union, continue to try to install a limited capitalism as the engine of socialist growth; but combining the two systems is precisely what Thatcher and other conservatives reject. The communist governments undertook economic reforms, including privatization, at some risk of destabilizing their own regimes—and indeed, succeeded in subverting their own rule—whereas conservative Western governments have been pursuing privatization with some hope of reinforcing their positions.

To be sure, it is possible to read each type of privatization program as enhancing the power of states, parties, or other powerful political actors. The legalization of the informal sector in the Eastern bloc is partly an effort at co-optation, and the moves to encourage private investment are part of a broader drive to modernize and strengthen the state as a whole. Similarly, divesting enterprises that need subsidies and provoke conflict is easily interpreted as a measure that strengthens the state. The same is true of contracting out, which weakens public employee unions. But if states are adopting privatization for rational power-related reasons, they are often being forced to do so because of new conditions, such as the growth of the second economy, the transformation of state enterprises into political liabilities, the post-industrial transition, and new demands on organizations for flexibility. To locate the "cause" of privatization within the state would be as foolish as to ignore the political interests that have helped advance it.

So what should we now think of the postwar view that the ground occupied by modern administrative states would never be given up? Several errors are apparent. In regard to the communist regimes, Western theorists mistook the abstract model of totalitarianism for the varied historical realities that shape each society, and they erroneously believed that the regimes could forever resist pressures from within and without. The Soviet Union's recovery from World War II and its success with Sputnik created a misleading perception of its capacities for economic growth and technological innovation. Its lagging development now exposes the endemic rigidities of an autarchic, centrally directed economy. Such a system may survive through political repression, but the possibilities of resistance and liberalization are clearly greater than were thought in the 1950s by Friedrich and Brzezinski (1956) as well as many others. In particular, they overestimated the regime's capacities to monopolize communication and to maintain closure against external influence. Either economic growth leads to greater communicative capacities in the society and to expanded international contact, or economic stagnation threatens the ability of the state to maintain its military and financial capacities for projecting power in the international arena. One way or the other (or even in both ways), communist states are prone to more pressure for liberalization than the postwar models of totalitarianism supposed.

In regard to the West itself, theorists were wrong to believe that political advantage one-sidedly favors government growth. As Musgrave (1981) points out, the "public choice" model of government bureaucracies as budget-maximizing firms ignores internal governmental checks on spending, such as finance ministries, as well as the potential voter coalitions for tax reduction. There is simply no a priori reason to believe that coalitions for government growth have any natural advantage. As recent experience shows, there are political gains to be made from privatization as well as from tax cuts and deregulation.

Moreover, just as Marxists were too committed to the idea that socialism is the stage of social development "beyond" capitalism, so too were many Weberian sociologists and political scientists too attached to the idea of bureaucratization as a secular tendency of advanced societies. Now we can see a different logic at work in economic organization, favoring flexibility, informality, and responsiveness to changes in taste. The same logic suggests the limits of bureaucratic organization and calls for more permeability along the boundary of the state with private firms and associations. The very tendency to impose greater bureaucratic control on the public sector to reduce corruption and improve accountability raises the cost differential with private firms and increases the incentive to use private service providers. These shifts toward flexibility, responsiveness to diverse tastes, and outsourcing counteract the tendency toward enlarged public sectors in post-industrial states. For although services may grow in size relative to manufacturing, their growth may take place increasingly outside the public sector as a result of wholesale shifts (for example, the privatization of telecommunications and broadcasting) or piecemeal changes (contracting out).

These trends, however, do not confirm the thesis that we are now entering a "post-socialist" era. Third World debt, war, ecological disaster—any of several possibilities could set off a new cycle of revolutionary activity in the West and the Third World, as unexpected today as the upheavals of the 1960s were unexpected the previous decade. The likelihood of new political eruptions is not the only reason that makes the "end of the socialist era" thesis unconvincing when applied to the West. To be sure, some parties of the left, such as Labour in Britain, have experienced a long-term decline of their electoral base. Others, however, have successfully reconstructed their bases of support. Moreover, the social democratic countries continue to perform well economically; their adoption of market-oriented policies is more an adjustment than a transformation. The more thorough and radical privatization programs of conservatives seem unlikely to be realized. What is returning, after all, is not the night-watchman state of nineteenth-century liberalism; the prospects of rolling back macroeconomic management, public education, and governmental programs of social protection are virtually nil. The politics of privatizing schools, social security, health care, and other human services differ sharply from the politics of privatizing state-owned enterprises. Some conservatives see the divestiture of industry as merely a first phase, to be followed by increasingly bold sallies against the central fortresses of the welfare and regulatory state. But more likely the conservative coalitions will break up as the battles turn to social provision, the environment, and other areas where the modern mixed, liberal, social democratic state enjoys wide support.

Furthermore, privatization policies are not yet so deeply entrenched as to be irreversible. In the West, the privatization of industry will be more strongly anchored where ownership is dispersed among citizens than where it is concentrated, particularly among foreigners. Thatcher's program has been aimed not only at putting the nationalized industries into the private sector but also at keeping them there. Any renationalization would have to confront, not some small group of owners, but a large body of shareholders. Similarly, if social security were privatized in other countries besides Chile, reversal would be difficult: social security privatization creates strong interests in its perpetuation (P. Starr 1988b; Sigmund, in this volume). But when privatized companies fail, or if privatized social security investment funds go bankrupt, political leaders are certain to be importuned to come to their rescue. And many will. Other forms of privatization are even more vulnerable to reversal. For example, it is relatively easy for governments to bring contracted-out functions back into the state since contracts come up periodically for renewal.

The larger question concerns the political future of liberal political and economic ideas. Internationally, respect for pluralism, civil society, and the market may now be greater than at any time in the twentieth century. Except in Latin America, communism scarcely counts as an ideological force; and where socialist governments thrive, they do so on liberal political foundations. "What we may be witnessing," writes Francis Fukuyama (1989), "is not just the end of the Cold War, but the universalization of Western liberal democracy as the final form of human government." The ink was scarcely dry on Fukuyama's words when the government of China put down demands for "bourgeois liberalism" in a brutal massacre.

History is a notoriously fickle ally. Anyone hearing the verdicts rendered today on the fate of ideologies and systems might recall that during the 1930s many thought the Depression had pronounced a final judgment on the struggle between capitalism and socialism. Not only socialists drew the conclusion that socialism was winning. In his great work, *Capitalism, Socialism and Democracy* (1942), Joseph Schumpeter celebrated the capitalist entrepreneur but concluded, regretfully, that socialism would ultimately triumph. After World War II, many said that the whole struggle between capitalism and socialism was irrelevant. If there was a new verdict then, it favored the mixed economy. In *Modern Capitalism* (1965), Andrew Shonfield could speak confidently of the great engine of economic progress that had been set moving by interventionist policy. By the 1960s, laissez-faire seemed dead and buried, and social democrats and liberals danced on its grave. But the coffin must have been empty: twenty years later the presumptuous dancers and the presumed dead have changed places. Yet if obituaries are now being written, not just for socialism but for American liberalism and European social democracy, the reason may be not that history has finally pronounced a verdict but that the current judges have a short memory. Such final verdicts seem to be good for, at most, thirty years. We should have learned from the failure of the Marxist theory of history not simply the mistake of believing in an inevitable transition from capitalism to socialism. We should have learned to be distrustful of all notions that history has in store for mankind the realization of a universal ideal. Even those of us who take satisfaction in the remarkable rebirth of civil society in the East and revitalization of the liberal state in the West ought to know that this is only another season of our passions and not history's last stop.

References

Arendt, Hannah. 1951. *The Origins of Totalitarianism*. New York: Harcourt Brace.

Baran, Paul A., and Paul M. Sweezy. 1966. *Monopoly Capital*. New York: Monthly Review Press.

Bauer, Tamas. 1988. "Hungarian Economic Reform in Eastern European Perspective." *Eastern European Politics and Societies* 2: 418–432.

Baumol, William J. 1967. "Macroeconomics of Unbalanced Growth: The Anatomy of Urban Crisis." *American Economic Review* 72: 1–15.

Bell, Daniel. 1973. *The Coming of Post-Industrial Society*. New York: Basic Books.

Berger, Peter L., and Richard John Neuhaus. 1977. *To Empower People: The Role of Mediating Structures in Public Policy*. Washington, D.C.: American Enterprise Institute for Public Policy Research.

Bernstein, Marver. 1955. *Regulating Business by Independent Commission*. Princeton: Princeton University Press.

Bird, Richard M. 1971. "Wagner's Law of Expanding State Activity." *Public Finance* 26: 1–24.

Block, Fred. 1987. *Revising State Theory: Essays in Politics and Postindustrialism*. Philadelphia: Temple University Press.

Borcherding, Thomas E. 1977. "One Hundred Years of Public Spending." In *Budgets and Bureaucrats: The Sources of Government Growth*, ed. Thomas E. Borcherding. Durham, N.C.: Duke University Press.

Brzezinski, Zbigniew. 1989. *The Grand Failure: The Birth and Death of Communism in the Twentieth Century*. New York: Charles Scribner's Sons.

Buchanan, James M. 1977. "Why Does Government Grow?" In *Budgets and Bureaucrats: The Sources of Government Growth*, ed. Thomas E. Borcherding. Durham, N.C.: Duke University Press.

Butler, David, and Donald Stokes. 1969. *Political Change in Britain*. London: Macmillan.

Butler, Stuart M. 1985. *Privatizing Federal Spending: A Strategy to Eliminate the Deficit*. New York: Universe Books.

Cameron, David R. 1978. "The Expansion of the Public Economy: A Comparative Analysis." *American Political Science Review* 72: 1243–61.

Cheung, Steven N. S. 1989. "The Experience of China's Economic Reforms: Privatization vs. Special Interests." *Harvard International Review* 11: 19–23.

Comisso, Ellen. 1988. "Market Failures and Market Socialism: Economic Problems of the Transition." *Eastern European Politics and Societies* 2: 433–465.

Curwen, Peter J. 1986. *Public Enterprise*. Brighton, Sussex: Wheatsheaf Books.

Derthick, Martha, and Paul J. Quirk. 1985. *The Politics of Deregulation*. Washington, D.C.: The Brookings Institution.

de Sola Pool, Ithiel. 1983. *Technologies of Freedom.* Cambridge, Mass.: Harvard University Press.

de Soto, Hernando. 1989. *The Other Path: The Invisible Revolution in the Third World.* New York: Harper and Row.

diIulio, John J. Jr. 1988. "What's Wrong with Private Prisons." *The Public Interest* no. 92: 66–83.

Ferrara, Peter J., ed. 1985. *Social Security: Prospects for Real Reform.* Washington, D.C.: Cato Institute.

Fitzgerald, Randall. 1988. *When Government Goes Private: Successful Alternatives to Public Services.* New York: Universe Books.

Friedrich, Carl J., and Zbigniew K. Brzezinski. 1956. *Totalitarian Dictatorship and Autocracy.* Cambridge, Mass.: Harvard University Press.

Friedman, Milton, and Rose Friedman. 1980. *Free to Choose.* New York: Harcourt Brace Jovanovich.

Fukuyama, Francis. 1989. "The End of History." *The National Interest* no. 16: 3–18.

Furubotn, Eirik G., and Svetozar Pejovich, eds. 1974. *The Economics of Property Rights.* Cambridge, Mass.: Ballinger.

Glade, William P. 1986. "Sources and Forms of Privatization." In *State Shrinking: A Comparative Inquiry into Privatization,* ed. William P. Glade. Austin: Institute for Latin American Studies, University of Texas at Austin.

Hall, Peter. 1986. *Governing the Economy: The Politics of State Intervention in Britain and France.* Cambridge: Polity Press.

Hanke, Steve H., and Stephen J. K. Walters. 1987. "Privatizing Waterworks." In *Prospects for Privatization,* ed. Steve H. Hanke. New York: Academy of Political Science.

Heilbroner, Robert. 1989. "The Triumph of Capitalism." *The New Yorker,* January 23, pp. 98–109.

Hindley, Brian, ed. 1983. *State Investment Companies in Western Europe.* New York: St. Martin's Press.

Hirst, Paul, and Jonathan Zeitlin, eds. 1989. *Reversing Industrial Decline? Industrial Structure and Policy in Britain and Her Competitors.* Oxford: Berg.

Holland, Stuart, ed. 1972. *The State as Entrepreneur.* London: Weidenfeld and Nicolson.

Jacobson, Charles. 1989. "Same Game, Different Players: Problems in Urban Public Utility Regulation, 1850–1987." *Urban Studies* 26: 13–31.

Jenkins, Peter. 1988. *Mrs. Thatcher's Revolution: The Ending of the Socialist Era.* Cambridge, Mass.: Harvard University Press.

Kay, John A., Colin Mayer, and David J. Thompson, eds. 1987. *Privatization and Regulation: The U.K. Experience.* Oxford: Clarendon Press.

Kennedy, Duncan. 1982. "The States of Decline of the Public-Private Distinction." *University of Pennsylvania Law Review* 130: 1349–1357.

Kirkpatrick, Jeane J. 1982. *Dictatorship and Double Standards: Rationalism and Reason in Politics.* New York: American Enterprise Institute/Simon and Schuster.

Kramer, Daniel C. 1988. *State Capital and Private Enterprise: The Case of the UK National Enterprise Board.* London: Routledge.

Letwin, Oliver. 1988. *Privatising the World.* London: Cassell.

Levy, Daniel C. 1986. *Higher Education and the State in Latin America: Private Challenges to Public Dominance.* Chicago: University of Chicago Press.

Lohr, Steve. 1987. "The Best of Times in British Business." *New York Times,* April 5.

———. 1989. "Has Thatcherism Really Worked?" *New York Times,* June 3.

Lowi, Theodore J. 1969. *The End of Liberalism.* New York: W. W. Norton.

Mayer, Colin, and Shirley Meadowcroft. 1987. "Selling Public Assets: Techniques and Financial Implications." In Kay, Mayer, and Thompson 1987.

Meltzer, Allan H., and Scott F. Richard. 1978. "Why Government Grows (and Grows) in a Democracy." *The Public Interest,* no. 52: 111–118.

Miliband, Ralph. 1969. *The State in Capitalist Society.* New York: Basic Books.

Musgrave, Richard A. 1981. "Leviathan Cometh—or Does He?" In *Tax and Expenditure Limitations,* ed. Helen F. Ladd and T. Nicolaus Tideman. Washington, D.C.: Urban Institute Press.

National Academy of Public Administration. 1989. "Privatization: The Challenge to Public Management." N.p.

Niskanen, William N. 1971. *Bureaucracy and Representative Government.* Chicago: Aldine-Atherton Press.

Noll, Roger G., and Bruce M. Owen, eds. 1983. *The Political Economy of Deregulation: Interest Groups in the Regulatory Process.* Washington, D.C.: American Enterprise Institute for Public Policy Research.

O'Connor, James. 1973. *The Fiscal Crisis of the State.* New York: St. Martin's Press.

Piore, Michael J., and Charles F. Sabel. 1984. *The Second Industrial Divide.* New York: Basic Books.

Piven, Frances Fox, and Richard A. Cloward. 1971. *Regulating the Poor.* New York: Random House.

Portes, Alejandro, Manuel Castells, and Lauren A. Benton. 1989. *The Informal Economy: Studies in Advanced and Less Developed Countries.* Baltimore: Johns Hopkins University Press.

Poulantzas, Nicos. 1969. "The Problem of the Capitalist State." *New Left Review* 58: 67–78.

Pryke, Richard S. 1971. *Public Enterprise in Practice.* London: MacGibbon and Kee.

———. 1981. *The Nationalized Industries: Policies and Performance Since 1968.* Oxford: Martin Robinson.

Rahn, Richard W. 1986. "Time to Privatize Money?" *Policy Review*, no. 36: 55–57.

Redwood, John. 1980. *Public Enterprise in Crisis: The Future of the Nationalised Industries*. Oxford: Basil Blackwell.

Roth, Gabriel. 1987. *The Private Provision of Public Services in Developing Countries*. New York: Oxford University Press.

Salamon, Lester M. 1986. "Partners in Public Service: Toward a Theory of Government-Nonprofit Relations." In *The Nonprofit Sector: A Research Handbook*, ed. Walter W. Powell. New Haven: Yale University Press.

Savas, E. S. 1987. *Privatization: The Key to Better Government*. Chatham, N.J.: Chatham House Publishers.

Schapiro, Leonard. 1972. *Totalitarianism*. New York: Praeger.

Schmitter, Philippe C., and Gerhard Lehmbruch, eds. 1979. *Trends Toward Corporatist Intermediation*. Beverly Hills, Calif.: Sage Publications.

Schumpeter, Joseph. 1942. *Capitalism, Socialism and Democracy*. New York: Harper and Brothers.

Shonfield, Andrew. 1965. *Modern Capitalism: The Changing Balance of Public and Private Power*. London: Oxford University Press.

Smith, Robert J. 1982. "Privatizing the Environment." *Policy Review* 20: 11–50.

Starr, Paul. 1987. "The Limits of Privatization." In *Prospects for Privatization*, ed. Steve H. Hanke. New York: Academy of Political Science.

———. 1988a. "The Meaning of Privatization." *Yale Law & Policy Review* 6: 6–41.

———. 1988b. "Social Security and the American Public Household." In *Social Security: Beyond the Rhetoric of Crisis*, ed. Theodore R. Marmor and Jerry L. Mashaw. Studies from the Project on the Federal Social Role. Princeton: Princeton University Press.

———. Forthcoming. "Television and the Public Household." In *Television in America's Future: A Search for the Right Public Policy*, ed. Michael A. Rice.

Starr, S. Frederick. 1988. "Soviet Union: A Civil Society." *Foreign Policy* 70: 26–41.

Stigler, George J. 1971. "The Theory of Economic Regulation." *Bell Journal of Economics and Management Science* 2: 1–21.

Tarchys, Daniel. 1975. "The Growth of Public Expenditures: Nine Modes of Explanation." *Scandanavian Political Studies* 10: 9–31.

Taylor, Charles, ed. 1983. *Why Governments Grow*. Beverly Hills, Calif.: Sage Publications.

U.S. President's Commission on Privatization. 1988. *Privatization: Toward More Effective Government*. N.p.

Vernon, Raymond. 1988. "Introduction: The Promise and the Challenge." In *The Promise of Privatization: A Challenge for American Foreign Policy*, ed. Raymond Vernon. New York: Council on Foreign Relations.

Wagner, Adolph. 1877. *Finanzwissenschaft*. Leipzig: C. F. Winter.
Weinstein, James. 1968. *The Corporate Ideal in the Liberal State: 1900–1918*. Boston: Beacon Press.
Wilensky, Harold L. 1975. *The Welfare State and Equality*. Berkeley: University of California Press.

3

Economic Rationales for the Scope of Privatization

Carl Shapiro and Robert D. Willig

In this chapter we seek to identify, at a fundamental theoretical level, the impacts of privatization on the operations of an enterprise. We conduct our analysis in an abstract framework that is rich enough to represent considerations of both efficiency in performance and ability to meet broader public objectives. Our goal is the delineation of various characteristics of an activity's structure and environment that point to either public or private forms of control as the most effective in accomplishing society's aims.[1]

Our approach focuses on informational and incentive differences between public and private enterprise. In particular, we suppose that in a public enterprise government officials possess intimate knowledge of the workings of the enterprise, while such information is controlled by private parties if the activity is privatized. Public enterprise is motivated to satisfy the goals of public management, while private enterprise is motivated to maximize profits, subject to whatever government regulation is imposed on it, and regulation is constrained by the need to attract private capital.

Our focus on information might appear peculiar and quite narrow to some readers. We shall argue, however, that at a fundamental level the intrinsic differences between public and private enterprise must ultimately be based on incentives, and these in turn are based on the available information. This information-theoretic perspective fits our work squarely into the recent and fast-growing economics literature on organizational design and performance, which focuses on the problems and opportunities posed by different patterns of control in settings distinguished by their structures of information and incentives.[2]

Our study of privatization thus asks how a shift from public to private ownership alters the structure of information, incentives, and controls facing the individuals operating the enterprise. These elements in turn determine the enterprise's operating decisions and hence its economic and social performance. Neither public nor private sector enterprises operate perfectly, and our organizational models of the two forms are designed to shed light on the conditions under which one can be predicted to perform better than the other.

In the following section we present the canonical models of private and public enterprise that we subsequently subject to comparative analysis. These models are designed to reflect a common technological and informational environment into which different governance structures can be imposed. We use our models of public and private enterprise in the third section to demonstrate a series of "neutrality results," that is, to identify informational environments in which there is no intrinsic difference in the performance of public and private enterprise. There we justify our focus on private information by showing that the presence of such information is necessary for privatization to have a genuine effect. We then focus on environments in which neutrality between public and private enterprise does not obtain, seeking to derive from our two models some qualitative results concerning the tradeoff between public and private enterprise. In particular, we identify those factors that would lead a public-spirited party to select private or public enterprise. In the fifth section we illustrate our theoretical findings by applying them to several stylized examples of public enterprise: a basic manufacturing operation, a hotel or tourist facility, the production of military equipment, prison management, and the operation of the postal or telecommunications system. There we take a step toward applying our framework to inform an inquiry into the relative merits of public versus private enterprise in practice.

Public Enterprise, Private Enterprise, and Regulation

The labels "public ownership" and "private enterprise" suggest two discrete and very different ways of structuring economic activity and utilizing productive assets. The corresponding simple view of privatization is that it inevitably and significantly alters the way in which resources are allocated. Certainly reading the country studies contained in this volume would not lead one to doubt that privatization "matters." Indeed, one might think it obvious that privatization has a significant influence on an enterprise's operating decisions and hence on the allocation of resources.

The conclusion that privatization typically has a major impact on the allocation of resources is probably correct. We seek, however, some general guidelines indicating the *nature* of the impact of privatization and how it varies with the underlying economic and political environment. Developing such guidelines requires a coherent comparative model of decisionmaking in public sector enterprises and in privately owned companies, the latter possibly subject to government control through taxes, subsidies, and direct regulation.

As one begins to think seriously about and to construct models of public and private sector enterprises, it soon becomes clear that the distinction between these two forms is not nearly so stark or so inevitable as it might appear upon casual consideration.[3] In particular, private enterprises that are subjected to carefully crafted taxes, subsidies, and regulatory oversight may be almost indistinguishable from public ones. Superficially, there might seem to be a stark difference between public and private enterprises because the former can be directed to serve entirely public goals, while the latter are entirely profit-oriented. In cases where there is no market failure, profit maximization coincides with public goals. But even where there is sharp deviation between public goals and profit maximization, private enterprise can be subjected to various forms of regulation to make it better serve public goals.

For example, consider an oft-cited motivation for privatization, namely, to achieve a reduction in the public sector borrowing requirement. Supposedly, privatizing a money-losing public operation will relieve the treasury of the ongoing drain of funds required to cover the enterprise's losses. Why privatization is necessary to achieve this goal is rarely articulated, however. If low prices are the source of the deficit, prices charged by the public enterprise could in principle be raised to generate more revenues. If inefficient operations are the cause, additional oversight or improved incentive mechanisms may be the solution. And if the enterprise's capital requirements are placing a strain on public sector borrowing, shifting these loans to the private sector may be a mere accounting change, not a genuine improvement in efficiency.[4]

Similar arguments can be applied to other common justifications for privatization. For example, if restrictive civil service rules hamper the operations of a public enterprise, relaxing these rules, perhaps on a selective basis, may serve the same goals for which privatization is touted. If trade unions are thought to be overly powerful in a public enterprise, why will they not be equally powerful in affecting the taxes and regulations imposed on the private enterprise? If an industry is thought to be vital for national security purposes or for general economic development, why is an arm's-length subsidy designed to promote domestic production not equally as effective as subsidized public sector enterprise?

We recognize that several of these arguments for privatization are likely to be valid, indeed overwhelming, in particular economic circumstances and especially when the political circumstances unique to each country are taken into account.[5] Our goal, however, is to look beyond these case-by-case considerations to elucidate some general principles regarding those activities most appropriate for privatization.

One way to analyze privatization would be to compare the operations of a public sector enterprise with those of an unregulated private company. Simply privatizing a public enterprise, without establishing any structure of regulatory oversight, taxes, or subsidies, will typically have a substantial effect on the allocation of resources, for the simple reason that an unfettered private company will seek to maximize shareholder profits, whereas a public enterprise is likely to be operated to serve social goals apart from the maximization of its profits. If market failures—externalities, monopoly power, and the like—are severe, then privatization without regulation may well be inferior to public enterprise.

We wish to pose a different question, however: What effect will privatization have if the private company is subjected to sophisticated *regulation*, as well as tax and subsidy policies, designed to account for public-interest goals? In posing the question this way, we can reject arguments such as the one that pursuit of national security goals alone mandates public ownership of an industry; rather, we ask whether national security goals can be better met by public enterprise or by private enterprise facing special tax treatment or regulation designed to promote those goals. Likewise, we do not accept the argument that an industry must be public merely because it is a natural monopoly; we ask whether a private company facing regulatory oversight could perform better than public enterprise.

When the effects of privatization are studied in this way, a surprising answer emerges: Under a remarkably general set of conditions, there is *no difference* between the performance of a public enterprise and that of a private company subject to an optimally designed regulatory and tax scheme.[6] We shall describe and comment below on these "neutrality theorems," which provide conditions under which public sector enterprise and regulated private enterprise are equivalent in terms of resource allocation. These neutrality theorems, which we have adapted from the economics literature on regulation and mechanism design, will be easier to describe after we present the components of our formal models.

In noting these neutrality results, we do not mean to suggest that any objective of privatization can in fact be achieved equally well with carefully chosen policies within the context of the public sector enterprise. Rather we take these neutrality theorems as our starting point in developing models rich enough so that privatization is *not* neutral. Such models are capable of revealing the intrinsic differences between public and private enterprise. The required richness is the presence of *private information* about both the costs and the benefits of the enterprise's operations. We turn now to the development of these models.

Comparative Models of Public and
Private Sector Enterprise

We present here our models of public and private sector enterprise. The models are designed to facilitate a comparison of these two forms of ownership and control of productive assets. Figure 1 presents a schematic diagram of our two models, which will become clearer as we describe them in the text.

Our analysis emphasizes private information, that is, information observed by one party that cannot be observed or verified by others. In contrast, public or *contractible* information is either commonly observed or can be verified by a neutral third party such as a court. To illustrate this distinction between public and private information, consider information about employment conditions. The published national unemployment rate contains some information about employment conditions, and we will allow for instructions of the form "increase employment during periods of high employment" to be given to the public official with responsibility for the enterprise. But government officials may have more detailed information about employment conditions that cannot be verified, such as qualitative information regarding unemployment rates in different regions, the extent of underemployment, the alternative opportunities of those who might be hired in the enterprise, skills and unemployment rates among different groups in the population, and so on. Our models are designed to allow for the possibility that hiring decisions at the enterprise more accurately reflect such qualitative, private information if the enterprise is operated in the public sector under the direct control of the public official with the private information about employment conditions.

We include three types of private information: information about the external social benefits of the enterprise's activities, which we call ψ; information about the divergence between the public interest and the interests of the public official who oversees the enterprise, which we call ε; and information about the profitability of the enterprise's operations, which we call θ. Each of these will be described in further detail below.

As we shall see, the form of ownership matters only if there is some private, noncontractible information. Yet our analysis is perfectly capable of including public, contractible information. In fact, our entire analysis could be made *contingent* on such public information.[7] For that very reason, and without affecting any of our comparisons between public and private enterprise, we suppress such public information in all that follows.

We postulate the presence of a public-spirited agent, the *framer*, who originally makes the choice between public and private enterprise and sets up the governance structure for the enterprise chosen. This choice is

FIGURE 1
Schematic Diagram of Public and Private Enterprise

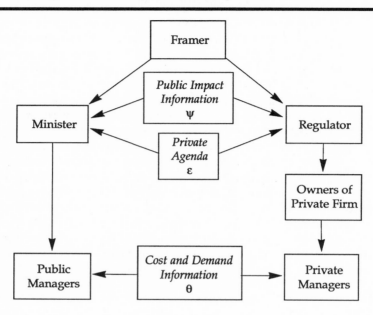

represented in Figure 1 by the two branches emanating from the box labeled "Framer." Our normative analysis is thus cast in the following terms: What is the optimal form of ownership and control for the framer to adopt, and how does this choice depend upon various features of the economic environment? The framer recognizes that political forces will influence subsequent public sector decisions, but he himself is above these forces, acting purely in the public interest.[8]

Public Enterprise

If the enterprise is public, it is controlled and operated by a public official, whom we call the *minister*. The minister may operate under restrictions put in place by the framer. If there are no such restrictions, we call the method of governance *discretionary public enterprise*. With restrictions, we have *nondiscretionary public enterprise*.

By virtue of his role in managing the enterprise, the minister receives private information, θ, regarding the technology of production and the state of demand.[9] We need not distinguish between demand and cost information; both are encompassed in the profit function. The profitability of taking action x is given by $\pi(x,\theta)$. We define θ so that profits are increasing in θ; $\pi_\theta > 0$, where subscripts denote partial derivatives. High values of θ correspond to conditions of high productivity or elevated demand. With the enterprise being run in the public sector, its contribution to the treasury is simply $\pi(x,\theta)$.

The profitability parameter θ is initially unknown at the time when the framer must choose between public and private enterprise. But the framer has prior beliefs about what θ will be; in particular, θ is distributed on the interval $[\theta_0,\theta_1]$ with probability density function $f(\theta)$ and cumulative distribution function $F(\theta)$.

Our notion of "action" is very general. We shall refer to x as "level of activity" (for example, output, quality, and the like) and θ as "level of profitability." We make the important assumption that $\pi_{x\theta} > 0$ at all x and θ, that is, that the marginal return to increasing the activity level is uniformly higher when the total return is higher. All other things being equal, efficiency requires higher levels of activity when costs are lower or demand is higher.

By virtue of his position in the public sector, the minister also observes information, ψ, that bears on the external social benefits generated by the enterprise's operations. The external social benefits associated with action x are given by $S(x,\psi)$. There are numerous examples of these benefits: consumer surplus generated by rail service; worker surplus generated by heavy industry; environmental damages caused by a manufacturing facility; spillover effects of a major factory on related industries or on overall regional development; national security benefits associated with the operation a defense facility; or the effect of the telephone system on national cohesion. $S(x,\psi)$ captures anything that affects the public interest but does not appear in the enterprise's profits.

We need not specify whether the enterprise receives revenues from the sale of its product. Any such revenue is included in the profit function; if there are no revenues, then the external benefits are correspondingly higher, since these include any surplus enjoyed by the enterprise's customers.

Our key substantive assumption is that the public-impact information that inherently resides in the public sector, ψ, does not appear in the profit function. In other words, ψ includes information not on the profitability of the enterprise but only on the external social effects of the enterprise's operations.

The minister makes two decisions. First, he must decide whether to authorize the investments required to operate the enterprise. For simplicity, we model this as a discrete, yes/no investment choice. If investment is not made, no further decisions in this domain are needed. We normalize all agents' payoffs to zero in this event. If investment is made, the minister makes the enterprise's operating decisions, that is, chooses x. Throughout this chapter, for the sake of simplicity, we assume that the investment is always warranted under the objectives of the framer and the public official.

The overall social welfare function that the framer seeks to maximize is given by

$$W = S(x,\psi) + k\pi(x,\theta).$$

This objective is simply external benefits plus enterprise profits, with a magnification factor applied to the net contribution made by the enterprise to the public treasury. This magnification factor, $k > 1$, equals the unit cost of raising public funds, including any distortions caused by the taxes required to finance public sector operations.[10]

The minister has objectives similar but not identical to those of the framer. In particular, the minister's objective is

$$V^M = W + \alpha J(x,\varepsilon).$$

We refer to J as the *private agenda of the minister*, but it could equally well represent divergences between the objectives of a public official, who is subject to short-run political pressure, and the genuine long-run public interest.

The variable α measures the extent of the divergence between the minister's objectives and those of the framer. Under the private-agenda interpretation of J, α measures the extent to which the minister is able to pursue his private agenda, as opposed to W. In this case, α could represent the effectiveness of the political system: a well-functioning political system limits the ability of public officials to pursue their personal interests, leading to a low value of α. Alternatively, ministers are more or less motivated by their personal agendas as α is large or small. Under the "short-run political pressure" interpretation of J, α measures the extent to which public officials are subject to political forces that in fact diverge from the long-run public interest.

The variable ε is observable only to the public official. It captures the idiosyncratic nature of his private agenda, which cannot be foreseen by the framer or observed by others while the minister is in power. The key point is that the framer cannot know just who the public official will be, or what his private aims will be, so it is difficult for the framer systematically to counteract such private agendas. Likewise, the minister's private goals will not be publicly observable, and hence the framer cannot charge a third party, such as the court, with the responsibility of penalizing the minister for pursuing his private agenda.[11]

Note that we are emphasizing certain control and governance problems and totally ignoring others. In particular, by assuming that the minister acts unilaterally to achieve a well-defined objective function, we ignore all of the internal control problems within the public sector bureaucracy. In terms of Figure 1, we are assuming away any agency problems between the minister and his public sector managers. We shall make an analogous assumption when analyzing private enterprise, namely, that no agency problems occur between the owners of the private firm and its managers.

Regulated Private Enterprise

Our model of regulated private enterprise is carefully constructed to capture the same underlying economic and informational environment as that just described for the public enterprise. As in that model, the public official, now playing the role of a *regulator*, observes the public-interest impact variable, ψ, and the private agenda variable, ε. We denote by $\rho = (\psi, \varepsilon)$ the private information of the regulator. And again, the party who will be operating the enterprise—in this case a private firm—observes the profitability parameter θ.

The private investment decision is necessarily more complex than was the public investment decision described above. But it is still a simple yes/no decision, and we assume that its outcome is commonly observable. The added complexity arises from the fact that, in order to attract private investment, the regulator must put into place a regulatory scheme that offers the expectation of at least a competitive rate of return on the private firm's sunk capital, be it physical investment or the purchase of assets previously owned by the public sector. So, in the case of private enterprise, a regulatory "contract" must be specified prior to the investment decision.

We model regulatory schemes as follows (see Caillaud, Guesnerie, and Tirole 1988 for a discussion of the generality of such schemes). The regulator offers a function $T(x)$ specifying that if the firm chooses action x it will receive a transfer $T(x)$ from the public sector.[12] If T is positive, this will constitute a payment; if T is negative it will be a tax or a franchise fee.[13] At this point, we focus on the case in which the regulator has complete freedom to select the regulatory scheme, $T(x)$. We denote this case by *discretionary regulation*. If the framer restricts the regulator's ability to choose $T(x)$, we have *nondiscretionary regulation*.

In response to the regulatory incentive scheme $T(x)$, the private firm first chooses whether to invest in the enterprise. The standard analysis postulates at this point that the private firm will in fact invest in the enterprise if and only if the regulatory contract $T(x)$ offers (expected) non-negative profits.[14] If investment does not occur, there are no further decisions to be taken and all parties earn the payoff of zero. If investment does occur, the private firm ultimately will choose an action x. Giving the firm the final choice of x allows that choice to be sensitive to the realized level of profitability, θ.[15]

This description of regulation has proven to be very powerful. One limitation is its focus on only a single period of production (see Caillaud, Guesnerie, and Tirole 1988 for extensions of this description to multiperiod contexts). It applies without alteration over time, however, if each period of production activity entails independent realizations of the informational random variables. Under this assumption, which we adopt here, the analytic approach is quite general if the regulator already is aware of the firm's public-interest impacts at the time the regulatory scheme is put into place.

The standard treatment is not suitable, however, if the regulator will receive further private information subsequent to investment by the firm. We seek an analysis that is general enough to include the possibility that the regulator will be better informed about public-interest impacts subsequent to investment than he is prior to the firm's investment. If the regulator can exert some discretion subsequent to the firm's investment, those components of $\rho \equiv (\psi, \varepsilon)$ that the regulator does not observe until after the firm's investment also can influence the choice of x by the private firm.

The regulator can give himself postinvestment discretion by using a generalized version of the regulatory scheme just described. In particular, the regulator can offer a *menu* of different regulatory schemes, $\{T(x)\}$, with the understanding that he will be allowed to pick any $T(x)$ from this menu subsequent to investment by the firm and the learning of ρ by the regulator. In fact, we can describe the menu as a single function, $T(x,\rho)$, with the interpretation that if the regulator announces ρ and then the firm chooses x, it will receive a transfer of $T(x,\rho)$.[16]

With this generalized scheme, the firm still must be given a non-negative expected return in order to induce it to make its initial investment. But now the firm must estimate the likelihood of various regulatory schemes being imposed, as well as figure out its own best response to each scheme for each realization of its own profitability.

Assuming that investment does take place, the regulator announces a value of ρ, that is, chooses a regulatory incentive scheme. Finally, the firm, observing its own profitability, chooses the profit-maximizing action in response to the regulatory scheme in force. The private firm's profits are defined as

$$\pi^P = \pi(x,\theta) + T(x,\rho).$$

The framer's objective, social welfare, is

$$W = S(x,\psi) + \pi(x,\theta) - (k-1)T(x,\rho),$$

again reflecting the cost of raising any public funds that must be used to pay the private company (or the benefit of collecting tax revenues from that company).[17] The regulator's objective function is again $V^R = W + \alpha J$.

What Constitutes Privatization?

The essential difference between public and private enterprises, as we are modeling them, is the location of private information about cost and demand conditions. We have postulated that the manager of the enterprise possesses the most detailed information about costs and demand, an assumption that strikes us as quite appropriate, and one that is common in the literature on regulation. Under public enterprise, the detailed cost and demand information resides public managers who report to a public official. Under privatization, this information resides with private managers who report to the owners of a private firm (see Figure 1).

The informational barrier that privatization erects between the public official and the mangers of the enterprise may not be totally impenetrable, however. If the government could audit the private firm sufficiently well to capture all of its managers' private information, then privatization would lose its uniqueness from public enterprise. We argue, therefore, that if privatization is to be meaningful, the government may need to make a commitment to respect private property rights to information by limiting its own ability to extract information from the private firm through an audit.[18] This commitment is above and beyond the well-known one that the government must make to respect private property rights to tangible assets by assuring private parties that their investments will not be expropriated.

The key distinction between public and private sector enterprise, in our view, is that privatization gives informational autonomy to a party who is not under direct public sector control. To put this another way, we have modeled privatization as the *deliberate* introduction of an informational barrier between the public sector official with responsibility for the enterprise—that is, the regulator—and the owners and managers of the enterprise. This barrier is reflected in the additional layer on the right-hand side of Figure 1.

Economists have given much attention to the inefficiencies associated with such informational barriers, which are more commonly called agency problems. In our model, the usual inefficiency is reflected in a reduced payoff *to the public official* if that official must motivate the private firm through regulation rather than control the public enterprise directly. What is novel about our approach is that we consider the *benefits* of introducing an agency problem from the perspective of a higher-level principal, namely, the framer. Since the public official does not precisely share the objectives of the framer—namely, social welfare—the framer sees some benefits to limiting the discretion of that official. Our analysis below compares these benefits with the inevitable costs of separating public-impact information, ψ, from profitability information θ.

When Discretionary Public Enterprise and Discretionary Regulation Are Equivalent

We now describe a number of cases in which the performance of public and regulated private enterprises are equivalent, given that the framer affords discretion to the public official.[19] These are cases in which the regulator can exert sufficient indirect regulatory control to achieve the same results he could obtain as minister with direct control of a public enterprise. If the regulator merely induces the private firm to duplicate the actions that he as minister would choose, the framer is indifferent between public and private enterprise.

First, consider the operation of an enterprise in an environment without any private information whatsoever. Suppose that all information about the external benefits of the enterprise, and all information about its profitability, is contractible. In such circumstances, the regulator could put in place a set of taxes or subsidies, contingent on what will become the commonly known realizations of the public costs and benefits of the enterprise's operations. These taxes and subsidies could be designed to induce the owners to operate the enterprise to serve precisely the regulator's objectives in every contingency.

Perhaps it is not surprising that one can obtain a neutrality result in the complete absence of noncontractible private information, for in such a case there is no truly active role for the managers of the enterprise. They need only carry out the detailed instructions left by the minister or the regulator, and he cannot claim that any new information or extenuating circumstances justify departures from that mechanical mandate. Of course, this description of the case only serves to underscore its lack of realism. In fact, the details of the operation of the enterprise are never commonly known, and thus the nature and identity of the party operating the enterprise can be expected to make a material difference.

Public enterprise and regulated private enterprise also may be equivalent in the presence of private information. There are three distinct cases of interest.

Private Information about Profitability Is Revealed after Investment

In the first case, the private information about profitability is not known before the private investment decision must be made; perhaps this information is revealed only through the physical process of investment or once the private owners have taken possession of the newly privatized public assets. In contrast, in this case, the private information concerning public impacts and private agenda, ρ, is known to the regulator when he must commit himself to the regulatory mechanism, before the time of the investment decision.

Under these conditions, the regulator can exert sufficient indirect control over the private firm to obtain the same outcome and payoff as under public ownership, so the framer is indifferent between public and private enterprise. The regulator's control is secured by paying the firm according to the following schedule:

(1) $\qquad T^*(x,\rho) = \frac{1}{k}(S(x,\psi) + \alpha J(x,\varepsilon)) + G(\rho).$

Here $G(\rho)$ is independent of the activity level x and is set as small as possible consistent with inducing the firm to make the required investment.[20]

With this schedule, the regulator induces the same actions and achieves the same payoff as does the minister under public enterprise. The mechanism operates by forcing the firm to *internalize* the objectives of the regulator. The optimality of the $T^*(x,\rho)$ schedule is clearest if k is taken to be equal to 1. Then, the transfer of T^* adds $S(x,\psi) + \alpha J(x,\varepsilon) + G(\rho)$ to the firm's payoff, thereby internalizing the benefits enjoyed by the regulator but otherwise ignored by the firm. For $k > 1$ these transfers are scaled back to account for the extra cost of public funds.

All Private Information Revealed after Investment

The second distinct case in which a surprisingly powerful neutrality result holds occurs when private information concerning both costs and public impacts is revealed only after the investment commitment must be made. Only the prior probability distributions of ρ and θ are known at the time the investment decision must be effected. By contrast, after the investment has been made, but before the activity level must be chosen, the value of ρ will be revealed to the regulator, and the value of θ will be revealed to the manager of the enterprise. Again, the regulator's optimal $T(x)$ results in the same choices of activity levels and the same expected drain on the treasury that would be the result of public enterprise.

The logic behind this result is a straightforward extension of the analysis of the first case. Here, the regulator commits himself to the menu of payment schedules given by $T^*(x,\rho)$, as in equation (1), with the understanding that he will choose a particular schedule from this menu by selecting a value of ρ after investment is made and the true value of ρ becomes known to him, but still before the activity level must be chosen by the firm. The firm is indifferent, ex ante, about which particular schedule will be chosen from the menu by the regulator, because each of them offers the same zero level of expected profits, that is, just enough to induce the firm to make the investment.[21]

Once the true value of ρ is revealed to the regulator, he will be motivated to select the payment schedule $T^*(x,\rho)$ corresponding to that value, because that schedule is optimal for his objective function. In the face of that payment schedule, the firm will be motivated to choose the same activity levels as in the first case above, and here too that is the optimum from the perspective of either the regulator or the public minister.[22]

No Cost of Raising Government Funds

In the third case of neutrality, unlike the first and second cases, the private firm may have private information about its costs before the investment commitment must be made. However, $k = 1$, so that transfers from the treasury are not a matter of concern to the framer, the regulator, or the public minister.

Because the firm knows its value of θ and the regulator is aware of that fact but does not know the pertinent value of θ, the regulator, to assure that the investment will be made, must commit to a payment schedule or to a menu of schedules that provides non-negative profit for all possible levels of θ.[23] Here, because of the stipulation that $k = 1$, this requirement poses no problem for the regulator: he is perfectly willing to add enough funds to any payment schedule to assure its profitability in the light of his indifference to transfers from the treasury. Consequently, it is optimal for the objectives of the regulator to offer the firm the internalization schedules $T^*(x,\rho)$ of equation (1), but with a different portion $G(\rho)$ that is here sufficiently large to guarantee the firm non-negative profit even if its profitability level θ is the worst possible.

In the end, the regulated private firm chooses the same activity levels that the public enterprise would choose, but the drain on the treasury caused by regulation is greater than that caused by public enterprise. Since in this case, however, that drain is not a matter of concern, the framer would find no difference between the performance of public and private forms of organization.

Summary of Neutrality Results

Our neutrality results indicate those elements of the environment that must be considered to develop insights into the fundamental differences between public and regulated private enterprises.[24] We can summarize our neutrality findings as follows:

Proposition 1. The framer is indifferent between permitting the public minister to control the enterprise and permitting the regulator to select a regulatory scheme under any of the following conditions: (1) all eventualities are contractible; (2) all private information about profitability is revealed only after the investment decision is made; or (3) the framer is unconcerned about transfers of funds from the treasury.

It follows from this result that to escape the neutrality between discretionary public enterprise and discretionary regulation we must consider an environment in which noncontractible private information about profitability is available prior to the investment decision and in which there is concern about the drain on the treasury ($k > 1$).[25] We turn now to a detailed analysis of this environment, with the aim of uncovering several dimensions of basic tradeoffs between public and private forms of organization.

Discretionary Public Enterprise versus Discretionary Regulation

Throughout this section we work in the context of the model in which all private information about profitability is revealed before the investment decision must be made.

Discretionary Public Enterprise

We begin by studying the behavior of the minister who exerts direct control over the public enterprise. Characterization of the outcome of such discretionary public management of the enterprise is straightforward. The objective function of the minister is

$$V^M = E_\theta[S(x,\psi) + \alpha J(x,\varepsilon) + k\pi(x,\theta)],$$

where the expectation is taken over the possible values of θ. The minister simply chooses the activity level x as a function of ρ and θ without any constraints. The first-order condition for the optimal choice of x, conditional on the values of ρ and θ, is

(2) $\quad S_x(x,\psi) + \alpha J_x(x,\varepsilon) + k\pi_x(x,\theta) = 0.$

Discretionary Regulation

We now turn to the much more complex problem of the regulator who, with knowledge of ψ and ε but in ignorance of θ, selects $T(x)$ to maximize his objective function,

$$V^R = E_\theta[S(x,\psi) + \alpha J(x,\varepsilon) + \pi(x,\theta) - (k-1)T(x)].$$

Below we shall extend this analysis to the case in which the regulator does not observe ρ until after $T(x)$ has been chosen and investment has occurred.

Facing the regulatory incentive schedule $T(x)$, and upon observing θ, the firm chooses its level of x so as to maximize its profits, $\pi^P = \pi(x,\theta) + T(x)$. The regulator chooses $T(x)$ in the fashion that is optimal for his objective function V^R, given this connection between the payment schedule, the actual value of θ, and the firm's choice of x. The constraint on the regulator's choice of $T(x)$ is that it must yield non-negative profits for the firm at all possible levels of θ; otherwise the firm would be unwilling to make the investment at some levels of θ, and we are assuming that the regulator finds it optimal to stimulate the investment at all levels of θ.

The following equation characterizes the actions x that the discretionary regulator optimally induces the private firm to take as a function of the firm's costs, θ:[26]

(3) $S_x(x,\psi) + \alpha J_x(x,\varepsilon) + k\pi_x(x,\theta) - (k-1)h(\theta)\pi_{x\theta}(x,\theta) = 0.$

Here $h(\theta)$ is the inverse of the hazard rate for θ, that is, $h(\theta) \equiv (1 - F(\theta))/f(\theta)$. Note that equation (3) is identical to equation (2) except for the addition of the final term on the right-hand side of (3).

We denote by $T^{**}(x,\rho)$ the regulator's optimal payment schedule that induces the actions given in equation (3). Under this regulatory scheme, the firm earns expected profits inclusive of transfer payments, which are given by

$$E_\theta[\pi(x,\theta) + T^{**}(x,\rho)] = E_\theta[\pi_\theta(x(\theta),\theta)h(\theta)] > 0.$$

These positive expected profits constitute a drain on the treasury; with $k > 1$ they impose a genuine welfare cost on the framer and the regulator. Nevertheless, as is well known, these *information rents* are a necessary feature of the optimal regulatory mechanism when the firm has superior information about its profitability before the time of the investment decision. Since the firm must be given enough payment to cover its costs when the firm knows that its profitability is minimal, the payments will necessarily yield the firm more than it needs to cover its costs when demand is high or costs are at a lower level.

Information rents are central for understanding the properties of optimal regulation. The larger the activity level sought by the regulator, the greater will be the concomitant level of information rent paid to the firm. As a consequence, the information rents not only deduct from the regulator's payoff, they also induce him to choose lower levels of activity for each value of θ.

So far in this subsection we have discussed the case where the regulator commits to a payment schedule when he already knows the pertinent value of ρ. It is more interesting and realistic to consider the case in which the value of ρ will not be revealed to the regulator until after the investment decision must be made, and a fortiori after the regulatory mechanism has been put into place.

Whether the regulator learns about public impacts before or after the investment decision must be made, discretionary regulation will result in the payment schedule $T^{**}(x,\rho)$. In either case, the activity levels will be characterized by equation (3), and the expected drain on the treasury will be identical.[27] As a consequence, we need not distinguish analytically between the cases in which the regulator learns about public impacts before and after the investment decision must be made.

Public versus Private Enterprise: Activity Levels

We are now prepared to compare the activity levels under public and private forms of ownership. As we noted above, condition (2) describing activity levels under public enterprise is the same as that in equation (3) characterizing the activity levels resulting from optimal discretionary regulation, with the exception that equation (3) has the extra negative term $-(k-1)h(\theta)\pi_{x\theta}(x,\theta)$. Consequently, for any values of ψ, ε, and θ, the value of x that solves equation (2) is greater than the value of x that solves equation (3).[28] Quite simply, under regulation the public official faces an added cost of increasing the activity level, namely the extra rents that must be paid to firms who will operate at that activity level or higher.

> **Proposition 2.** In equivalent circumstances, activity levels are lower under discretionary regulation than under discretionary public management.

Intuitively, under regulation the regulator must give the firm greater informational rents to induce higher activity levels. Such rents are not necessary under public management, so activity levels are uniformly higher under that form of ownership and control. Remember that "activity level" here refers to anything that is more profitable at the margin when overall profitability is high.

We also are interested in determining how changes in the underlying economic environment differentially affect public vs. private enterprise. To answer such questions requires placing additional structure on some of the functions that comprise the model.

Definition. In the *normal case,* (i) $\pi_{xx\theta} \geq 0$, and (ii) the second partial derivative with respect to x of the left hand side of equation (2) is nonnegative.

Stipulation (i) of the normal case follows, for example, if θ is a cost parameter and $C(x,\theta) = c + m(\theta)n(x)$ with $m' < 0$ and $n'' \geq 0$. Stipulation (ii) holds in a conventional quadratic model, or, if x were output, with convex inverse demand, convex marginal revenue, and concave marginal cost functions.

Proposition 3. In the normal case, the activity level under discretionary public management is more responsive to changes in its marginal value than under discretionary regulation.

Proposition 3 captures the notion that public enterprise responds more fully than does regulated private enterprise to changes in the objectives of public officials, whether these changes reflect the public interest or merely the private agenda of the public official.

Bounding the Advantage of Public Enterprise

What are the implications of these different activity levels for the relative performance of discretionary regulation and discretionary public management from the perspective of the framer? We have just shown that it is more costly for the regulator to influence the private firm's actions than it is for the minister to alter the actions of the public enterprise. To the extent that the public official's objectives coincide with those of the framer, this reduced flexibility lowers performance. To the extent that the public official is pursuing his or her own private agenda, however, this reduced flexibility raises performance.

In this section and the next we identify those factors that tip the balance, from the framer's perspective, in favor of private or public enterprise. Figure 2 offers a preview of our normative findings in these sections. It compares the framer's expected payoff under discretionary public enterprise, $E[W^P]$, with that under discretionary regulation, $E[W^R]$. As drawn, Figure 2 shows that public enterprise is preferred if the public official's private agenda is sufficiently muted, that is, if α is sufficiently small. At the same time, Figure 2 shows that privatization is welfare-enhancing if the public official's private agenda is sufficiently influential. Our aim in this section and the next is to establish conditions under which Figure 2 is accurate as drawn.

To this end, we begin by comparing the payoff to the *public official,* as distinct from the framer, under the two forms. Clearly the public official

FIGURE 2
The Effect of the Public Official's Private Agenda on the Framer's Payoff

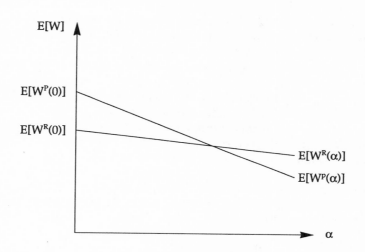

prefers public enterprise, since this gives him an entirely free hand in choosing the activities of the enterprise. We now derive a set of bounds on the increased payoff available to the public official under public enterprise.

Let $E[V^{M*}]$ and $E[V^{R*}]$ be the optimized levels of the expected values (taken over θ) of the objective functions of the minister and regulator that are obtained under discretionary public management and discretionary regulation, respectively. Denote by $\bar{\theta}$ the expected value of θ. Finally, denote the maximal and minimal values of (π_θ) over the support of θ and over the corresponding relevant set of activity levels by $\max(\pi_\theta)$ and $\min(\pi_\theta)$, respectively.

Proposition 4. The public official prefers discretionary public management over discretionary regulation to an extent that depends on the harm associated with treasury drain and the variability in the enterprise's profitability. Analytically,

$$(k-1)(\bar{\theta}-\theta_0)\max_\theta(\pi_\theta) > E[V^{M*}] - E[V^{R*}] > (k-1)(\bar{\theta}-\theta_0)\min_\theta(\pi_\theta).$$

Proposition 4 reflects the information rents that must be paid from the treasury under regulation. These rents are a drain on the treasury that lowers the objective function of the public official and the framer at the rate of $(k-1)$ per unit.

To prove Proposition 4, we observe that the regulator could always induce the same actions as does the minister if he is willing to pay additional rents to the firm. Conversely, we observe that the minister could always choose the same actions as does the regulator and save on the information rents that the regulator is forced to offer. These two observations lead to the two-sided bound in Proposition 4.

Now recall that when $\alpha = 0$ the objectives of the framer and the public official coincide. Clearly, in this case the framer cannot do better than under discretionary public management. After all, if $\alpha = 0$ the framer need not fear that the public official will pursue his private agenda, so it is best not to raise the costs to that official of redirecting the activities of the enterprise. Simply put, in this extreme case there is no reason to impose an agency problem on the minister so as to limit his pursuit of his private agenda. Combining this observation with Proposition 4 we have

Corollary 1. If $\alpha = 0$, so there is no salient private agenda, then the advantage of public enterprise over regulated private enterprise from the framer's perspective satisfies the same bounds as given in Proposition 4.

Corollary 1 tells us that the bounds in Proposition 4 apply to the distance $E[W^P(0)] - E[W^R(0)]$ in Figure 2.

More Pronounced Private Agendas Favor Privatization

We next ask how an increase in the relative importance of the public official's private agenda affects the framer's choice between public and private enterprise. Our aim is to show that an increase in α, that is, an increase in the salience of the public official's private agenda, makes privatization more attractive from the framer's perspective. In terms of figure 2, we seek to show that the $E[W^P]$ curve falls more steeply than the $E[W^R]$ curve. Let $E[W^P(\alpha)]$ and $E[W^R(\alpha)]$ represent the expected values of the framer's objective function under discretionary public management and regulation respectively, when the salience of the private agenda is measured by α.

Proposition 5. Suppose that the conditions of the normal case apply and the public official's private agenda places a constant marginal value on increased activity, that is, $J(x,\varepsilon) = \varepsilon x$. As the salience of the private agenda grows, the expected value of the framer's objective function falls faster under discretionary public management than it does under discretionary regulation. Analytically,

$$E[W^P(0)] - E[W^P(\alpha] > E[W^R(0)] - E[W^R(\alpha)] > 0.$$

Summary

We now have painted a complete picture of the comparison between discretionary public management and discretionary regulation of private enterprise. Absent a salient private agenda, the information rents that must be paid from the treasury mean that the public form of organization is superior and yields greater levels of desirable activity. On the other hand, activity levels typically are less responsive under regulation than under public management to the vicissitudes of the private agenda, due to the costliness of regulatory control. As a consequence, and as shown in Figure 2, the private agenda diminishes the objective function of the framer less under regulation than under public management.

In sum, we have found that discretionary regulation of private enterprise is more desirable in comparison with discretionary public control, the more salient the private agenda of the public official and the less significant the private information concerning profitability. A poorly functioning political system, or the absence of substantial information at the operating level of the enterprise, imply that privatization is superior to public enterprise.

Nondiscretionary Governance Systems

We now consider governance systems in which the framer gives *no* discretion to the public official. Such nondiscretionary governance systems are the opposite extreme from the completely discretionary systems studied above. Analysis of systems in which the public official is given partial discretion—for example, in which the framer imposes rewards and penalties on the public official that depend on the official's action, or in which the public official is allowed to pick from a restricted set of actions—is beyond the scope of this chapter.

If the framer mandates the actions to be taken by the minister, then the minister is effectively removed as a decisionmaker. Likewise, if the framer mandates the regulatory mechanism to be employed by the regulator, the regulator's role is passive and mechanical. He observes the contractible state of nature and follows the instructions left by the framer, perhaps in the enabling legislation, for the corresponding regulatory mechanism.

The choice between discretionary and nondiscretionary systems presents the framer with a tradeoff. If the public official will receive private information that is pertinent to the public interest, then the framer's objectives might be better served if that official were given some discretion. This same discretion, however, would also allow the public official to influence the enterprise in accordance with his private agenda, to the harm of the framer's objectives. Despite the complexity of the tradeoff between discretionary and nondiscretionary systems, and that between public and private enterprise, we can identify an informational environment in which nondiscretionary regulation is unambiguously the most preferred governance form:

> **Proposition 6.** Private enterprise subject to nondiscretionary regulation is the best organizational form if there is no private information about public impacts and all private information about profitability is revealed only after the investment decision must be made.

The key to Proposition 6 is that nondiscretionary regulation allows the framer to limit sharply the discretion of the public official, who has no socially valuable private information, while still giving discretion to the managers of the enterprise, who possess socially valuable private information about the enterprise's profitability. The only way for the framer to give discretion to the managers of the enterprise but not to the public official is to remove the operation of the enterprise from the public official's control, that is, through privatization.

The argument behind Proposition 6 runs as follows. Observe first that with private profitability information revealed only after investment, there are no information rents paid under regulation. As we showed above, without such rents, discretionary regulation and discretionary public enterprise are equivalent. But with no private information about public impacts, the framer has no reason to give any discretion to the public official, so nondiscretionary regulation is clearly superior to discretionary regulation. Finally, the inability of nondiscretionary public management to yield activity levels responsive to cost and demand conditions renders it too inferior to nondiscretionary regulation in the eyes of the framer. Under the conditions of Proposition 6, nondiscretionary regulation induces choices of activity levels that respond to private information about cost and demand conditions in fashions that are optimal for the objectives of the framer, while avoiding any influence of the private agenda and while requiring the minimal possible expected drain on the treasury.

A general lesson emerges in stark form from the analysis of this case. A regulator of private enterprise can be more effectively monitored and thus more effectively constrained by the framer than can a public minister because the regulator does not have access to the private information on costs and demand that is possessed by the public minister. With less private information, the regulator is less able to disguise his pursuit of his private agenda. Under the privatized form of organization, it is the firm that possesses the private information about profitability, and the firm is motivated to use this information for the pursuit of its profits and not for the pursuit of the private agenda of the public official. In contrast, under public management, the minister is the party with both the private agenda and the private information about profitability; any discretion accorded him to use the cost and demand information beneficially also permits the influence of the private agenda to be exercised banefully.

In short, one general effect favoring privatization arises from its intrinsic separation of cost and demand information from the power to influence activities for the sake of public impacts and private agendas. As a result of this separation, the framer can better restrain the influence of the private agenda on the interventions of the regulator of the private enterprise.

In the most dramatic form of this effect, optimal nondiscretionary regulation is no regulation at all. Then, private enterprise with a commitment of laissez-faire from the framer yields optimal results from the framer's perspective. In this case, discretionary public management would yield lower net social benefits due to the influence of the private agenda on the activities of the enterprise, and nondiscretionary public management would yield lower net social benefits due to the unresponsiveness of the enterprise's activities to cost and demand conditions.

Analytically, this case arises when the revenues provided by the market to the firm are an accurate measure of the gross social benefits of the firm's activities. A very special instance of this arises, for example, if x represents the firm's output of a good or service sold in a perfectly competitive market. More generally, without external benefits, $S(x,\psi) = 0$ for all pertinent values of ψ, and equation (3) shows that with α set equal to 0, T^* is just a lump-sum tax (possibly zero) that does not interfere with the profit-maximizing market incentives of the firm. In summary of this discussion, we have:

Corollary 2. Where market revenues equal the gross social benefits of the enterprise's activities, as under perfect competition, private enterprise with a commitment of laissez-faire is the best organizational form.

More generally, suppose that $S(x,\psi) = -ex$, as would be the case, for example, if x were the firm's output of a good sold in a perfectly competitive market and each unit of the good caused external harm of e to the environment. Then optimal nondiscretionary regulation would impose a Pigouvian (externality-correcting) tax on the firm's output but otherwise permit the firm to maximize its profits. The framer would explicitly deny to the regulator any additional powers of intervention but could stipulate that the size of the Pigouvian tax be determined on the basis of contractible information on the magnitude of the externality effect e. Here, again, public enterprise would perform worse from the framer's viewpoint due to the intrusion of the private agenda or to the unresponsiveness of output resulting from the restrictions designed to chill the influence of the private agenda. Hence we have:

Corollary 3. Under perfect competition with output externalities, private enterprise with a commitment to laissez-faire and externality-correcting taxes is the best organizational form.

Examples

We now briefly illustrate how the reasoning of our general model can be used to inform the choice between public and private enterprise in several different contexts. All of the examples here concern the possible privatization of existing public facilities. In some cases, the private parties bidding to take over public assets have no special information regarding the cost or demand conditions that are likely to face the enterprise. In other cases involving the sale of public assets, particular private firms with experience in related areas will have superior information about cost or demand conditions. In terms of our model, this important distinction is between cases in which θ is known prior to investment and cases in which θ is observed only subsequent to investment.

A Basic Manufacturing Operation

Consider a basic manufacturing operation in a small country. Suppose the output of the manufacturing facility competes with imports that are supplied at a constant world price. If all externalities caused by the operation will be commonly observable, then ψ is absent and there is no reason for the framer to give discretion to the public official. The relevant choice is between nondiscretionary public enterprise and nondiscretionary regulation.

If those bidding for the public assets have no private information concerning the technology of production, then Corollary 3 applies and privatization along with nondiscretionary regulation is called for. Even if those bidding for the public assets do have private information about cost and demand conditions, nondiscretionary regulation is still the preferred form if more than one bidder has this information, for no informational rents need be forfeited if the manufacturing facilities are auctioned off and the bidders cannot collude.

If a single party bidding for the assets enjoys superior cost and demand information, then privatization will surrender profits to that party and increase the drain on the treasury. If this is of little concern, privatization again is the preferred choice. Even if drain on the treasury is a genuine concern ($k > 1$), privatization will still be desirable if the political system is ineffective at controlling the public official's private agenda or will force the public official to serve short-term goals at the expense of the long-term public interest.

A stronger case can be made for retaining the manufacturing operation in the public sector if the externalities caused by the operation will be observable only to future public officials. For example, the true environmental costs of running the operation may be difficult to prove in court, or the benefits to workers of increased employment may be difficult to measure objectively and thus difficult to use as a basis for rewards paid to a private firm. If these externalities will be measured much more accurately by future public officials than by neutral third parties, then privatization may worsen performance. But privatization may be desirable even under these circumstances if the political system functions badly.

A Hotel or Tourist Facility

The analysis of whether to privatize a government hotel or other tourist facility is much like that above for the basic manufacturing operation. The major difference concerns the nature of the externalities generated by the hotel in contrast to the factory.

Many of the externalities generated by a tourist facility are likely to be positive ones, as when a hotel serves the public-good function of attracting tourists into the country. If government officials are likely to have valuable private information about the size of these positive external benefits, then keeping the hotel in the public sector may be the best course of action. On the other hand, if the minister will locate new hotel facilities in regions of the country where he has friends and relatives, rather than regions where demand is greatest or unemployment highest, then this intrusion of his private agenda argues for privatization.

Postal and Telecommunications Services

Postal and telecommunications services are important elements of the economic infrastructure. They tend to generate significant externalities: an improved telecommunications system benefits a broad range of industries, even after accounting for the charges levied on those industries for the services. Additionally, national growth and national cohesion are promoted by improved communications capabilities. Some of these externalities can be measured, but many cannot; external benefits that are difficult to measure objectively but that are known to public officials are captured in our variable ψ. Costs associated with providing these services that are not commonly known are captured in our variable θ.

The decision of whether to privatize the postal service, for example, can be analyzed using the same logical structure as sketched above for a basic industry. One difference is the likely magnitude of market power that a postal and telecommunications monopoly would have.[29] Another difference is the nature of the informational variables ψ and θ. The externalities generated by the telephone system are much more widespread than those generated by a steel factory, and the public official's informational advantage in measuring these externalities, ψ, may be all the more significant. The greater significance of market power argues for the importance of regulatory oversight if privatization is selected. The greater importance of information that resides in the public sector argues against privatization altogether.

Production of Military Equipment

The production of military equipment is different from the examples above in that the entire output of the enterprise is to be used in the public sector. It is quite likely that public officials will have superior information about the national security benefits of producing better or more military equipment. Even if these benefits could be demonstrated in court to enforce contracts with private parties, there may well be national security reasons not to reveal such information. In terms of our notation, ψ is likely to have significant information content.

Given the important informational role played by public officials, it is crucial that the framer allow these officials discretion. Consider, then, the choice between discretionary regulation and discretionary public enterprise. If private companies have superior information about costs, discretionary regulation will require the surrender of informational rents; this drain on the treasury may be a significant factor if $k > 1$. As against this, the importance of the public official's private agenda, α, must be considered. In some countries, concern about such private agendas is very grave in the military context, and production is contracted out to private companies. In other countries, the unwillingness to yield profits to the private sector and the concern about losing control over military secrets and technology keep military production within the public sector.[30] In such countries, our analysis suggests, political structures such as civilian oversight, which are designed to limit the intrusion of the public official's private agenda, are a necessary part of the efficient production of military equipment.

Prison Management

As our final example, consider the management of a prison facility and the choice of whether to hire a private prison management company.

Now we can interpret our public-impact variable ψ as reflecting the importance of protecting the civil rights of prisoners.[31] The framer and the public official are concerned about prisoners' rights, but these rights may be of little matter to a private, profit-oriented prison management company, except insofar as that company is motivated through fines or rewards to respect those rights.

In this example, x represents the choice of how to treat prisoners. Higher levels of x correspond to more lenient treatment of prisoners, with less likelihood of infringing on their rights or less severity of such infringements. Finally, θ measures the severity of a given potential riot situation. Higher levels of θ correspond to situations that are *less* threatening (and thus more profitable for the prison operator).[32]

The ultimate decision to be made is how favorably to treat the prisoners: better treatment is preferred by the prisoners and also by the framer and the public official because it makes violations of their rights less likely and less severe when they do occur. But more favorable treatment may be more expensive and can increase the likelihood that the prison officials lose control and face a riot.[33] Privatization runs the risk of placing officials in charge who will undervalue prisoners' rights as they seek merely to maximize their profits. And prison regulators may not want to the treatment of prisoners, because in some circumstances harsh treatment will in fact be desirable to retain control.

Discretion for the public official is important if the framer does not know what value will be placed on prisoners' civil rights in the future.[34] At the same time, sensitivity to θ, the specific conditions at the prison, is important, since such conditions can and do vary greatly across prisons and across time.

If the intrusion of public officials' private agenda is small, because the officials' private benefit varies little with the different levels of prisoner treatment ($\alpha \ni 0$), then public prison management is superior to privatization. Public management of prisons also is called for if the protection of prisoners' rights is viewed as very important and if any variations in the explosiveness of prison conditions is either small or easily observed. If, however, public officials will tend to depart from the long-term public interest—so as to avoid unfavorable publicity in the immediate term, for example—then the framer may choose to tie the hands of public officials, at least partially, by privatizing the prison.[35]

Conclusions

In this chapter we have developed models of public enterprise and of regulated private enterprise and subjected them to comparative analysis to identify the effects of privatization. Privatization in our models means that the government commits itself to a particular regulatory scheme (or possibly no regulation at all) and limits its own ability to extract information from the private company that is being regulated.

The public-spirited framer who initially chooses between public and private enterprise recognizes that subsequent public officials will not be acting totally in the public interest, either because they will pursue their private agendas or because they will be subjected to short-term political pressures that diverge from the long-term public interest. Under these circumstances, the framer will see some advantages to limiting the discretion afforded to public officials or to making it more costly for officials to redirect an enterprise's activities.

We have shown how privatization naturally raises the cost to the public official of redirecting an enterprise's activities. These increased costs stem from the informational rents that the regulator must surrender to the private firm if he wishes to encourage investment by firms that have private information about profitability prior to making their investment decisions.

There is thus a tradeoff involved in choosing whether to privatize. Privatization has the undesirable effect of raising the cost to the public official of inducing an enterprise, via regulation, to serve legitimate public-interest goals. These increased costs are an obstacle to coordinating the public official's information and the owners' information to achieve the socially preferred outcome. On the other hand, privatization, by eliminating the minister's direct control over the enterprise, limits the minister's ability to redirect the enterprise's activities in ways that promote his personal agenda or succumb to short-run political pressure at the expense of market efficiency.

We have explored the factors that influence this tradeoff. For example, a pronounced private agenda on the part of the public official or a poorly functioning political system favor privatization. On the other hand, if public officials are likely to have significant private information regarding the public impact of the enterprise's activities, then public ownership is the preferred form, even though we permit the privatized firm to be regulated in complex and sophisticated ways by the public-sector official. Likewise, if those who operate the enterprise are likely to have significant private information about the cost and demand conditions under which the enterprise will operate, and if there is a deadweight-loss burden associated with raising funds in the public sector, then public enterprise is the preferred form of ownership and control.

Our analysis is novel in that it identifies the effects of *deliberately introducing* an information problem through privatization. Privatization creates an agency problem between the public official as regulator and the private firm. Standard analyses identify the costs associated with such agency problems. What may be a cost from the viewpoint of the principal, the public official, can be a benefit when viewed by another party with a different objective, namely, the public-spirited framer. Thus our results have a distinct second-best flavor: Given an imperfect political system in which public officials do not purely serve the public interest, it may be desirable to limit their discretion by deliberately introducing an agency problem between them and the owners of a privatized firm. We see the tradeoff between the costs of such an agency problem and the benefits of restricting the discretion of public officials as fundamental to privatization.

Notes

We thank Henry Bienen and John Waterbury for valuable comments on an earlier draft, Mark Dutz for cheerful and competent research assistance, and seminar participants at Carnegie-Mellon, Bell Communications Research, Princeton, and the University of California, Berkeley, for valuable comments. The formal claims in this paper are proven in our technical companion paper, "Privatization to Limit Public-Sector Discretion." Both authors acknowledge the financial support of the John M. Olin Foundation and the Pew Foundation. This paper was completed while Shapiro was a Fellow at the Center for Advanced Study in the Behavorial Sciences.

1. Our analysis is complementary to the existing economics literature on privatization, as exemplified by Kay and Thompson (1986), Yarrow (1986), and Vickers and Yarrow (1988).

2. For excellent surveys and descriptions of this burgeoning literature, see Hart and Holmstrom (1987), Holmstrom and Tirole (1989), and Sappington (1989).

3. Paul Starr (1987, 1988) also argues that the distinction between "public" and "private" is not necessarily so great or so stark as it might appear. He points out, for example, that a government agency can contract out to private companies for many of its services.

4. Of course, in some situations shifting loans from the public to the private sector is more than an accounting change. For example, in countries facing severe debt crisis, a private company may have more credibility as a borrower than does its own government.

5. In terms of realpolitik, needed reforms of public sector control may be infeasible, and the drama, shock, and coalition-creation of privatization may be the only effective route to real change. See our colleagues' case studies for elaboration of these political themes.

6. This statement assumes that the same party who would operate the public enterprise would administer the regulations and set the tax rates.

7. For example, under either public or private enterprise the managers of the enterprise could be instructed to increase employment in times when the

overall unemployment rate is high, to make additional investments when interest rates are low, or to base their capital-labor mix on the statutory minimum wage, which is commonly known.

8. This fiction is simply our way of conducting a normative analysis within a decision-theoretic and game-theoretic framework.

9. For example, the state of the enterprise's capital equipment is likely to affect costs but may be difficult for those not working for the enterprise to observe. Likewise for the state of technological expertise at the enterprise. Alternatively, the managers of the enterprise may have superior private information about the demand facing the enterprise.

10. If the enterprise operates at a loss, then its drain on public funds will lower social welfare and increase the excess burden associated with taxation, just as net proceeds will raise welfare and reduce the excess burden.

11. Alternatively, if the minister is subject to short-run political pressures, we assume that the divergence between these forces and the long-run public interest is unpredictable and, if observable, would not be controllable by a neutral third party such as a court. Under either interpretation of J, we assume that the direction of the minister's bias cannot be anticipated. Formally, we assume $E[\partial J / \partial x] = 0$, where $E[\cdot]$ is the expectations operator, in this case conditioned on the framer's information. This assumption is unrestrictive, since any anticipated bias can readily be counteracted by the framer.

12. We are assuming throughout that the action taken by the private firm is commonly observable.

13. These transfers are defined to include any applicable franchise fees or payments for newly privatized public assets.

14. Here we make the implicit assumption that the government is able to make a commitment to a regulatory arrangement. Without any commitment or an effective reputation mechanism, privatization would be impossible, as potential investors would expect their investments to be expropriated.

15. The regulator *could* directly control the private firm by imposing a large penalty for any action other than the one specified by the regulator. Such rigid regulatory control will not typically be desirable, however.

16. Since only the regulator observes ρ, there is nothing forcing the regulator to announce the true ρ.

17. To see that our specification of social welfare here is indeed consistent with the one used under public enterprise, suppose that the regulator could perfectly capture the firm's profits for each realization of θ. Then the firm could be charged a franchise fee equal to its profits, making $T = -\pi(x,\theta)$. Substituting this value of T into W above returns the framer's objective function under public enterprise, namely $S(x,\psi) + k\pi(x,\theta)$.

18. It is our understanding that the British government finds it much more difficult to obtain detailed information about the operations of British Telecom now that the company is privately owned.

19. We shall return below to a comparison between discretionary and non-

discretionary forms from the framer's viewpoint. At this point we simply note that the framer will likely want to give discretion to the public official if that official's private information is highly pertinent to the efficient operation of the enterprise from a public-interest perspective, that is, if ψ is significant.

20. This internalization procedure was inspired by the work of Loeb and Magat (1979), who were the first to show that a firm with private information about costs could be motivated with a schedule of transfer payments to produce optimally for social welfare, and by Sappington and Stiglitz (1987), who argued that other features of the environment must underlie choices between private and public enterprise, since the Loeb-Magat mechanism could make the two equivalent where it is applicable.

21. Here we need to assume that θ and ρ are independently distributed, and we are relying on the assumption that the regulator and the firm share common priors on the distribution of ρ.

22. This proposition is an adaptation of the results derived in a somewhat different context by d'Aspremont and Gerard-Varet (1979), and explicated and applied by Pratt and Zeckhauser (1986).

23. Recall that for the sake of simplicity we assume that the investment is desirable in all possible environments.

24. This is the same approach taken by Sappington and Stiglitz (1987) in an analytic setting without private information about public impacts and without a private agenda for the public official.

25. Even under these conditions, neutrality still emerges in two environments that are beyond the scope of this chapter. First, if the regulator can partially observe the firm's private information (that is, can observe a variable that is correlated with the firm's information), if there is no limit to the penalties that the regulator can impose on the firm, and if the firm is risk neutral, then Baron and Besanko (1984) show that the information problem between the regulator and the firm is inessential. Second, if two identical firms with knowledge of θ compete to win a government franchise, then, as Sappington and Stiglitz (1987) point out, the regulator need surrender no profits, and neutrality again applies.

26. Baron and Myerson (1982) derived the original version of this equation, which has been much utilized in the recent literature on regulation and mechanism design. See Baron (1989) for a discussion of this literature. Derivation of this equation in our particular model is contained in our companion piece, Shapiro and Willig (1990). The characterizing equation is valid so long as the resulting solution for x is increasing in θ.

27. This claim is proven using an argument similar to that on pp. 69–71. See Shapiro and Willig (1990) for the technical details.

28. Of course, if k were equal to 1, the first-order conditions in equations (3) and (2) would be the same and the optimal activity levels would be the same, as already established in Proposition 1.

29. We assume a monopoly here because telecommunications services may be provided according to economies of scale: there may well be a natural monopoly, at least for some components.

30. The concerns over military secrecy may be overwhelming in practice. It may be more difficult for the government to keep military information secret if private parties are privy to it and indeed if the crucial know-how resides in private organizations.

31. The importance attached to such rights, both for the prisoners themselves and for broader social perceptions of justice, may not be known in advance by the framer and certainly cannot be quantified and used to reward or penalize private prison operators.

32. Our assumption that $\pi_{\theta x} > 0$ now has the interpretation that the costs to the prison operator of treating the prisoners more leniently are less when the situation is less threatening. In a more threatening situation, such treatment increases the likelihood of a riot that may be very costly (both in terms of facilities and personnel and in terms of possible loss of life).

33. If in fact more favorable treatment is no more expensive and eases tensions in the prison, then it is clearly superior. The interesting questions arise in the range of behavior where more lenient treatment is costly or poses certain dangers to prison control.

34. Discretion is less valuable if strategic behavior by prisoners is important. With such behavior, it may be valuable for the framer to commit subsequent officials to certain actions (via a nondiscretionary governance form) so as to deter certain uprisings or riots by prisoners. For example, if regulators were required to fire wardens of prisons where riots occurred, and if wardens were given extensive authority, prisoners might accept as unavoidable a harsh response by the warden to any uprising.

35. In terms of our model, the public official would have to pay the private prison company more for operating the prison if more lenient treatment of prisoners were demanded.

References

Baron, David. 1989. "Design of Regulatory Mechanisms and Institutions." In *Handbook of Industrial Organization*, ed. Richard Schmalensee and Robert Willig. Amsterdam: North-Holland.

Baron, David, and David Besanko. 1984. "Regulation, Asymmetric Information and Auditing." *Rand Journal of Economics* 15: 447–470.

Baron, David, and Roger Myerson. 1982. "Regulating a Monopolist with Unknown Costs." *Econometrica* 50: 911–930.

Caillaud, B., R. Guesnerie, and J. Tirole. 1988. "Government Intervention in Production and Incentives Theory: A Review of Recent Contributions." *Rand Journal of Economics* 19: 1–26.

d'Aspremont, C., and Gerard-Varet, L. 1979. "Incentives and Incomplete Information." *Journal of Public Economics* 11: 25–45.

Hart, Oliver, and Bengt Holmstrom. 1987. "The Theory of Contracts." In *Advances in Economic Theory, Fifth World Congress*, ed. Truman F. Bewley. New York: Cambridge University Press.

Holmstrom, Bengt, and Jean Tirole. 1989. "The Theory of the Firm." In *Handbook of Industrial Organization*, ed. Richard Schmalensee and Robert Willig. Amsterdam: North-Holland.

Kay, J. A., and D. J. Thompson. 1986. "Privatization: A Policy in Search of a Rationale." *Economic Journal* 96: 18–32.

Loeb, M., and W. Magat. 1979. "A Decentralized Method for Utility Regulation." *Journal of Law and Economics* 22: 399–404.

Pratt, J., and R. Zeckhauser. 1986. "Incentive-Based Decentralization: Expected Externality Payments Induce Efficient Behavior in Groups." In *Kenneth Arrow and the Ascent of Modern Economic Theory*. New York: New York University Press.

Sappington, David. 1989. "Incentives." Bell Communications Research, June.

Sappington, David, and Joseph Stiglitz. 1987. "Privatization, Information and Incentives." *Journal of Policy Analysis and Management* 6: 567–582.

Shapiro, Carl, and Robert Willig. 1990. "Privatization to Limit Public-Sector Discretion. Princeton University, January.

Starr, Paul. 1987. "The Limits of Privatization." In *Prospects for Privatization*, ed. Steve H. Hanke. New York: Academy of Political Science.

———. 1988. "The Meaning of Privatization." *Yale Law and Policy Review* 6: 1120–1136.

Vickers, John, and George Yarrow. 1988. *Privatization: An Economic Analysis.* Cambridge, Mass.: M.I.T. Press.

Yarrow, George. 1986. "Privatization in Theory and Practice." *Economic Policy* 2: 324–377.

4

The International Spread of
Privatization Policies: Inducements,
Learning, and "Policy Bandwagoning"

G. John Ikenberry

It is striking how widely and quickly privatization—the selling of state enterprises and other public assets to private parties—has spread among developed and developing countries. Regimes of very different political types and at different levels of socioeconomic development are embracing various sorts of privatization programs; indeed, the spread of privatization policies has not seemed to discriminate among liberal democratic, authoritarian, or socialist governments. Just as striking is the rapidity with which this phenonemonon has unfolded. Most analysts trace its beginnings to proposals stumbled onto and subsequently pushed with great zeal by Margaret Thatcher's government after 1979. In just a very few years, similar types of experiments could be found in dozens of countries and on every continent. "Rarely in history," says the *Financial Times* (Sept. 16, 1987), "has an innovation in economic and monetary policy caught on as quickly in as many different countries as privatisation."

Government elites in otherwise disparate political and socioeconomic circumstances have chosen to rethink and rework the relations of the public and private sectors. To the extent that it represents a reorientation of prevailing modes of public thought on the relations of state and economy, the broad historical sweep of this movement is quite intriguing. Why so many countries and why now?

Given the wide-ranging nature of the phenomenon, it is necessary to inquire into the international sources and dynamics of the privatization movement. Are governments responding to similar sorts of economic dilemmas that are comprehensible only on an international scale? Are government elites copying or learning from innovations developed elsewhere? In what way and to what extent is the spread of privatization linked to its promotion by leading liberal countries through political and financial inducements and sanctions? Finally, what can we learn from other historical periods when innovations in economic policy spread throughout the international system?

I shall argue that privatization policy is not comprehensible simply in terms of national governments responding to the interests and power of domestic groups. That is, privatization programs across developed and developing countries can be understood only with an appreciation of their international context—an international context that influences policy at several levels. At one level the international context is economic. Governments have faced common patterns of economic change since the late 1970s: slower growth and enlarged state sectors have put pressure on the fiscal stability of governments. Also, technological changes in telecommunications and financial sectors have altered the constraints on government economic management. Common problems and changes of this sort have discredited or rendered problematic the earlier appeal of enterprises managed in the public sector. At another level, the international context is political (or even sociological): government elites monitor and, at times, emulate or learn from policy innovations developed elsewhere. This is a more obscure but equally profound aspect of the privatization movement. A sort of common "international policy culture," to be a bit vague for the moment, appears to attend the unfolding of privatization on a global scale and gives impetus to its course. This is both a process of emulation (copying successes achieved elsewhere) and learning (redefining one's interests on the basis of new knowledge).

Probing the international dimensions of the movement toward privatization has a healthy methodological warrant. It is a mistake to focus too narrowly on the domestic sources of privatization: one may miss larger forces at work that extend beyond individual countries or that are shared by several countries. The general point is captured by Robert Keohane: "Without an analysis of common patterns, comparative political-economic studies can be quite misleading. Analysts focusing on the domestic politics and economics of one or a few countries may ascribe patterns of behavior and outcomes to distinctively national causes, without recognizing the degree to which common forces affecting a range of countries operate powerfully in each" (Keohane 1984: 15). Countries occupy different positions or niches within the international system, of course, and common forces and pressures will be mediated through distinctive political and economic (particularly financial) systems. But when privatization programs are as widespread and appear as rapidly as our initial observations suggest, there is reason to keep an eye on the common features and international dimensions of the process.

There are three general ways of characterizing the international dimensions to the phenomenon. The first regards them as spurious correlations and denies the existence of real international connections. Different countries are reacting to very different types of problems; the determinants of policy are wholly domestic, and only the policy outcomes have a vaguely common appearance. The international pattern is only in the eye of the analyst and not in the underlying forces. In this case, we have not a privatization "movement" but a diverse set of goals, plans, and initiatives that can only loosely be called privatization. Privatization, in this view, may be a global phenomenon, but it is not a global process that requires a global explanation. It can be thought of as a bit like rust: you find it everywhere, but you can study it in individual countries or locales without missing some larger set of dynamics.

The second interpretation appeals to common underlying economic and technological changes. Here the international dimension lies in the similar and connected economic problems that governments confront. Problem X tends to produce policy Y. For a variety of historical and economic reasons, many countries began to experience problem X in the early 1980s. In this case, governments are not interacting with, learning from, or inducing change in others; they are simply reacting independently to a common underlying set of stimuli.

The third interpretation stresses international interaction. Countries may or may not be experiencing problem X, but governments copy policy Y either willingly or through external inducements. Underlying problems may also be similar, but the adoption of similar policy comes through learning from or interacting with other governments (or international institutions). Alternatively, the underlying problems may be quite disparate, but governments copy the innovations for reasons that are quite local and specific.

In what follows I want to pursue the latter two theses: common underlying conditions and the emulation of policy innovations (or what could be called policy "bandwagoning"). I begin by examining what appears to be the basic set of rationales that lie behind privatization policies. The focus is on what government officials might themselves have in mind in pursuing these policies. I shall then explore several models that specify the international sources and dynamics of privatization.

The Logic of Privatization

Privatization is not a social movement. It is more accurately understood as a government reform movement pushed forward by politicians and public officials within government rather than by social groups or classes.[1] This observation will be important later when I discuss the various international pressures that have given impetus to privatization experiments—pressures that impinge most directly on government officials. Now, however, it is necessary to sort out the reasons that would induce state officials to take an interest in privatization policy. What types of "state goals" might be served by privatization?

Response to Fiscal Crisis

In the late 1970s a wide variety of countries encountered a similar sort of fiscal crisis. A long period of expansion of the public sector in many countries was sustained in the postwar period by strong growth in their economies. With the second oil shock, economic growth decelerated, which simultaneously accelerated the growth of public sector expenditures on subsidies, welfare, and the like. The result was soaring public deficits and increased public borrowing. Under these circumstances, the sale of public assets was seen as an expedient to increase state revenues and decrease public borrowing. In effect, privatization became a way for governments to finance spending by offering the public equity instead of debt.[2]

Evidence of this rationale is found when governments sell public enterprises under implicit or explicit guarantees that the firms' monopoly profits will be maintained. That is, states show more interest in dressing up a public enterprise to increase its asset value, even at the expense of not promoting the competitive breakup of the monopoly. (A state interested in increasing competition and efficiency or in increasing its control over the economy would nurture competition in the private sector and therefore would break up public monopolies as it privatized them.)

In summary, this rationale is a short-term response to the budget crisis. The firms themselves may or may not currently be profitable, but the goal is to liquidate assets for current cash flow purposes.

Efficiency Goals

Efficiency is perhaps the most frequently mentioned reason for privatization. This goal would be evidenced by privatization policies that remove monopoly privileges and constraints (and by a concern with the problems of the displacement of real private capital formation). This goal may also be seen in concern over enterprise management. Whether the focus is on the promotion of competition or the reform of management, the goal is greater levels of efficiency: to increase productivity, improve quality, and reduce costs.

In Britain, expectations of increased efficiency through competition have attended many of the privatization initiatives. Even when privatization simply involves a public to private transfer of monopoly, expectations of future competition and increased efficiency may still be present. Although the selling of British Telecom did not involve a breakup of the enterprise, government officials have sought to encourage competition: there is hope that Mercury, a Cable and Wireless subsidiary, will act as a small competitor, and the regulatory Office of Telecommunications has insisted that British Telecome publish performance targets. The government is also seeking to establish a competitor for British Gas (*The Economist*, Dec. 19, 1987).

Even when future competition is not expected, government elites often justify privatization with the claim that firms improve their performance in the private sector. Managers come under pressure from new constituencies; workers are exposed to the discipline of a share price; projects have to be attractive to private capital markets rather than public officials. Moreover, the privatization of some enterprises may indirectly stimulate more efficient management of firms that remain in the public sector.

*Reworking the Instruments of State Economic
and Political Management*

The diverse goals that lie behind the creation of public enterprises include economic development, employment, social welfare, and national security (see Vernon and Aharoni 1981). It is scarcely surprising, therefore, that privatization also serves widely varying goals. Privatization can reflect either a change in the nature of state goals or it can involve a reconsideration of the means or instruments whereby those goals are effectively pursued (for example, a nationalized steel firm is no longer seen as necessary for national security). The rationale for privatization considered in this section is of the latter sort, that is, government elites seeking to rework the mechanisms or instruments of state policy. In this case, privatization does not signal a decline or change in the government's interest in controlling a set of economic or political outcomes; rather, the means to do so are under active reform.

There is evidence that the relationship between central government elites and state enterprises is evolutionary: a state enterprise at the moment of its establishment may be an effective tool of government policy, with control flowing from government to enterprise, but this control frequently diminishes over time. In a study of French state-owned petroleum firms, N.J.D. Lucas noted that "the close relationship between state enterprise and government, deliberately constructed to ensure the precise operation of state policies, can work both ways; state enterprises can use the apparatus to impose its ideas on government." In the French case in particular, relations between the state and national firms changed: "State direction was clear and control was tight" in the years immediately after nationalization, but control shifted. In a later period, the national oil industry sought to influence the energy priorities of government, to extend operational control over adjacent aspects of the industry, and to ensure financial access to state resources without political control by the state (Lucas 1977: 120, 93, 110; see also Feigenbaum 1985). Evidence of this loss of control can also be found in Italy.

State elites with an interest in retaining political autonomy and control over official policy goals may well find the increasing encroachments of public firms to be a liability. State interventions in the society (in this case, public ownership), initially indicative of a certain capacity of government elites to shape internal political and economic practices, may eventually lead to commitments and obligations that subsequently constrict state decisionmaking (Ikenberry 1986). The efficacy of particular instruments changes over time; a set of interventions may well initially achieve the goals of a government elite but eventually leave it enfeebled. Privileged access to state policy and revenue is created for public firms, and it is often consolidated by a set of clientelistic relations (Suleiman 1988).

Problems of privileged access and declining control are often accompanied by an evolution in the autonomy and goals of the public enterprise itself. In a study of European state-owned petroleum enterprises, for example, one analyst has found that the problem of government control was exacerbated by a universal tendency of the firms in France, Italy, Norway, and the United Kingdom to expand into new fields of the oil industry and to do so at great financial risk.[3] The diversification of the goals of state enterprises, as Raymond Vernon notes, may not be due simply to the aggrandizing actions of the firms' managers, but may also stem from the political constituencies that impinge on their missions. "The enterprise that is created to support a branch of high technology may soon find itself diverted to maintaining jobs. The enterprise that comes into being to support farm incomes may soon discover that its principal role is to hold down urban food prices" (Vernon 1981: 12). Taken together, the expansion of state enterprise goals and the quest by managers for access to and autonomy from the state generate pressures within the state to recast the relationship.

On the other hand, some public enterprises have had clientalism and patronage as their rationale from the very beginning. The growth of the public sector in the Philippines, for example, took place under martial law and aptly became known as "cronyism." As Stephan Haggard notes, "cronyism rested on the extension of various economic privileges to favored firms—monopoly power and preferential loans and contracts—in return for political support. A number of state-owned enterprises and banks became conduits for this political patronage" (Haggard 1988: 91). In this case, privatization exhibits, at least in part, a political rationale: to shed costly clientelistic relations and reconstitute the bases of government control over economic management.

Coalition Building

Privatization can serve the broader political goals of government elites by allowing them to build or rebuild ruling coalitions. This goal seems to go hand in hand with the others already mentioned. To the extent that privatization threatens established and privileged groups within the public sector, in particular, new bases of support may be necessary; for managers and workers threatened by the selling of public firms, new sorts of incentives may have to be created to re-establish their support for the government. For both these reasons, privatization often carries with it arrangements that bring voters, workers, and owners of capital into the program. These efforts at coalition building become all the more important to the extent that my earlier observation carriers weight: privatization is not typically a policy that responds to popular societal pressures; rather, it comes about as a reform movement within the government. In such cases, coalition building is not the impetus for privatization but a necessary (if secondary) ingredient for its implementation.

The most obvious mechanism of coalition building is the characterization of privatization as a form of "popular capitalism." This sort of emphasis has attended British privatization; and indeed, through tax incentives, employee stock ownership plans, and other programs the number of private shareholders has grown substantially in the wake of the British programs, from 3 million in 1979 to about 9 million last year (*The Economist*, Dec. 19, 1987; see also Cowan 1987: 4). This emphasis on building a social consensus on privatization is perhaps most striking in Chile, where a radical form of "popular capitalism" has been integral to the "second wave" of privatizations that began in 1985. The clear image that emerges from this case is of government elites pushing an extreme, ideological version of privatization, divesting the state of even core social welfare roles, but simultaneously attempting to reintegrate workers in a private system of welfare provision. At the broadest level, Chile presents a case of a state shedding its social responsibilities but also attempting to structure a set of incentives so as to recreate a private basis for social well-being (Sigmund, this volume).

In the Philippines as well, privatization has become a tool of political coalition building. To be sure, the public sector has become a financial burden to the government of Corazon Aquino. But privatization has served also to sever ties with the supporters of Ferdinand Marcos and to solidify relations with other parts of society. According to Stephan Haggard,

The most important factor in creating an initial consensus around the goals of privatization and market-oriented policies was the blatant abuses of the Marcos years. While the right embraced the new course as placing proper emphasis on the private sector, privatization could also be tied to a populist agenda. Reform of the government had broad appeal, and Aquino linked the proceeds from privatization to the financing of the government's land reform program. (1988: 103)

The logic of coalition building might be simplified as follows. From the perspective of state elites, the expansion and the contraction of the public sector might both be understood, at least in part, as strategies of increasing political support and building coalitions. Both involve coalition building; but they involve the building of different coalitions, in support of different regimes. The former coalition would involve government employees and recipients of (subsidized) public services; the latter would embrace "capitalists" large and small. In one case, the state provides services; in the other, it sells assets.

We might cautiously take this point one step further. The expansion of the public sector as a strategy of coalition building will be easier at times of rapid growth and loose fiscal constraints. Periods of slow growth and tight fiscal constraints favor coalition building based on the contraction of the public sector. The relationship between coalition-building strategy and underlying economic circumstances, however, is not tight or straightforward. A coalition strategy organized around contracting the public sector may well be sustained during periods of high or moderate growth; and the obverse is equally plausible (Pen 1987). There is no reason to believe, for example, that the Thatcher government will alter its privatization policies and coalitional strategies if higher growth levels are achieved and as budget constraints loosen. What can be argued is that rapid growth favors the continuation of a particular strategy of coalition building and that slow growth and crisis favor change. Yet, for present purposes, I want to make an even more modest point: privatization, as it anticipates the shrinkage of the public sector, can indeed be pursued as a strategy of coalition building.

Depoliticizing Economic and Social Outcomes

This last rationale may be the most diffuse of the entire group, and evidence of its role is difficult to adduce. Yet it follows from what are very powerful observations about the growth of the public sector and state-owned enterprises in the postwar period. The growth of the public sector has not simply been an enlargement of its aggregate size; it also has involved an expansion in the roles and responsibilities that states have assumed in the management of the economy and society. It is not just that an increasing share of the GNP is being spent in the public sector, but governments have increasingly been judged accountable for the country's social and economic conditions. These roles and responsibilities were taken on by the state in an earlier period, when politicians and experts were optimistic about their ability to manage socioeconomic outcomes. According to this view, privatization represents an attempt by government elites to shed roles and responsibilities that set up conditions for political failure.

The growth in the duties and obligations of the state in the early postwar period is most strikingly evident in the rise of Keynesian "social democracy." From the vantage point of the late 1980s, the view seems quite fanciful and naive. Yet after the war and into the 1960s, public officials in the Western democracies were confident that governments could become masters of their economies. "In [Keynes's] system," David Marquand argues, "the unemployment figures would be the products of conscious political choice, and therefore subject to political scrutiny and debate" (Marquand 1987: 22). The early success of postwar economic growth across the industrial world seemed to only confirm the new promises and expectations. "The progressive acceptance of Keynesian economic theory and associated techniques of economic management," writes John Goldthorpe, "together with the growing control exercised by public authorities over the functioning of the economic system, seemed to have inaugurated a new era of capitalism in which stability and dynamism were reconciled and guaranteed" (Goldthorpe 1987: 363). The triumph of Keynesianism was, in one sense, the victory of an alternative to centralized planning and extensive public ownership of the economy (Skidelsky 1979). Keynesian interventions were limited, and the market remained the central instrument of control. Yet, in a more profound sense, the government's role as guarantor of full employment and growth was no less plenary. The instruments were more limited, but not the political responsibility.

The public attitudes that emerged in support of Keynesian policy also gave impetus to other forms of state management of the economy. The growth of the public sector and state-owned enterprises proceeded within this permissive political setting. "Perhaps the most general reason," Raymond Vernon notes, "for the growth [of public enterprise] has been a shift in public opinion regarding the appropriate role of the state in economic affairs" (Vernon 1981: 8). Very gradually and in subtle ways, the rising expectations that citizens had in the capacities and responsibilities of government followed the rising optimism that politicians and civil servants themselves had for public management of the economy.

The story of slow growth, higher levels of unemployment and inflation are a matter of recent historical record. The disillusionment in state economic management has been widespread, to say the least, and throughout the 1970s and early 1980s ruling political parties felt the electoral consequences. It follows that government elites might well wish to alter the political foundations of Keynesian social democracy, to scale back the institutions—and thus the expectations—that set up political failure. In these terms, privatization is part of a larger process to define the proper and accountable spheres of government. Political elites want not just to shrink the public sector but to shrink the boundaries of what is considered political.[4]

There is a neat symmetry in this process: the rise in expectations about the capacities of the state to manage the economy was itself pushed forward primarily by government elites (again, not a social movement). Likewise, government officials again lead the campaign to redefine public duties and responsibilities. Privatization becomes an attractive goal for regimes that wish to reshape the boundaries between state and society; by returning enterprises to the private sector and to the market, the state is removed as an object of judgment.

The Spread of Privatization Policies

Governmental elites, as the foregoing suggests, may well have a variety of reasons for finding privatization programs attractive. The far-flung goals that privatization seems to serve should make us skeptical of any simple characterization of the phenomenon as a single, unidimensional "movement." But to understand why so many countries are turning to privatization, and why now, it is necessary to focus more explicitly on the international dimensions of privatization policy. At the outset, I mentioned two useful ways to talk about these international dimensions (the third was simply a null set): as change in underlying economic and technological setting (simultaneous and linked international change), and as interaction effects (patterns of emulation and external inducement). I now turn to these considerations.

Underlying Economic and Technological Change

I have already noted the postwar changes in rates of growth that, together with an expansion of the public sector in many countries, produced rising public deficits and vast increases in public borrowing. At this level, the international setting is in the common circumstances that governments confront. Moreover, these circumstances that have produced fiscal pressures on governments are themselves the result of a confluence of trends and not a single underlying force. But the trends are clear. Amidst slower levels of growth, the size of public sectors has steadily expanded.

The International Monetary Fund (IMF) reports that from 1960 to 1980 the public expenditures of most countries rose by 2 to 3 percent a year in real terms (especially from 1960 to 1975). In the early 1970s, thirteen countries were spending nearly 30 percent of their GNP in the public sector; by 1980 about forty countries were spending at least a third of their GNP in the public sector (E. Hanke 1987: 23).

These underlying trends have provided new circumstances that many governments share, but the policy that emerges is not inevitable. Some countries that have experienced slower growth and tighter fiscal constraints, such as Sweden, have not moved toward privatization. Other countries, such as Japan, have not come under intense fiscal pressures but nonetheless have selectively pursued privatization initiatives. Economic growth and public sector trend lines provide a background condition, but other levels of change are also. operating. A particular set of economic circumstances (such as fiscal crisis) does not inexorably produce a single policy response (privatization).

One of those other levels is technological change. In a variety of sectors, such as telecommunications and finance, evolving technologies have reduced the institutional bases of monopoly and, hence, state control. In telecommunications, technological change has lowered the costs of entry to potential competitors. At the same time, changes in the financial services sector have also given impetus to the proliferation of intermediaries. Within the United States, Japan, and Great Britain the movement toward privatization and the deregulation of telecommunications and financial services are bound up together: a rapid rise in demand for financial services has occurred since 1982; at the same time, costs of advanced technology have dropped; and these circumstances have created pressures and opportunities for new transnational telecommunications services (Vickers and Wright 1989).

Several observations can be made about the role of technological change. First, this factor is particularly important for explaining policy change in a limited set of sectors in several advanced industrial nations (primarily the United States, the United Kingdom, and Japan). Second, incentives for deregulation and privatization are produced in part from cross-sector interactions: changes in telecommunications costs create new opportunities for financial services, which in turn feed back as pressure for deregulation in telecommunications. Finally, the technological dimension is bound up with changes in government policy: it is not a politically unmediated force, and it is driven, at least in part, by international competition.

The upshot is that underlying economic and technological changes are an important part of the international context, but only a part. To focus exclusively on this level is to miss important political and interactive aspects of the spread of privatization policy. It is to the specification of these interactive processes that I now turn.

Models of the Diffusion of Privatization Policy

The fact that privatization programs have appeared in countries of very different political character and levels of socioeconomic development is a clue that a process of diffusion may well be at work. The fact that these initiatives are often pushed by government elites themselves only strengthens the likely importance of international processes of inducement, competition, and learning. Government elites do not just have their collective eye on domestic groups and developments; they also monitor and respond to changes that occur abroad.

If we conceive of privatization as a form of *policy innovation*, we are led to the same sorts of questions that analysts ask when studying the diffusion of technological or organizational innovations (for example, new farming techniques or breakthroughs in military hardware; see Rogers 1962). What are the patterns of diffusion? Through what processes does the spread of innovation occur? What variables influence the likelihood that the innovation will be adopted in secondary countries?

In the following sections I shall outline three varieties of diffusion: external inducement, emulation (or "policy bandwagoning"), and social learning. Each model helps to explain aspects of the spread of privatization ideas and links this phenomenon to other episodes of policy diffusion.

External Inducement. This model refers to the role of direct external political pressure that may induce some governments to pursue privatization. According to this model, one state (or its agents) provides incentives or inducements that lead other states to adopt the preferred policy. External inducements can range widely in their severity, from overt coercion to the loose structuring of incentives and sanctions.

The most obvious cases of external inducement in regard to privatization are the activities of the IMF and American foreign policy. For a large number of developing countries, the IMF and the World Bank have made financial credits and development aid contingent on liberalizing reforms of the the domestic economy (Babai 1988). Policies of the American State Department and Agency for International Development (AID) have worked in accord with the reform programs pushed by the major multilateral financial and development organization (McPherson 1987).

The role of external inducement is more complex than the simple image of a coercive outside actor forcing policy change on dependent regimes. In some countries what emerges is a coalition of groups that form around a growth strategy that includes a policy of privatization. In the Philippines, for example, a market-oriented model of development has been pushed by multilateral development and lending organizations, but in coalition with portions of the bureaucracy and the private sector. Privatization in the Philippines began with the economic crisis of late 1983, which produced a financial panic and a reassessment of the country by external creditors. Investigations by the IMF and domestic development agencies revealed that the most serious problems were tied to growth of the public sector. The role of the IMF, World Bank, and Asian Development Bank were crucial in generating new information about the problems of a poorly performing public sector and in developing financial controls on the largest nonfinancial public enterprises. A reform program was put forward in order to meet IMF ceilings on public borrowing and transfers to the private sector (Haggard 1988: 102–103). Information, monitoring, and contingent financial arrangements by outside multilateral agencies served to mobilize private sector and bureaucractic opposition to Marcos and an overextended public sector. The reform program eventually adopted by the Aquino government followed the outlines of a World Bank reform and loan package.

External agencies, therefore, play an important role in helping to bolster national coalitions that favor privatization and public sector reform. We have already noted that government elites might well favor privatization for reasons of efficiency and political coalition building. What these government elites often face are old clientalistic, rent-seeking groups. External pressure helps government officials put into action the policies they already desired. Multilateral agencies and other external actors provide information and resources that serve to create or strengthen reform coalitions. A sort of "triple reform alliance" takes root between outside agencies, state officials, and private sector groups.

We can broaden this point about the role that external agents play in strengthening the domestic hand of the state. External involvements of states may heavily influence the nature of domestic restraints on government action. Paradoxically, when states become enmeshed in international commitments or negotiations, these external constraints may actually reduce domestic obstacles and impediments to policy (and for this reason states may actually court these external commitments). This is the case for developed as well as developing countries. Stanley Hoffmann notes that negotiations during the 1970s between the IMF and the British and Italian governments resulted in a set of commitments on social and budgetary policy that "partly liberated these governments from the grip of left-wing socialist ideologies in one case, and a host of pressure groups in the other" (Hoffmann 1987: 274). Likewise, in the United States the movement toward decontrol of oil prices was facilitated by a set of interlocking international agreements actively pursued by President Jimmy Carter so as to strengthen his domestic position with Congress (Ikenberry 1989).

In summary, external inducement may limit the policy options of government elites and provide pressure for the adoption of privatization. At the same time, external pressure may actually be welcomed and manipulated by reform elites so as to strengthen their domestic political position. Together, these variations on external inducement help account for the spread of privatization policy.

Emulation and Policy "Bandwagoning." Privatization may also spread when its adoption in one country creates "successes" that other countries seek to emulate. According to this model, privatization policy is an innovation or breakthrough that other governments copy or adapt. Often these innovations emerge from the core nations and spreads to the periphery. The process of emulation is driven by several forces. Most overt are the imperatives of international competitive pressures. But government elites may also simply emulate successful policy innovations as those officials anticipate similar political or economic rewards. Finally, and perhaps least significant here, political elites within a country may copy similar normative standards for state involvement within the economy and society. In all these cases, emulation is a process whereby elites monitor policy change abroad and, seeking similar successes, import the appropriate policies. What emerges is a sort of "policy bandwagon."

International competition is a powerful force in spreading ideas and policies. "Perhaps the most obvious fact about a state system," John Hall notes, "is that it leads to a high degree of emulation" (Hall 1988: 139). Similarly, Kenneth Waltz argues that "competition produces a tendency toward the sameness of the competitors" (Walz 1979: 127). This model seeks to capture the process whereby political and economic policy innovations in one national setting prompt other governments to embrace similar policies.[5]

This competitive emulation can be seen at a very general level within the international system. International competition, for example, led political elites to copy the efforts of leading capitalist countries to rationalize their economies and societies. John Hall notes that "the adoption of local agricultural societies and the attack on state interference in eighteenth century France, were self-conscious attempts to copy capitalist innovations. Such emulation has a long history in European society for the brutal reason that a state which did not advance its economy would not be able to pay for sufficient military might to survive in the competitive international arena" (Hall 1988: 24). The competitive system provided incentives for states to attend to the efficient organization of their economy and society; the common cultural system within which the European states emerged allowed innovations to be diffused with relative ease (Hall and Ikenberry 1989).

There are several ways in which competition appears to drive policy bandwagons. Where a particular set of policies seems to generate economic success in one country, government officials in other countries are likely to reconsider their own strategies in light of the innovations they observe abroad. In recent years, the dramatic economic success of Japan has led other capitalist nations, including the United States, to consider the incorporation of Japanese-style economic policy. In many respects the political debates over "industrial policy" in the early 1980s and the current rhetoric of "competitiveness policy" exemplify efforts to emulate Japanese success.

In the area of privatization, international competition may not be as powerful a direct force in driving the emulation process as it is in other areas of public policy.[6] Nonetheless, in specific sectors, such as financial markets, competition may well give impetus to privatization and deregulation. Japanese deregulation and London's "big bang" are both associated with establishing more efficient and competitive financial markets. In other areas, it is not competition as such that pushes the process but a general pattern of copying success. There is evidence that officials in many governments have kept an eye on the experiments in Britain. In Thailand, the deputy minister in charge of privatization noted: "We are moving slowly and at the moment I am just trying to float off parts of one or two state sector corporations, profitable and one not. So in a way we are starting to follow the policies of Mrs. Thatcher which seem to have been very successful in Britain" (*Financial Times*, Sept. 16, 1987, sec. 3, p. 8). At other points, policy bandwagoning is driven by the political successes of the British model. The Conservative party of Canada, impressed by the electoral successes of its counterpart in Britain, incorporated privatization into into its platform in the early 1980s.

Finally, emulation may involve the copying of particularly attractive social or political standards of state involvement in the economy. As before, government elites monitor policy innovation abroad, but what constitutes "success" in this area is more a normative orientation than a specific set of economy outcomes. Some scholars, for example, have noted the transnational diffusion of constitutionalism and patterns of social provision, such as education systems. Although the shape and content of state activities are highly mediated by domestic economic and social structures, these analysts argue, the rapid spread of particular types of state practices can be understood only in terms of a process whereby government elites copy the social commitments made by others (see Mayer and Hannan 1979). "Elites are highly susceptible to demonstration effects," one author concluded, "copying each other's commitment to new social programs or enforcement procedures rather readily" (Boli-Bennet 1979: 232). According to this variant of emulation, political elites monitor changes in the social and economic commitments of other states and come to expect similar standards at home. There is evidence that this sort of process has attended the *expansion* of state involvement in the economy and society (see Meyer 1984). What is interesting for our purposes is the manner in which this normative emulation process might be working to *contract* the state.

To summarize, emulation is an important process by which policies spread because states tend to have similar general goals. All states are interested in doing better rather than worse; they prefer economic and political success to any alternatives; and the experiences of other states provide lessons and examples for how success might be achieved. The guiding rule is: copy what works.

We can take this point a bit further. It appears that emulation will be most pervasive when international competition is most intense, inasmuch as competition provides a powerful incentive to monitor and respond to innovations developed abroad. In cases of intense competition, the costs of failing to innovate are highest. Moreover, the diffusion of policy practices is most likely to occur when states share underlying cultural or social settings (although a highly competitive environment might serve to transcend obstacles presented by divergent cultural or societal circumstances). Finally, policy bandwagoning, where the watchword is "copy what seems to work," is most likely to operate when levels of information about policy are low.[7] In lieu of direct information about appropriate policy, officials turn to the successes of others as guides. In a country where old political and economic strategies appear to be faltering, the reflexive logic of policy bandwagoning will become more attractive.

Social Learning. Social learning refers to the spread of new information with which governments make policy choices. The outcome of social learning may look very similar to that of emulation. Governments do copy policies that are developed elsewhere. But the process is not driven by intergovernmental competition and bandwagoning. Rather it is the diffusion of policy-relevant knowledge about, for example, the way public enterprises influence economic growth or the likely impact that sales of state assets will have on financial markets. What emerges from this model is a view of the evolving "consensual knowledge" that undergirds policymaking in the international system.

Social learning refers to the spread of new knowledge about the way the world works. Ernest Haas, who has done pathbreaking work in this area, notes that "knowledge is the sum of technical information and of theories about that information which commands sufficient consensus at a given time among interested actors to serve as a guide to public policy designed to achieve some social goal" (Haas 1980: 367–368). In this model, therefore, policy spreads in the wake of the diffusion of "consensual knowledge," that is, a shared fund of knowledge among social and political elites about the nature of socioeconomic change and effective policy.

But who is knowledgeable? Social learning surely involves the spread of knowledge among specialists; but to be a meaningful model of policy diffusion, that knowledge must also permeate the policymaking apparatus of government. The spread of Keynesian policy is instructive. Keynesian ideas existed in the professional literature prior to 1944, when they came to influence the agreements reached at Bretton Woods; efforts were made as early as 1933 to use them in international negotiations. As Haas describes it, "Knowledge becomes salient . . . only after it has seeped into the consciousness of policy makers and other influential groups and individuals. In 1945, Keynesian economics was widely accepted by economists and labor leaders, had made important inroads into the U.S. bureaucracy, but was still being resisted by the business community; a few years later, some key business groups made their peace with it" (Haas 1980: 269–270).

Similarly, during the same period that Keynesian ideas spread across the industrial nations, the concept of import substitution industrialization (ISI), fashioned by Raul Prebisch and the Economic Commission on Latin America (ECLA), was transmitted and adopted across the developing world, although it sometimes followed complicated pathways. Chinese adoption of ISI programs came primarily from the Soviet model. In India, Nehru clearly admired Fabian socialism and Soviet industrialization. The hybrid model was one that the Egyptians found attractive. In Latin America, ISI ideas emerged from experience with open economies from the 1930s and from internal economic analysis. The work of Prebisch and the ECLA gave programmatic expression to this model that other developing countries came to accept as a matter of doctrine or truth (Hirschman 1961; Kahler 1988). The pathways of diffusion were not straightforward, however, as if radiating outward from an single epicenter. One can note mavericks and anomalies in the process of diffusion; Turkey, for example, adopted state-led ISI simultaneously with the USSR and long before ECLA came up with the prescriptions.[8]

Social learning involves a set of interlocking processes. New forms of theoretical and policy knowledge must make their way into a professional community. These ideas, in turn, need to find their way into the councils of government. Moreover, to the extent that these two processes take place in a *transnational* setting, the movement of policy will be evident on an international scale. Behind this model of diffusion is an image of government itself as, at least in part, an organization that engages in "puzzling" as well as "powering" (Heclo 1974). That is, politicians and bureaucrats are attempting to solve problems and therefore are open, at particular historical moments, to new information. Those moments may be provoked by crisis: old reigning ideas are discredited. Or those moments may come with a change in regime (itself provoked, perhaps, by crisis). In these various ways, a new conventional wisdom emerges.[9]

In the area of privatization, a question remains concerning what constitutes the new knowledge. Some have argued that privatization policy really does not flow from a very well-developed new body of consensual knowledge; it does not have the full set of theoretical underpinnings that Keynesian policy, for example, seemed to manifest (Goldthorpe 1987). From this perspective, one would not expect privatization to have the same powerful impact on government that Keynesian economics had in an earlier period (unless privatization was driven by forces captured in the other models). Indeed, some might argue that what governments are currently experiencing is a crisis in economic theory. Old conventional wisdom is tarnished, but a new consensual fund of knowledge has yet to emerge. It may well be that social learning, as it relates to privatization, is at a more shallow level than that of Keynesianism. What governments have "learned" is that privatization can proceed without triggering massive economic and political dislocations. The lesson of the privatization of British Telecom was that the sale of huge public assets could take place without disaster; it did not result in the crowding out of private capital formation (S. Hanke 1987).

It remains a matter for further investigation, but privatization policy does seem to have been bolstered by the arguments put forward by economists working in close proximity to policymaking. In this sense, a sort of common international "policy culture" has attended and buttressed the international dimensions of the process.[10]

But the story of the spread of Keynesian policy suggests a final point about the limitations of the social learning model. The diffusion of Keynesian ideas and policy was clearly facilitated by the power and prestige of the United States. "The hegemonic position of the United States," writes Ernest Haas, "meant that other countries had little choice, even if they had wished to opt differently (which most did not)" (Haas 1980: 365). Similarly, Albert Hirschman notes that Keynesianism, although developed as an intellectual doctrine in Britain, gained its first success in the United States after 1938 and during the war. "Through the war's outcome the United States was then propelled to super-power status, and proceeded to promote Keynesian-type policies not only because of its general position in the world, but also because it acquired, through postwar aid programs, considerable direct influence on the economic policies of other major countries. In spite of many resistances . . . [Keynesianism] acquired a good measure of intellectual hegemony."[11] The presence of a well-articulated set of ideas was important and served to nurture a consensus on economic policy within the academic community; but the emergence of the United States as a powerful nation seeking to project those policy ideas onto others was also crucial.

The emergence of consensual knowledge provides a necessary but not sufficient condition for the spread of policy. The spread of Keynesianism, and one suspects the spread of privatization, needs to be understood by references to all three of the models of diffusion. Power matters, linking the flow of financial and other resources to the reform of economic policy. Likewise, the adoption of the preferred policies of the dominant nation will be greatly facilitated when those policies come to be associated with economic and political success. Finally, the presence of a coherent body of theoretical knowledge (a persuasive statement of the new theoretical orthodoxy) will help propel the spread of policy. In the Keynesian story, all three elements were present (see Baffi 1985). In the case of privatization, the package of policy ideas is less well bundled (there is no treatise like the *General Theory* to serve as an intellectual guide); Keynesian ideas are clearer and form a more discrete, more easily tracked package.[12] For this reason, the models of external inducements and emulation become all the more important in the process of diffusion.

Conclusion

We are now in a position to reflect on these various pieces of the privatization puzzle. It is evident that the diffusion of privatization is more complicated than the specifications of any single model will allow. Each model is, to borrow Dean Acheson's memorable phase, clearer than the truth. The answer to the question, "Why so many countries and why now?" needs to emphasize a confluence of events and processes. The common underlying trajectory of economic growth and expansion in the public sector of many countries is a necessary preliminary to the rest of the discussion. At the same time, an economic reductionism of the problem will not do. There are critical political and sociological processes at work, both transnational and internal to particular countries, that propel the spread of privatization policy. The answer to the basic question must involve several levels of analysis and a variety of intervening clauses.

This chapter seeks only to present some of the analytical tools to explore the international context within which privatization programs appear to be unfolding. It is not a substitute for detailed case studies, but the types of arguments I present would seem to be necessary to an understanding of the phenomenon on a worldwide scale. Privatization is not rust.

Several general conclusions seem to follow from the discussion. First, the spread of new policy ideas seems to proceed most rapidly following a crisis, when old policy ideas break down or are discredited. The exhaustion of old reigning policy ideas clears the way for new ones. Such crises will trigger a search for new approaches to policy; they may also serve to discredit old elites and policies and open up the way for new coalitions and new policies. This sort of historical disjuncture was clearly a part of the Keynesian story: the problems of economic disorder opened up opportunities for policy experimentation. The recent economic crisis served similarly to shake loose the orthodoxy of Keynesianism and public sector economic management, providing opportunities for new experiments in privatization.

Second, individuals, groups, and governments will adopt new policy approaches that serve their own internal needs. It surely has been crucial that privatization experiments took place in the leading capitalist nations (initiatives begun in Britain and pushed by the United States). But the movement of those policies to other developed and developing nations has taken place only because domestic groups and state officials have found their own reasons to pursue them. Moreover, the adoption of those policy ideas has also involved their adaptation to local circumstances. Even in the extreme cases of external inducement, local groups have found ways to use that pressure to build political coalitions and strengthen the government's hand in reform.

Notes

1. There is evidence in some cases that the impetus for privatization has come from the managers of state enterprises.

2. The early British privatization initiatives (British Airways, British Telecom, and British Gas) took place when the government was running a budget deficit (no longer the case). Moreover, despite some government statements to the contrary, these assets were not promoted with the explicit goal of encouraging competition. These sales merely turned public monopolies into private ones. See "Who Needs Privatisation Now?" *The Economist*, Dec. 19, 1987, p. 49.

3. See Oysten Noreng (1981: 141–142): "Historically, private enterprises in these countries have chosen to remain cautious and conservative rather than involve themselves in risky investments and uncertain business propositions. One explanation for the apparent audacity of state-owned oil companies is that they are not subject to the same set of sanctions as are private enterprises. Dynamic private firms that err in judgement by expanding too fast or misusing funds are punished by the market; they may have to reduce their rate of growth or, in extreme situations, declare bankruptcy. State oil companies, operating under a *raison d'être* that carries them to some extent above mar-

ket forces, are able to mobilize additional funding in the event of mistaken judgement."

4. Albert Hirschman (1982) presents a variant of this thesis when he argues that Western Europe oscillates between periods of preoccupation with expanding the public sector and periods of concern with strengthening the private sector and market.

5. A variant of diffusion by emulation is diffusion by avoidance. Some countries may be observing the course of privatization in other countries to see if it is something they want to emulate or avoid.

6. It is likely that competitive emulation is a more relevant factor in those areas of public policy that have a direct or immediate bearing on international standing, for example, trade policy.

7. There is another possibility. Privatization is so wide-ranging in terms of policies and outcomes that it may not be clear what consitutes "success." Precisely because there is often poor information, some countries may wish to "wait and see" rather than join the bangwagon.

8. I am endebted to John Waterbury and Atul Kohli for bringing this material to my attention.

9. In the case of Chile, the policy change emerged with the well-known recruitment of "Chicago school" economists in government. This may be an episode of forced consensual knowledge.

10. I have taken the term "international policy culture" from Paul Starr.

11. Hirschman 1989; see also Hirschman 1988: 4–7. According to several sources, Keynes wrote the *General Theory* after he had been unable for several years to persuade the British government to implement his ideas. He hoped that by first convincing the academic community he might then influence policy. This is precisely what happened in the United States and elsewhere. Keynes' ideas in the *General Theory* would thus have already been familiar to many of this readers.

12. One could argue that the intellectual sources of privatization are clear enough and can be found in the works of F. A. Hayek (1960, 1973–1979) and Milton Friedman (1962). A more recent statement of these views can be found in Samuel Brittan (1973, 1977).

References

Babai, Don. 1988. "The World Bank and IMF: Backing the State versus Rolling It Back." In *The Promise of Privatization: A Challenge for U.S. Foreign Policy*, ed. Raymond Vernon. New York: Council on Foreign Relations.

Baffi, Paolo. 1985. "The Bank of Italy and Foreign Economists, 1944–53: A Personal Memoir." *Rivista Di Stori Economica* 2nd ser., 2 (international issue): 1–40.

Boli-Bennet, John. 1979. "The Ideology of Expanding State Authority in National Constitutions, 1870–1970." In Meyer and Hannan 1979.

Brittan, Samuel. 1973. *Capitalism and the Permissive Society*. London: Macmillan.

───. 1977. *The Economic Consequences of Democracy*. London: Temple Smith.

Cowan, L. Gray. 1987. "A Global Overview of Privatization." In S. Hanke 1987.

Feigenbaum, Harvey. 1985. *Politics of Public Enterprise: Oil and the French State*. Princeton: Princeton University Press.

Friedman, Milton. 1962. *Capitalism and Freedom*. Chicago: University of Chicago Press.

Goldthorpe, John H. 1987. "Problems of Political Economy after the Postwar Period." In *Changing Boundaries of the Political: Essays on the Evolving Balance Between the State and Society, Public and Private in Europe*, ed. Charles Maier. Cambridge: Cambridge University Press.

Haas, Ernest. 1980. "Why Collaborate? Issue-Linkage and International Regimes." *World Politics* 32, no. 3: 357–405.

Haggard, Stephan. 1988. "Privatization in the Philippines." In *The Promise of Privatization: A Challenge for U.S. Foreign Policy*, ed. Raymond Vernon. New York: Council on Foreign Relations.

Hall, John A. 1988. *Liberalism: Politics, Ideology and the Market*. London: Paladin.

Hall, John A., and G. John Ikenberry. 1989. *The State*. Milton Keynes: Open University Press.

Hanke, Elliot. 1987. "The Role of Divestiture in Economic Growth." In S. Hanke 1987.

Hanke, Steve H., ed. 1987. *Privatization and Development*. San Francisco: Institute for Contemporary Studies.

Hayek, F. A. 1960. *The Constitution of Liberty*. London: Routledge.

───. 1973–1979. *Law, Legislation and Liberty*. 3 vols. London: Routledge.

Heclo, Hugh. 1974. *Social Policy in Britain and Sweden*. New Haven: Yale University Press.

Hirschman, Albert. 1961. "Ideologies of Economic Development in Latin America." In *Latin American Issues: Essays and Comments*, ed. Albert Hirschman. New York: Twentieth Century Fund.

───. 1982. *Shifting Involvements: Private Interests and Public Action*. Princeton: Princeton University Press.

───. 1988. "How Keynesianism Spread from America." *Challenge* 31, no. 6: 4–7.

───. 1989. "How the Keynesian Revolution Was Exported from the United States, and Other Comments." In *The Political Power of Economic Ideas: Keynesiansim across Nations*, ed. Peter Hall. Princeton: Princeton University Press.

Hoffmann, Stanley. 1987. "Domestic Politics and Interdependence." In Hoffmann, *Janus and Minerva: Essays in the Theory and Practice of International Politics*. Boulder: Westview Press. Originally published 1978.

Ikenberry, G. John. 1986. "The Irony of State Strength: Comparative Responses to the Oil Shocks in the 1970s." *International Organization* 40 (Winter): 105–137.

_____. 1988. *Reasons of State: Oil Politics and the Capacities of American Government*. Ithaca: Cornell University Press.

_____. 1989. "Manufacturing Consensus: Private Interests and International Trade Negotiations." *Comparative Politics* 21, no. 3: 289–305.

Kahler, Miles. 1988. "Orthodoxy and Its Alternatives: Explaining Approaches to Stabilization and Adjustment." Unpublished.

Keohane, Robert O. 1984. "The World Political Economy and the Crisis of Embedded Liberalism." In *Order and Conflict in Contemporary Capitalism*, ed. John H. Goldthorpe. Oxford: Clarendon Press.

Lucas, N.J.D. 1977. "The Role of Institutional Relationships in French Energy Policy." *International Relations* 5 (November), 87–121.

McPherson, M. 1987. "The Promise of Privatization." In S. Hanke 1987.

Marquand, David. 1987. *The Unprincipled Society: New Demands and Old Politics*. London: Cape.

Meyer, John W. 1984. "The Expansion of the State." *Annual Review of Sociology* 10: 461–482.

Meyer, John W., and Michael T. Hannan, eds. 1979. *National Development and the World System: Education, Economic and Political Change, 1950–1970*. Chicago: University of Chicago Press.

Noreng, Oysten. 1981. "State-Owned Oil Companies: Western Europe." In Vernon and Aharoni 1981.

Pen, Jan. 1987. "Expanding Budgets in a Stagnating Economy: The Experience of the 1970s." In *Changing Boundaries of the Political: Essays on the Evolving Balance Between the State and Society, Public and Private in Europe*, ed. Charles Maier. Cambridge: Cambridge University Press.

Rogers, Evertt M. 1962. *Diffusion of Innovation*. New York: Free Press.

Skidelsky, Robert. 1979. "The Decline of Keynesian Politics." In *State and Economy in Contemporary Capitalism*, ed. Colin J. Crouch. London: Croom Helm.

Suleiman, Ezra. 1988. *Private Power and Centralization in France: The Notaires and the State*. Princeton: Princeton University Press.

Vernon, Raymond. 1981. "Introduction." In Vernon and Aharoni 1981.

Vernon, Raymond, and Yair Aharoni, eds. 1981. *State-Owned Enterprise in the Western Economies*. New York: St. Martin's Press.

Vickers, John, and Vincent Wright. 1989. "The Politics of Industrial Privatization in Western Europe: An Overview." In *The Politics of Privatization in Western Europe*, ed. Vickers and Wright. London: Frank Cass.

Waltz, Kenneth. 1979. *Theory of International Politics*. New York: Wiley.

PART TWO

Advanced Industrial Countries

5

The Politics of Privatization in Britain and France

Ezra N. Suleiman

Privatization represents, in both Britain and France, a definite break with the postwar tradition of state ownership of economic enterprises. Yet the underlying motivations that impelled privatization were not the same in the two countries. Also, the decisions regarding the companies that were to be privatized, the timing and sequence of privatization, and the modalities of privatization all reflected different priorities.

The differences in the privatization policies of Britain and France are the result of each country's experience with nationalization, as well as of the specific context in which each found itself in the late 1970s and 1980s.[1] In the first place, nationalization for the British Labour party and for the left in France was more than a response to the failures of the market. State ownership was a fundamental part of the ideological structure of the left in both countries. Still, there were marked differences in the original impetus to nationalize industries in the two countries, and these differences are reflected in the privatizations that the two societies have undertaken.

Second, the political context in which the French right found itself in 1986 was very different from that surrounding the Conservative government of several years earlier in Britain. The center-right government of Jacques Chirac was reacting to the massive drive to nationalize industries and financial institutions that the socialists undertook in 1981. It must be said that in making denationalization a priority in its electoral program, the RPR-UDF (the center-right) coalition took few risks, for by then privatizations had become an international phenomenon, and even the socialists had begun putting forth measures that sought to stimulate competition (Cerny 1987; see also Zysman 1983 and Suleiman 1987).

It should be clear that privatization is used in this chapter to refer only to the selling of equity. Contracting out has been widely employed in Britain and France, particularly at the local level. Jacques Chirac, for example, has used this method frequently as mayor of Paris to ensure that the city does not undertake to perform all social services itself. In Britain, the sale of local authority–owned council houses has bought receipts of about £15 billion and has been widely seen as influential in accounting for the substantial number of crossover votes from the Labour to the Conservative party. Important as contracting out is as a means of achieving privatization, it is only one among a number of ways to achieve the reduction of state ownership and control. Among those others are deregulation, user fees, voucher systems, and load shedding, whereby the state ceases completely to take on responsibility for providing certain services (see Hartley and Huby 1986; Asher 1987; Henig, Hamnett, and Feigenbaum 1987).

Great Britain

The Background

Privatization began in Britain in 1979, but it did not suddenly spring onto the Conservative party's agenda in that year (Vickers and Yarrow 1985; Yarrow 1986). The extent of state intervention in the economy had long been a divisive issue between the Conservative and Labour parties. It should not be forgotten that some of the industries nationalized by the first postwar British government in 1945 were denationalized by the Conservatives in 1951–1955, only to be renationalized by Labour in 1964. (This ping-pong game concerned mostly the iron and steel industries.)

Privatization in Britain has cast a remarkably wide net and has included British Airways, British Gas, British Aerospace, the National Freight Corporation (created by the Labour government in 1964), Rolls-Royce, British Telecom, British Shipbuilders, and British Petroleum. The British government expects to raise £5 billion a year from the sale of such assets in the 1987–1990 period.

In view of the large role that the public sector came to have in Britain, there had long developed within the Conservative party a voice that called for the sale of public assets in order to reduce the level of the public sector borrowing requirement (PSBR). Reduced government expenditure was seen by the monetarist wing of the Conservative party as necessary to prevent the crowding out of private investment. Although the sale of government-held equity would not normally be expected to reduce crowding out (it would be more likely to do precisely the reverse), it would, by standard British accounting procedures, be considered as a re-

TABLE 1
Privatization Proceeds in Britain

Year	£ Million	Year	£ Million
1978–1980	377	1983–1984	1,142
1980–1981	405	1984–1985	2,132
1981–1982	493	1985–1986	2,702
1982–1983	488	1986–1987	4,750
1987–1988 to 1989–1990: 5,000 annually			

Source: Vickers 1988: 1.

duction of the PSBR (rather than a method of financing it at a given level). The PSBR was seen as the main indicator of government expenditure, and its reduction was a goal that the newly elected Conservative government was to set itself.

It is interesting to note that, although there may have been a monetarist wing within the Conservative party, the party itself had not demonstrated an unequivocal desire to pursue a broad program of privatization. In 1979, as John Vickers has noted, the Conservative party manifesto had little to say about privatization. Aside from references to "rolling back the frontiers of the state," the party offered no specific program (Vickers 1988). Indeed, the privatization program seemed to gain momentum, as the years passed, running today at ten times its size in 1979 (see Table 1).

The first equity sold by the Conservative government consisted of a 5 percent tranche of British Petroleum (BP). BP operated in a competitive environment and, despite a government majority shareholding, had never been subject to much government interference. Thus the sale simply represented a way of raising money. The government continued a policy started by the Labour government, which had sold a 17 percent tranche in 1977, and concluded with sales of the remaining shares in 1981, 1983, and 1987.

The BP sale was followed by a number of minor sales, most notably of shares that had been acquired by the National Enterprise Board (NEB), a body that had been created by the Labour government to invest predominantly in high-technology companies. The NEB was disbanded, shares in a number of small companies (including ICL, Ferranti, and Fairey) were sold off, generally to other companies, and the NEB's two largest concerns, British Leyland and Rolls-Royce, were transferred to direct government ownership. The next major sale, a 50 percent stake of British Aerospace (BAe), was seen as a major success. The issue was three and a half times oversubscribed and attracted 155,000 new shareholders. But neither it nor the other sales of the government's first term, which included Cable and Wireless, Amersham, Associated British Ports, Britoil, and Enterprise

Oil, were major events for the government in terms of political impact or of revenue raised. These were mainly small companies, and little economic justification for keeping them in the public sector could be given.

It was with the Conservative government's second term, and in particular the sale of British Telecom (BT), that the policy of privatization underwent major evolution, in two ways. First, there was a change in the way in which privatizations were carried out. Increasingly, privatizations became major political events, as an attempt was made to sell large proportions of the shares to the general public. The massive advertising campaigns that were needed to achieve this goal also succeeded in generating much publicity for the program itself.

Second, there was a change in the type of company sold. Larger companies were involved, and they were no longer sold in slices, as had been the case earlier, but rather in their entirety (Vickers 1988). Moreover, although the government continued to sell companies that were operating in competitive markets, the sale of BT inaugurated the policy of selling public utilities that many considered to be natural monopolies (or at least de facto monopolies)—companies about which economic arguments could be given that they should remain in the public sector.

These two changes were closely connected. Although large proportions of competitive companies such as Rolls-Royce were sold to the general public, it was the sale of the big utilities, especially BT, that was central in arousing public interest in privatization. More important, it would have been politically very difficult to sell utilities like BT in such a way that a large proportion did not end up in the hands of the general public. Despite the utilities' huge size, it is conceivable that institutional buyers could have been found, although this might have led to some crowding out of the equity markets. But it would have been politically difficult to sell to a small number of private buyers. By presenting privatization as an instance of popular capitalism, the government was able largely to avoid the charge that it was giving a small group of investors a licence to make monopoly profits.

As the privatization program has progressed, the order of its priorities appears to have changed. Its initial impetus came from dissatisfaction with the growth of the public sector and the inefficiencies of the nationalized industries. The desire to make these industries efficient through the transfer of ownership to the private sector no doubt motivated the privatization program in its early stage. As the revenues that were raised by the sale of public assets increased, however, the program came to be seen as having important macroeconomic advantages and effects. In its current phase, the program's main advantage is believed to be the spreading of ownership (Vickers 1988). Indeed, it is for this reason that the shares of the public assets have been consistently underpriced. The restrictions placed on the number of shares that can be acquired was intended to spread ownership thinly but broadly. The purpose here was not economic; rather, the intention was to grant ownership both to employees and to the public and so reduce the power of trade unions. A second advantage of mobilizing popular demand for shares in privatized companies was that it increased the total funds available and hence reduced the need to place shares overseas. The risk of foreign takeover did not become a big issue in the debate on privatization until the government entered negotiations with General Motors in 1986 over the possible purchase of that part of British Leyland that included the commercial vehicles sector and Land Rover. Backbench outcry forced the government to harden its negotiating stance, and General Motors withdrew. It has been generally thought that most of the nationally important companies the government privatized were too big to be likely targets for takeovers. (The purchase of 19 percent of BP by the Kuwaiti Investment Office, however, shows that even the largest companies are not immune to the purchase of shareholdings in numbers sufficient to be influential.) Nevertheless, the government has retained a special "golden" share in all but two (BP and Associated British Ports) of the companies that it has privatized by public issue. These shares place various conditions on who may own the rest of the equity in the company, often limiting single shareholdings to 15 percent.

In the case of strategically sensitive companies, such as British Aerospace, British Airways, and Rolls-Royce, the government has limited total overseas holdings to between 15 and 25 percent. Britoil, in which the government holds a golden share that is activated only if some buyer obtains more than 50 percent of the stock, but that is then empowered to outvote all the other shareholdings, will provide a test case of government policy. Unlike the golden share in Amersham and Enterprise Oil, it has no fixed date of expiration. BP has bought 54 percent of Britoil's shares; and although the government has decided not to refer the takeover to the Monopolies and Mergers Commission, how it will use its golden share remains to be seen.

Case Studies

British Telecom.   British Telecom was, in many respects, the central privatization. It was the first utility to be privatized; it was the first for which the general public was targeted as the main buyer; and it was, at the time, by far the largest sale—seven times larger than the largest flotation to have taken place in the United Kingdom (Vickers and Yarrow 1985; Holton 1986).

Until 1981 telecommunications had been part of the Post Office. International comparisons showed the operation to be inefficiently run: 1984 figures estimated the number of subscribers per employee as 83 for BT, 125 for the PTT (France), and 181 for Bell Atlantic (United States). The government split telecommunications from the Post Office to form a separate company, BT. In 1984, 50.2 percent of BT was privatized. The offer of three billion 130-penny shares was four times oversubscribed. The shares opened at a premium of 45p on their partly paid price of 50p, giving a 90 percent profit to those who sold immediately (Newman 1986).

The BT sale came in for much criticism, which centered on two areas. First, the government underpriced the issue, giving a windfall profit to those who had bought the shares (this included an estimated £180 million capital gain going to overseas buyers). Although intentional underpricing seems unlikely, it is clear that the government was keen, with its first big issue, to err on the side of under- rather than overpricing. The BT issue worked as a form of loss leader, with most of the windfall profits going to people who were potential Conservative voters. The loss to the community as a whole through underpricing was hard to perceive; the gain to individuals was readily recognized. In a situation where the flotation of an unquoted company made it almost impossible to pitch the issue price exactly right, underpricing rather than overpricing made sound political sense.[2]

The second criticism concerned the claim that the government had turned a public monopoly into a private one. The government had two responses to this criticism. It created a regulatory body, Oftel, with power to control BT's pricing policy and to investigate complaints. It also introduced some measure of competition by licensing Mercury, a subsidiary of Cable and Wireless (and, originally, of BP and Barclays Bank, which later withdrew), to set up a rival fiber optics telephone network interconnected with the BT network. Both of these measures have had some effect. Despite its small size, Oftel, led by Bryan Carsberg, a professor of accounting, has shown every sign of avoiding capture by BT. It made an important decision in 1986, allowing Mercury to interconnect with the BT network at a rate that many commentators saw as favorable and that has ensured Mercury's continued existence. By targeting business users, Mercury hopes to have 5 percent of the UK telecommunications market by 1990, and 10 percent within ten years.

BT's profitability has increased from £1.5 billion in 1984–1985 to £2.1 billion in 1986–1987; and by taking a controlling stake in the Canadian company Mitel, BT has moved into equipment manufacturing. But many problems remain. Under the conditions of its contract, BT must make its prices conform to the "RPI-3" formula: total price increases on a basket of goods must be three points less than the rate of inflation. But this has allowed BT to rebalance its fees to the advantage of high-volume users and business customers. This practice, together with evidence that the public call-box network is deteriorating, has brought many complaints from the general public. A Mori poll in mid-1987 showed that 52 percent of BT customers considered their prices unreasonable, compared to 40 percent in 1980. Business customers also complain about poor service: late deliveries, faulty lines, poor quality of transmission. In short, BT behaves much as might be expected of a company with no effective competition for most of its services.

Rolls-Royce. During the 1960s, Rolls-Royce was largely forced out of the American market by GE and Pratt and Whitney. In the late 1960s the company decided to develop a new engine, the RB211, with which to re-enter the American market; but technical and financial problems arose, and the company went into receivership in 1971. The Conservative government of the time, worried at the prospect of high redundancies and the loss of Britain's only aero-engine manufacturer, sold off the profitable car and diesel engine sectors and nationalized what remained.

During the 1970s Rolls-Royce received large injections of government money, enabling it to complete the development of the RB211, which proved successful worldwide. But in the early 1980s, with the recession in the civil aircraft market, Rolls-Royce began losing money once again. Employees were reduced from 62,000 in 1980 to 41,000 in 1984. In 1984 the group recorded a consolidated profit, following losses in all but one of the previous five years. Substantial increases in profits were recorded in 1985 and 1986.

In 1983 the government announced that it intended to privatize Rolls-Royce. As was generally the case for privatizations in Britain, this required a change of status to public limited company, which took place in 1986. Two million people applied for shares when the company was finally privatized in 1987, the offer being 9.4 times over subscribed. On the first day of trading the shares went to a premium of 73 percent on the partly paid price. The government kept a golden share, and there were further conditions that no individual could hold more than 15 percent of the total equity and that no more than 15 percent could be held overseas.[3] Rolls-Royce provides a good example of a company that came into the public sector only as a result of its commercial failure. Once it was successful again, there was no reason to hold on to it. The company's behavior would not likely be much changed by its changed status. The most significant change was that most of its employees became shareholders: 96.2 percent took up the initial offer of free shares, 76.6 percent an offer of two free shares for every one bought, and 42 percent an option to buy further shares at preferential rates. Here again, it was most uncertain that this share ownership would have much effect on industrial relations.

Gas, Water, Ectricity. After the sale of BT, the government decided to go ahead with the privatization of some other public monopolies. In the case of telecommunications, changes in technology made it possible to envisage some competition, even at the level of national networks. There is little likelihood that competition could arise in the gas or water industries, however, or in the distribution (but not the generation) of electricity. One of the government's main arguments for the privatization of BT—that privatization is necessary to promote competition and that competition increases efficiency—thus had no relevance here.

British Gas was sold in 1986. The flotation of £5.4 billion of stock was, at the time, the largest in the world. A £40 million advertising campaign attracted many buyers from different social classes, which had not been the case in earlier privatizations. British Gas gained a total of 4.5 million shareholders—more than any other privatized company. The government had decided against breaking the company up; in the total absence of competition, the only control was the regulatory body, Ofgas.

The plan to privatize the water industry was delayed during the government's second term by technical and legal problems, and the enabling legislation was shelved in 1986. The government has since reintroduced a new project to privatize water. Although the government believes that the water industry is a natural monopoly, it hopes that efficiency can be ensured on the free market by selling the industry as ten separate companies (corresponding to the ten existing water boards, divested of their responsibility for environmental control). In this way the companies will be small enough, and comparisons between them will give likely buyers enough information, for inefficiently run companies to be subject to takeover.

The sale of the electricity industry provides an opportunity to introduce greater competition. The Central Electricity Generating Board (CEGB), which currently controls generation and, through its control of the National Grid, coordinates distribution, argued that it should keep this role. But the government seems to have heeded the criticism of its sale of BT and British Gas and, even though proceeds from the sale will probably be reduced, has decided to split up the industry. The National Grid will come under the control of twelve regional companies, which will be privatized separately; 30 percent of CEGB will be split off to form a rival generating company, and the two companies thus created will then be privatized.

Conclusion

During its term of office the Conservative government has seen a marked turnaround in the profitability of a number of state-owned companies. In virtually all cases this turnaround came before privatization;

indeed, it was necessary for successful privatization. On the other hand, a strong argument could be made that only the spur of future privatization was sufficient to force this turnaround; and profits have gone on increasing (*The Observer*, Oct. 25, 1987). In evaluating the desirability of this increase in profitability, we must distinguish between companies operating in competitive markets, such as Rolls-Royce and BAe, and those, such as British Gas and BT, that hold monopoly positions. Although the profitability of the former is probably the result of increased efficiency, the latter may simply have discovered how to exploit a monopoly position effectively.

Where the policy has been unambiguously successful is in increasing the number of shareholders. Following the British Gas privatization, an estimated 9.4 million people–23 percent of the adult population–were direct shareholders, compared 2 million shareholders before the BT sale. It was only with the sale of British Gas, which attracted 4.4 million buyers, that this imbalance was largely corrected.

A claim by the government, however, that it radically altered the nature of shareholding in Britain is liable to two caveats. First, most new shareholders have invested only in privatized companies; 56 percent own shares in only one company, 22 percent in two, and only 22 percent in three or more. The government has, in effect, been as successful in creating a new class of shares as in creating a new class of shareholders. Whether the new shareholders will buy shares in other, nonprivatized, companies is bound to depend to some extent on the success of the privatized shares. Second, although the total number of private shareholders has increased, the proportion of shares held by them rather than by institutions continues to fall, from 54 percent in 1963, to 28 percent in 1981, to 24 percent in 1986. Moreover, it is uncertain whether the gain in popularity that is often attributed to the government as a result of its privatization policy will be permanent.

The effect upon workers' attitudes has been mixed (Thomas 1986). In the case of the National Freight Corporation there has even been something of a revolution. The company was privatized in 1982 in a management-led staff buy out (McLachlan 1983). The company is still owned by its staff, who by September 1987 had seen their shares rise to 54 times their original value. In other companies the effects have been less dramatic. Trade unions at BT have, as we have seen, been weakened by privatization; but worker morale appears to be low, and the unions have become more militant. At Jaguar, only 19 percent of the workers took up the offer of concessionary shares. The union responded to the increased efficiency of the company by requesting that the increased profits be distributed in increased wages, and it backed up this request with an effective strike.

France

The Background

Privatization in France is bound to represent a more severe break with the past than it does in Britain. The long tradition of government ownership and direction of the economic sector, to which both the left and the right had been committed,[4] meant a more drastic shock for a state seeking to "roll back its frontiers." Yet the speed with which the privatization program has been pursued in France is its most notable feature.

In 1986, the Gaullist party (the RPR) and its center-right allies (the UDF) declared in their joint manifesto that they would privatize the banks, the insurance companies, the audiovisual sector, and the major industrial groups (*Le Monde*, Jan. 19–20, 1986). After the conservative government was elected in March 1986, these plans were made more precise with the publication of the *projet de loi de habilitation*, which was intended to enable the government to privatize sixty-five companies in the period up to 1991. The government committed itself to the privatization of the five industrial groups nationalized in 1982, together with the banks, insurance companies and Elf Aquitaine; and it held open the option of privatizing Matra, CGCT, Bull, and CCF (*Le Monde*, Apr. 12, 1986). By 1988, the conservative government had completed the privatization of four industrial groups (Saint-Gobain, CGE, CGCT, and Matra), two investment banks (Paribas and Suez), two commercial banks (CCF and Société Générale), two media companies (TF1 and Havas), and a number of smaller banks, bringing in net receipts of over 55 billion francs. Why was implementation so much faster than in Britain? There are three principal reasons.

First, the idea of privatization was no longer novel. Margaret Thatcher had certainly helped to pave the way and shown that she could remain popular into the bargain. Also, the expertise needed to carry out the program was readily available. There were extensive contacts between the British Treasury and the French Ministry of Finance over the issue of privatization. The minister of finance himself noted that there were important differences between the French and British attempts at privatization: the French project was larger than the British one; French cultural, economic, and financial attitudes were different; and the French wanted a juridical system that was simple and flexible and that was to be uniformly applicable so that a new law would not be required for each individual company or bank privatized. Nonetheless, the minister recognized that "the British experience was, without any doubt, the best example, and the one that had the greatest similarities with what we wanted to do" (Balladur 1987: 93). In fact, one can draw a distinction between "the Franco-British radical models and the piecemeal and limited measures of other [European] countries" (Vickers and Wright 1988: 22). In no other European country that have embarked upon a privatization program—Spain, Italy, Portugal, Austria, Belgium—has the scope of or the commitment to privatization been as far-reaching as in Britain and France.

The second reason the government of Jacques Chirac proceeded so rapidly was that it sought, through a massive program of privatization, to counter the nationalization program undertaken by the left in the early 1980s. Although the left's program had followed the precedents set by two earlier waves of nationalization—by the Popular Front government in 1936–1937 and by the Liberation government in 1944–1946—the fact remains that it came at a time when other countries were beginning to reduce the weight of their public sectors. Moreover, its scope had been all-encompassing.

It has been argued that nationalizations were originally intended to democratize French industry by increasing worker participation but that "their real importance derived from the enhanced control they offered the state in restructuring, rationalizing, and improving the competitive posture of the French economy, particularly in those sectors involving advanced technologies" (Cameron 1986). This justification may have been derived ex post facto, since the nationalizations were, as Richard Holton has argued, necessary concessions that the Socialist party had to make in order to reach an accord with the Communist party (Holton 1986). They were met in 1982 with strong parliamentary criticism on economic and political grounds: nationalization raised, as the right claimed, the specter of the collectivization of the French economy.

The legislative elections of March 1986 returned the right to power. Just as nationalization (and decentralization) had become the hallmark of socialist rule, so privatization was intended to become the distinguishing—equally revolutionary—feature of the right. Chirac's government had an additional reason for proceeding at a breakneck pace: it had a maximum life of two years, after which Chirac himself would be the right's candidate in the presidential elections. The government thus wanted a policy that signaled a decisive break with socialism and that could be implemented rapidly. Nor did the prospect of privatization lack popularity. According to a Gallup poll, 61 percent of the public thought it a good idea, while 24 percent were opposed to it.[5] It was also fortunate that, given the status of the nationalized companies under socialist rule, privatizing these companies would not pose undue complications.

This brings us to the third reason privatization proceeded much more quickly in France than in Britain: the state of the nationalized companies. Most of them, including all of those that had been nationalized in 1982, remained public limited companies whose shares were owned by the government.[6] Moreover, they were not strangers to the stock market. The five industrial concerns nationalized in 1982 were basically holding companies, and the Socialist government allowed minority shareholdings in their subsidiaries to remain in private hands.[7] Their share values provided an important indicator of the total values of the holding companies themselves, as did the various forms of nonvoting stock, in particular *certificats d'investissement* and *titres participantifs*, which the Socialist government had permitted the companies to issue in order to raise capital.

The rapid sale of public assets was greatly facilitated by the financial condition of the nationalized companies. It is true that the enormous handouts that the French government offered the nationalized companies to compensate them for operating losses (and to shore up employment), at least in the early years, were substantial. Between 1982 and 1986, it is estimated, government subsidies totaled 40 billion francs, which "represented an amount twenty times larger than the total investment by all private shareholders in the firms in the twenty years prior to nationalization!" (Cameron 1987). But this record needs qualification. In the first place, a substantial portion of this subsidy went to the steel industry and to Renault, which experienced substantial losses in the first part of the decade.[8] The profitability of these firms began to rise, so that by 1986 most of the newly nationalized sector was in a better financial position than it had been prior to nationalization.

The financial condition of the nationalized companies in France contrasts sharply with that of the British companies on the eve of privatization. When the Conservative government came to power in Britain, many of the large companies, including Rolls-Royce, British Airways, British Steel, and British Leyland, were losing money. The return of these companies to profitability, and the increased efficiency and profitability of BT and British Aerospace, came largely as a result of their privatization. Restructuring and redundancies were implemented in order to make the companies sufficiently attractive for privatization. The result was that most of the firms saw their profits increase, while those losing money (Sacilor, Usinor and Renault) saw their loses decrease. Consequently, the nationalized companies destined for privatization were all in good financial health by 1986.

Principles of Privatization

Openness.   Partly because the sale of public assets is an enormous undertaking, and partly because of the ties between big business and the center-right, the Chirac government claimed that the privatization process had to be totally open and above suspicion. "It was important," noted the minister of finance, "that the privatizations should be as incontestable as possible. Because of the inherent moral and political questions, the process had to be carried out with much scruple, precision, and rigor. I was determined that my action would follow strict principles and rules" (Balladur 1987: 81).

The principle of transparency required that all legal procedures be followed. Consequently, a law was drawn up that encompassed all sixty-five companies to be privatized. A separate law had to be passed for the privatization of one of the major public television stations (TF1) and for the privatization of the foremost cooperative bank in the world (the Caisse Nationale de Crédit Agricole), particularly since the latter did not involve sale of shares to the public.

There is no doubt that the entire process of privatization was strongly guided and controlled by the state—an apparent contradiction of the liberalism that it was seeking to put into effect. The minister of finance justified the even greater degree of centralization that was needed to effect the privatization process on the grounds that disposition of the state's assets required extensive cooperation among many economic and financial institutions. "A similar concentration of powers in the same hands is not necessarily desirable in ordinary times. It was necessary during the two-year period that we were embarking upon because economic policy had to be conducted in a coherent manner" (Balladur 1987: 81).

The procedure chosen by the government, in keeping with the principle of transparency, was the creation of the Commission on Privatization, whose seven members were selected by the government. The commission's main task was to evaluate the financial condition of each company and suggest a price for the company's shares. The companies and the government were also to have the advice of French and foreign investment banks, which could analyze each company's accounts and advise it on the risks that it would run in the event of a sale under a particular condition.

Foreign Control. An additional issue that confronted the French government was the degree of foreign investment that would be considered tolerable. The original *ordonnance* included a clause, inserted by Balladur (*Le Monde*, July 2, 1986), that limited the total holdings that the government could sell directly to foreigners to 15 percent. This was the text that François Mitterrand refused to sign (*Le Monde*, July 17, 1986), on the grounds that it threatened national independence. Ironically, the bill that Chirac was forced to submit subsequently to Parliament raised the limit to 20 percent to ensure conformity to EEC law. Once the shares are in private hands, however, this limit no longer applies.

The government had three responses to criticisms that companies would be vulnerable to foreign takeover. First, it argued that any takeovers would be subject to EEC law, which prohibits non-EEC buyers from buying more than 20 percent of a company without the permission of the national government concerned. Second, it reserved the right to take a golden share in companies that were especially sensitive or vulnerable, a share that would give the government the right to veto any purchase of 10 percent or more of the company concerned for a period of five years after privatization (Balladur 1987: 107). The government has such shares in Havas, Elf Aquitaine, and Bull. Third, the government has had recourse to a *noyau dur*: a small number of institutional investors, mainly French, who have been guaranteed an allotment of shares (normally not more than 2 percent) in return for paying a premium over the normal issue price and for accepting controls on their ability to sell their shares for a period (normally five years) after privatization.

Noyau Dur. The most controversial of the procedures used by the government in connection with privatization has been the creation of a stable core of investors in order to avoid a dispersed, and hence potentially unstable, shareholding population. Having reserved 10 percent of the shares to the employees of the privatized company (at preferential conditions), the government sought to protect the companies from raids by foreign companies having access to substantial capital. Consequently, a company's total shares could not be offered to the general public, a "dispersed and atomized" group. What was needed, according to the minister of finance, was "a stable group of shareholders, each one having 2 percent to 5 percent of the capital, with the entire group possessing 20 percent" (Balladur 1987: 85). A third argument has been advanced for the creation of this *noyau dur*, composed essentially of the largest French industrial and financial groups: the size of the French capital market. In other words, French Bourse would be unlikely to absorb the ambitious program of privatization; consequently, an adequate provision of capital had to be assured for the success of the program, and only the largest industrial and financial groups could provide this capital. In retrospect—that is, in view of the oversubscription of the shares—this argument now appears dubious.

The policy of creating the *noyau dur* has been criticized on the grounds that it gives disproportionate economic power to a few giants and concentrates capital even further (see the criticisms by the socialists, *Le Monde*, Oct. 9, 1987). Moreover, the choice of the companies that in each separate case came to constitute the *noyau dur* belonged solely to the minister of finance.[9] The minister was accused of using privatization as a means of rewarding friends (most often, the political friends of the Gaullist party) and of maintaining a substantial part of the ownership of the privatized companies within a circle close to the minister's own political party.[10]

Although the finance minister maintained that the *noyau dur* was a necessary step in the direction of changing French capitalism (*Le Monde*, Sept.

17, 1988), others have seen the revival of the specter, if not of the "two hundred families," then of the "fifty-two friends."[11] François Morin has traced what he calls "the financial circles" of privatisation: the first links the already private firms through their *noyau dur*; the second links the stake of the firms to be privatized to the already privatized firms; and the third links the stake of the private firms in the already privatized ones. He sees the beginnings of a renaissance of a "financial capitalism" that will lead to a further restriction of ownership once the *noyaux dur* are no longer obligated to hold on to their shares. "Financial capitalism" is to be feared because it is not productive capitalism. Morin maintains that of the 90 billion francs spent on purchasing the public assets, none of this amount has gone into productive investment (Morin 1987). Hence, the role granted the *noyau dur* has had political consequences in the short term and is expected to have economic consequences in the long run. At any rate, for the government, the *noyau dur* made the ambitious privatization program possible by providing the necessary capital, by not overly dispersing ownership, and by protecting the firms against foreign raids.

Finally, because of the strong hand that the government has had in the privatization process and in the choice of the stable core of investors, it has been suggested that the aim has been to preserve the state's role in industrial policy and in the economy. Privatization is thus seen as a continuation of government intervention by other means (Bauer 1988). Chirac himself said that privatisation was not be construed as "désétatisation."[12] Yet one should be careful not to confuse the short and long terms. It may well be that in the present postprivatization period, the government has lost little control over the direction of industrial policy. In the long run, however, private ownership is bound to lead to greater independence from—or at least to a greater capacity to resist—the state. This outcome may take some time, but it is likely to come about simply because new institutional structures and expectations eventually lead to a changed relationship among institutions.

Popular Ownership. "Privatisation is the veritable nationalization of the economy," said Jacques Chirac (*Le Monde*, Apr. 14, 1987). The French government has throughout maintained that workers should be more closely associated with their enterprises and that people should come that they have a stake in the economy. It was a question of "power, of participation, of belonging," and even a modest shareholding would make the shareholder feel "at home" (Balladur 1987: 67). A new era was going to open up for a new category of partners: "the employee-shareholders. They would be both capitalists and employees at the same time" (ibid.: 69).

In order to attract the largest number of shareholders, the government offered a series of benefits to the small investor. Applications for ten or fewer shares were to be honored; payment could be made on an install ment basis at no additional cost (though the shares could not be resold until they had been fully paid for); one free share was to be given to investors for every ten purchased (up to a maximum of fifty shares) and held for eighteen months; and finally, neither the free shares nor the interest-free installment payments were to be subject to income taxes.

The government's policy of encouraging a broad, "popular" investment in the stock market appears to have succeeded. Thirteen percent of the French people purchased at least one share (Le Boucher 1987), so that, whereas there were fewer than two million shareholders in France prior to the privatization program, there are more than six million today, and of those, 50 percent are under forty-five years of age (ibid.). Clearly, the profile of the shareholders has changed since privatization, "different from the image that one had of this group, that of the old Parisian rentiers. More stable, affecting the French heartland of the provincial bourgeoisie and the active France of managers. Not really popular therefore, but popularized, and affecting the middle class" (ibid.).

To be sure, the popularization of shareholding and the creation of "employee capitalists" brings in capital. But underlying this intent is a political goal that aims at the creation of a stable order by reducing the allegiance of workers to the left and to the trade union movement. Unions, like the organization of the *patronat*, do not like "small production units" because "both bureaucracies have the same interest: to be the only repository of power, which is why they are always opposed to decentralization" (Balladur 1987: 46). Finance Minister Balladur was ready to recognize that decentralization was likely to have less impact on the union hierarchy, but nonetheless he expected them to play a less obtrusive role in the economy. That privatization helps, by the inducements offered to workers, to diminish their opposition to privatization while strengthening that of the trade union leadership is evident in both France and Britain (Vickers and Wright 1988).

Perhaps the small shareholder can be induced to hold on to his few shares through mere "loyalty." But perhaps other investments will appear more attractive. Still, in both France and Britain, the conservative governments have attached an unusual degree of importance to the small (employee) shareholder. There is no evidence to indicate that this involvement will revolutionize the labor-capital relationship.

A New Managerial Elite.   Although France is reputed to have a better trained managers than Britain, it has traditionally been a homogeneous group that passed through state service (Suleiman 1978). Competence in a given industry has not been a requirement for the top positions. How is privatization expected to change the profile of the top managers?

The sale of public firms to the private sector implies the removal of the state's authority over the running of the firms. Hence, top managers will be named to their positions not by the state but by the boards of the corporations. Second, the performance of the firms will be an open matter reflected in stock prices; concern for the shareholders and for profits will lead to a greater emphasis on competence when choosing corporate executives. Finally, the greater separation between the private and the public sector engendered by privatization is expected to end, or at least to dilute, the network that facilitated the transfer from the public to the private sector of many civil servants (*Le Monde affaires*, Mar. 19, 1988). Expected instead are "executives coming from a variety experiences or having acquired competence within the firms" (Balladur 1987: 210).

It is interesting to note that the finance minister included in his defense of privatization a scathing attack on the strengthening of what he calls "the state bourgeoisie," which was occasioned by the nationalization program of 1982. He argues, as the left did in the past, along the same lines and in equally harsh terms, that there has been a

> collusion between political power and economic power that has worked to benefit a small group of technicians. Its ramifications have extended to the entire state apparatus, to the administration and to the public enterprises. Originating as a system based on merit, it now constitutes a veritable state bourgeoisie. . . . This state bourgeoisie recruits and reproduces itself within a small circle whose limits are traced by the grandes écoles and also by political considerations. (Balladur 1987: 48–49)

Balladur maintains that the system did not value competence; had been able to do that, he might have accepted all its faults. "In the final analysis," notes Balladur,

> the choice is simple: should all the key posts be reserved for those who have received a privileged training, or should confidence be placed in life experiences which reorder talents and which give rise to competence? The second solution is the more preferable; it is more flexible, more just, and more democratic. In order to have this, the state has to restrict its field of action and pull out substantially from the economy. (Balladur 1987: 52)

Will privatization be able to produce a more democratic business elite? Will it be able to drive a serious wedge into the existing "old-boy" network? Will it be able to give rise to a truly competent managerial class? The evidence thus far does not lead to an affirmative response to any of these questions (see *Le Monde affaires*, Mar. 19, 1988).

It is evident that the policy of privatization represents something of a relocation of political debate in France. One of the effects of the Socialists' period in office (and of the Socialists' moderate policies), after thirty-five years of conservative rule, has been to force the right to reconsider its positions on what had been considered nonpolitical issues. Questions of industrial policy, which had been largely the concern of technocrats, and to which the same answers had been given since the Fourth Republic, became political questions. Unlike the situation in Britain, where privatization was the result, at least initially, of increased political polarization, in France it was seemingly accompanied by decreased polarization, by an increased application of ideological beliefs to concrete policy proposals, and by a general shift to the right.

Conclusion

Although similar political and economic factors (or rationales) inspired the privatization programs in Britain and France, the modalities of privatization differed considerably in the two countries, largely because of the condition of the nationalized companies in the two countries. In France, it was the successful nationalized companies that were sold off first, thus giving an impetus to the widespread shareholding that the government desired to put into motion in order to legitimize the privatization program and to create a workers' stake in the so-called "new capitalism." In Britain, there were no limits set to the privatization program, which meant that the government had to offer money-losing industries for sale.

With respect to the goals of privatization, it is clear that these change over time. In the case of Britain, John Vickers has argued that whereas privatization began as a mere manifestation of a general dissatisfaction with nationalized industries, its macroeconomic potentials soon came to have an important place (Vickers 1988). The government then became much more preoccupied with the distribution of shareholding in society. In other words, privatization has different rationales at different phases.

In France, privatization began as a reaction to the massive nationalization program of 1982. It was seized upon by the Gaullist party both as a means of distinguishing itself from the left and as a way of preventing the small parties of the right from pre-empting the liberal program. The program was strongly controlled by the government, which, by creating a stable core of investors (the *noyau dur*), both used the program in a politically adroit way and ensured the availability of capital. Privatization was legitimized by the emphasis placed on the diffusion of shareholding, but the important place accorded the fifty-five companies that make up the *noyaux dur* continues to be questioned. Moreover, the "worker-capitalist" has seen his representation on the company boards decrease substantially from what it was during nationalization.

If privatization is intended to decrease state intervention in the economy, the government in France will need to make a greater effort at non-intervention than has been the case in Britain, where government intervention has been confined to nationalized companies. Consequently, the argument is made that privatization in France will not entail the end of an interventionist industrial policy (Bauer 1988). The French state is likely to become less interventionist in the competitive sectors of the economy. Whether it will remain so will depend in the final analysis on the performance of the privatized companies, for intervention has often resulted from demands made by the companies.

There has not yet been sufficient time to evaluate whether privatization will greatly affect the behavior of the companies concerned in France or Britain. Given the way that the nationalized industries were run by the Socialists in France, it seems unlikely that their behavior will change greatly. The most likely difference will be in the area of divestments and takeovers, which were largely blocked while the companies were in state hands for fear of criticism of creeping privatization or nationalization. CGE, with its surprise bid for Generale Occidentale some two weeks after privatization, has shown that it, at least, is prepared to use its new freedom. Moreover, their easier access to the Bourse means that the privatized companies are less likely to be hampered by a shortage of funds in their acquisitions activities.

The most immediate effect of privatization has not been on the companies involved, however, but on the level of shareholding in France. The sale of Saint-Gobain, perhaps intentionally somewhat underpriced, was very successful; but two-thirds of those who subscribed were already shareholders in other companies. In the sales that followed, the group of buyers widened. According to a *Le Monde*–IPSOS survey, at least five million people have bought shares in a privatized company (*Le Monde*, Aug. 5, 1987). To avoid either crowding out the small Paris Bourse[13] or placing a large proportion of the shares overseas, the government was forced to appeal to small investors. In this it has been successful: the Bourse does not seem to have been financed by a reduction of personal savings.[14] In so doing, the government has created a new set of shareholders, predominantly middle class, but neither predominantly male (48 percent are women) nor predominantly old. Whether they will constitute a sizable political bloc for the government, as some argue has happened in Britain, remains to be seen. The outcome is likely to depend in part on the performance of the privatized shares. These are not as underpriced as similar shares in Britain. In the wake of the stock market crash of October 1987, the shares of a few privatized companies were trading below their original offer price. According to some estimates, one-quarter of the new shareholders sold their shares during the crash (*New York Times*, Nov. 2, 1987). The privatization of Matra and the sale of 15 percent of Air France were postponed. Claims that this marked the end of the government's privatization policy were premature: the Matra sale went ahead in January 1988 and was two times oversubscribed. Still, the dramatic claims about the emergence of a "new capitalism" as a result of employee shareholding appear for the moment to lack serious foundations.

Privatization is not merely one shift in a continually swinging pendulum. Renationalization is not envisaged by the left in either country. This is all the more remarkable in the case of the British Labour Party, for which public ownership of the means of production has formed a central core of its ideology. The transfer of ownership of economic assets from the public to the private sectors represents a turning point in both Britain and France. This historic change should not be confused with the abandonment or decline of the welfare state, for in both countries (particularly in France) the commitment to key tenets of the welfare state have not been put into question.

The return of the socialist government to power in France in 1988 shows no indication of a reversal of the privatization program. Mitterrand stated during the campaign that there would be "neither privatization nor nationalization" in the next five years (*Le Mond affaires*, May 28, 1988). Although the privatizations carried out during the previous two years will not be put into question, the privatization program will not be accelerated. This is now clear. What has been brought into the question is the means that the Chirac government used to effect privatization. In particular, the socialists, as was noted earlier, never accepted the principle of the *noyau dur*, since the choice of these shareholders always appeared to them to be suspect. No sooner had he succeeded Balladur as minister of finance than Pierre Bérégovoy declared that it was essential to "break the 'noyau dur' of the privatized groups" (ibid.). But how and when? There is no clear answer to either of these questions. The need to preserve the capital injected into the privatized firms, the difficulty of replacing this capital, and the budgetary constraints that the government faces may mean that the socialist government will be able to do no more in the short run than control the *noyau dur* so as to be able to influence ownership and change of ownership (through fusions, raids, and the like) of the privatized companies.

The replacement in July 1988 of the head of the Union d'Assurance de Paris (the largest insurance company in France), a major shareholder in the privatized groups, by the socialist Jean Peyrelevade can be read as more than the usual settlement of accounts between left and right. Jean Dromer, Peyrelevade's predecessor, was the first head of a major company to be replaced. This was clearly no accident, given UAP's strength in the privatized companies. The support that the Caisse des Dépôts, a strong financial arm of the government, gave a private investor, Georges Peberean, in his attempt to obtain a controlling share in the Société Générale bank (which is part of the *noyaux dur* in several privatized firms) shows how political is privatization in France. The socialists might not have been willing to roll the frontiers of the state "forward," but they were not going to sit back and accept as a *fait accompli* the control of the nation's enterprises by "the friends of the RPR." The attempt to influence the *noyau dur* by governments of both the left and the right suggests that this is the chief means now left to governments to influence the actions of the major corporations. The process of privatization may not continue in France at full pace as it does in Britain. But it has not been halted, and nationalization no longer has defenders in either country.

The basic difference between Britain and France, insofar as the consequences of privatization are concerned, lies in the fact that the *économie mixte*—an economy based on the combination of public and private ownership of the means of production *and* of stakes in the ownership of the one by the other—may yet turn out to be a "novel" form of economic organization. The novelty, which is likely to have a strong appeal to the countries of Eastern Europe, lies in what might be called "mutual ownership," that is, of the largest industrial, financial, and insurance firms, *whether public or private*, all having a share in the ownership of one another. This is the concept of the *noyau dur* that is intended to permit firms to exist within a relatively stable world and to adopt long-term investment outlooks.

Notes

This chapter was written under the auspices of the Center of International Studies, Princeton University. The research was undertaken with the support of the German Marshall Fund of the United States and the Fulbright Commission. I also wish to thank Richard Holton for his invaluable assistance.

1. The state's postwar ownership of economic enterprises and the subsequent divestiture of these assets are the subject of a full-length study currently being undertaken by the author.

2. Compare the reaction to the sale of BT with the reaction to the one sale that the government did seriously overprice: that of Britoil. Although the 75 percent of shares that remained unsold were bought by the underwriters the sale is widely perceived as a failure that set the government's privatization program back.

3. By the time of the payment of the second installment in September 1987, the proportion of shares held overseas was 21 percent. This put the government in the difficult position of having to instruct overseas holders, who had only recently been encouraged to buy, to sell back their shares.

4. This commitment is what is meant by the "Jacobin" tradition; see Hollifield 1987).

5. *L'Express*, Sept. 19, 1986. It was only slightly less popular with employees of nationalized companies, who might have been expected to be adversely affected by it: 44 percent of bank employees, 43 percent of insurance company employees, and 42 percent of industrial workers thought it was a good idea, compared with 36 percent, 39 percent, and 36 percent, respectively, who were opposed.

6. The most notable exceptions were the public utilities, including Electricité de France, Gaz de France, the railway company (SNCF), and Renault. None of these has been privatized, and even the government's move to change the status of Renault from that of a *régie* to that of a public limited company has now been dropped.

7. This was the issue on which the Union de la gauche had split in 1977. The French Communist party wanted complete nationalization, that is, 100 percent holdings, of all subsidiaries.

8. The two major steel firms, Sacilor and Usinor, had been a drain on the treasury since the 1970s. Renault had previously been a profitable firm—the model of a competitive nationalized firm—but had seen its share of the auto market drop in the early 1980s. On the steel industry, see Padioleau 1981 and Hayward 1986: 68–104.

9. "The choice of companies to be privatized, the price of the shares, the selection of the principal shareholders. . . . It's always Balladur who decides." See "Privatisation: temps des copains," *Le Nouvel Observateur*, June, 18, 1987, p. 55.

10. Blandin 1987. One of Balladur's own mentors, Ambroise Roux, has said in the case of one privatization that "the only real shareholders were the R.P.R." (cited in Denis 1988: 87).

11. Blandin 1987. In almost all of the privatized companies, the level of participation by the *noyaux dur* has increased at the expense of private and public shareholding. See *L'Express*, Apr. 15, 1988.

12. *Le Monde*, Apr. 14, 1987. The argument that privatization in Western Europe will not entail a reduction in the role of the state is also made in Vickers and Wright (1988).

13. Total capitalization is about 25 percent of GNP, compared to 60–100 percent in Britain, Japan, and the United States.

14. In mid-1986 deposits in personal savings accounts amounted to about 50 percent of all new investments; by mid-1987 this amount was down to 20 percent. *Financial Times*, Sept. 16, 1987.

References

Asher, K. 1987. *The Politics of Privatization: Contracting Out Public Services*. London: Macmillan.

Balladur, Edouard. 1987. *Je Crois en l'Homme plus qu'en l'Etat*. Paris: Fayard.

Bauer, Michael. 1987. *Les 200: Comment on devient patron*. Paris: Seuil.

————. 1988. "The Politics of State-Directed Privatization: The Case of France, 1986–88." *West European Politics* 11 (October): 49–60.

Blandin, Claire. 1987. "Privatisation en circuit fermé." *Le Monde*, Sept. 17.

Cameron, David R. 1986. "The Nationalized Industries after March 16." *French Politics and Society* 14 (June): 16–26.

————. 1987. "The Colors of a Rose: On the Ambiguous Record of French Socialism." Working Papers, Center for European Studies, Harvard University.

Cerny, Philip G. 1987. "The 'Little Big Bang' in Paris: Financial Market Deregulation in a *dirigiste system*." Unpublished.

Denis, Stéphane. 1988. *Le Roman de l'argent*. Paris: Albin Michel.

Hartley, K., and M. Huby. 1986. "Contracting-out Policy: Theory and Evidence." In Kay, Mayer, and Thompson 1986.

Hayward, Jack. 1986. *The State and the Market Economy*. Brighton: Wheatsheaf Books Ltd.

Henig, J., C. Hamnett, and H. Feigenbaum. 1987. "The Politics of Privatization: A Comparative Perspective." Unpublished.

Hollifield, James. 1987. "Jacobinism: Moribund or at Bay? An Essay on the Evolution of the French State." Paper delivered at the American Political Science Association.

Holton, Richard. 1986. "Industrial Politics: Nationalization in France under Mitterrand." *West European Politics* 9 (January): 67–80.

Holton, Richard. "Privatization and Deregulation of Telecommunications in the U.K."

Kay, J., C. Mayer, and D. Thompson, eds. 1986. *Privatization and Regulation— The UK Experience*. Oxford: Oxford University Press.

Le Boucher, Eric. 1987. "Français moyen cherche privatisée." *Le Monde*, Aug. 5.

McLachlan, S. 1983. *The National Freight Buy-Out*. London: Macmillan.

Morin, François. 1987. "Les trois cercles des liaisons financières." *Le Monde*, Sept. 17.

Newman, K. 1986. *The Selling of British Telecom*. London: Holt, Reinhart and Winston.

Padioleau, Jean. 1981. *Quand la France s'enferre*. Paris: Presses Universitaires de France.

Suleiman, Ezra N. 1978. *Elites in French Society: The Politics of Survival*. Princeton: Princeton University Press.

————. 1987. *Private Power and Centralization in France*. Princeton: Princeton University Press.

Thomas, S. 1986. "The Union Response to Denationalization." In Kay, Mayer, and Thompson 1986.

Vickers, John. 1988. "Privatization in the U.K.: An Overview." Lecture delivered at Princeton University, March 19.

Vickers, John, and Vincent Wright. 1988. "The Politics of Industrial Privatization in Western Europe: An Overview." *West European Studies.*

Vickers, J., and G. Yarrow. 1985. *Privatization and the Natural Monopolies.* London: Public Policy Centre.

Yarrow, G. 1986. "Privatization in Theory and Practice." *Economic Policy* 1,
no. 2.

Zysman, John. 1983. *Governments, Markets and Growth: Financial Systems and the
Politics of Industrial Chance.* Ithaca: Cornell University Press.

6

The Politics of Public Enterprise in Portugal, Spain, and Greece

Nancy Bermeo

Scholars who have tried to explain the size of the public sector as a whole have focused on three sorts of variables. Some scholars find economic factors (both domestic and international) to be determinant (Wilensky 1975: 27; Lehmbruch 1977: 98; Cameron 1978). Others offer essentially value-centered arguments, asserting that the size of the welfare state and/or the public budget is determined essentially by "national values" or "the desires of the electorate" (Downs 1960: 541; Wildavsky 1985: 255). A final set of explanations focuses primarily on institutions. Proponents argue that the size of the public sector derives from the nature of class organizations outside the state (Stephens 1978), bureaucracies within the state (Heclo 1974; Weir and Skocpol 1985), or, most often, the socialist or nonsocialist identity of ruling parties. The idea that "partisan control of government is a major determinant of policy outputs" (Castles 1981: 88) is one of the most widely accepted conceptions in the comparative public policy literature (see Hibbs 1977; Tufte 1978; Vernon and Aharoni 1981: 9).

It is plausible to expect that the expansion and contraction of the public enterprise sector is determined to some degree by all of these factors. But how, precisely, do they work? Which are the most important? Do domestic factors carry more weight than international ones? Are there other factors that ultimately tell us more about patterns of privatization?

In this chapter, comparing policies toward public enterprise in Spain, Portugal, and Greece, I do not pretend to explain patterns of privatization everywhere. Nor do I offer a "test" of the approaches mentioned above. Instead, I provide an explanation that works in three cases, that can be evaluated elsewhere, and that allows us to speculate about which of these approaches may be most promising in future research.

The cases themselves offer three advantages. First, they provide an excellent opportunity for assessing the impact of ruling party ideology because each of these states has undergone both a major regime change and major changes of ruling party through democratic elections. Second, although these states differ in many respects, they are similar in that they are the three poorest nations in Europe and the three most recent entrants to the European Economic Community (EEC). All are dependent on imported energy, and Portugal and Greece have small, open economies that are highly vulnerable to market changes abroad. If international economic actors such as the EEC do play a pivotal role in pressuring domestic decisionmakers and in shaping the size of the public sector, we might expect to see very similar patterns in Portugal and Greece and a somewhat similar pattern in Spain. Third, each country has been a liberal democracy since the mid-1970s. The three thus afford us a relatively clear picture of who the adversaries and advocates of policy change are and how they rationalize their groups' positions.

Patterns of Nationalization and Privatization since the 1960s

Portugal

When Portugal became a full member of the EEC in 1986, it had the largest public enterprise sector in Western Europe. Yet under the Salazar-Caetano dictatorship (1932–1974), the opposite was true. As Eric Baklanoff described it, "private enterprise ownership dominated the Portuguese economy to a degree unmatched in other Western European countries" (Baklanoff 1987: 15). State-owned enterprises were virtually nonexistent in the manufacturing sector, and private capital even controlled the ownership of railways, electricity, air transportation, and telecommunications. Salazar's state certainly interfered in the national economy through tariff controls, the granting of monopolistic privileges, and complicated licensing legislation, but it never played an unmediated role in the ownership and management of productive resources. Marcelo Caetano, who headed the Portuguese dictatorship from 1968 until 1974, left Portugal's public enterprise sector more or less as he had found it.

The Portuguese revolution of 1974 dramatically changed the state's role in the economy. In an early phase, approximately 300 small- and medium-sized enterprises were brought into the state sector; but in the sixteen months following the installation of the radical fourth provisional government in March 1975, the Portuguese state directly nationalized 244 enterprises, including most of the nation's largest firms in all the key sectors of the economy. All domestically owned banks and insurance firms were nationalized within two weeks. Electricity, petroleum, shipbuilding, railway, tobacco, paper, glass, mining, chemical, and beer companies were nationalized during the following months, along with most air and ground transportation, radio and television stations, and newspapers.

Civilian political parties offered little resistance to these nationalizations. In fact, when a freely elected constitutional assembly met in 1975–1976, the nationalizations were given constitutional status as "irreversible conquests of the working classes." Although parties on the right abstained from supporting this provision, no political party actually voted against it (Caldeira and Silva 1976: 604). By the end of the nation's first constitutional government, public enterprise in Portugal encompassed 22 percent of the economy's value-added, 34 percent of all fixed capital investment, 9 percent of all employment, and 76 percent of fixed investment in manufacturing (Baklanoff 1987: 15).

Despite the rise and fall of nearly a dozen constitutional governments of various political colorations, the size of Portugal's public enterprise sector did not diminish in the aftermath of the revolution. Although new private banks were officially sanctioned in November 1983, by the end of 1987 no government had succeeded in denationalizing any bank or any other enterprise.

The July 1987 electoral victory of the center-right Social Democratic party (PSD) may mark a watershed in the history of Portuguese public enterprise. Cavaco Silva, the party leader, campaigned on a promise to denationalize major sectors of the economy and won 51 percent of the vote—the first absolute parliamentary majority in Portuguese history. The PSD had to amend the constitution to start making good on this promise, and it had to muster the support of the Portuguese Socialist party (PS) to do so. Late in 1989 the PS finally agreed to back the constitutional change.

Public enterprise in Portugal began as a very small component of the national economy, grew dramatically during the mid-1970s, and maintained its scale throughout the 1980s. Only now, sixteen years after the revolution and some thirteen years after the country petitioned for membership in the EEC, has a center-right party put a program for partial denationalization on the national political agenda.

Spain

The history of Spain's public enterprise sector is markedly different from that of its neighbor to the west. Francisco Franco, unlike Salazar, backed the idea of state-led industrialization and founded a holding company for a wide range of public firms in 1941, just three years after he came to power. By 1954 the Instituto Nacional de Indústria (INI) owned more than a dozen firms, had controlling interest in thirty-seven, and held minority interest in another twelve. These firms were located in virtually all of Spain's basic industries. In addition to running airline, telegraph, and telephone services, the Spanish state was directly involved in the production of steel, hydroelectric power, ships, chemicals, aluminum, fertilizers, textiles, and automobiles (Anderson 1970: 40).

The political actors who led Spain's transition to democracy inherited a large, diverse public enterprise sector from the old regime. In this respect, they differed dramatically from their counterparts in Portugal. They also differed in their party affiliation: the leaders of the Spanish transition were, by and large, men of the center-right. Despite these differences, policymakers in Spain, like those in Portugal, expanded the size and role of public enterprise during the period of redemocratization. Between 1975 and 1980, employment in public enterprises increased by 11 percent; and in the five-year period prior to the 1982 victory of the Socialist party, budgetary transfers to public enterprise increased fivefold, reaching nearly 50 percent of all transfers to enterprises (OECD 1985: 71).

The 1982 elections brought a new party to power and a new policy toward public enterprise. For the first time in Spanish history, the state began a deliberate effort to pare down public enterprise employment and to privatize a large number of public firms. Ironically, this redirection of policy was carried out by Spain's Socialist party, the PSOE. Groups within the Union of the Democratic Center (UCD) had made efforts to restructure Spanish industry in 1981, but it was not until the PSOE gained control of the government that a privatization drive was finally launched.

Between 1984 and 1986, the Socialist government sold off or dissolved more than thirty enterprises (*Cambio*, Nov. 3, 1986). The list of privatized firms included the SEAT Car Company (sold to Volkswagen), the National Truck Company (sold to General Motors), and dozens of other firms producing a broad range of products, from paper to canned fish to ballbearings. The Socialist party's policies provoked a great deal of popular resistance, but at the end of 1987 party leaders showed no signs of changing course.

The scope of public enterprise in Spain seems to have gone through several phases; rapid growth during the early 1940s, a gradual increase in the 1950s and 1960s, and another fairly rapid expansion during the mid-1970s. The triumph of the Socialist party in 1982 marked a surprising reversal of a forty-year trend of expansion.

Greece

The history of public enterprise in Greece charts yet a third pattern. Prior to World War II, Greece, like Portugal, had very little public enterprise. A rough estimate made by a Bank of Greece official suggests that public enterprises contributed about 7–8 percent to the gross national product (GNP) between 1959 and 1961 (Lenoudia 1963: 288). The colonels' dictatorship (1967–1974) did not affect the size of the public enterprise sector in any significant way. When democracy was restored in 1974, the public enterprise sector was still "relatively small by European standards" (Keefe 1977: 112). As one analyst put it, "unlike the U.K., France, Italy, and Germany, Greece's economic policy stood out in its pathetic reliance on free markets" (Freris 1986: 217).

As happened in Spain and Portugal, however, the role of public enterprise expanded substantially during the period of redemocratization. The center-right government of Constantine Karamanlis nationalized Olympic Airways, established the Public Petroleum Corporation, took control of lignite development, and, most important, nationalized the Commercial Bank of Greece, through which it gained control of many other enterprises (Tsoukalis 1981: 35).

But although the size of the public enterprise sector expanded during the mid-1970s, the Greek state has never assumed the role in industry of its Spanish or Portuguese counterpart. Until recently, state ownership in the manufacturing sector has been almost negligible. A Greek minister of industry has argued that, historically, "the state has been absent as a producer from the Greek economy" (Vaitsos 1986: 81).

As happened in Spain, when a socialist party triumphed in national elections in the early 1980s, the contours of the public enterprise sector began to change. Change in Greece and change in Spain took opposite forms, however. The Spanish Socialist party began to privatize, while the Greek Socialist party (PASOK) began to nationalize—expanding the public enterprise sector more than any previous government in Greek history.

In 1983 alone, eight firms were added to the public sector. By 1984, nineteen out of the top fifty industrial concerns in the nation were controlled either directly or indirectly by the state (EIU 1985a: 10). In the remaining years of PASOK's first term in office, the trends of expansion continued. The major Greek businessmen's association complained that the state controlled "60 percent of the nation's textile potential, all large paper mills and pharmaceutical companies," and more than half of all production in "shipbuilding, mining, fertilizer, sawmills, and cement" (EIU 1985b: 8).

In the first quarter of 1987 state policy toward the public enterprise sector altered course. As the year began, Economics Minister Kostas Simitis announced that nineteen problematic firms would have to be closed and that the government agency founded to help them would be converted into a holding company (EIU 1985b: 12–13). As of 1989, the fate of public enterprise in Greece was uncertain. Simitis himself was replaced as soon as this initiative began, and PASOK lost the 1989 national elections.

Whatever happens in the future, however, the Greek case differs from the others reviewed here in that the Greek Socialist party expanded state enterprise, while its counterpart in Spain took an opposite position and its counterpart in Portugal held a middle ground. Summing up the Greek chronology, we see a very small public enterprise sector in the early 1960s, then rapid, but moderate (compared to the Portuguese case), growth during the mid-1970s, and, finally, rapid expansion between 1981 and 1985.

Explaining Nationalization and Privatization

Some preliminary conclusions based on our three cases are now in order. First, periods of expansion and contraction of public enterprise are not related in any simple way to whether the ruling party is socialist or nonsocialist. Spain's public enterprise sector was initiated by a right-wing authoritarian regime, expanded by a democratically elected center-right government, and then successfully challenged, for the first time in history, by a democratically elected socialist party. In Greece, New Democracy, a democratically elected center-right party, expanded the small public sector during the mid-1970s, and the Socialist party expanded it further in the 1980s. In Portugal, the Socialist party supported the nationalization of banks and industry and then maintained tacit support of a massive state enterprise sector for at least twelve years. For these cases, at least, a ruling party's position on the ideological spectrum tells us little about national policy toward public enterprise.

A second conclusion that emerges from this overview is that periods of expansion and contraction of public enterprise are not related in any simple way to susceptibility to pressure from the international community. If privatization were always a function of pressures from international lending agencies or international traders, Portugal and Greece—the two small, open, poor, and therefore extremely vulnerable economies—would have privatized first. Portugal was forced to seek IMF loans on two occasions. Although Socialist leaders instituted highly unpopular austerity plans as a result, they never attempted to privatize public enterprise. Greece, as illustrated above, expanded public enterprise in both the mid-1970s and the early 1980s under two different parties—even though Greece was both the earliest petitioner for EEC membership and the earliest entrant to the community. If EEC pressures were the decisive factor explaining privatization, Greece would have been the first state to privatize rather than the last.

A third conclusion immediately apparent from the chronology above is that regime type seems to explain little about the shape of public enterprise: there is great variation in the size and nature of public enterprise across dictatorships and across democracies. Dictators in Iberia and

Greece shared important similarities; but they differed greatly in their view of state enterprise, and their public enterprise sectors differed as well. The democratic leaders who followed them held equally divergent views. There is no reason to expect that regime type per se is associated with any particular pattern of public enterprise.

The differences between these three national policy chronologies indicate that ruling party identity, vulnerability to outside economic pressure, and regime type are inadequate explanations for the scope of public enterprise. But the similarities between these cases are instructive too. One of the few consistent patterns we see across the three countries is rapid expansion of public enterprise in the mid-1970s, just as redemocratization gets under way. The scope varies, but the expansion itself is not coincidental. In all three cases, democratizing forces used the public enterprise sector to mitigate the conflicts that the process of democratization unleashed. This use of the public sector took a variety of forms. Firms that might have been allowed to go bankrupt under a previous authoritarian regime were often taken into the state sector to prevent job loss among a newly mobilizing working class. Firms that were owned by individuals with strong ties to the old regime were sometimes incorporated into the emerging state because democratic leaders sought to dissociate themselves in a concrete way from the old order and to control more resources to meet new demands.

In all three cases the redemocratizing state used public enterprise as a means of legitimating itself and absorbing the many shocks associated with regime transition. In Portugal, for example, the democratizing state mitigated the disruption caused by 800,000 refugees by absorbing thousands of ex-colonials into nationalized enterprises. The center-right transitional government in Greece helped to legitimate itself by nationalizing the property of Stratis Andreadis, the owner of the Commercial Bank of Greece and a supporter of the dictatorship. In Spain, much of the success of the "pacted" transition resulted from the state's ability to reward labor with public enterprise resources. Although the expansion or contraction of public enterprise seems to have little to do with regime type, it seems to be related in a very clear way to regime change.

The convergence of policy that occurred in the mid-1970s happened only once again, and on a lesser scale. In the last quarter of 1987, in all three states, public enterprise seemed especially vulnerable. Only the Spanish government had moved very far toward denationalization; but in all three cases, nationalizations ebbed (at least temporarily), and socialist parties openly promoted some form of privatization for the first time in history. Why was the most consistent privatization drive lead by the PSOE, a socialist party in a state with the highest level of unemployment in Europe? Why did the Greek Socialist party have a policy that was so dissimilar? Finally, why did the Portuguese socialists resist pressures toward privatization until now? The answer to these questions derives from the origins of the public enterprise sectors themselves, the organization and autonomy of domestic capital, the technocratic traditions of each state, and the extent to which liberal technocrats succeeded in permeating ruling parties.

Explaining Privatization

The Origins of Public Enterprise

It is no coincidence that Spain has gone farther toward denationalization than Portugal or Greece, for the PSOE is unique in facing an inherited public enterprise sector with a long and complex history. The fact that public enterprise in Spain was a legacy of the old regime left the PSOE with two problems and a major opportunity. All three contributed to the likelihood of privatization.

A long-established, inherited public enterprise sector poses a particular problem in that it is especially difficult to permeate and control. The INI had been in continuous operation for more than forty years when the Socialists came to power. Its central office in Madrid employed at least a thousand people (Boyer 1980: 607)—probably more than the PSOE itself—and though the Socialists moved quickly to replace many of the top administrators, most of the managerial staff in both the INI central bureaucracy and in INI firms continued to to hold their positions after democratization.

The origins of Spain's public enterprise sector were especially problematic for the PSOE. Not only did the INI represent a deeply entrenched bureaucracy; it represented a bureaucracy with longstanding links to the "great Spanish banks and other elements of monopoly capital" (Anderson 1970: 257). These groups stood well outside the PSOE's network of support.

The historical associations of Spain's public enterprise sector determined the sorts of firms that were owned by the state, and these posed a second serious problem for the PSOE. The state-owned steel, shipbuilding, automobile, and truck industries created by Franco suffered badly in the late 1960s, when the newly industrializing countries began producing the same products at lower cost. Yet longstanding practices and alliances were slow to change, and the authoritarian state continued to expand investments in noncompetitive areas even in its last years. The early democratic government acted much like its predecessor. In the year before the PSOE victory, subsidies to INI doubled (EIU 1982: 5), and the number of nationalized firms increased. INI losses rose from 25,681 million pesetas in 1977 to 161,500 million in 1983 (Ministerio de Economia y Haci- enda 1984: 64).

The history of Spanish state enterprise had thus given the sector a com- position that proved highly problematic for the PSOE; but because that sector had been shaped by nonsocialist parties, the PSOE could divorce itself from public enterprise with greater ease. Felipe Gonzalez could ar- gue—as he did on several occasions—that "the idea of nationalization was not an idea of the left" and, implicitly, that privatization was not an idea of the right (*Cambio*, Oct. 4, 1982, p. 38).

The origins of public enterprise in Portugal and Greece presented so- cialist leaders with very different situations. Neither set of leaders con- fronted an entrenched bureaucratic agency comparable to INI—indeed, neither party confronted a state holding company at all—and bureau- cratic resistance was lessened by other factors as well. Much of the Greek public enterprise sector was either nationalized by PASOK itself or was a relatively recent legacy of the postauthoritarian center-right adminis- tration. Portugal's public enterprise sector did not come into being until 1974 and was endorsed from the outset by the Socialist party.[1] These fac- tors made both Portuguese and the Greek socialists more hopeful about their abilities to permeate these structures and to control them to their party's—and their nation's—advantage.

The Organization and Autonomy of Industrial and Finance Capital

Capitalists' associations opposed public enterprise in all three states by the mid-1970s. The organization and resources of these associations dif- fered, however, and these differences—due in large measure to contrasts in economic history—also explain the varied patterns of privatization in the three cases.

In Greece, economic growth was heavily concentrated in the service sector, especially tourism and shipping. During the period 1960–1976, overall investment in manufacturing as a percentage of gross domestic product (GDP) was lower in Greece than in any other member country of the Organization for Economic Cooperation and Development (OECD)- (Ioakimidis 1984: 38). Low investment meant concentration in traditional industrial activities, such as textiles and food processing (Tsoukalis 1981: 45), and a plethora of what might be called industrial minifundios. In 1978 more than 93 percent of all Greek manufacturing firms employed fewer than ten people. In Spain, the comparable figure was less than 77 percent (Hudson and Lewis 1984: 200).

The peculiar configuration of the Greek economy meant that domestic industrialists were relatively weak both in number and in organization. They were also key in any privatization lobby, since they were most dependent on domestic interest rates and thus most disadvantaged by the diversion of state funds to public enterprises. The Federation of Greek Industrialists (SEV) was "probably the best organized and certainly the most active and effective Greek interest group," but it was "essentially run by the biggest of Greek industrialists" (Tsoukalis 1981: 113). In a nation with such a highly traditional industrial sector the typical businessman has little time for structured political participation, and organizations like the SEV have difficulty claiming to be truly representative. The fact that SEV is the most powerful of the Greek interest groups says little about its potential effects because Greek interests groups in general are extremely weak. Nicos Mouzelis argues persuasively that the Greek state is much more autonomous than its Western counterparts because Greek capitalists have been so dependent on the Greek central government for so long (Mouzelis 1978: 132).

The capacity of industrialists to affect state decisionmaking has also been relatively low in Portugal, again as a result of the nation's economic history. Even prior to the revolution, "the owners as a class, with the exception of the seven largest cartels, were weak in influence" (Bruneau and Macleod 1986: 109). In the aftermath of the dictatorship, the position of Portuguese capital only worsened. Not only were the cartels destroyed, but many of the politically active members of the Portuguese business community were driven abroad (Bermeo 1987). Contemporary studies of Portugal assert that groups and associations in general "seem to have a relatively minor role in influencing government policies," and they conclude that industrialists' associations in particular have "little coherence and apparently slight influence" at any level of government (Bruneau and Macleod 1986: 100, 111). The fact that capitalists are divided into two separate associations contributes to divisiveness, as does the attitude of owners who had property expropriated and who thus favor compensation and return rather than privatization.

Of the three business communities under review here, the Spanish is clearly the best organized and the most influential. A founder of the Spanish industrialists' organization, the Employers' Federation of Spain (CEOE), writes that recent history has given Spanish employers' associations "a role they do not have in other countries" (Pascual 1984: 139). Not only was the CEOE a major actor in the all-important Moncloa Pacts; its leaders played a role in the writing of the new Spanish constitution, and one of its founders composed article 38, which guarantees that Spain will be a market economy (Pascual 1984: 11).

Neither Greek nor Portuguese industrialists played such a role. On the contrary, the popularly elected constitutional assembly of Portugal drafted and ratified a document that guaranteed "the transition to socialism through the democratic exercise of power by the working classes"

(Caldeira and Silva 1976: 366). The 1976 Greek constitution is not nearly so radical, but it "foresees expropriation in the public interests" (article 17:2) and states that "the Law may regulate the acquisition [of productive property] by purchase of enterprises or the compulsory participation therein of the State" (article 106:3). Neither Portuguese nor Greek entrepreneurs made a successful attempt to formulate corporatist pacts.

One of the reasons that Spanish industrialists succeeded where their counterparts elsewhere failed relates to the autonomy of the banking sector, which varies greatly in these three states. Spain's private banking sector is extremely large and powerful. One analyst has described it as "the guiding member" of the nation's "public policy decision-making coalition" (Lancaster 1985: 169). The Spanish Banking Association (AEB) is one of the most powerful, if not the most powerful, organizations within the CEOE. Where three-quarters of CEOE affiliates have one vote in national assemblies, the AEB has ten. Yet the power of the AEB "far surpasses its formal rights" (Martínez 1984: 54).

Private banks have much less power in Portugal and Greece. Indeed, Portugal nationalized all its domestic private banks in 1975. None of these banks was denationalized before 1989, and no new private banks were licensed until 1985.

The Greek banking industry has more autonomy than the Portuguese but less than the Spanish. The state owns the two largest banks in Greece, which control approximately 85 percent of all deposits. Private banks exist but are tightly regulated by the state. At least one scholar believes that the role of government authorities in controlling credit goes farther in Greece than in any other European country (Siotis 1983: 63).

The different relations between these states and their domestic banking sectors had important ramifications as the costs of public enterprise rose. In all these states, public enterprise losses and debts drove up the public sector borrowing requirement, escalated interest rates, and decreased the amount of capital available to private domestic investors. But only the Spanish banking sector provided these investors with allies who functioned relatively independently of state control. With autonomous control of a huge network of economic resources and easy access to the media through the ownership of several important publications, the private banking sector became a strong and effective lobby for privatization in Spain. No doubt many bankers in Portugal and Greece sought to play the same role, but the tighter political controls on finance capital prevented them from doing so as effectively.

A comparison of capitalists' associations in Spain, Portugal, and Greece does much to explain why Spain launched its privatization drive first. The Socialist party in Spain was subject to pressures from both a comparatively well-organized employers' group and a powerful private banking network. But as important as these pressures were, the activities of capitalists' organizations should not be seen as a sufficient explanation for privatization patterns in any of our three cases. After all, a party like the PSOE, with an absolute majority in government, could conceivably have nationalized the material resources of these groups and decreased their power considerably. (This indeed is what the party promised five years before it was elected.) But one of the problems with the nationalization scenario was that the resources called upon by Spain's class associations were not only material ones. They marshaled "cultural" resources as well, for privatization found a ready audience with large sections of the Spanish people. This audience was a reflection of the nation's technocratic tradition, and it is to this factor that we now turn.

Technocrats and Technocratic Traditions

Technocratic arguments have a longer and more revered history in Spain than in either of our other cases, for the Franco regime was unique in its emphasis on technocratic planning. It drew up and implemented a stabilization plan in 1959 and three national development plans, running from 1964 through 1975.

State planning produces more than just plans and state-initiated economic change; it also produces "planners" and a whole series of "backward linkages" in university education. Just as the number of students in Spanish universities rose from 77,000 in 1960 to 241,000 in 1972 (Wright 1977), economics became the most popular area of study for Spanish males. Francisco Umbral, the Spanish journalist observed that "young economists replaced cadets as sex symbols" in the 1960s. As the one area of the university community where criticism of the regime was "more or less tolerated," economics became "a fashionable novelty" (Carr and Fusi 1986: 59). One of the more traditional leaders of the Franco regime bemoaned the technocratic trend in unambiguous terms: "Dogmas have gone out the window. Now we have the *solucionadores*—the problem solvers—the managers, the boys who have been to the university in the last few years, especially in the Faculties of Economics" (ibid.: 81)

The triumphs of the *solucionadores* were closely associated with the growth and power of Opus Dei, an organization of Catholic professionals dedicated to a traditional Church but a greatly modernized economy. Opus Dei members began to permeate the upper reaches of the Franco regime in the late 1950s and by 1969 controlled each of the seven ministries concerned with economics and culture.

By the late 1960s, "the period of the 'primacy of the economy' and of the economists" was well under way. Raymond Carr and Juan Pablo Fusi claim that the watchwords of the sixties were "rationality, efficiency [and] the maxims of the . . . competitive business corporation" (Carr and Fusi 1986: 80). The language used to justify the Socialists' privatizations is riddled with these same terms. As the INI president who launched the party's largest privatizations put it, "the fundamental objective is to reduce losses." Carlos Solchaga is more specific. He asserts that "no one in the PS today thinks that the state by itself can or should design an industrial profile which will bring us out of the economic crisis. This we can only do with [more] recourse to the market [and] its General Laws" (*El Pais*, Jan. 20, 1985).

How did this sort of argument find favor with a socialist party? It is important to recognize that privatization is an innovation—both for the Socialist party (which until the early 1980s promised an expansion of nationalized industries) and for Spanish policymakers in general. As the chronology of public enterprise policy illustrates, privatization in Spain has been extremely rare. The key to understanding why the Socialists adopted this particular innovation lies in understanding how policy innovations in general emerge. Here, Hugh Heclo's work is extremely useful. He argues that policy innovation is "most directly influenced by middlemen at the interface of various groups," typically people "with transcendable group commitments 'in' but not always 'of' their host body [with] access to information ideas and positions outside the normal run of organizational actors" (Heclo 1974: 308).

Spain's privatization policy was designed and implemented by men who fit Heclo's model. Even a brief review of the biographies of the PSOE's main industrial policymakers illustrates the point. Miguel Boyer, the man who became the PSOE's first minister of economics, finance, and commerce, had worked for a major explosives firm, the INI, and the Bank of Spain (EIU 1983: 8). Luis Solchaga, who became minister of industry, came to government after years in the research department of the Banco de Viscaya, a commercial banking group (*Financial Times*, Sept. 16, 1987). Luis Carlos Croissier, who developed the PSOE's economic program and then became president of INI, had been an economics professor in Madrid and program director for the Ministry of Industry and Energy under the center-right government (*El Pais*, Oct. 4, 1984). Claudio Arzandi, who replaced Croissier as president of INI, had a degree from France in economics and had worked for the Bank of Vizcaya and the Grupo Bancaya (*Cambio*, Mar. 8, 1982).

It would be foolish to argue that technocrats "at the interface of various groups" did not exist in Portugal and Greece, but Portuguese technocrats certainly worked from a weaker historical tradition and were, as a result, relatively few in number. Salazar's ambivalence about industrialization and his hostility to state planning delayed the structural incentives for technocratic thinking. The Opus Dei organization in Portugal was relatively weak, and the nation's economics faculties allowed less debate and criticism than their counterparts in Spain. (Liberals were much more likely to be found in faculties of law.) A small group of European-oriented technocrats emerged within the Caetano government, but their position was extremely tenuous. In sharp contrast to the Spanish case, none of the technocrats ever gained a full ministerial position (Baklanoff 1987: 5). Their influence was "only marginal," and in 1972 they were all forced to resign (Tsoukalis 1981: 52).

The revolutionary nature of Portugal's transition to democracy put many technocrats on the defensive. Some were purged, and many went abroad voluntarily. Since all banks and many major industries were nationalized (and multinationals were temporarily scared away), there was a narrower range of groups that technocrats could enter. Moreover, the deep hostility existing between even centrist parties in Portugal decreased the professional mobility that one finds so often in Spain. It is hard to imagine that a figure like Fernández Ordoñez, who was once president of INI under Franco, then a major industrial policymaker under the UCD, and is now a member of the Socialist cabinet, would ever have emerged in the Portuguese context.

Greece, like Portugal, had a weak planning tradition. There was no Greek version of Opus Dei and no equivalent structural impetus for domestic technocracy. The technocratic community that did develop differed from its Spanish counterpart in important ways. Because the Greek state had no clear commitment to economic planning, neither the government nor private organizations put much money into public policy, economics, or business programs. While Opus Dei was founding its own business schools and controlling Spain's Ministry of Education, Greeks who were interested in policy-oriented fields were often forced to study abroad. With limited opportunities and political turmoil at home, they often stayed abroad, the advance guard of a brain drain that was unmatched in Spain and Portugal. The seven-year dictatorship exacerbated the problem, and the migration increased.

When democracy was restored, many diaspora technocrats came home, and some resembled the portrait of the ideal innovator described by Heclo. Andreas Papandreou came close to the model himself, although he had more personal power than the sort of innovator Heclo had in mind. Under the pre-coup government of Constantine Karamanlis, he had been an advisor to the Bank of Greece and had headed the nation's major economics research organization. He had studied economics at Harvard, joined the U.S. Navy, and lived abroad for more than two decades, mostly as an economics professor in the United States. He also held cabinet positions under the short-lived administration of his father, George Papandreou. With such a complex amalgam of experiences and ideas, Papandreou was likely to be an "innovator" (as Heclo might have predicted), but the innovation he promoted in Greece differed from that advanced by technocrats in Spain. For Spain, with a long tradition of public enterprise, the innovation was privatization. For Greece, with a much more modest tradition of public enterprise, the innovation was nationalization.

Technocratic innovators who backed privatization certainly existed in Greece, even within PASOK; but compared with their counterparts in Spain, their role in policymaking was and remains much more precarious. In Portugal, technocratic innovators were comparatively rare, due to the peculiarities of Portuguese history summarized above, and technocrats who favored privatization have only recently made their way into stable policymaking positions within the Socialist party. To understand why technocrats in the three states gained access to different parties at different times, we must look at the contrasts in the nature of party governance and support.

Party Permeability and the Power of Technocrats

The socialist parties of Greece, Spain, and Portugal are all considered parties of the center-left. But there are some dramatic differences in the way these parties are governed, and these differences have had critical effects on the power of proprivatization technocrats.

PASOK. Technocrats have been most disadvantaged by the nature of party governance in PASOK, where decisionmaking power is heavily concentrated in the person of Andreas Papandreou. As the party's charismatic founder and only leader, Papandreou has been able to impose his political will on virtually all challengers. Party structure reflects and facilitates this concentration of power. PASOK candidates are chosen through straight party lists—composed by the party leader himself (Mavrogordatos 1984: 160)—and the party's central and departmental committees (where decisionmaking power is supposed to reside) operate "like sounding boards or rubber stamp organizations," imposing no "serious limits on the leader's decisionmaking powers" (Mouzelis 1986: 277).

Papandreou's strong leadership role presents a problem for all party officials, but for technocratic innovators the constraints are especially severe. Like all officials, they can be removed from office—as they often are—when controversy breaks out; but because Papandreou can claim to be a technocrat himself, they have special difficulty challenging his authority. It is surely not coincidental that Papandreou changed his "economic team" constantly during his administrations, while in Spain and Portugal Felipe González and Mário Soares (who are both labor lawyers) left theirs more or less intact.

PASOK's policy toward nationalization is also explained by its voting public. In October 1981, 69 percent of Greeks favored more nationalizations, and 71 percent agreed that the government should play a greater role in the management of the economy. The corresponding figures for other Western European countries were 50 percent and 39 percent, respectively. Later, as PASOK actually took control of firms, public support continued. A Eurobarometer poll in March 1983 reported that 59 percent of the Greek public agreed with PASOK policy toward problematic firms. In October 1983, 64 percent considered government takeovers of such firms to be "beneficial to Greece" (Dimitras 1987: 71). In the period under study, PASOK and Papandreou showed no signs of ignoring the preferences of the voting public: at election time the party leaned leftward. The fact that PASOK, unlike PSOE, faced a well-entrenched Communist party contributed to the trend.

PS.   The privatization policies of the Portuguese socialists can also be explained by party governance and support. The party resisted pressures to denationalize nonagricultural property throughout Mário Soares's tenure as party leader (that is, from the time of the nationalizations themselves in 1975 until 1986). The party's recent willingness to support privatization corresponded with a new era of leadership under the economist Vítor Constâncio. The change of policy and the election of Constâncio represented a triumph of the technocratic wing of the PS—a triumph that distinguished the Portuguese socialists from their Greek counterparts. Although Portugal's relatively weak technocratic tradition and highly divisive transition to democracy delayed the process for years, the nature of the party's governance and its public support eventually allowed liberal technocratic innovators access to the most important offices in the party. Soares was much more tolerant of open factionalism than Papandreou. The Portuguese secretary general made public reference to different "sensibilities" within the party, meaning four well-known groups: the *históricos*, who had founded the party in exile in the early 1970s; the moderates, who were social democrats, like the first group, but younger; the ex-GIS (Grupo de Intervençao Socialista), who came from a small far-left group that emerged during the revolution; and, finally, the technocrats—men like Constâncio who emphasized economic development and economic liberalism (Opello 1985: 98; *Expresso*, Apr. 17, 1981). Most históricos and moderates were lawyers, like Soares himself; most of the ex-GIS were in the "soft" social sciences; and most of the technocrats were (and are) economists.

Socialist party structure eventually worked to the advantage of the technocrats. One important factor that distinguished the PS from PASOK was that the former had frequent national congresses. In the Congress of

April 1979, party factions began to battle openly. In an attempt to resolve the situation, Soares agreed to bring ex-GIS and technocrats into the National Commission, but he alienated the moderate and histórico factions as a result. When three históricos left the party secretariat in January 1980, technocrats gained a majority (Bruneau and Macleod 1986: 70). Thus, Soares's willingness to tolerate and even make compromises with party factions eventually meant that the groups with which he was most closely identified lost hegemony in the party.

The nature of PS support beyond its formal membership eventually worked to the advantage of the technocrats as well. The change in party policy toward public enterprise coincided with important changes in the ideas of Portugal's voting public, which has grown more conservative since the period of nationalizations. In the mid-1970s, nationalization was justified on punitive grounds, and also in the hope that new state leaders would have the capacity to use these resources to the nation's advantage. Arguments about the inefficiency of public enterprise have gained appeal over time, as revolutionary fervor has waned and as the costs of the public enterprise sector have risen. Two major surveys of public opinion dealt with the issue of denationalization in 1987. Before the July elections, 67 percent of the public backed total or significant denationalization; after the elections, more than 80 percent agreed. The primary justification for privatization was that "public enterprises are seen as a barrier to economic development" (*Expresso*, Mar. 16, 1987). The electoral victory of the Social Democrats in July 1987 provides further evidence of changed attitudes toward public enterprise, for the party's main platforms promised to initiate a process of denationalization and to remove the "ideological" sections of the constitution. The fact that the PSD won the election with the largest majority in Portuguese history is highly significant.

Given these changes in public attitudes and the fact that support in national elections dropped from 37.9 percent in 1975 to 20.8 percent in 1985, it is not at all surprising that the Socialist party chose Vítor Constâncio as its leader. The party had the internal structure to make change possible and the external incentives to make change essential. In the aftermath of the revolution, the PS was known as the "party of culture," while the PSD was known as the "party of technology" (*Expresso*, Aug. 22, 1987). Important elements in the PS are trying to change this image and convince the public that the PS can be a force not simply for "democratization" but also for "modernization" (ibid., Mar. 15, 1986). The choice of Constâncio as party leader marks an important step in this direction. Constâncio—like Boyer and Solchaga in Spain (and the less fortunate Simitis in Greece)—is a young, foreign-trained economist with years of experience in banking. Sociologically, he is remarkably similar to Prime Minister Cavaco Silva of the PSD, who is also a young, foreign-trained economist.

PSOE. The peculiar nature of Socialist party organization worked to the advantage of proprivatization technocrats in Spain—even before the PSOE took control of government. Contrasts in party governance and support thus explain not simply where privatization policies were adopted but when as well.

How did technocrats with proprivatization ideas succeed in permeating the party so successfully? The answer may begin with the election of Felipe González as party leader in 1974. González's accession was not the victory of a technocrat—he was an activist lawyer and a labor lawyer at that—but it was the triumph of a man from the *generation* to which most of the PSOE technocrats belonged.[2] In this sense, González's victory was an opening to a decisive reorientation of party priorities.

A second factor that worked to the advantage of the technocrats was González's recognition that success on the national level would depend on the incorporation of smaller political parties and groups. In 1978 the PSOE succeeded in attracting several smaller socialist parties, each of which contained important technocrats in its leadership group. In exchange for agreeing to join the PSOE, these leaders were promised and given important positions in their new party. Some, such as Enrique Baron, Eduardo Barrionuevo, and Julián Campo, became ministers in the first PSOE government (*Cambio,* Mar. 19 and Apr. 23, 1978). Few socialists predicted what the incorporation of these parties would mean in terms of future policy, but there is little doubt that the change advanced the position of the technocrats.

Technocrats gained further advantages from the sophistication of Spanish public opinion polling. Until the late 1970s, polling was almost non-existent in Portugal and Greece, but it was relatively well developed in Spain. Poll results were a major factor in González's insistence that the PSOE drop its Marxist label in 1978. By 1979, polls showed that the PSOE's electoral success was "dependent on the consolidation of a social democratic image" (Preston 1986: 154). González made it clear that technocratic programs were key to this consolidation. As he put it in an interview before his election: "Whoever sits behind a desk in the national assembly begins to lose his ideological sentiment and begins to transform himself into a person who wants to *solve problems*" (*Diário 16,* Aug. 17, 1979).

El cambio—the change—that González promised in the 1982 national campaign was defined in terms of efficiency, a characterization that the "problem solvers" of Spain's older technocratic tradition would not have found alien. As González defined it in a nationwide campaign address, the change meant that "the country would finally function" (Garcia Santesmases 1985: 70). Technocrats were bound to play a key role in a party that promoted such an image. By the early 1980s one could observe within the PSOE "not only the tendency toward higher professional qualifications but also a change in the professions themselves." In parliament especially, one could observe "a smaller percentage of lawyers and unionists and an increase in economists, *técnicos*, engineers, and public functionaries" (Tezanos 1985: 54).

The party made these radical changes in image and program without losing votes: its support base not only grew greatly between the 1979 and 1982 elections but weathered the PSOE's first term as well. The party had less need to move leftward before elections because the weakness of the Spanish Communist party meant that its left wing had no where else to go.

The Implications of the Three Cases

What factors explain the very different patterns of privatization in Portugal, Spain, and Greece? Are they primarily domestic or international in origin? Do they relate most closely to materialist concerns, to political and cultural values, or to differences in institutional structure?

The explanation presented thus far relies wholly on domestic factors, but not because international actors such as the International Monetary Fund (IMF) and the European Investment Bank (EIB) exert no effect on domestic policymaking. Quite the contrary. The austerity measures adopted by PASOK in 1985—and the curtailment of nationalizations that followed—were almost exclusively responses to demands from the EIB. There should be little doubt that the recent convergence of what have heretofore been very different public enterprise policies is due in large part to the role of international actors.

Yet the effects of international actors should not be overstated. Even in the Greek case, where the dictates of the EIB loan agreement were unambiguous and well known, Papandreou eventually proved willing and able to reverse austerity measures and take wholly independent action because of domestic electoral concerns. When the Socialist government of Mário Soares decided to seek a loan from the IMF in 1977, it was forced to reduce its balance of payments current account dramatically and, accordingly, alter interest rates and credit policies, adjust exchange rates, and cut the national budget. Yet denationalization was never put on the policy agenda. Even when the PS was forced into a coalition government with the conservative Social Democratic Center in 1978, the party refused to endorse denationalization. At the end of 1987, with a strong center-right government in power, another loan from the IMF, and full integration in the EEC, Portuguese policymakers still formulated a program for only partial sale of some nationalized companies. Domestic factors militated against any more dramatic changes.

It would be easy to attribute privatizations to the dictates of the EEC, but this too would be misleading. EEC reports and leaders have voiced preferences for changes in the level of state intervention. The Commission Report on Spain's Application for Membership recommended that sectors in crisis be restructured "as rapidly as possible" and that Spanish "state aids" be aligned with community rules. But this advice is not synonymous with mandating privatization (Commission of the European Communities 1978: 19). Moreover, in Portugal (according to Vítor Constâncio himself) the commission "disappointed many people by saying that the size of the public sector was certainly not incompatible with the Treaty of Rome" (*Diário de Notícias*, Mar. 3, 1979), and the commission's report on the application of Greece contained no explicit remarks about state enterprise at all.

Essentially, the EEC's position was sometimes ambiguous and often ignored. The Greek law that granted assistance for problematic firms prompted EEC complaints, but these went unacknowledged for at least three years. Even unambiguous treaty provisions, such as the prohibition on state monopolies, are meaningless if a state chooses to ignore them. Greece was supposed to start dismantling its state petroleum monopoly in 1979 but still had not done so by the end of 1987. Cases like these are too numerous to allow us to attribute privatization to EEC pressures alone.

Materialist or economic factors contribute surprisingly little to the explanation of the varied patterns of privatization in Portugal, Spain, and Greece. On the macro level, we cannot argue that a "fiscal crisis" will lead to privatization, for each of the three states has experienced fiscal crises, and each reacted in a different way. On the micro level, we cannot state that money-losing firms will be sold off first. Nor can we argue alternatively that money-making firms will be the first to be transferred. In terms of profitability, public enterprises were often in miserable condition in all three states, but they have endured everywhere and have been successfully challenged only in Spain. One reason is that each government has used the public enterprises for a variety of economic goals. Maintaining price controls and controlling unemployment are obvious uses, but equally important and less well known is the fact that each state used its larger public firms as collateral for its loans abroad in order to help finance the overall state deficit (Ministerio de Indústria e Energia 1984: 166; EIU 1985b: 13). The same enterprises that are policy problems can thus be policy solutions as well.

The complex economic roles played by public enterprise in these three states cannot be understood with the very simple sorts of economic arguments that political scientists and sociologists offer for the size of the public sector generally. Macro-level arguments about economic growth or decline or openness may explain a good deal about other public policies, but they are not particularly helpful as explanations of nationalization or denationalization.

The importance of values emerges clearly at several points in the preceding analysis. We see this most dramatically when we consider the expansion of public enterprise in the mid-1970s, when each of these states redemocratized. For the most part, expansion followed no economic rationale. Nor was it the result of pressures from foreign actors. Expansion during this period was based first and foremost on the redemocratizing politicians' desire to mitigate conflict and hold the emerging democracy together—even at enormous cost.

Values figure prominently as well in two of the factors used to explain different policies toward public enterprise in the post-transition governments. The contrasting technocratic traditions of these three states are important for institutional reasons (as I discuss shortly), but their impact on the mentality of elites and large sectors of society is crucial to explaining both when the drives for privatization emerge and how large sectors of the population perceive them. Spain's experience with liberal technocrats in the early 1960s (and the economic development that followed this) created a constituency for capitalism that was broad enough to affect not only capitalists and the natural constituency of parties on the right but also large sectors of the middle, lower-middle, and even working class. Values left behind by the technocratic tradition of the past help explain why the PSOE could move ahead with privatizations and not suffer greatly at the polls.

Public values and opinions play a key role in determining whether liberal technocrats permeate the upper reaches of each party organization. The leaders of the PSOE assessed Spanish political values in the late 1970s and concluded that they had to eschew nationalization to get elected. Papandreou assessed Greek public opinion and concluded that he had to expand or at least maintain the nationalized sector to stay in power. The Portuguese socialists began to consider privatization only after they had lost power to a proprivatization party and, relatedly, after public opinion about Portugal's nationalized sector had changed considerably.

Before privatizations became commonplace, Raymond Vernon attributed the *growth* of the public enterprise sector in Western economies to "a shift in public opinion regarding the appropriate role of the state in economic affairs." He recognized that "the exact circumstances and extent of the shift have varied from one country to the next" (Vernon and Aharoni 1981: 8). Shifts in public opinion clearly affect the *contraction* of the public enterprise sector as well. But because the "exact circumstances and extent of the shift" vary from case to case, patterns of privatization vary too. It is only through careful attention to shifts and continuities in public values that the patterns of privatization in Portugal, Spain, and Greece can be understood.

The argument presented here has strong institutional components, but it also calls for a modification of some of the more standard institutional approaches in the public policy literature. Understanding the origins of public enterprise enables us to judge whether the institutional structure of the state sector is likely to serve the institutional needs of the ruling party. This seems a likely way of predicting policy, yet even conscientious studies of public enterprise exhibit a disturbing ahistoricism. When we are told that "the existence of public enterprise seems to provide a reasonable index of the power of the state" (Feigenbaum 1982: 102), we are encouraged to forget that public enterprises are often inherited. Every public enterprise sector, and indeed every public enterprise, has a history, and this institutional history has dramatic effects on whether a ruling party will try to dismantle, maintain, or expand it.

Similarly, a close look at class associations is important to understanding the size of the public sector. A cursory look at these institutions might lead one to conclude that privatization emerges first and strongest where capital is well organized and labor is relatively weak. The recent change in Portuguese privatization policy supports this line of argument. Portuguese policymakers took their first steps toward privatization only after capitalists' associations had had more than a decade to recover from the social revolution, after private banks had started to operate, and after organized labor appeared to be losing its ability to mobilize strikes. In Greece too, trade unions clearly played a role in Papandreou's decision to reverse Simitis's austerity policies and resist pressures from the EIB.

One can thus note the effects of class associations on several different occasions in each of our three cases, but a narrow focus on class associations leaves many questions unanswered. For example, if nationalization is a function of strong labor and weak capital, why would nationalizations have gone farthest under Franco, and how would one explain the fact that privatizations in Spain did not take place until the socialists were in power?

Political parties are the institutions that figure most prominently in this analysis—but not for the reasons that are so frequently cited in the literature on the public sector. We illustrated clearly that the center-right or center-left position of a party told us little about its policy toward public enterprise. Socialist parties privatize and nonsocialist parties nationalize.

An understanding of the ruling party, however, is essential to predictions about whether public enterprise will expand or contract. We must understand how the origins of the public enterprise sector affect the party's ability to use the sector to partisan advantage. We have to know how party governance facilitates or impairs the access of policy innovators, liberal technocrats in particular. Finally, we have to understand the nature of party support and electoral vulnerability. The voting public's attitudes toward public enterprise are relevant only if party leaders know what they are and choose to respond to them.

Strictly speaking, the bureaucracies of our three cases do not figure prominently in the explanations for privatization offered here, but bureaucrats of a certain type are extremely important as a source of innovation. To understand bureaucratic innovators, the study of institutions is essential, but we should not confine ourselves to the institutions that political scientists might first consider. Institutions like Opus Dei, or the ministry of education in an old regime, or the research department of a private bank may ultimately be as important to contemporary economic policymaking as parts of the formal economic bureaucracy itself.

Patterns of privatization in Southern Europe cannot be explained with a materialist or a value-centered or an institutional approach alone. The explanation I offer here points instead to the relevance of all three approaches. The value-centered approach and a modified version of the institutional approach appear to be the most useful.

Notes

1. The Socialists did not have ascendancy in the postrevolutionary provisional government that actually nationalized most of the Portuguese firms; but they did not attempt to block the action and quickly moved to colonize the nationalized firms themselves.

2. The fact that the PS was led by Soares (who was a *histórico*) probably delayed the advance of the new generation of leaders in the Portuguese case. The generational factor also operates in Greece with younger technocrats thinking more like Simitis than Papandreou.

References

Anderson, Charles W. 1970. *The Political Economy of Modern Spain*. Madison: University of Wisconsin Press.

Baklanoff, Eric N. 1987. "Portugal's Economy, Old and New." Paper prepared for a conference on "Portugal: Ancient Country, Young Democracy," Woodrow Wilson Center, Washington, D.C., May 18–21.

Bermeo, Nancy. 1987. "Redemocratization and Transition Elections: A Comparison of Spain and Portugal." *Comparative Politics* 19: 213–232.

Boyer, Miguel. 1980. "La empresa pública en la estrategia industrial Española:

el I.N.I." In *Crecimiento Económico y Crisis Estrutural en España 1959–1980,* ed. Roberto Carballo, Antonio G. Temprano, and José A. Moral Santín. Madrid: Akal.

Bruneau, Thomas C., and Alex Macleod. 1986. *Politics in Contemporary Portugal.* Boulder, Colo.: Lynne Rienner.

Bustelo, Carlos. 1982. "Tendéncias económicas internacionales, La nueva estratégia industrial del sector público español." *La Política Industrial Española para los Próximos 10 Años.* Madrid: INI Empresa.

Caldeira, Reinaldo, and Maria do Ceu Silva, eds. 1976. *Constituição Política da República Portuguesa 1976.* Lisbon: Bertrand.

Cameron, David. 1978. "The Expansion of the Public Economy: A Comparative Analysis." *American Political Science Review* 72: 1243–1261.

Carr, Raymond, and Juan Pablo Fusi. 1986. *Spain: Dictatorship to Democracy.* London: George Allen and Unwin.

Castles, Francis. 1981. "The Impact of Parties on Public Expenditure." In *The Development of Welfare States in Europe and America,* ed. Peter Flora and Arnold Heidenheimer. New Brunswick, N.J.: Transaction Books.

Commission of the European Communities. 1978. "Opinion on Spain's Application for Membership 29 November 1978." *Bulletin of European Communities Supplement,* no. 9–78.

Dimitras, Panayote. 1987. "Changes in Public Attitudes." In *Political Change in Greece Before and After the Colonels,* ed. Kevin Featherstone and Dimitris Katsoudas. London: Croom Helm.

Downs, Anthony. 1960. "Why the Government Budget Is Too Small in a Democracy." *World Politics* 12: 541–563.

EIU (Economist Intelligence Unit). 1982. *Country Report Spain.* London: Economist Publishers Inc.

EIU. 1983. *Country Report Spain.* London: Economist Publishers Inc.

EIU. 1985a. *Annual Supplement for Greece.* London: Economist Publishers Inc.

EIU. 1985b. *Country Report Greece.* London: Economist Publishers Inc.

Feigenbaum, Harvey. 1982. "Public Enterprise in Comparative Perspective." *Comparative Politics* 15, no. 1: 101–122.

Freris, A. F. 1986. *The Greek Economy in the Twentieth Century.* London: Croom Helm.

Garcia Santesmases, Antonio. 1985. "Evolucíon Ideológica del Socialismo en la España Actual." *Sistema* 68–69: 61–79.

Heclo, Hugh. 1974. *Modern Social Politics in Britain and Sweden.* New Haven: Yale University Press.

Hibbs, Douglas. 1977. "Political Parties and Macroeconomic Policy." *American Political Science Review* 71: 1467–1487.

Hudson, R. and J. R. Lewis. 1984. "Capital Accumulation: The Industrialization of Southern Europe?" In *Southern Europe Transformed,* ed. Allan Williams. London: Harper and Row.

Ioakimidis, P. C. 1984. "Greece: From Military Dictatorship to Socialism." In *Southern Europe Transformed*, ed. Allan Williams. London: Harper and Row.

Keefe, Eugene, et al. 1977. *Area Handbook for Greece.* Washington, D.C.: U.S. Government Printing Office.

Lancaster, Thomas D. 1985. "Spanish Public Policy and Financial Power." In *Politics and Change in Spain*, ed. Thomas Lancaster and Gary Prevost. New York: Praeger.

Lehmbruch, Gerhard. 1977. "Liberal Corporatism and Party Government." *Comparative Political Studies* 10: 91–126.

Lenoudia, Pella. 1963. "Public Enterprises in Greece." *Public Finance* 28, no. 3–4: 287–309.

Martínez, Robert. 1984. "Business Elites in Democratic Spain." Ph.D. dissertation, Yale University.

Martínez-Alier, Juan, and Jordi Roca. 1987. "Spain after Franco: From Corporatist Ideology to Corporatist Reality." *International Journal of Political Economy* 4: 56–87.

Mavrogordatos, George. 1984. "The Greek Party System: A Case of 'Limited But Polarised Pluralism'?" *West European Politics* 7, no. 4: 156–169.

––––––. 1984. *The Rise of the Green Sun.* Kings College London Occasional Papers. Athens: Sakoulas.

Ministério de Economia y Hacienda Secretária General de Economia y Planificacíon. 1984. *Programa Económico de Medio Plaza 1984/87. Reformas Estructurales e Institucionales.* Madrid: Ministério de Economia y Hacienda.

Ministerio de Indústria e Energia. 1984. *El Ciclo Industrial en España.* Madrid: Ministerio de Indústria e Energia.

Mouzelis, Nicos. 1986. "Continuities and Discontinuities in Greek Politics: From Elefterios Venizelos to Andreas Papandreou." In *Political Change in Greece Before and After the Colonels*, ed. Kevin Featherstone and Dimitris Katsoudas. London: Croom Helm.

––––––. 1978. *Modern Greece Facets of Underdevelopment.* New York: Holmes and Meier.

OECD (Organization for Economic Cooperation and Development). 1985. *Economic Survey: Spain 1983/1984.* Paris: OECD.

––––––. 1987. *Economic Survey: Spain 1985/1986.* Paris: OECD

Opello, Walter. 1985. *Portugal's Political Development.* Boulder, Colo.: Westview.

Pascual, Julio. 1984. *En Defensa de la Empresa: Alegato en Crónica (1976–1984).* Madrid: Unión Editorial, S.A.

Preston, Paul. 1986. *The Triumph of Democracy in Spain.* London: Methuen.

Siotis, Jean. 1983. "Greece: Characteristics and Motives for Entry." In *The Enlargement of the European Community*, ed. José Luis Sampedro and Juan Antonio Payno. London: Macmillan.

Stephens, John. 1978. *The Transition from Capitalism to Socialism.* London: Macmillan.

Tezanos, José Felix. 1985. "Continuidad y Cámbio en el Socialismo Español. El PSOE durante la Transición Democrática." *Sistema* 68–69: 19–61.

Tsoukalis, Loukas. 1981. *The European Community and Its Mediterranean Enlargement*. London: George Allen and Unwin.

Tufte, Edward. 1978. *Political Control of the Economy*. Princeton: Princeton University Press.

Vaitsos, Constantine. 1986. "Problems and Policies of Industrialisation." In *Socialism in Greece: The First Four Years*, ed. Zafiris Tzannatos. Brookfield, Vt.: Gower Publishing.

Vernon, Raymond, and Yair Aharoni, eds. 1981. *State-Owned Enterprises in the Western Economies*. New York: St. Martin's Press.

Weir, Margaret, and Theda Skocpol. 1985. "State Structures and the Possibilities for Keynesian Responses to the Great Depression." In Peter Evans et al., *Bringing the State Back In*. Cambridge: Cambridge University Press.

Wildavsky, Aaron. 1985. "The Hope of Public Sector Growth." In *State and Market: The Politics of the Public and the Private*, ed. Jan Erik Lane. London: Sage Publications.

Wilensky, Harold. 1975. *The Welfare State and Equality*. Berkeley: University of California Press.

Wright, Alison. 1977. *The Spanish Economy 1959–1976*. New York: Holmes and Meier.

7

Public Corporations and Privatization in Modern Japan

Kent E. Calder

As in many late-modernizing nations, the state has loomed large and ambitious in the economic life of Japan. To industry and finance it has been a defender, collaborator, and at times a confining regulator. For a century and more the state has been a primary agent of Japan's broad and rapid economic transformation (Lockwood 1968; Nakamura 1974; Johnson 1982).

But for all its influence on the course of economic development in Japan, the state has only intermittently and incompletely been an owner or a manager of public assets. To be sure, the early Meiji era, from 1868 through the 1880s, brought an initial proliferation of public enterprise, as government sought to educate fledgling private firms in entrepreneurial ways through the example of the public corporation. Yet these early public businesses were virtually all privatized within a decade of creation. Similarly, public enterprises emerged once again during the early 1930s, only to be largely dismantled by the end of 1951. And almost all of the enterprises still public at the end of the Allied Occupation in 1952 returned to the private sector in a third major wave of privatization between 1984 and 1987.

Japanese Privatization Patterns in Comparative Context

There are prima facie reasons why one might expect substantial public ownership in postwar Japan. The Japanese state has historically taken intense strategic interest in economic development, often viewing the successful emergence of competitive basic industry as central to national security. Public corporations were the Japanese state's initial vehicle for

FIGURE 1
The Limited Scale of Public Ownership in Japan

	Brazil	*Britain*	*France*	*West Germany*	*India*	*Japan*	*United States*
Posts	■	■	■	■	■	■	■
Tele-communications	■	■	■	■	■	□	□
Electricity	■	■	■	75%	■	□	25%
Gas	■	■	■	50%	■	□	□
Oil Production	■	25%	NA	□	■	NA	□
Coal	■	■	■	50%	■	□	□
Railways	■	■	■	■	■	75%	25%
Airlines	25%	75%	75%	■	■	25%	□
Motor Industry	□	50%	50%	25%	□	□	□
Steel	75%	75%	75%	□	75%	□	□
Shipbuilding	□	■	□	25%	■	□	□

Source: Adapted from "The State in the Market," *The Economist*, Dec. 30, 1978, p. 39.

Key: □ privately owned all or nearly all.
■ publicly owned all or nearly all.
75 percent.
50 percent.
25 percent.
NA: not applicable or negligible production.

achieving industrial prowess during the early Meiji period, and they were revived once again during the late 1940s and the early 1950s.

Yet, as Figure 1 suggests, by the late 1970s there was remarkably little public enterprise in Japan, compared with patterns in Western Europe and some of the major Third World nations. Electricity, gas, coal, airlines, and steel—all sectors where public ownership is common in Europe, not to mention the Third World—have remained under private ownership in post–World War II Japan. Only the United States and a few extremist outliers such as Pinochet's Chile exhibited a comparable prevalence of private ownership. And in some sectors, such as electric power, private ownership has been more pervasive in Japan than in the United States.

TABLE 1
Japanese Privatization in the 1980s

Public Corporation	Number of Employees (1984)	Status as of April 1, 1988
Japan National Railways (Nihon Kokuyū Tetsudō, or JNR)	358,045	Privatized, 4/1/87. Split into six successor firms
Japan Telephone and Tele-graph (Nihon Denshin Denwa Kōsha, or NTT)	326,546	Privatized, 4/1/85.
Japan Monopoly Corporation (Nihon Sembai Kōsha)	36,959	Privatized, 4/1/85, through legislation passed 8/10/84
Japan Air Lines (Nihon Kōku K.K., or JAL)	20,782	35.5 percent of total capitalization held by government as of 4/1/85, with a program of phased sale of government shares in effect.
Japan Broadcasting Corpora-tion (Nippon Hōsō Kyōkai, or NHK)	16,310	Remains a government corporation, although the issue of its privatization has been raised in the Administrative Reform Council

Source: General Affairs Agency Administrative Management Bureau (Sōmuchō Gyōsei Kanri Kyoku), *Tokushū Hōjin Sōran* [Almanac of Special Legal Entities], 1985 ed. (Tokyo: Gyōsei Kanri Kenkyū Center, 1985).

Notes: (1) The five enterprises in question in 1984 had the largest numbers of employ-ees of any government-affiliated enterprises in Japan. (2) The total Japanese employed labor force in 1984 was 57.66 million, so the five corporations listed above accounted for 1.28 percent of the total employed Japanese labor force.

During the mid-1980s the realm of public ownership in Japan became even more constricted. Within the space of two years (1985–1987) the three largest remaining public corporations in Japan, employing more than 90 percent of all public enterprise workers, were privatized. Japan Air Lines (JAL) and the Japan Broadcasting Corporation (NHK) were the only remaining government-affiliated enterprises in early 1988 with more than 12,000 employees (Administrative Management Agency 1988). As of March 1988, the next largest government-affiliated enterprises, in terms of employees, were: Teito Rapid Transit Authority, responsible for running the Tokyo subway, with 11,137 employees; Japan Road Corporation (Nihon Dōrō Kōdan), 8,584; and International Telegraph and Telephone Corporation (Kokusai Denshin Denwa, or KDD), 6,829 (Administrative Management Agency 1988). At JAL, the state held less than two-fifths of total shares; and, as Table 1 suggests, government ownership was steadily declining. Pressures were mounting for privatization of NHK as well.

Although in comparative perspective an unusually small and rapidly declining proportion of Japan's manufacturing and public utilities is under public ownership, the state retains an important and direct role in finance. In contrast to France, Japan has never nationalized any major commercial or investment banks. But the Japanese state has developed a powerful system of government financial institutions, linked to a huge, publicly operated postal savings system holding more than 30 percent of all savings assets in the country (Calder 1988a: chap. 4).

In 1988 Japan had eleven government financial institutions, including the Japan Development Bank, the Japan Export-Import Bank, the Housing Loan Corporation, and a range of small business, regional, and agricultural-support banks, which together borrowed ¥1,493 billion from the postal savings, postal life insurance, and related government savings programs and disbursed it to a broad range of industrial, agricultural, and welfare-policy purposes (Yonezawa, Noguchi, and Kubota 1987: 230–234). They did so in accordance with an annual Fiscal Investment and Loan Program laid out by the Ministry of Finance and coordinated with the national General Account Budget. A broad range of parastatal enterprises also had lending functions under the Fiscal Investment and Loan Program, including thirty-five public units (kōdan and jigyōdan) and ten mixed public-private enterprises. (For details on their substantial lending activities, see Ministry of Finance [Ōkurashō], "Zaisei Tōyūshi Tokushū" [Special Edition on the Fiscal Investment and Loan Program], an annual special issue of the Ministry of Finance's authoritive monthly journal Zaisei Kinyū Tōkei Geppō.)

These government institutions operated on the whole like private banks, except that their lending activities were explicitly directed toward public-policy objectives, and loans were generally offered at lower cost and with less onerous restrictions than comparable funds available from the private sector. The concessionary element generally came from the willingness of government banks to lend at close to cost from their nominally low-cost savings pool, rather than from direct subsidies; general account subsidies to the Japan Development Bank, for example, came to only ¥5.5 billion on ¥769 billion in lending during 1985 (Ishizaka, Yoshimoto, and Nakajima 1986). For projects of special national importance, particularly overseas resource extraction ventures with a high risk element, government institutions have typically engaged in consortium lending with major private institutions to help reduce the risk implicit for the private sector (Japan Export-Import Bank 1971: 226–281.)

This system provides the Japanese state with a mechanism for supplying investment capital to the private sector that complements that of the private banks; it defuses risk in large, capital-intensive ventures that private firms might otherwise hesitate to undertake. The scale of government finance relative to the private financial system grew substantially during the 1960s and the 1970s, remaining largely unchanged during the 1980s, even as government ownership in manufacturing and public utilities receded significantly from previous levels.

Apart from the government financial institutions and the postal savings system, the Japanese state's primary vehicle for direct involvement in the economy is through an extraordinary number and variety of parastatal organizations. Besides the three public corporations (*kōsha*) described above, all of which were privatized during 1985–1987, and eleven government financial institutions discussed above, there were in 1985 also thirteen "public units" (*kōdan*), one *eidan* (wartime term for kōdan), ten special companies (*tokushū kaisha*), and forty-two other government-affiliated entities. Japan Air Lines was a special company, and NHK Broadcasting was one of the "other government-affiliated entities" (General Affairs Agency Administrative Management Bureau, annual; Johnson 1978: 34–48).

These parastatals proliferated particularly rapidly in the 1950s and 1960s, but they have not increased substantially in number since the oil shock of 1973. They generally do not employ a large number of workers; the only one with more than 10,000 employees, as noted above, is the Teito Rapid Transit Authority. But these parastatals continue to play a major role in the Japanese economy and, unlike the largest public corporations, have not been dismantled through privatization.

Seen in comparative context, then, public enterprise in Japan exhibits four major features. First, fully public corporations play a remarkably small role at present in the Japanese industrial and public utility sectors. Second, the role of government financial institutions and the public postal savings program, in contrast to the fluctuating role of the state elsewhere in the economy, has remained consistently strong. Third, public ownership in manufacturing and public utilities has fluctuated broadly over time, with two major waves of privatization (1880s and 1950s) preceding that of the 1980s. And, finally, parastatal enterprises play an unusually large role in Japanese economic life. The analytical task here is to explain the contours and pace of the Japanese privatization program in the light of these four features. Ultimately this requires an integrated consideration of both state and private institutional structure and incentive patterns, because it is the interaction of the two that has determined the profile of the Japanese privatization process.

Japanese Public Corporations and Privatization: Historical Perspectives

The tradition of public enterprise in Japan antedates the Meiji Restoration of 1868. At that time the government inherited a small number of plants and four shipyards from the Tokugawa shogunate and subordinate domains, such as the Nagasaki Shipyards and the Sakai spinning mill (Hirschmeier 1964: 143–144). But the earliest major expansion of the Japanese public sector came after 1870. In 1872 Japan's first railway line, eighteen miles of track between Tokyo and Yokohama, was opened under government auspices; between 1872 and 1886 it carried an average of 1.5 million passengers annually and averaged around a 20 percent return on its capital investment (Hirschmeier 1964: 139). In 1877 the government also completed a line between Kyōto and Kōbe. But in contrast to the practice in Belgium and several other European nations, the Japanese state did not suppress the construction of private railways; its model from the beginning was the mixed public-private railway system of Prussia.

Beginning in the 1870s the Ministry of Public Works (Kōbushō), the Home Ministry (Naimushō), and the Hokkaidō Colonization Office inaugurated an expanded program of state industrial enterprise, designed to teach production techniques to private firms, to stimulate import substitution, and to foster industries important for national security purposes. Among the first government efforts was a large-scale construction plant in Akabane, which produced steam engines, boilers, and machinery for cotton spinning and silk reeling. There were also mines and chemical factories producing cement, bricks, and glass, as well as several cotton-spinning, weaving, and thread-plying mills (Smith 1955; Yoshitake 1973; Kobayashi 1977).

In terms of profitability, the government factories were total failures and proved a constant drain on government finances, in contrast to the relatively profitable railroads. The contrast in profitability, of course, flowed from state objectives and prevailing economic realities: the factories were import-substitution ventures in a world where unequal treaties with the industrialized West denied the Japanese state the tariff autonomy to ensure that its ventures would be profitable. Imperatives of national economic security nevertheless compelled the Meiji government to plunge ahead. Between 1868 and 1884 total state investment in public industrial enterprises totaled more than ¥32 million—greater than naval expenditures for much of this period (Yoshitake 1973: 72). But total profits were little better than half that amount: ¥17.2 million (Hirschmeier 1964: 151).

Ultimately, this poor profitability, combined with the rise of an entrepreneurial class confident enough to assure national industrial autonomy themselves and the government's need for cash for more direct pursuit of military activities, induced Japan's first major wave of privatization. Starting in November 1880, the government began actively selling its industrial assets, other than those with strategic military importance, at highly concessionary rates. The Shinagawa Glass Factory, for example, was sold for ¥79,950, to be paid in installments over fifty-five years, beginning ten years after the sale (Hirschmeier 1964: 152). Total government investments in that factory had been ¥350,000, or nearly five times the government's proceeds from its sale. This sort of wholesale concessionary privatization greatly strengthened a small clique of private entrepreneurs close to government, such as Mitsubishi group founder Iwasaki Yatarō; it also gave birth to a wealthy, cohesive private sector.

For ruling elites in quest of both a private sector and a mechanism for stabilizing and perpetuating their rule, the Meiji privatizations served as a potentially useful point of reference. Like much of Meiji Japan's modernizing experience, the interrelated political and economic implications of the Meiji privatizations were not lost on other countries, for example, the Park Chung Hee government in South Korea during the 1970s. The Meiji practice of devolving ownership of government enterprises to politically supportive private investors also resembles the controversial *noyau dur* (stable core) strategy employed under the Chirac-Balladur privatization program in France during 1986–1987, although many details and circumstances were obviously very different and there is no evidence that France consciously emulated Meiji Japan, as the South Koreans have often done.

Reasons of state also inspired some expansion of public enterprise after the Sino-Japanese War, as Japan began a headlong buildup of strategic industries to support its military's rise to world-power status. Thus in 1896 was born the Yawata Iron and Steel Works, the largest of Meiji government enterprises, financed through indemnity payments from China. In 1906 the railways were by and large nationalized, and a major expansion of government investment in railway equipment and rolling stock began, ostensibly for military reasons. During 1906–1907 the government acquired seventeen of the major private lines, boosting the proportion of government-owned railway mileage from 32 to 91 percent (Lockwood 1968: 24–25).

Otherwise the expansion of government enterprise took place almost entirely in the colonial sphere, where the large zaibatsu were less active than in the home islands and hence less intent on and capable of opposing expansion of state enterprise. Among the major new national policy companies (*kokusaku kaisha*) in the colonial development area were: the Nippon Kangyō Bank (founded in 1897); the Bank of Taiwan (1899); the Hokkaidō Development Bank (1900); the Industrial Bank of Japan (1902); the South Manchurian Railroad Company (1906); the Oriental Development Company (1908, operating mainly in Korea); the Yalu River Extraction and Lumber Company (1908); the Bank of Korea (1909); the Japan-Russia Fishing Company (1914); the Korea Industrial Bank (1918); and Taiwan Electric Power (1919) (Johnson 1978: 66). Only in the cases of the Yalu River Company and the South Manchurian Railroad did the government own a majority of the shares, however.

Although unemployment and growing ideological opposition to monopoly capitalism among nationalist military officers tended to increase support for state involvement in the economy, including nationalization, such factors were less salient in Japan than in the major industrial democracies of the West. Japanese manufacturing, which underwent severe retrenchment following World War I, expanded rapidly after 1931, stimulated by a sharp depreciation of the yen and the expansionary domestic policies of Finance Minister Takahashi Korekiyo, just as the Great Depression was assuming its most painful and threatening dimensions in the West (Nakamura 1986: 61–100). In the shadow of the Manchurian incident of 1931 and rising tensions throughout the Pacific, the logic of state-led industrial rationalization was becoming ever more persuasive to Japanese planners, but with a more heavily military rationale than was common in the non-Axis Western world (Johnson 1982: 105–115).

The security-related expansion of state enterprise in Japan passed a critical milestone in 1934 with the creation of Japan Steel, the first true domestic national policy company, or Kokusaku Kaisha (Johnson 1978: 67). As noted above, the Japanese state had managed Yawata Steel since 1896; the creation of Japan Steel essentially represented an expansion and a rationalization of Yawata's operations through its merger with other, smaller firms. One large private firm, Nippon Kōkan, never joined Japan Steel. But Japan Steel's establishment meant effective state ownership of the steel industry from 1934 to 1950.

By 1939 the Finance Ministry was a major shareholder in a wide range of strategic firms in Japan, including Japan Steel, a synthetic fuels corporation, and several metals, fabricating, and trading firms (Samuels 1987: 84). Despite a long, bitter struggle with private interests, particularly the five largest electric power generating firms, in which it enjoyed the support of farmers and small businessmen as well as state planners and large industrial users, the government had not been able to secure passage of its national-management proposals for electric power by the Diet, even amidst the Sino-Japanese War (Samuels 1987: 143–148). But in March 1938 it obtained Diet passage of legislation creating a joint public-private special company to construct new thermal and hydroelectric generating plants and transmission lines, which would also sell power to the private companies (Johnson 1978: 132–133). This enterprise, the Japan Electric Power Generation and Transmission Company (Nippon Hassōden K.K.), together with Japan Steel, became one of the key domestic national policy companies of the World War II period. As the war intensified, Nippon Hassōden expanded its operations, resulting in de facto nationalization of the electric power industry in Japan.

Public enterprise expanded still further in the immediate aftermath of World War II. Between April and December 1947, the Diet established fifteen new state corporations to replace the control associations (*tōsei kai*) through which most of the Japanese economy, aside from steel and electric power, had been administered during World War II (Johnson 1978: 78). Eight of these state enterprises were in the field of domestic distribution, four were in foreign trade, two were related to industrial recovery, and one was established to administer price controls. All were tax-exempt and staffed by government employees; they obtained their fixed capital from the government and working capital from the Reconstruction Finance Bank.

The high-water mark of public management in the postwar Japanese economy was the Katayama Cabinet of 1947–1948, the only Socialist-led government in Japanese history (Katayama Naikaku Kiroku Kankōkai). During the brief nine months of this coalition cabinet's existence, six new public corporations were created, in a pattern strikingly similar to sweeping contemporary nationalizations in Western Europe. Socialists in the Katayama Cabinet were committed, as the Atlee government in Britain had been, to nationalizing the domestic coal industry, and it was on this issue that the government ultimately fell in February 1948, in the face of opposition from Democratic party coalition partners.

Following the accession of the unambiguously conservative third Yoshida cabinet during February 1949, over which organized labor had little influence, a sharp retrenchment in both the scope and the workforce of Japanese public corporations—without parallel in either Western European or Third World experience—began. Japan's second wave of privatization came as part of the so-called Dodge Line shift in Occupation economic policies of 1949. Named after Occupation economic advisor Joseph Dodge, who drafted and supervised them, these were reforms that the United States, increasingly restless at the continuing costs of supporting the Japanese economy, saw as necessary to make that economy more efficient and self-supporting. The Occupation proposed to do so through a reduction of the direct state role in economic affairs and a concomitant rationalization of a public sector workforce swollen by repatriates from overseas and other redundant workers.

The early postwar labor force of Japan National Railways, for example, reached 610,000 employees by late 1948—2.7 times prewar levels. It was reduced by 95,000 in the wholesale cutbacks of 1949–1950. This largely economic objective of public sector retrenchment coincided with the shared interest of SCAP and the new conservative Yoshida government in curbing militant, left-oriented labor, whose principal supporters were public employees (Satō 1976: 120–159). In December 1950 the Nippon Hassōden electric power corporation was dissolved (Johnson 1978: 135). Japan Steel was also privatized; and by the spring of 1951, all fifteen of the new kōdan established in 1947 had been abolished.

The number of public employees also fell sharply, from 1,679,000 in 1948 to 1,568,000 in 1949, according to Ministry of Finance data, and controls were introduced on the subsequent expansion of the public sector labor force. (Prime Minister's Office Statistical Bureau 1953: 404). These workforce cutbacks were especially controversial and led to several bombing incidents (Johnson 1972), as well as a sharp, albeit temporary, decline in the popularity of the ruling Democratic Liberal party. Almost simultaneously, however, several new government financial institutions came into existence, and the state assumed major new responsibilities in off-budget finance. The Japan Export-Import Bank was founded in 1950, for example, and the Japan Development Bank in 1951. A comprehensive Fiscal Investment and Loan Program—the so-called "second budget" of the Japanese government, covering the off-budget financial operations of virtually all government financial institutions—was established in April 1951 and began formal operations in fiscal 1953 (Takehara 1988: 100–120).

In contrast to the privatizations of the Meiji period, no windfall profits seem to have accrued to the private firms assuming custody of state assets during the late Allied Occupation. But these privatizations did sharply cut back the presence of state enterprises in the industrial and public utilities area and detached operations in telecommunications and railways from government ministries just as the Japanese state was expanding and diversifying its activities in the field of finance. The Japan National Railways and Nippon Telephone and Telegraph, for example, had been bureaus of the Transport (formally Railway) and Communications ministries, respectively, but during 1949–1952 they became independent public corporations (kōsha).

Events of this period thus were crucial in establishing the distinctive contours of the Japanese public sector, seen in comparative context. The profile of public enterprise in Japan was relatively close to Western European patterns before the Dodge Line of 1949 and the privatizations flowing from it, with major segments of the Japanese steel and power sectors in public hands. The strong divergence came with Japan's subsequent privatizations of 1950–1951, which had no immediate analogues in most of Western Europe or in the developing world.

An unusual salience of parastatal enterprise, it was noted above, is among the most distinctive traits of current Japanese state involvement in economic life, seen in comparative context. Although such parastatal enterprises had been common in Japanese colonial administration and in Manchuria during the 1930s, only with the onset of rapid post–World War II growth did they gain prominence in Japan proper. In 1955, for example, there were only two "public units" (kōan) participating in the Fiscal Investment and Loan Program; by 1965 the number had increased to twenty-five, only five fewer than the thirty of 1984 (Ishikawa and Gyōten 1977: 106; General Affairs Agency 1985: 1–2).

Rapid economic growth, and the expansion of both budgetary resources and state industrial-coordination responsibilities that flowed from it, clearly aided the expansion of the Japanese parastatal enterprises. But growth and resource expansion alone cannot explain this distinctive organizational form and its rapid emergence in Japan after 1955. Also important in fueling the expansion of parastatals have been the structure of the Japanese government employment system and the persistent interest of Japanese conservative politicians in both compensating important private sector constituencies and enhancing their personal leverage with the powerful bureaucratic world.

Key to the expansion of the parastatals has been the after-retirement employment and fringe-benefit opportunities that these organizations typically provide to the bureaucracy. In late 1983, 78 percent of the 462 senior executives of Japanese parastatals were retired officials of the central government (Nishida 1984: 205, 283). Salaries of these officials were much higher than they had been in the bureaucracy, and retirement pay was also lavish, averaging ¥11.99 million (roughly $50,000 at prevailing exchange rates) per person, provided in a lump-sum payment after fifty months of service (Nishida 1984: 169). This pay was, of course, supplemental to basic bureaucratic retirement allowances, and it applied whenever an official retired from any given parastatal enterprise or state corporation. Short service at a succession of parastatal enterprises, resulting in a progression of lucrative retirement payments, was thus not uncommon.

Policy implementation through parastatals has also been attractive for the ruling Liberal Democratic party because it circumvents restraints that might otherwise be imposed by either legislative review or budgetary constraints. Conservative politicians have found it much easier to compensate supporters quietly through off-budget funding or other assistance from the parastatals, less subject than the government proper to accounting and reporting requirements, than to work through government ministries themselves. Some of the parastatals—particularly the Japan Motorboat Association, headed by Sasakawa Ryōichi—play active roles in support of conservative politicians, little constrained by the minimal legal restrictions on their activities.

Privatization in the 1980s

Explaining Japan's sudden wave of privatizations in the mid-1980s requires first making a fundamental distinction between background enabling circumstances and proximate catalytic factors. As noted earlier, there had been no major privatization in Japan between the early 1950s and the mid-1980s. Nevertheless, the Japanese political economy, like those of other industrialized nations experiencing substantial privatization during the 1980s, had been changing gradually in ways that eroded support for public management of the economy, and indeed actually strengthened resistance to state ownership. Then big business initiative, coupled with strong support from Prime Minister Nakasone Yasuhiro (1982–1987) and the mass media, provided the direct incentives that led once again to large-scale privatization in Japan.

The Candidates for Privatization

To understand the Japanese privatizations of the mid-1980s, it is important first to recognize the distinctive and somewhat contrasting characters of the public corporations being privatized. The largest of these, in terms of both employees and overall significance for the Japanese economy, was Japan National Railways (JNR), which was split into six private, regionally based successor companies on April 1, 1987. The JNR in 1984 had more than 358,000 employees and revenues exceeding ¥3 trillion. More important, however, were its huge operating deficits, which required subsidies of ¥648.8 billion (more than 20 percent of revenues), borrowings of ¥836 billion, and government-guaranteed bond issues of ¥620 billion in 1984 alone (General Affairs Agency 1985: 8–9). Throughout the early 1980s the JNR was known in Japan as one of the "three Ks"—*kokutetsu* (JNR), *komei* (rice), and *kokumin kenkō hoken* (national insurance)—the largest contributors to Japan's substantial national budgetary deficits.

The JNR's huge operating deficits were the result of a series of implicit agreements struck betewen the ruling Liberal Democratic party (LDP) and the opposition Socialists (JSP) during the high-growth 1960s, the consequences of which did not become either evident or financially burdensome until nearly two decades later. To obtain JSP parliamentary cooperation on a broad range of policy issues, the LDP acquiesced in large-scale wage increases for public employees, which had a major impact at the JNR because of its large workforce. For its part, the JSP acquiesced in the 1964 creation of the Japan Railroad Construction Corporation (Nihon Tetsudō Kensetsu Kōdan), which exposed JNR routing decisions to vastly expanded political influence. Throughout the late 1960s and the 1970s, JNR continued both to increase the salary and benefit packages of its employees and to expand its network of unprofitable local lines, leading to an accumulation of deficits that attracted growing opposition from both the big business world and the Ministry of Finance.

The Japan Telephone and Telegraph Company (Nihon Denshin Denwa Kōsha, NTT) was, like JNR, a major presence in the Japanese political economy throughout the postwar period. Established in August 1952 through a reorganization of the Communications Ministry (Teishinshō) that also gave birth to the current Ministry of Posts and Telecommunications, NTT in 1984 had sales exceeding ¥4.5 trillion—the largest of any public corporation in Japan (General Affairs Agency 1985: 11). It was second only to JNR in number of employees, with 326,546.

In sharp contrast to JNR, however, NTT was in strong, and improving, financial condition, thanks to regulatory policies that kept long-distance charges high even as transmission costs declined and demand for telecommunications services grew rapidly in Japan during the late 1970s and early 1980s. With autonomous sources of financing through a compulsory NTT bond-purchase system for new telephone subscribers, and without external debts requiring government subsidy, NTT enjoyed far more autonomy from the political world than did JNR. Its operations were also less distorted by political pressure for inefficient, welfare-oriented practices. But the powerful Zendentsu telecommunications workers union, with the support of the Japan Socialist party and intermittently of the LDP as well, was able to curb NTT management efforts at labor rationalization. As in the case of the JNR's relationship to public sector unions, the JSP-Zendentsu coalition was also able to secure wage and benefits increases for NTT employees far above those available to the private sector. NTT thus experienced important internal inefficiencies, which became more pronounced as technological change in the 1970s and the 1980s created prospective labor-rationalization opportunities to which NTT could not easily respond.

The Japan Monopoly Corporation (Nihon Sembai Kōsha) had a traditional monopoly on the production and marketing of tobacco and salt. Although significantly smaller than JNR and NTT in number of employees, with 36,959 in 1984, it enjoyed sales of more than ¥3 trillion (General Affairs Agency 1985: 1). Through its dual monopoly on both trading in leaf tobacco (including imports) and producing cigarettes, the Monopoly Corporation was, like NTT, quite profitable and required no government subsidies.

Rising Incentives for Privatization

Common to all three public corporations by the early 1980s were salary scales, benefit packages, and labor-productivity patterns—relative to existing technology—that were significantly more favorable to labor than their private-sector counterparts provided or than market forces alone would likely generate. Salary and benefit levels were sustained politically—indeed, systematically raised—through JSP and labor union pressure. But by 1980 both the strength of the JSP and that of organized public sector labor—entities with destinies ever more deeply intertwined—had begun to significantly decline. In the 1976 general elections the JSP polled 20.7 percent of the total popular vote; its support declined to 19.3 percent in 1980 and to 17.2 percent in 1986 (Seiji Kōhō Center 1987: 210). Conversely the LDP's popular vote rose from 41.8 to 49.4 percent over the same 1976–1986 period, with LDP Diet strength rising to nearly 60 percent of total seats. With the conservative LDP in an increasingly commanding position, a declining JSP was ever less able to demand compensation on behalf of public labor clients.

Those clients were also losing their direct leverage with the political process. To be sure, over the course of the 1960s and 1970s the Sōhyō public sector labor union came to enjoy increasing dominance over the JSP. In 1958 union leaders accounted for less than 30 percent of JSP candidates; this ratio doubled over the next two decades (Curtis 1988: 116). But by the 1980s membership in public sector unions was beginning to decline. At its high point in 1949 the major Japan National Railway workers union (Kokurō) had around 600,000 members; in December 1987 the comparable figure was less than 95,000 (*New York Times*, Jan. 14, 1988). Between April 1985 and the end of 1987 alone Kokurō membership declined by more than 40 percent, due to worker disillusionment with the union's militant refusal to negotiate an employment security agreement recognizing the breakup of JNR, which it opposed (*Japan Labor Bulletin*, Nov. 1986, p. 3). The unionization ratio for Japan as a whole dropped steadily, from 34.4 percent in 1975 to 30.8 percent in 1980 and to only 28.2 percent in 1986, little more than half the corresponding ratio in Britain (Keizai Kōhō Center 1988: 73).

Paralleling the declining political strength of organized public sector labor in Japan—the major advocates of public ownership—was the increasingly insistent effort of big business to dismantle Japan's system of extensive support for inefficient groups. To be sure, big business had been intermittently involved in politics during the political crises of the early 1960s and the early 1970s, pragmatically urging social concessions and providing large-scale political funding when it appeared that continued conservative political pre-eminence was at stake (Calder 1988a: chap. 2). It had also consistently expressed its concerns in the area of industrial policy and remained a financial mainstay for the ruling LDP. But as the greater stability of conservative rule became evident in the early 1980s, the business world grew increasingly confident in its attempts to dismantle the network of inefficient welfare-oriented policies built up when conservative pre-eminence was more precarious. Thus emerged the administrative reform movement, chaired by longtime Keidanren chairman Doko Toshio.

Business pressures for cutbacks in the role of the Japanese public sector were given particular urgency by what the private sector perceived as a serious fiscal crisis. Between 1974 and 1979 Japan's national fiscal deficit rose from 1.6 to 6.1 percent of gross national product (GNP), with the national debt service burden also increasing from 5.3 percent of general account expenditures in 1975 to 11.0 percent in 1979 (Ministry of Finance

Budget Bureau 1987: 32–33; *Nomura Investment Review*, Feb. 1987, p. 9). Although the current fiscal deficit fell to 5.9 percent of GNP in 1980, and to 3.9 percent in 1985, the national debt service burden began to rise rapidly, increasing from 12.6 percent to 19.5 percent of the national budget over those same years (Bank of Japan Research and Statistics Department 1987: 227, 343–344). Looking to the future, Japanese big business saw the prospect of rising welfare expenditures accompanying the rapid aging of Japanese society in the 1990s, as well as the need for increased military spending and, in their view, a major corporate tax reduction to match those provided by the Reagan administration in 1981 for their competitors in U.S. business.

On the need for general fiscal retrenchment, big business and the Ministry of Finance concurred. On the desirability of increased budgetary slack and economic efficiency through labor-related reforms at the public corporations, the LDP also agreed. Given the prevailing configuration of political forces in Japan after 1980, this was an unassailable coalition.

The Catalytic Role of Foreign Pressure and Domestic Leadership

Of course, background circumstances enabling privatization do not fully explain either the form or the timing of privatization itself. This appears to be particularly true in technocratically dominated developmental states such as Japan and France, where privatization can involve an especially broad redefinition of government-business relations even when it does not produce a net reduction of the state's economic role. The stakes of such redefinition are often so high, and uncertainties regarding prospective outcomes so great, that catalytic forces capable of stimulating and then organizing an inherently complex private sector outcome are crucial even when privatization may accord with dominant interests.

In France the catalytic role appears to have been played during 1986–1987 by Finance Minister Eduoard Balladur. Although the three major privatization episodes of the 1980s in Japan have to some degree different dynamics, they are united in the central role that Doko Toshio, chairman of the Administrative Reform Commission, and Nakasone Yasuhiro, prime minister from 1982 to 1987, played with respect to all of them. It was Doko who put administrative reform, including privatization, clearly on Japan's national policy agenda, just as the configuration of broader political forces was becoming increasingly auspicious. And it was Nakasone, director-general of the Administrative Management Agency immediately before assuming the prime ministership, who orchestrated the process of privatization itself.

The role of foreign pressure, both political and economic, in determining the profile of Japanese privatization in the 1980s also should not be underestimated (Calder 1988b; Calder 1989). Direct diplomatic pressure for privatization seems to have been strongest in the case of the Japan Monopoly Corporation, where U.S. negotiators intent on finding expanded markets for American products felt that privatization would significantly aid the efforts of U.S. firms to sell American tobacco in Japan. But even in the case of telecommunications, foreign negotiators felt privatization could potentially open new opportunities by increasing competition and accelerating market growth within Japan that could naturally increase demand for imports. The Reagan administration in the United States and the Thatcher government in Britain both strongly advocated privatization at home; stressing the beneficent effects of privatization abroad—for their own nations as well as for Japan—was virtually an article of faith.

Japanese officials and businessmen regarded the global logic of privatization less rhetorically but nevertheless with seriousness. Conceding sufficiently to foreign, especially American, pressures to forestall Western protectionism has been a consistent imperative of Japanese trade policy throughout the postwar period, particularly in sectors such as telecommunications, where exports constitute a high proportion of total production and half of total exports go to the United States. In 1986, for example, 52.3 percent of Japanese wireless telecommunications equipment exports and 43.2 percent of all Japanese telecommunications equipment exports went to the United States (Japan External Trade Organization 1987: 111–112). But despite the rhetoric of Western trade negotiators, there had been little concrete evidence, especially under the early Reagan administration, that foreign retaliation for market-access difficulties experienced in Japan might be in prospect.

The most persuasive international reasons for privatization, in the Japanese view, had to do not with fidelity to the abstraction of global free trade but with the long-term prospective evolution of Japanese industry itself. In the wake of Computer Inquiries I and II, the ATT divestiture, and the ensuing process of deregulation in the United States, the American informatics industry was beginning to develop, through the operation of competitive market forces, a sophisticated telecommunications services sector, especially important to the financial services industry. Such services were not emerging nearly as rapidly in Japan, although prospective demand was being spurred by the emergence of a large and globally oriented Tokyo capital market. Many in Japan thus felt that for strategic reasons the nation needed a deregulation process that could enhance competitiveness in rapidly expanding, market-driven telecommunications service sectors. This view was held especially strongly within Keidanren, the Federation of Economic Organizations, in which the voice of financial institutions and other large users of telecommunications services is influential.

A final range of catalytic considerations governing the time and form of Japan's privatization process related to public finance. In the midst of the escalating boom in global capital markets from 1982 until Black Monday of October 1987, sales of Japanese public assets—as of public assets elsewhere—promised to be highly profitable to the state, as well as to the financial intermediaries involved in underwriting them. A 12.5 percent tranche of NTT shares sold in November 1987, for example, fetched nearly ¥5 trillion (around $38 billion), with each share selling at issue for the equivalent of $19,000—270 times earnings (*Japan Economic Journal*, Nov. 28, 1987). The proceeds to the government came to more than 11 percent the size of total fiscal 1987 central government revenue and more than two-fifths the scale of total government deficit bond issues for that year (Ministry of Finance Budget and Finance Bureaus 1987: 27, 58). Underwriting fees to the politically influential Big Four Japanese securities houses (Nomura, Daiwa, Nikko, and Yamaichi Securities) were also substantial: the bulk of the ¥62.7 billion expended by the government in connection with privatization went to underwriting and associated costs (*The Economist*, Sept. 5, 1987; *Japan Economic Journal*, Nov. 28, 1987).

In France, Britain, and several other nations, shares in privatized corporations have been distributed widely among the general public and have been important in building mass political support for the incumbent administration. This does not appear to have been a central objective of the Japanese privatizations. The ruling Liberal Democratic party is now firmly entrenched and does not appear to need the prospective mass support accruing from broad-based share distributions.

Thus, the 1985–1987 privatizations in Japan increased the community of corporate shareholders by under one million, or less than one-quarter the increase in France; the bulk of the Japanese increase is accounted for by the 752,000 individual holders (by November 1987) of NTT shares (Tōyō Keizai Shinpōsha 1988: 1160). Shareholders increased further with the expanded public issues of railway, tobacco, and telecommunications shares at the end of the 1980s, but still not to the broad levels of the earlier Western European privatizations. Windfall profits made by subscribers to the initial NTT issue of February 1987, which more than doubled in value within six months of issue, appear due more to speculative frenzy in the Japanese capital markets on the eve of the Black Monday crash, and to the Ministry of Finance's desire to begin Japan's privatization program auspiciously, than to any systematic attempt to create a new class of small-scale, conservatively oriented capitalists. The government's approach to the second NTT issue of November 1987, priced 3.5 percent below market and only marginally profitable thereafter for investors, confirmed this Japanese strategy of maximizing short-run government revenue, even at the expense of broader political considerations.

Implications of Privatization

In contrast to patterns in many privatizations elsewhere in the world, little labor rationalization was undertaken in Japan prior to the privatizations of the 1980s. To the contrary, management and the LDP made commitments to organized labor (such as those of NTT chairman Shintō Hisashi to the Zendentsu telecommunication workers union that layoffs would not occur following privatization) in order to obtain labor's cooperation in the privatization process (Komori 1988: 1–102). The major short-run effects of the privatization process have been financial and political, although broader consequences may well emerge as the Japanese state divests itself of shares still held in formerly public entrepises. This process of de facto state divestiture is unusually prolonged in the Japanese case, with levels of private ownership announced as targets during 1987–1988 unlikely to be attained until the 1990s in most instances.

Financially, as noted above, privatization has been a windfall to the Japanese government, especially in the case of NTT. Boasting the highest capitalization of any corporation in the world, NTT was worth on paper more than $300 billion at the end of 1987. Provided that the prevailing share prices of 1987 were to hold, the government could look forward to revenues upward of $100 billion from additional scheduled sales of NTT shares alone over the 1988–1990 period. A small portion of these revenues has been earmarked for accelerated telecommunications research and development. But the bulk will apparently flow back into the national government's general account or into public construction funds, allowing for an acceleration beyond original expectations of public works and other domestic demand stimulation programs.

Politically, the privatizations of the 1980s are having a calamitous effect on the political fortunes of the Japan Socialist party and the public sector unions, thus further entrenching LDP dominance in Japanese politics. As indicated earlier, the Japan National Railway Workers Union (Kokurō), which militantly opposed privatization, and was once a principal political supporter of the JSP, has declined to less than 20 percent of its greatest membership strength. Smaller losses are occurring in telecommunications union membership. Indirect effects of privatization and its implications for public sector unions can also be seen in disarray at Nikkyōsō, the major teachers federation, where membership is declining and a leadership struggle has broken out. In view of the almost simultaneous decline at all the major public sector unions except Seirōkyō, the association of workers within the government ministries themselves, a major realignment within the Japanese labor movement as a whole is in prospect. The 4-million-member strong public sector union federation Sōhyō, of which the railway, telecommunications, and teachers unions are the principal elements, merged in the fall of 1989 with Rengō, the 5.5-million-member umbrella federation of private sector workers formed in November 1987. Although this merger created a single Japanese labor movement of unprecedented dimensions, the public sector voice has been considerably diluted. And the strong personal ties of dominant LDP politicans to private sector elements make it unlikely that reorganization of the Japanese labor movement will pose a major political threat to the LDP.

In a homogeneous Japan with a strong sense of national destiny and a powerful technocracy, public purposes are keenly and broadly felt. Over the 120 years since the Meiji Restoration, those purposes have intermittently, albeit erratically, been filled by public enterprise, followed by periodic waves of privatization. Such cycles may well occur again. But given the current and foreseeable configurations of Japanese politics and of the broader economy within which those politics are embedded, parastatals and private enterprise seem the more likely future tools of public purpose in Japan than public corporations. The Japanese state of the 1990s will thus likely be smaller in terms of employment and more restricted in functions than heretofore, although it may also be a more autonomous and decisive state—shorn through privatization of some previous clientelism and inefficiency, but perhaps less sensitive to popular welfare demands as well.

References

Bank of Japan Research and Statistics Department. 1987. *Keizai Tōkei Nenpō* [Economic statistics annual]. 1986 edition. Tokyo: Nihon Ginkō.

Calder, Kent E. 1988a. *Crisis and Compensation: Public Policy and Political Stability in Japan, 1949–1986*. Princeton: Princeton University Press.

———. 1988b. "Japanese Foreign Economic Policymaking: Explaining the Reactive State." *World Politics* (July 1988): 517–541.

———. 1989. *International Pressure and Domestic Policy Response: Informatics Policy in the 1980s*. Princeton: Princeton University Center of International Studies.

Curtis, Gerald. 1988. *The Japanese Way of Politics*. New York: Columbia University Press.

General Affairs Agency Administrative Management Bureau. Annual. *Tokushū Hōjin Sōran* [Almanac of special legal entities]. Tokyo: Gyōsei Kanri Kenkyū Center.

Harada Katsumasa, Aoki Eichi, Imashiro Mitsuhide, and Nakanishi Kenichi. 1988. *Tetsudō Seisaku Ron no Tenkai* [The unfolding of railway policy]. Tokyo: Chikuma Shobo.

Hirschmeier, Johannes. 1964. *The Origins of Entrepreneurship in Meiji Japan*. Cambridge, Mass.: Harvard University Press.

Ishikawa Itaru and Gyōten Toyoo. 1977. *Zaisei Tōyūshi* [The fiscal investment and loan program]. Tokyo: Kinyū Zaisei Jijō Kenkyū Kai.

Ishizaka Masumi, Yoshimoto Jyūji, and Nakajima Katsumi. 1986. *Zaisei Tōyūshi* [The fiscal investment and loan program]. Tokyo: Tōyō Keizai Shinpōsha.

Japan Export-Import Bank. 1971. *Ni Jyū Nen no Ayumi* [A twenty-year course]. Tokyo: Nihon Yūshutsunyū Ginkō.

Japan External Trade Organization. 1987. *White Paper on International Trade: Japan, 1987*. Tokyo: Japan External Trade Organization.

Johnson, Chalmers. 1972. *Conspiracy at Matsukawa*. Berkeley: University of California Press.

———. 1978. *Japan's Public Policy Companies*. Washington, D.C.: American Enterprise Institute.

———. 1982. *MITI and the Japanese Miracle*. Stanford: Stanford University Press.

Katayama Naikaku Kiroku Kankōkai, ed. 1980. *Katayama Naikaku: Katayama Tetsu to Sengo no Seiji* [The Katayama Cabinet: Katayama Tetsu and postwar politics]. Tokyo: Katayama Naikaku Kankōkai.

Keizai Kōhō Center. 1988. *Japan 1988: An International Comparison*. Tokyo: Keizai Kōhō Center.

Kobayashi Masaaki. 1977. *Nihon no Kōgyōka to Sangyō Haraisage* [Japan's industrialization and the sale of government enterprises]. Tokyo.

Komori Masao. 1988. *Denden Mineika no Butai Ura* [The inside story of NTT privatization]. Tokyo: Orange Shuppan.

Lockwood, William W. 1968. *The Economic Development of Japan: Growth and Structural Change, 1868–1938*, Princeton: Princeton University Press.

Ministry of Finance Budget and Finance Bureaus. 1987. *Shōwa Roku Jyū Ni Nendō Yosan oyobi Zaisei Tōyūshi Keikaku no Setsumei* [Explanation of the fiscal 1987 budget and fiscal investment and loan program]. Tokyo: Ōkurashō Insatsu Kyoku.

Ministry of Finance Budget Bureau. Annual. *Zaisei Tōkei* [Financial statistics]. Tokyo: Ōkurashō Insatsu Kyoku.

Nakamura Takafusa. 1974. *Nihon no Keizai Tōsei* [Japan's economic controls]. Tokyo: Nikkei Shinsho no. 208.

———. 1986. *Shōwa Keizai Shi* [An economic history of Shōwa]. Tokyo: Iwanami Shoten.

Nishida Tatsumasa, ed. Annual. *Amakudari Hakusho* [Amakudari white paper]. Tokyo: Seifu Kankei Tokushū Hōjin Rōdō Kumiai Kyōgikai.

Prime Minister's Office Statistical Bureau. Annual. *Nihon Tōkei Nenkan* [Japan statistical yearbook]. Tokyo.

Samuels, Richard J. 1987. *The Business of the Japanese State*. Ithaca, N.Y.: Cornell University Press.

Satō Kōichi, ed. 1976. *Sengo Nihon Rōdō Undō Shi* [A history of the postwar Japanese labor movement, 1949–1954]. Tokyo: Satsuki Sha.

Seiji Kōhō Center. Annual. *Seiji Handbook* [Politics handbook]. Tokyo: Seiji Kōhō Center. February.

Smith, Thomas C. 1955. *Political Change and Industrial Development in Japan: Government Enterprise, 1868–1880*. Stanford: Stanford University Press.

Takehara Norio. 1988. *Sengo Nihon no Zaisei Tōyūshi* [Postwar Japan's fiscal investment and loan program]. Tokyo: Bunmeido.

Tōyō Keizai Shinpōsha. Spring 1988. *Japan Company Handbook: First Section*, Tokyo: Tōyō Keizai Shinpōsha.

Yoshitake Kiyohiko. 1973. *An Introduction to Public Enterprise in Japan*. Beverly Hills, Calif.: Sage Publications.

PART THREE

Developing Countries

8

Capitalism in Colonial Africa: A Historical Overview

Robert L. Tignor

In October 1986 a distinguished group of government officials, businessmen, and representatives of private agencies gathered in Nairobi, Kenya, to discuss ways in which the private sector could contribute more powerfully to African economic development. The Enabling Conference, as this body was called, agreed that African communities should consider "how environments can be created, within the constraints imposed by the international economy, that will supplement important government initiatives and those of public enterprises by permitting the extensive resources, imagination, and creativity of the private sector—both people and institutions—to participate fully in the development process" (*Enabling Environment Conference* 1986). This statement is an African echo of the emphasis on capitalism and private initiatives that has been sweeping through the developed and developing world, as well as the Communist countries, in the 1980s.

The ability of African societies to invigorate their private sector and to promote capitalist development should be set within a historical framework. In particular, observers should look at Africa's colonial experience with a view to determining whether this crucial era in Africa's recent history helped to lay firm foundations for a vigorous private sector. On the surface, it should have, for Africa came under the control of capitalist Europe at the height of its economic development. Surely it would be reasonable to expect the Europeans to have imported into Africa some of their essential economic institutions.

In this chapter I propose to examine the historical evolution of the private sector under colonial rule and to focus on the indigenous or African position within that sector. The aim is to understand how relatively little

articulated the private sector was during the colonial period, how monop-
olized it was by a few powerful European firms, and how subordinate the
African participation in it was. Africans started almost from the beginning
when they took over the positions of power at the end of the colonial era.
Now, when their leaders and outside experts call upon them to set loose
the creative energies of private, free market capital, it behooves them to
reflect on this immediate historical experience and judge how well it
prepared them for these new economic arrangements.

In truth, the colonial experience did not lay firm foundations for vigorous private sector development. Quite the contrary, colonialism inter-
rupted some important indigenous private initiatives, including the emergence of wealthy and influential Creole businessmen in West Africa. It
also endowed Africa with a strong public sector relative to the private
sector and tended to implant a suspicion of private initiatives in the ethos
of public sector officials, who were expatriates in the beginning but Africans at the end of the colonial period and during the period of independence. Finally, the colonial period witnessed the rise of relatively large,
oligopolistic firms that drew their capital and talent from Europe, leaving
little room for indigenes except as petty traders subordinate to the big
firms and/or locked in an unequal struggle with East and West Asian
immigrant groups for the retail trade.

Many of these trends were confirmed and some broken at the end of the
colonial period. It would be difficult to contend, however, that the era of
decolonization favored the private sector. African nationalists were critical of the business elites (mainly European and Asian) who dominated
commerce and finance. Those with business inclinations tended to es-
pouse a populist form of capitalism. The majority of African nationalists,
however, were interested in seizing control of the public sector and using
it as the primary instrument of economic change.

There are many ways to approach the study of the private sector under
colonialism. I would like to focus on three topics: the discontinuities in
entrepreneurial elites; the firm as a manifestly exogenous force; and the
public sector's predominance over private initiatives.

Discontinuities in the Entrepreneurial Tradition

A vigorous private sector requires entrepreneurs willing to take risks in
combining capital and labor and able to manage enterprises. Although
Africa's long entrepreneurial tradition is well documented in recent schol-
arship, its entrepreneurial groups have lacked continuity. Consequently,
a strong, relatively autonomous commercial and industrial middle class
was not able to coalesce in colonial and postcolonial societies.

The African entrepreneurial tradition in the precolonial period re-
volved around long-distance trade and was controlled by ethnic minorities. Africans living in different ecological zones and cultivating different
crops traded across these regions. The beginnings of this trade can be
traced to the employment of the camel in the Sahara in the second to the
fifth centuries A.D. Gold was sent to North Africa and copper was
brought south. At first the trade stopped at the edge of the Sahel, beyond
which camels could not go. But in time new groups of merchants, many of
them converts to Islam, brought the savannah and rain forest areas of
West Africa into these trading networks (Curtin 1975, 1984).

Critical in the evolution of this trade was the appearance of dispersed,
usually ethnically related trading communities. Although these groups
existed all over Africa, they have been most carefully studied in West
Africa. There the Hausa, Juala, Borgu, and Wangara peoples, to mention
only a few, spread out along the trade lines and facilitated trade in salt,
kola nuts, gold, cloth, and many other commodities (Lovejoy 1980, 1983,
1986).

In the nineteenth century, especially along the coast of West Africa, the
private sector had its fullest flowering in precolonial times. The primary
export commodities of this so-called legitimate commerce, peanuts and
palm products, were handled by new ethnic minorities—the Creole populations of mixed European-African ancestry and customs: the *habitants* of
Senegal and the Creoles of Sierra Leone. Christopher Fyfe (1981) has re-
counted the history of one such individual. In the process of organizing
exports in peanuts and palm kernels, Charles Heddle, a half-Scottish, half-
Senegalese merchant, amassed nearly £500,000, a fortune larger than that
of any other African or European entrepreneur in the West African trade.

We should not, however, exaggerate the extent of this development, the
size of these mercantile communities, or the sophistication of their economic institutions. Only rudimentary private sectors existed in the midst
of economies dominated by kin organizations or by a slave mode of production. The institutional framework of Africa's commercial activity was
not well developed. Businesses were organized by individual proprietors
or as partnerships; larger corporate entities had yet to appear. The long-
distance caravans—which could number as many as five thousand travelers from Egypt or two thousand in West Africa—were usually under the
control of a single administrator when they were under way. But they
seemed to have no regular or corporate existence (Curtin 1975: 271ff.;
Walz 1978; Lovejoy 1980: 102; Roberts 1980). They were formed by individual merchants and travelers who neeeded to band together for security
reasons in order to make the journey. Nor had banks appeared in those
parts of North Africa, Egypt, or West Africa where it would appear that

the volume of trade and exchange would have supported such institutions. Perhaps the Islamic injunction against usury proved a deterrent. Still, at the end of the eighteenth century, the Cairene merchants who engaged in trade with black Africa and the Arabian peninsula had not accumulated great fortunes, and their inventory of stocks on hand was surprisingly small (Raymond 1973: 243ff.).

Any likelihood that these minority entrepreneurial groups in Africa would be a driving force in forging a capitalist economy and a vigorous private sector was cut short by the onset of colonialism. Just what happened to these African proto-middle-class elements under colonialism is an issue still little studied. But there seems no doubt that they were pushed aside by the great European export-import firms (to be discussed later) and over time lost out in the agricultural export-oriented colonial economies to immigrant ethnic minorities—Syrians and Lebanese in West Africa, Indians in East Africa, and Greeks, Italians, and Mediterranean Jews in Egypt and North Africa.

This important transformation and discontinuity in Africa's entrepreneurial tradition has many explanations. According to one, the new emigrant groups brought linguistic and commercial skills lacking in African societies and were prepared to live on profit margins regarded as unacceptable by European and also by potential African mercantile competitors (Winder 1962; van der Laan 1975). The columns of the two leading Nigerian nationalist newspapers, the *West African Pilot* and the *Daily Service*, charge that aspiring African merchants were subject to discrimination when applying for loans. Recent scholarly studies have contended that specific colonial policies undermined the most successful West African trading groups and opened up the commercial arena to Europeans, Syrians, and Lebanese.

According to these views, big West African traders, some of them employing as many as several thousand people, endeavored to break into the export business and develop an indigenous capitalism in the second half of the nineteenth century but encountered opposition from expanding European commercial houses. In league with the newly established colonial states, these firms eliminated the African middlemen (using land and taxation policies and the colonial courts) to clear the way for the European firms. In southern Nigeria, African merchants enjoyed a brief period of prosperity (1900–1905) as they spearheaded the European export-import thrust into the interior. But soon afterward the European merchants sought direct trading connections with producers and consumers and ultimately turned these powerful and wealthy businessmen into subordinate, petty traders. A similar development occurred in Dahomey, where a local bourgeoisie, spearheaded by the Adjovi family, envisaged a domestic form of capitalism, only to be defeated by the French colonial administration in alliance with the big export-import firms (Garlick 1967; Codo and Anignikin 1981; Manning 1981; Nwabughuogu 1982). The general point to be made here, however, is that, although the numbers of these emigrant groups were not large (except for some selected areas like Asians in Kenya) and although African long-distance trading was not completely eliminated (Hausa merchants still engaged in the kola trade), a major reordering of the commercial hierarchy occurred at the expense of the indigenous population. New ethnic minorities—West and East Asians—supplanted the African ethnic long-distance trading minorities of the precolonial period.

Africa has lacked continuity in the development of entrepreneurial experience. The precolonial indigenous and Creole elites did not become the agents of choice for the new European shipping, banking, mining, and export-import companies of the colonial era. They were discriminated against and forced into subordinate niches within the colonial economy. Their ability to accumulate capital was limited. In their place emerged new ethnic minorities who used the protections of colonial rule to accumulate capital and in some cases to position themselves to compete with the great European firms. But their standing was in turn jeopardized by rising nationalist sentiments in the late colonial and postcolonial eras.

The Exogenous Firm

Perhaps no institution better represented late-nineteenth-century European and American capitalism than the limited-liability joint-stock company. This organization was destined to play a large role in the development of the colonial private sector in Africa. Under the impulse to mobilize larger amounts of capital and to diversify economic activities, the joint-stock company centralized vast financial, technical, and managerial resources in a single institutional and corporate entity. This new organization, in which ownership was separated from management, facilitated Europe's economic domination of the rest of the world and became a model of rationalized business enterprise to be copied by late developing societies (see Stopford 1974; Chandler 1977; Hannah 1983; Jones 1986).

It was hardly surprising that large-scale European-financed and -run companies made their presence felt in colonial Africa. They formed the core of the large-scale commercial and financial private sector; and when industrialization was the order of the day during the decolonizing era and the immediate postcolonial period, they were at the forefront there too.[1] Unfortunately, these companies did not encourage African involvement. Nor, contrary to conventional wisdom, did they create economic change where there had been none before; instead they preferred to expand economic initiatives already under way in Africa. Their capital, technical, and managerial talent nonetheless accelerated the incorporation of Africa into the world economy while ensuring European corporate domination.

Having supplanted African efforts, the joint-stock companies were then slow to involve Africans in their higher management levels—a development that occurred only under strong nationalist pressure in the post–World War II era. They also made the entry of purely African firms into the private sector difficult. Indeed, immediately after World War II, when nationalist pressure and the accumulation of capital in the hands of local businessmen led African merchants to press for inclusion in the corporate private sector, their entry was blocked by strong coalitions of expatriate firms, the most powerful and best organized being the Association of West African Merchants.[2] Good examples of these generalizations can be seen in the organization of the export and import trade in West Africa, though similar developments could be described elsewhere in colonial Africa.

The gradual emergence of the big firm has been well described for francophone West Africa. By the twentieth century two major French enterprises were the primary actors: Compagnie Francaise de l'Afrique Occidentale (CFAO, known as la Compagnie), founded in 1887, and La Societe Commerciale de l'Ouest Africain (SCOA), established around 1906. Both firms rested on a long tradition of French business activity in West Africa, CFAO having been formed by the merging of a number of smaller French trading companies.

The French, like the other European powers, had engaged in commerce with West Africa from the beginning of the slave trade era. That trade had altered in the nineteenth century under the impact of gradual abolition and the rise of new cash-crop exports. Bordeaux traders pioneered this new activity, and small firms like Les Etablissements Manuel et Prom encouraged the cultivation of peanuts. The latter enterprise started trading at Goree in 1822 and established the first peanut oil factories at Marseilles and Bordeaux. A large advance in this trade occurred with the foundation of CFAO in 1887. Although many of these smaller French mercantile firms continued to prosper, CFAO became the dominant export and import enterprise, for quite understandable reasons. The new firm suppressed barter and spread the use of money, opposed usurious forms of credit, fixed affordable prices for European imports, and encouraged higher levels of agricultural production by offering better prices to farmers. CFAO was first installed at Marseilles but soon opened offices at Paris, Bordeaux, Liverpool, Manchester, New York, and Osaka.[3]

Soon after its inception, SCOA brought further advances in commercial relations. The founders of the new firm objected to what they considered the old-fashioned, even anti-African practices of CFAO and committed themselves to a higher volume of trade between Africa and Europe. In particular SCOA placed emphasis on the import trade, which it believed to be potentially more lucrative than profits from exports. To this end, the firm sought to pay attractive prices for peanuts and to promote a high volume of European manufactures through fair pricing. It did in fact achieve a fast turnover in sales, prompting customers to call SCOA's retail shops "la chaine avion."

Similarly, in anglophone West Africa the great export-import firms battened onto African agricultural initiatives, accelerated the raw-material export revolution, especially by providing large amounts of capital, and imported European manufactures as consumer incentives. They thus came to dominate this trade. Here, too, although oligopoly, price fixing, and market-sharing arrangements existed, firms were eager to promote a high-volume trade and to encourage the African farmer as both a producer and a consumer.

Although European colonial authorities attributed African agricultural expansion to European capital and colonial rule, in fact, as scholarly studies have indicated, the original innovations, such as the decision to cultivate cocoa, a new crop in West AFrica, were taken by African farmers with little European input (Hill 1963; Berry 1975). Only after the profitability of the crop had been established did European capital direct its attention to this enterprise.

Even though European capital fastened onto African initiative and probably took much of the profit from the expanding international trade and agricultural activity (though we know little about the reinvestment or repatriation of the profits of this trade), we should not view these private sector actors in a wholly negative light. As P. T. Bauer (1954) first suggested, the export-import firms were compelled to be large-scale and heavily capitalized. Large amounts of capital, available at first only in Europe, were required to organize far-flung cultivation and trade. Cocoa was grown on numerous small plots. Cultivators themselves, as well as the small-scale merchants who played an essential role in transmitting the crop from the small farms to the various collection points, needed credit advances. Additionally, the export trade required a widespread network of import traders to keep it flourishing. Firms provided services ancillary to the trade itself, such as building wharves and large storage facilities and creating numerous retail shops where trade commodities were marketed. They had to have ample financial resources to withstand the slumps of the trade and the decline in world market prices. In all respects, companies needed to maintain large reserves of capital and to be capable of diversified export and import functions.

Banking and shipping in Africa were even more oligopolistic and centralized than they were overseas. It is hardly surprising that the first modern banks appeared in the two different poles of African economic growth—Egypt and South Africa—at roughly the same time in the mid-nineteenth century and that with the passage of time smaller establishments were absorbed by larger ones. In South Africa the first of the large-scale banks to appear was the Standard Bank of South Africa, established in 1862 with a nominal capital of £1,000,000 and a paid-up capital of £280,000. Already this bank—which subsequently expanded into Central and East Africa—aspired to regional influence. It drew capital from Britain, attempted (unsuccessfully at first) to open offices in the Orange Free State, contemplated an entry into Mauritius, and was energetic in absorbing numerous small banks that had preceded it in South Africa (Henry 1963: 37–130).

In a similar fashion Egyptian banking came to be dominated by a few firms. After an abortive effort to establish a state bank failed in the first half of the nineteenth century under Muhammad Ali, no further experiments in banking occurred until 1856, when a joint-stock bank called the Bank of Egypt was created by means of a khedivial decree with £250,000 in capital. A group of banks was then established in the 1860s to lend to Khedive Ismail (1863–1879), largely on the basis of the cotton boom of the early 1860s. One of these firms—the Anglo-Egyptian Bank, established in 1864—grew through mergers into Barclays Bank, Dominion Colonial and Overseas (1925); at the same time, numerous branches of European banks came into being, notably the Ottoman Imperial Bank (1864), Credit Lyonnais (1874), and Credit Nationale d'Escompte. After the deposition of Khedive Ismail in 1879 and the British occupation of the country in 1882, Egyptian banks turned almost exclusively to the financing of the cotton crop and its export (Antonini 1927; Jiritli 1960; Davis 1983).

It is worthwhile remembering that in Europe at this time, as Cameron (1967) and Gershenkron (1962) have demonstrated, banks mobilized capital for new industrial projects and promoted economic change. What then of their role in Africa? Here the banks were more circumspect. To begin with, there were no true central banks; the metropole issued currency and served as banker to the regular commercial bank. In anglophone Africa currency boards were established and issued sterling currency backed by holdings in the Bank of England (Newlyn and Rowan 1954). A similar arrangement existed in the French colonies. Ostensibly, Egypt had a central bank when the National Bank of Egypt was founded in 1898, largely with British capital. But the National Bank, although a bank of issue, was linked with the Bank of England, which held the backing for the Egyptian currency. Until World War II it had a separate London-based consulting committee (*National Bank of Egypt* 1949).

Nor were these banks primarily interested in attracting deposits or mobilizing capital. Their overarching responsibility was facilitating trade between Africa and Europe, and they did so by advancing funds to merchants and cultivators. Clearly, then, their goal was the closer integration of Africa into the world economy in a particular way as a supplier of raw materials and an importer of European manufacturers. Their well-defined and limited functions made them eager to deal with well-known and reputable commercial agents—mainly Europeans and to a lesser extent Asians—and loathe to entertain projects outside these boundaries or to advance funds to businessmen not yet established, most particularly aspiring African entrepreneurs. These banks were general commercial banks, requiring a fairly high degree of liquidity and poorly equipped to serve as development banks.

The same tendency toward oligopoly existed in shipping and can be well illustrated for West Africa through the career of Alfred Jones. Jones brought the Elder Dempster line to an unrivaled status in West African shipping in the second half of the nineteenth century and also founded the leading bank in the area, the Bank of British West Africa. Jones's shipping ring tied mercantile firms and the colonial governments to his company. He accepted freight from merchants and government agents only if they signed a declaration that all of their shipments would be made via his line for a period of six months; he then offered a rebate for payments if they adhered to the agreement. Although merchants had previously arranged their own shipping, Jones's Elder Dempster line provided a regular and reliable service, though without any rate competition (Leubuscher 1963; Davies 1973).

In such a fashion the modern private sector in Africa was largely a European colonial importation. It did not grow from African roots, and it afforded little play to African participants, except on the lowest clerical, proletarian, and peasant levels. The joint-stock companies, whether export-import firms, banks, or shipping lines, were incorporated in Europe under European commercial laws, drew on European capital, and were managed by European personnel. Capital was raised in European money markets, thus obviating the need to develop such bourses in Africa. When African colonial governments introduced commercial legislation into their territories, the codes were nearly exact replicas of European law. In Nigeria, for instance, the law enacted to make possible the formation of a purely Nigerian joint-stock company was based almost word for word on the British joint-stock legislation (Nigeria 1922). A similar piece of legislation was introduced into Egypt in 1927 (Tignor 1984: 179).

The overall impact of colonial rule was to establish an exogenous modern private sector, to which, however, a small group of African and Asian businessmen aspired after World War II. To a very large extent—particularly in West Africa—the Asian business aspirants made some inroads into the modern business world, creating their own limited-liability firms. But Africans had greater difficulties and enjoyed considerably less success. In Nigeria a wing of the nationalist movement was composed of new businessmen who wanted to break the monopolistic stranglehold that European firms held on the Nigerian economy. The two most powerful Southern Nigerian nationalist parties—the NCNC and the Action Group—both succeeded in creating indigenous banks and a group of newspapers (Post 1963; Sklar 1963). But these institutions owed their success to the appeal of nationalism rather than to business efficiency; indeed, as the Foster-Sutton Commission of 1956 and the Coker Commission of 1962 pointed out, they were badly managed, often corrupt, and compelled to place political concerns above business matters (Nigeria 1963).

Efforts to indigenize the private sector and to promote a local or native bourgeoisie have not been notably successful thus far. In Nigeria foreign businessmen generally succeeded in evading the indigenization decrees enacted in the 1970s (Biersteker 1987). Even in Egypt, where a more vigorous local bourgeoisie had come into being in the first half of the twentieth century, laws requiring a high proportion of Egyptian directors and Egyptian shareholders in business firms operating in the country did not eradicate the foreign presence. Foreign capital remained powerful until it was forcibly removed by the Nasser regime in the mid-1950s.

The most dramatic effort to Egyptianize the private sector was taken by the Nasser government in 1956–1957 following the British-French-Israeli invasion of November 1956. The government sequestered British, French, and Jewish assets and placed most British, French, and Jewish companies under the jurisdiction of a parastatal body called the Economic Organization, with the announced intention of turning these firms over to worthy Egyptian businessmen. Although some of these foreign firms did end up in the hands of Egyptian businessmen, most stayed with the Economic Organization and came to constitute the core of an expanding public sector. What appeared on the surface to be a policy for promoting a truly indigenous private sector proved finally to be a major step in dismantling private enterprise and making the public sector dominant. In the late 1950s and early 1960s the Nasser government absorbed virtually all large-scale commercial, industrial, and financial undertakings.

The general conclusion to be drawn from this discussion is that Africa's large-scale private sector was dominated by overseas capital and personnel in the colonial period and has been resistant to takeover by local entrepreneurs. Most African governments have only the option of tolerating the foreign influence or incorporating the institutions into the public sector.

The Ambiguous State

The state has always played a major, albeit often supportive, role in societies where strong private sector development has occurred. As Alexander Gerschenkron (1962) has observed in analyzing the different European routes to economic change, late developing countries have often had to rely on centralizing financial institutions and the powers of the state to overcome gaps within the private sector. Thus, a strong state possessing a well-developed public sector need not be a detriment to private initiatives. Quite the contrary, as the nineteenth-century Japanese experience demonstrates: the state can initiate key economic change, as it did in the textile, iron and steel, and other industries and then privatize these enterprises (Smith 1955; Marshall 1967).

In contrast, the colonial state had a profoundly ambiguous attitude toward private actors, even though the colonial administrators who came from Europe at the end of the nineteenth century had left societies with highly developed free market economies and a strong commitment to the virtues of laissez-faire economies. Yet in the colonies their economic policies betrayed suspicion of business firms and a preference for statist solutions to economic difficulties. More to the point, these officials left a legacy of relatively strong and powerful centralized polities for African nationalists whose aspiration was to seize control of these bureaucracies and use them as the primary instruments of economic change.

We begin this discussion of colonial states with an obvious but important fact: the colonial polities were conquest states. Even though European powers everywhere, except in Ethiopia, prevailed over African adversaries, resistance occurred at the time of conquest, continued to erupt after the era of pacification, and was an ever-present fear in the minds of colonial administrators. To be sure, Europeans ruled Africans with a modicum of European administrators and a small expenditure of metropolitan funds. They did so by practicing divide-and-rule techniques and by relying on willing African collaborators. Nonetheless, the instruments of coercion remained important in the colonial system, and the overriding concern for political stability and fear of the consequences of political disturbances meant that important economic endeavors would always be subordinated to political tranquility.

Even after the colonial administrative structures were in place, the commitment to private sector growth was not necessarily a determined one. As A. G. Hopkins has observed, "colonial capitalism ought not to be regarded as an extension abroad of the interests of metropolitan industry." Indeed, his suggestion that there were varying relations between the state and the private sector seems correct. In some colonial polities the state restrained private enterprise; in others, it was closely identified with European commercial groups; and in yet others, it "sought to combine business and administration in a form of colonial corporatism" (Hopkins 1987: 130). The most extreme examples of this varying commitment were Leopold's Congo, where business and administration were completely intermeshed in large concessions companies, and, at the other end of the spectrum, Britain's status quo and antibusiness orientations as practiced in the prime areas of indirect rule like northern Nigeria and the southern Sudan (Harms 1975;Luc-Vellut 1981; Shenton 1986; Watts 1987). A further vivid example was the British decision not to allow Lever Brothers to establish oil palm plantations in Sierra Leone and Nigeria for fear of legal hassles over the land and the need for permanent government assistance to make the enterprise a success (Meredith 1984). Nevertheless, as an overarching generalization, it can be argued that the colonial state assumed vast economic responsibilities—well beyond those exercised by metropolitan states at the time. The colonial state's powers were exalted at the expense of private business, and a suspicion of business activity permeated the higher levels of the government bureaucracy.

A brief resume of the state's major economic obligations should lend support to the assertion that the colonial state was large relative to the private sector. In the first place, colonial land policy put restrictions on private landholding and the emergence of independent landholders, be they Africans or European agrobusinesses. Almost everywhere in colonial Africa the state assumed power over so-called vacant or unoccupied land. In many territories this crown land, as the British called it, could be made available to concessionary companies or sold off or leased to European settlers—a practice that did of course foster the emergence of private landholding among Europeans. As for African areas, the prevailing policy was based on the assumption that Africans did not own land privately but possessed it communally. European colonial administrators therefore sought to maintain communal traditions, often by grouping Africans into reserves (especially in colonies of European settlement), and refused to recognize individual African landed rights even when rich and successful farmers petitioned the state for such recognition (Buell 1928; Hailey 1938).

In addition to restraining the evolution of private landholding among Africans, the colonial state assumed responsibility for many types of economic activity clearly in the domain of the private sector in Europe at the time. In colonial Africa nearly the entire economic infrastructure was controlled by the state. The colonial governments built and administered the railroads, were responsible for port and harbor development and administration, and took charge of roadways.

In several colonial territories—Egypt and the Sudan under British control and Morocco under the French—irrigation and hydraulics swelled the responsibilities of the public sector. In Egypt, Lord Cromer at first contemplated putting the hydraulic system in private hands, but the whole weight of Britain's experience in India, as well as Egypt's own traditions, worked against this idea. The extremely large capital expenses involved, the state's traditional responsibility for the distribution of precious irrigation waters, and the fear that private actors would show favoritism ruled against resort to private firms (Tignor 1966: 100–101; Swearingen 1987: 36–77).

Colonial state involvement in public utilities also contrasted with the more common European pattern. Here the record is a mixed one. In many cities in Africa electricity, filtered water, urban public transportation, sewerage, and so forth were in the hands of private concessionaires that provided the services under some form of state regulation and some guarantee against competition; such was true, for example, of most of the public services in Cairo and Alexandria up until the 1950s. In other cities, however, sometimes as a consequence of the failure of private firms, the state ran public utilities or became an important shareholder and member of the board. Two examples must suffice. In East Africa electricity was supplied by the East Africa Power and Lighting Company, a subsidiary of the British engineering firm Balfour Beatty, until intense complaints led the Uganda government to expropriate the company's license and properties in 1946. In Kenya a new public-private conglomerate, the Kenya Power Company, was created in 1955 (East Africa Power and Lighting Company, various years; Kenya Power Company 1955). Similarly, the Sudanese government established a construction company (Sudan Construction and Equipment Company) and a public utility (the Sudan Light and Power Company) when private capital failed to show interest in providing such services (Tignor 1987b: 191).

There were numerous reasons for the relative enlargment of the colonial state, many of which would not have precluded a subsequent evolution of the private sector. In the early colonial era, *raisons d'état* were sufficient. Railroad construction, for example, had to be carried out quickly, often in conjunction with campaigns to conquer territories or to maintain control over them. The political urgency lying behind the railroad from the border of Egypt to Khartoum in the Sudan or from Mombasa to Lake Victoria virtually precluded the involvement of private business firms. The substantial sums involved in railroads, although they were regarded as a charge against the colonial territory and its tax-paying peoples, came in the first instance from the metropole, usually in the form of guaranteed colonial loans. But the actual construction of the railways, the mobilization of labor, and the administration of railways once completed invariably remained in the hands of state bureaucrats.

A second factor was a lack of interest on the part of private business. As S. H. Frankel (1938: 168) has shown, the amount of private investment in the French colonial empire was exceedingly small. Although private capital flows were larger in the British territories, these tended to be located in a few areas, like South Africa, where a growing population of European settlers and the superabundance of raw materials assured a substantial rate of return. Elsewhere, capitalists failed to take the lead and forced the state to become a major economic actor.

Finally, the state's powers were magnified because it had to mediate among competing interest groups at widely varying levels of economic development. To use the expression of John Lonsdale and Bruce Berman, the colonial state had to cope with the contradictions of colonial capitalism. Lonsdale and Berman (1979, 1980) argue that the colonial administration in Kenya came under pressure from metropolitan business and investment interests but could not be wholly responsive to these factions because European settlers in Kenya clamored for attention and agitated for independent economic and fiscal policies. Nor could the administration neglect African populations, which might rise in revolt if policies impinged severely upon them. The colonial state then became a mediating agency and assumed a size, authority, and interventionist capacity hardly warranted by the actual economic resources it was capable of extracting from local populations.

A powerful state need not be a hindrance to the growth of the private sector. Indeed, most colonial officials contended that the state assumed major infrastructural duties in order to prepare the way for private firms in other areas. But in reality the colonial administrators were profoundly suspicious of business and did little to encourage the activities of businessmen. Their reservations about the private sector stemmed from a paternalistic ethos toward so-called primitive African populations and from their own class and antibusiness biases.

Paternalism expressed itself in administrators' suspicion of the greed of businessmen and their fear that business firms would corrupt and exploit innocent African populations. Paternalism undergirded indirect rule in northern Nigeria and the British administration of the Sudan. Not surprisingly, in northern Nigeria and the Sudan administrators feared (with much justification and ample historical example) strong movements of Islamic opposition and looked upon other European colonial agents, such as missionaries and businessmen, as likely to stir up opposition through misguided and overzealous educational, proselytizing, and business ambitions.

Recent work on the class backgrounds of colonial officials indicates that

British colonial officials tended to be drawn from the upper landed gentry and professional classes, to have been educated in elite public schools (Eton, Harrow, and the like), and to have attended Oxford and Cambridge universities. Not only did this background equip these officials with a noblesse oblige toward African subject populations, but it also caused them to look down upon mercantile classes, European and African, as a lower group on the social ladder (Kirk-Greene 1982).

Anti-business paternalism is seen most clearly in the Gezira project in the Sudan. Although most colonial African states took responsibility for hydraulics, railways, and agricultural research, they left the actual cultivation of the land and the marketing of crops to independent farmers and traders. Not so in the development of cotton cultivation and marketing in a large area of land located between the White and Blue Niles just south of Khartoum. The British colonial administration not only provided the requisite irrigation water through a dam built on the Blue Nile after World War I; but in conjunction with a large European-based, -financed, and -managed land concessionaire it controlled the cultivation of the crops and their marketing. The British government refused to turn the Gezira development over to private business because of its distrust of agrobusiness. By the same token, the colonial government kept African cultivators as tenant farmers because of it believed that independent cultivators would fall into debt (which in fact they did) and would fail to cultivate the land efficiently or benefit from it without state oversight.

The large colonial state is an important ingredient in the evolution of the African private sector. The relationship of the state to private business firms was profoundly ambiguous. In theory, the state's widespread responsibility for economic infrastructure was meant to foster a favorable environment for private investment. But in practice colonial bureaucrats were so supicious of private actors that they often put obstacles in the way of these firms. As independence approached, the state became a target for nationalists, much more so than private businesses. Once independence came, and also under the impulse to use the state as an instrument for promoting economic growth, the size of the bureaucracy and its functions expanded. Bureaucrats soon were organized to protect their interests and saw to it that the private sector remained stunted.

Decolonization and Capitalism

The era of decolonization—roughly from 1945 to 1963—was a decisive and unsettling one for the evolution of the private sector in Africa. Many of the characteristics of colonial capitalism were greatly strengthened, but there were some dramatic ruptures with the past.

Continued Growth of the Public Sector

The two decades following World War II witnessed a steady growth in the activities and functions of the public sector. In anglophone Africa the single most important development was the establishment of marketing boards. These parastatal bodies, composed of government officials and representatives of the private sector, had been brought into existence during World War II as part of a program to regulate production in Africa for the war effort. Although they were intended to be abolished at the close of the war, they continued to function, as more and more commodities were taken under their jurisdiction. The marketing boards set the prices to be paid to cultivators at the beginning of the selling season. The old export-import firms that previously had handled the purchase of African cash crops now became the commissioned buying agents of the boards. In this critical respect the purchasing and exporting of Africa's main agricultural commodities was removed from private hands and given over to the state (Bauer 1955; Helleiner 1966).

The original justification for the boards was that they would smooth out the price paid to cultivators and thereby lessen the risk to them of fluctuations in world market prices. Additionally, the boards were empowered to use any accumulated surpluses to enhance the productivity of cultivators. But even in the immediate postwar years, when the boards were still controlled by British colonial officials rather than African bureaucrats responsive to nationalist pressures, the clause permitting boards to invest surpluses was given a wide interpretation.[4] Funds were set aside for development projects that only with difficulty could be rationalized as benefiting the cultivators of the regions from which the funds had been raised. As the number of African representatives on the boards increased and as specialized regional development and finance bodies were created, the funds began to be used in expansive ways, often for little concealed political purposes.

The accumulation of substantial surpluses in the marketing boards presented opportunities for the state to promote private, indigenous enterprise. The early discussions of these boards indicated that nationalist leaders were alive to these possibilities. Unfortunately, the substantial sums, which were turned over to development boards, were often squandered on political and personal programs. The 1963 Coker Commission Report (Nigeria 1963) contains the fullest record of the misuse of these surpluses in Nigeria.

In other crucial ways public responsibilities for economic matters were growing. All of the colonial territories drafted economic plans in the 1940s and 1950s; and although private enterprise was expected to play a large role in these plans, the public sector was not minimized. The consensus of

development economists was that the key to industrialization and economic diversification was an increase in the savings rate. Here the state
was expected to play a crucial role. By using its taxation powers as well as
the resources of the marketing boards, it could launch society into self-
sustaining economic growth (Killick 1978).

The great European commercial firms were surprisingly sensitive to the
changing political and economic trends in postwar Africa. They were
quick to see that Africanization and economic diversification were the
keys to their continued activity in Africa. In Nigeria, where the United
Africa Company led the way, firms created new industries and put themselves at the forefront of economic change (Holt 1944).

Nationalist Rhetoric and Capitalism

The main stream of nationalist sentiment and most legislative enact-
ments during the era of decolonization were favorable to capitalist enterprise. Many decolonizing countries, mindful of their technical and capital
deficiencies, endeavored to attract foreign capital through special concessions. The Sudanese and Nigerian pioneer industries bill encouraged investment, particularly foreign investment, in critical new industries and
provided incentives for such firms through tax breaks and generous allowances for the repatriation of profits (Nigeria House of Representatives
1952; Sudan House of Representatives 1955: 116ff.). Between 1952 and
1956 the military regime in Egypt made concessions to foreign capital by
undoing the binding company legislation that civilian regimes had enacted in 1947 and 1948 (O'Brien 1966: 68–84). In Nigeria Azikiwe had a
conglomerate of businesses and was as deeply engaged in business and
finance as he was in politics. One of his close associates was Louis
Ojukwu, a wealthy and successful trucking magnate and probably Nigeria's most eminent business person (Post 1963: 58–60).

But the nationalist impulse was profoundly ambiguous to the private
sector and was especially critical of the dominant position enjoyed by big
business in Africa and the influence of foreign businessmen. The nationalist parties had a populist orientation and tried to incorporate Africa's
working classes. Close ties were established with trade union leaders, and
their critique of capitalism was incorprated into the nationalist attack
against colonial rule. In virtually every decolonizing territory at least one
respected and well-established nationalist leader became a focal point for
anticapitalist sentiments. In Nigeria, Obafemi Awowolo, despite the privileges of his upbringing and education, used the Nigerian parliament to
criticize the prevailing capitalist programs.[5] A similar position was taken
in Kenya by Oginga Odinga (Odinga 1967). In Egypt, during the brief
capitalist phase of the Nasser regime (1952–1956), Gamal Salam and other

young military officers worked behind the scenes against accommodations with business groups (Tignor 1987a).

Decolonization Outcomes

In spite of the undercurrent of populist and antibusiness sentiment, the private sector emerged largely intact in decolonized Africa. As Gary Wasserman (1976) has shown for Kenya, alliances were formed between moderate African nationalists and foreign and local business leaders to thwart a challenge from a radicalized peasantry, the urban working class, and inflexible settlers, a challenge that would have taken Kenya away from moderate economic policies.

Only where the struggle for independence was protracted and led to confrontations and deep-seated bitterness, as was the case in Egypt, or where the severing of the colonial ties was traumatic, as in Guinea, was the conferral of political independence accompanied by strong anticapitalist measures. In Egypt, despite impressive attempts to involve foreign capital in the development effort, the withdrawal of Western financial support for the High Dam project, the resultant nationalization of the Suez Canal Company, and the British-French-Israeli invasion persuaded the Egyptian military junta to nationalize a large portion of the local economy and then incorporate it into the public sector. The nationalizations of 1956 led in an almost logical sequence to the takeover of virtually all large-scale financial, commercial, and industrial companies in the period 1959–1962 (Tignor 1986).

Although at independence the African states had large private sectors and counted on private sector contributions to development plans, there had been enough criticism of capitalism, even from established and conservative nationalist politicians, to create a mood of uncertainty among business elites. In particular, the minority communities, still deeply involved in commerce and industry, felt exposed and vulnerable. Much of the legislation of the decolonizing period posed a threat to their existence in Africa. Their status was confused, and new nationality laws drafted by African governments in anticipation of independence were exclusive rather than inclusive, stressing racial rather than residential and place of birth criteria. Also, requirements for obtaining visas and residency permits were tightened, making it more difficult for aliens to remain in a country. Finally, company legislation stressed the employment of higher proportions of nationals and put additional pressures on the foreign communities.

The continuities and ruptures of the turbulent era of decolonization were familiar and predictable ones for the private sector, in keeping with earlier twentieth-century experience. The emigrant, non-European business minorities were placed under nationalist pressures, and their futures were in jeopardy. The exogenous firms remained powerful despite efforts on the part of colonial and postcolonial states to establish their own currencies, national banks, commercial legislation, and stock exchanges. The powers of the public sector grew at the expense of private actors.

Notes

1. The most powerful of these firms were usually joint-stock, limited-liability, multinational firms like Unilever, the oil conglomerates, and the banking and shipping concerns. But not all of them were joint-stock companies. John Holt and Company was a private limited-liability company. For insight into the activities of Unilever in Africa, see Pedler (1974) and Fieldhouse (1978).

2. One need only read the chief Nigerian nationalist newspapers in the post–World War II era to get a sense of these complaints. The champion of purely Nigerian enterprise against the Association of West African Merchants was the Association of Nigerian African Exporters and Importers. See *The Daily Service* and *The West African Pilot* for the years 1945–1948.

3. This interpretation draws heavily on the work of Jean and Rene Charbonneau (1961: esp. 67–85). One should also consult the appropriate sections of A. G. Hopkins (1973). Decidedly more negative views of the French export-import houses may be found in Jean Suret-Canale (1964) Catherine Coquery-Vidrovitch (1975).

4. See the minutes of the sixteenth meeting of the Nigerian Cocoa Marketing Board, March 28, 1951, where the Oni of Ife favored the allocation of board funds for the endowment of a medical college, arguing that the "distinction between the use of marketing board and government monies for particular purposes would not be obvious to the communities as a whole who wanted to see great and good things accomplished." Public Record Office, London, Colonial Office 852/1150/7.

5. In the Nigerian House of Representatives, Awolowo attacked the bill on the grounds that it was "designed to encompass the economic slavery of this country so as to reduce to a sham and a mockery its political independence when it shall be attained." *Debates*, April 7, 1952, p. 988.

References

Antonini, Emile. 1927. *Le credit et la banque en Egypte*. Lausanne: Vaney-Burnier.
Bauer, P. T. 1954. *West African Trade: A Study of Competition, Oligopoly, and Monopoly in a Changing Economy*. Cambridge: Cambridge University Press.
Berman, Bruce, and J. M. Lonsdale. 1979. "Coping with the Contradictions: The Development of the Colonial State in Kenya, 1895–1914." *Journal of African History* 20, no. 4: 487–506.

_____. 1980. "Crises of Accumulation, Coercion, and the Colonial State: The Development of the Labor Control System in Kenya, 1919–1929." *Canadian Journal of African Studies* 14, no. 1: 55–83.

Berry, Sara. 1975. *Cocoa, Custom and Socio-Economic Change in Rural Western Nigeria.* Oxford: Clarendon Press.

Biersteker, Thomas J. 1987. *Multinationals, the State, and Control of the Nigerian Economy.* Princeton: Princeton University Press.

Buell, Raymond. 1928. *The Native Problem in Africa.* New York.

Cameron, Rondo, ed. 1967. *Banking in the Early Stages of Industrialization: A Study in Comparative Economic History.* New York: Macmillan.

Chandler, Alfred Jr. 1977. *The Visible Hand: The Managerial Revolution in American Business.* Cambridge, Mass: Harvard University Press.

Charbonneau, Jean, and Rene Charbonneau. 1961. *Marches et Marchands d' Afrique Noire.* Paris.

Codo, Bellarmin C., and Sylvain C. Anignikin. 1981. "Pouvoir colonial et tentatives d'integration africaines dans le systeme capitaliste: Le cas du Dahomey entre les deux guerres." In Laboratoire "Connaissance du Tiers-Monde," Actes du Colloque, *Enterprises et entrepreneurs en Afrique,* vol. 1. Paris: Editions l'Harmattan.

Coquery-Vidrovitch, Catherine. 1975. "L'impact des interets coloniaux: SCOA et CFAO dans l'Ouest Africain, 1910–1965." *Journal of African History* 15, no. 4: 595–621.

Curtin Philip. 1975. *Economic Change in Precolonial Africa: Senegambia in the Era of the Slave Trade.* Madison: University of Wisconsin Press.

_____. 1984. *Cross Cultural Trade in World History.* Cambridge: Cambridge University Press.

Davies, P. N. 1973. *The Trade Makers: Elder Dempster in West Africa, 1852–1972.* London: Allen and Unwin.

Davis, Eric. 1983. *Challenging Colonialism: Bank Misr and Egyptian Industrialization, 1920–1941.* Princeton: Princeton University Press.

East African Power and Lighting Company. Various years. *Annual Report.*

The Enabling Environment Conference: Effective Private Sector Contribution to Development in Sub-Saharan Africa. 1986. Nairobi: Printed privately.

Fieldhouse, D. K. 1978. *Unilever Overseas: The Anatomy of a Multinational, 1895–1965.* Stanford: Hoover Institution Press.

Frankel, S. H. 1938. *Capital Investment in Africa.* London.

Fyfe, Christopher. 1981. "Charles Heddle, An African 'Merchant Prince.' " In Laboratoire "Connaissance du Tiers-Monde," Actes du Colloque, *Enterprises et entrepreneurs en Afrique,* vol. 1. Paris: Editions l'Harmattan.

Garlick, Peter C. 1967. "The Development of Kwahu Business Enterprise in Ghana since 1874—An Essay in Recent Oral History." *Journal of African History* 8, no. 3: 463–480.

Gerschenkron, Alexander. 1962. *Economic Backwardness in Historical Perspective.* Cambridge, Mass.: Harvard University Press.

Hailey, William Malcolm. 1938. *An African Survey*. London: Oxford University Press.

Hannah, Leslie. 1983. *The Rise of the Corporate Economy*. London: Methuen.

Harms, Robert. 1975. "The End of Red Rubber: A Reassessment." *Journal of African History* 16, no. 1: 73–88.

Helleiner, Gerald. 1966. *Peasant Agriculture, Government, and Economic Growth in Nigeria*. Homewood, Ill.: Irwin.

Henry, J. A. 1963. *The First Hundred Years of the Standard Bank*. London: Oxford University Press.

Hill, Polly. 1963. *The Migrant Cocoa Farmers of Southern Ghana: A Study of Rural Capitalism*. Cambridge: Cambridge University Press.

Holt, John. 1944. Quarterly Report, September 18, 1944. John Holt Papers, Rhodes House Library, Oxford University.

Hopkins, A. G. 1973. *An Economic History of West Africa*. New York: Columbia University Press.

———. 1987. "Big Business in African Studies." *Journal of African History* 28: 119–140.

Jiritli, Ali. 1960. "Tatawwur al-Nizam al-Misrafi fi Misr." In al-Jama iya al-Misriya lil-Iqtisad al-Siyasi wal-Ahsa wal-Tashr, *Buhuth al-Id al-Khamsini, 1909–1959*. Cairo: Egypte Contemporaine.

Jones, Geoffrey, ed. 1986. *British Multinationals: Origins, Management, and Performance*. Aldershot, England: Gower.

Kenya Power Company. 1955. *Annual Report*.

Killick, Tony. 1978. *Development Economics in Action*. New York: St. Martin's.

Kirk-Greene, A.H.M. 1982. *The Sudan Political Service: A Preliminary Profile*. Oxford: Oxford University Press.

Leubuscher, Charlotte. 1963. *The West African Shipping Trade, 1909–1959*. Leyden: A. W. Sythoff.

Lovejoy, Paul. 1980. *Caravans of Kola: The Hausa Kola Trade, 1700–1900*. Zaria, Nigeria: Ahmodu Belle University Press.

———. 1983. *Transformations in Slavery: A History of Slavery in Africa*. Cambridge: Cambridge University Press.

———. 1986. *Salt of the Desert Sun: A History of Salt Production and Trade in the Central Sudan*. Cambridge: Cambridge University Press.

Luc-Vellut, Jean. 1981. "Articulation entre entreprises et etat: Pouvoirs hegemonique dans le bloc colonial belge, 1908–1960." In Laboratoire "Connaissance du Tiers-Monde," Actes du Colloque, *Enterprises et entrepreneurs en Afrique*, vol. 2. Paris: Editions l'Harmattan.

Manning, Patrick. 1981. "L'affaire Adjovi: La bourgeosie fonciere naissante au Dahomey face a l'administration." In Laboratoire "Connaissance du Tiers-Monde," Actes du Colloque, *Enterprises et entrepreneurs en Afrique*, vol. 1. Paris: Editions l'Harmattan.

Marshall, Byron K. 1967. *Capitalism and Nationalism in Prewar Japan: The Ideology of the Business Elite, 1868–1941*. Stanford: Stanford University Press.

Meredith, David. 1984. "Government and the Decline of the Nigerian Oil
   Palm Export Industry, 1919–1939." *Journal of African History* 25: 311–329.
National Bank of Egypt, 1898–1948. 1949. Cairo: Printed privately.
Newlyn, W. T., and D. C. Rowan. 1954. *Money and Banking in British Colonial
   Africa: A Study of the Monetary and Banking Systems of Eight British Territories.*
   Oxford: Clarendon Press.
Nigeria. 1922. *Companies Ordinance.* Lagos.
_____. 1963. *Report of the Coker Commission of Inquiry into the Affairs of Certain
   Statutory Corporations in Western Nigeria.* Lagos.
Nigeria, House of Representatives. 1952. *Debates,* April 7.
Nwabughuogu, A. I. 1982. "From Wealthy Entrepreneurs to Petty Traders:
   The Decline of African Middlemen in Eastern Nigeria, 1900–1950." *Journal
   of African History* 23, no. 3: 365–379.
O'Brien, Patrick. 1966. *The Revolution in Egypt's Economic System: From Private
   Enterprise to Socialism, 1952–1965.* New York: Oxford University Press.
Odinga, Oginga. 1967. *Not Yet Uhuru.* London: Heinemann.
Pedler, Frederick. 1974. *The Lion and the Unicorn: A History of the Origins of the
   United Africa Company, 1787–1931.* London: Heinemann Educational.
Post, Kenneth W. J. 1963. *The Nigerian Federal Election of 1959: Politics and Ad-
   minstration in a Developing Political System.* London: Oxford University
   Press.
Raymond, André. 1973. *Artisans et commercants au Caire.* Vol. 1. Damascus:
   Institut français de Damas.
Robert, Richard. 1980. "Long Distance Trade and Production: Sinsani in the
   Nineteenth Century." *Journal of African History* 21: 169–188.
Shenton, Robert W. 1986. *The Development of Capitalism in Northern Nigeria.*
   Toronto: University of Toronto Press.
Sklar, Richard L. 1963. *Nigerian Political Parties: Power in an Emergent Nation.*
   Princeton: Princeton University Press.
Smith, Thomas C. 1955. *Political Change and Industrial Development in Japan:
   Government Enterprise, 1868–1880.* Stanford: Stanford University Press.
Stopford, John M. 1974. "The Origins of British-Based Multinational Manufac-
   turing Enterprises." *Business History Review* 48 (Autumn): 303–335.
Sudan, House of Representatives. 1956. *Weekly Digest of Proceedings,* January
   26.
Suret-Canale, Jean. 1964. *Afrique Noire Occidentale et Centrale: l'ere coloniale,
   1900–1945.* Paris: Editions Sociales.
Swearingen, Will D. 1987. *Moroccan Mirages: Agrarian Dreams and Deceptions,
   1912–1986.* Princeton: Princeton University Press.
Tignor, Robert L. 1966. *Modernization and British Colonial Rule in Egypt, 1882–
   1914.* Princeton: Princeton University Press.
_____. 1984. *State, Private Enterprise, and Economic Development in Egypt, 1918–
   1952.* Princeton: Princeton University Press.

————. 1986. "Foreign Capital, Foreign Communities, and the Egyptian Revolution of 1952: The Importance of Events." Typescript.

————. 1987a. "Decolonization and Business: The Case of Egypt." *Journal of Modern History* 59 (September): 479–505.

————. 1987b. "The Sudanese Private Sector: An Historical Overview." *Journal of Modern African Studies* 25, no. 2: 191.

van der Laan, H. L. 1975. *The Lebanese Traders in Sierra Leone*. The Hague: Mouton.

Walz, Terence. 1978. *Trade between Egypt and Bilad as-Sudan, 1700–1820*. Cairo: Institut Français d'archeologie Orientale du Caire.

Wasserman, Gary. 1976. *Politics of Decolonization: Kenya Europeans and the Land Issue, 1960–1965*. New York: Cambridge University Press.

Watts, Michael, ed. 1987. *State, Oil, and Agriculture in Nigeria*. Berkeley: University of California Press.

Winder, R. Bayly. 1962. "The Lebanese in West Africa." *Comparative Studies in Society and History* 4, no. 3: 296–333.

9

State, Economy, and Privatization in Nigeria

Peter M. Lewis

Nigeria possesses the largest public enterprise sector in sub-Saharan Africa, and one of the most troubled; yet serious consideration of privatization did not begin in Nigeria until the mid-1980s. As in many African countries, economic crisis provided the immediate impetus for public sector reform, and international financial institutions have played an important role in promoting the policy. The military regime of President Ibrahim Babangida has undertaken a domestic Structural Adjustment Program (SAP), closely linked with multilateral negotiations to reschedule the country's burdensome foreign debt and to obtain renewed sources of external financing. Privatization has been an increasingly significant element in that program. The present government of Nigeria, while making concerted efforts to articulate a privatization policy, has moved cautiously toward implementation.

Privatization policy in particular, and public sector reform in general, must be viewed against Nigeria's history of contentious ethnic and regional rivalries, institutional weakness, and political instability. The Nigerian state has historically exercised little autonomy from diverse societal interests seeking access to public resources. Distributive pressures dominate Nigerian politics, and political imperatives hold sway over the nation's economy; these circumstances have substantially contributed to the current economic crisis. Distributive politics, and the private appropriation of state resources, have impeded the public sector's ability to achieve a modicum of productivity or efficiency. The same factors militate against a rapid or effective privatization exercise.

This chapter considers the development of Nigeria's privatization policy within the context of the state's expanding and increasingly problematic economic role during the past thirty years. The following section provides a sketch of Nigeria's development strategy and a historical outline of the growth of the nation's public sector. This is followed by an elaboration of some theoretical considerations relevant to an understanding of public-private sector relations in Nigeria. We conclude with a discussion of privatization policies and issues.

Development Strategy and State Sector Expansion

Nigeria has experienced two broad phases in development strategy since the conclusion of the colonial era. Throughout the 1950s and 1960s, the government's economic role was interventionist and tutelary, but limited. The state acted as a "catalyst" for private sector development by creating the physical, institutional, and financial environment for economic progress (Berry and Liedholm 1970: 76–77; Schatz 1977: 3). During the final years of British rule, the colonial government initiated efforts to establish a nationwide economic and social infrastructure and to foster the emergence of a viable domestic private sector. This orientation did not change appreciably after independence in 1960. The civilian regime ruling Nigeria until 1966 emphasized the development of physical infrastructure and the creation of an institutional framework for economic growth. The government also intensified efforts to attract foreign capital and participation in the economy.

The military coups of 1966 and the ensuing civil war marked a decisive change in the pattern of Nigerian development. The war experience accentuated nationalist and statist tendencies among Nigeria's leadership. Furthermore, during the 1970s three successive military regimes inherited a windfall in resources from petroleum exports and attempted a strategy of de facto state capitalism. Central planning efforts and regulatory authority were greatly expanded. Public investments increased and diversified as the state moved directly into strategic productive areas of the economy. The state became a central source of economic growth, accumulation, and entrepreneurship.

State capitalism is a term often used yet rarely defined. The strategy appears as a particular response by certain ruling coalitions in developing countries to the problems of economic dependency and domestic class formation. State capitalism typically describes a concerted, programmatic effort by state elites to reduce the power of foreign capital and to foster an integrated, dynamic national capitalist economy. The goals of state capitalism are to limit or usurp the influence of foreign economic forces, to create a framework for national economic integration and endogenous growth, and in many instances to foster indigenous entrepreneurship (Petras 1977; FitzGerald 1979; Waterbury 1983). The state assumes greater control of and participation in the economy, particularly through direct involvement in productive ventures; but it does not seek to reorder relations of production or to constrain the prerogatives of indigenous private capital. The public enterprise sector, though expanded in scope and diversity, is predominantly run along capitalist lines, that is, as a complex of profit-making ventures embodying hierarchical labor relations and managerial organization.

The elite coalition initiating state capitalism typically unites nationalist military rulers, or leaders of a dominant or single party, with technocratic elements in the public sector, especially higher civil servants and public enterprise managers. The state takes on a dual role: the public sector acts in lieu of an absent or incipient domestic bourgeoisie, while government intervention is also intended to foster a domestic capitalist class. These objectives are often in tension, as contradictions arise between the state's roles as substitute and patron for indigenous capital.

The earliest state enterprises in Nigeria date from the late colonial period. As in many African countries, the colonial government established agricultural marketing boards during World War II. The boards purchased export crops from producers at prices below those of the world market, retaining the surplus for stabilization and welfare purposes. After 1954, marketing board funds were turned over to regional development corporations with a mandate to promote production and development. These resources were controlled by three semiautonomous regional governments, each dominated by a different nationalist political party with distinct communal and ethnic constituencies.

Major federal enterprises in utilities and transportation evolved from colonial government departments. The regional development corporations acquired numerous holdings, concentrated in commercial agriculture and small- to medium-scale import-substitution industries. The beginnings of public finance capital were established with the introduction of agricultural and industrial loan schemes and the founding of indigenous commercial banks funded by the development corporations (Helleiner 1966; Forrest 1987).

During this period state planners were reluctant to commit substantial public resources to direct production, preferring to emphasize social services, utilities, transport, and finance. The postindependence regional governments increased their efforts to attract external investment and to foster the activities of indigenous business. The federal government sought to provide incentives for foreign investors and to rationalize and upgrade the national planning apparatus. For the most part, however, the state remained an agency of private sector development in the early years after independence (Kilby 1969: 23–24). In 1966, amid increasing regional competition, communal conflict, and political upheaval, the civilian regime of the First Republic was overthrown by the military, setting into motion a chain of military factionalism and ethnic violence culminating in civil war. This episode signaled a significant shift in Nigeria's development strategy and a decisive change in the role of the public sector.

The civil war, 1967–1970, naturally disrupted production, curtailed nascent petroleum activities, and diverted public funds. The war effort necessitated strict economic austerity measures, including trade, monetary, and fiscal controls. The experience of financing a costly military campaign without recourse to heavy foreign borrowing convinced Nigerian leaders of the need to utilize state intervention to achieve national autonomy (1970: 29; Ayida 1987: 187). These proclivities were expressed in the Second National Development Plan for 1970–1975, which in newly resolute nationalist terms called for the state to assume control of the "commanding heights" of the economy.

The Second National Development Plan was promulgated by a military government determined to cement federal unity and promote rapid postwar reconstruction. It coincided fortuitously with Nigeria's entry into the world arena as a major oil producer. At independence in 1960, the petroleum sector accounted for less than 1 percent of Nigeria's gross domestic product (GDP) and export revenues. Beginning in 1970, oil production expanded rapidly. Average production stood at a little over 500,000 barrels per day (bpd) in 1969. The following year production topped 1,000,000 bpd, and in 1973, 2,000,000. The international oil crisis of 1973–1974 increased prices dramatically. By 1974 oil production constituted 30 percent of GDP, nearly 70 percent of government revenues, and more than 92 percent of export earnings. Subsequently, petroleum accounted for between 93 and 98 percent of Nigeria's export values. The steady increases in Nigerian production and international prices created a windfall in revenues, prompting a rapid expansion of the economy. The GDP increased fourfold (at current prices) between 1973 and 1981 (Nigeria Federal Office of Statistics 1982: 1), and the rapid increase in petroleum rents fostered an abrupt expansion in government activities (World Bank 1981: 42).

The government's economic role changed dramatically during the oil boom. By creating more states and changing national revenue allocation formulas to make the states more reliant on federal revenues, the federal government centralized its fiscal and administrative authority (Bienen 1985: 11). Public economic activities expanded along several fronts: planning became more ambitious, comprehensive, and detailed; public investments experienced tremendous growth and diversification; federal and state governments participated in a variety of productive ventures in agriculture and industry; the regulatory scope of the state increased greatly as the government implemented substantial nationalizations in the petroleum and financial sectors and widespread indigenization throughout the economy. Administrative restrictions on imports, exports, and foreign exchange allocations were introduced (or revived from the war era) in an effort to control trade and monetary flows. The government moved from a supportive to a vanguard role in the process of economic growth. This role was articulated in planning documents and in the "mixed economy" model of the 1979 constitution (1979: 16–17). It was widely accepted throughout the public and private sectors.

Although the extent and zeal of government economic intervention looked very much like state capitalism, appearances were sharply at variance with capabilities, and state strategies failed to produce a positive structural transformation of the Nigerian economy. State expansion in Nigeria was not structured by a coherent program of state-led economic reform; and perhaps most important, the Nigerian public sector had no effective or competent technocracy to implement such a program. The economy became suffused by political authority, with no corresponding development of administrative or managerial capacity. The result was an ineffectual and wasteful state sector and a private sector simultaneously co-opted and stifled by public tutelage.

The emergence of a state capitalist strategy in Nigeria was signaled by two central policies: the indigenization program and the expansion of public enterprises. The two policy thrusts were ostensibly intended to promote development of the indigenous private sector and rapid accumulation within the state sector. The indigenization decrees of 1972 and 1977 required companies under foreign ownership—including those held by Lebanese nationals—to relinquish a substantial portion of their shares to Nigerian control (Biersteker 1987). The foreign divestiture process facilitated widespread, though limited, acquisition of equity in foreign-owned companies by the federal and state governments.[1] This coincided with a tremendous expansion of state investments and a proliferation of state-owned enterprises.

Public enterprises were a central instrument of state economic policy during the oil boom. The federal government took a mandatory 60 percent share in foreign petroleum companies and financial institutions. Dozens of new companies were established, many as joint ventures with foreign capital, as well as numerous wholly-owned public enterprises.

The state governments followed with equal enthusiasm as state-level elites, like their regional predecessors, apprehended new opportunities for patronage, personal enrichment, and local development (Wilson 1983: 62–63). Many investments at the state level echoed the import-substitution activities of the 1960s. They also reflected considerable replication and haste, as civil servants and politicians sought control over bounteous public resources.

The Public Enterprise Sector:
Scope and Performance

Accurate figures are lacking, but it is likely that Nigeria has the largest state-owned enterprise (SOE) sector in sub-saharan Africa: as of 1990, about 900 enterprises. Of this total, 275 are federally owned, and more than 600 are owned by the states. Government enterprises may be distinguished among commercial and noncommercial categories; about two-thirds of the federal enterprises are commercial ventures. Significantly, the SOE sector is estimated to contribute about 35 percent of GDP (Okigbo 1981: 170), which, when matched against comparative data, again places Nigeria's SOE sector among the largest in sub-Saharan Africa.[2] Employment in the public enterprise sector is approximately 500,000, about a third of public sector employment and nearly 22 percent of total employment in the formal sector of the economy (Sanda 1986).

These enterprises make a huge claim on government resources. In 1986 the federal government estimated that about 40 percent of nonsalary recurrent expenditure and 30 percent of its capital budget have gone annually toward public enterprises (Nigeria 1986b: 24). Total investments may exceed $35 billion, including $11.2 billion in equity, $10.2 billion in government loans, and another $11.5 billion in unspecified (and largely unrecorded) "subventions" to various enterprises. These investments have provided meager returns, yielding less than $1 billion in dividends and loan repayments from 1980 to 1985.[3] Net outflows from the government to public enterprises may total as much as $2 billion annually (Callaghy and Wilson 1988).

The magnitude, extent, and persistence of failure among Nigeria's public enterprises have been extraordinary. Only a handful of companies, mostly those representing "passive" shareholding in foreign financial and petroleum enterprises, have yielded dividends on public investment. Public utilities and government-controlled transport require continuous, massive subsidies while delivering intermittent, substandard services. Industrial enterprises typically operate at 20–35 percent of capacity. As in many other developing countries, public enterprise failure in Nigeria carries severe and far-reaching consequences for public finances, economic growth and adjustment, income distribution, and even political stability.[4]

Since the early 1960s, the operational causes of public enterprise failure have repeatedly been identified by commissions of inquiry convened by the federal, regional, and state governments.[5] These reports document a familiar set of problems: political and bureaucratic interference with managerial autonomy; multiple goals and uncertain policy and economic environments; unstable and often mediocre management; poor information and accounting systems; inadequate financing and inappropriate capital structures; and a lack of performance targets and accountability.

Government investigations have periodically reiterated suggestions for reform. Government leaders have intermittently attempted to obtain better performance and financial discipline in the public sector. But change has scarcely been effected at the enterprise or the sectoral level. Political instability, administrative weakness, and a lack of mangerial accountability have frustrated reform efforts. Public enterprise personnel are often flagrant in flouting the authority of government, as was exemplified in 1983 when employees of Nigerian External Communications (NET) set the company's Lagos headquarters ablaze rather than risk seizure of records revealing official misconduct.

The Politics of Distribution

Adverse public sector performance, and the resistance of SOEs to reform efforts, may be traced to an enduring syndrome of Nigeria's political economy, usefully termed the "politics of distribution." Nigeria's political economy is conditioned by diverse cleavages among the nation's governmental and business elites. Ethnic and regional divisions, the most basic and pervasive distinctions in Nigerian society, are augmented by identities of locality, language, and religion, yielding a complex array of communal tensions. Communal divisions are expressed politically in factional struggles over access to state offices and competition for the apportionment of public resources. Nigerian state institutions are permeated by these heterogenous and competitive societal elements, and public policies reflect this rivalry.

State capitalism in Nigeria has embodied a basic paradox: fiscal and administrative authority have progressively been centralized under a rentier state, as state capacities have become increasingly strained and ineffectual. The Nigerian state is fraught with division and instability; there is no public sector technocracy to provide autonomous, politically neutral economic management; and Nigerian governments have historically experienced tenuous popular legitimacy. The fractious nature of Nigerian society, and the relative weakness of class politics, have created fragile social bases for Nigerian regimes; consequently, Nigerian leaders, whether civilian or military, have emphasized short-term political strategies incorporating a large component of material inducement.[6]

The Nigerian economy has been thoroughly politicized since the end of the colonial era; control of economic resources and opportunities resides with state offices and policies (Rimmer 1981: 40). As fiscal centralization advanced and state economic activities expanded during the oil boom, increased public resources became the focus of distributive demands from diverse sectional interests.

Distributive pressures are often satisfied at informal levels, as patronage networks and corruption provide widespread access to public largesse. An implicit moral economy governs state patronage: all major actors in a highly factionalized system expect access to state bounty, and the state contends with private interests over the control of such wealth.[7] The widespread tendency toward private appropriation of public resources has been characterized by Richard Joseph (after Weber) as the "prebendalization" of the state (Joseph 1983).

Distributive politics hinder state-led accumulation, as the public sector serves as an avenue of distribution at the expense of its productive goals. The formal purposes of public enterprises, ostensibly intended to produce goods and services, are undermined as these organizations become hostage to a raft of separate acquisitive interests. At the levels of both policy formation and enterprise operations, production is subverted and ultimately frustrated by political criteria. The ubiquitous politicization of economic activity, prevalent throughout Africa, stands in direct contradiction to the realization of capitalist development. It is inimical to the conditions of calculability and rationality that have historically facilitated the growth of rational, systematic accumulation in nascent capitalist economies (Berry 1984: 92; Callaghy 1988).

As suggested earlier, public and private sector growth have proceeded simultaneously in Nigeria. These processes have been not antagonistic but complementary and symbiotic (Bienen 1985: 17). The proliferation of public enterprises occurred in tandem with the expansion of the domestic private sector into territory previously held by foreign capital. Public sector growth, in fact, has been a central source of private accumulation. Private business has benefited immeasurably from state patronage and government resource allocations. Contractor/supplier/distributor relationships have been the basis for substantial entrepreneurial development in the private sector (Forrest 1987: 336). Indigenous business interests have not sought to constrain state economic expansion; rather they work informally and individually to secure public favors.

Background to Reform: Crisis in the 1980s

Nigeria followed a disheartening course throughout the 1970s, as the lofty expectations accompanying petroleum-led growth turned to profound failures. The oil boom ended abruptly in the early 1980s. Nigeria's petroleum revenues peaked at nearly $25 billion in 1980; by 1982 that figure was halved; and in 1986 petroleum netted less than $7 billion (World Bank 1981: 52; Central Bank of Nigeria 1987).

A fiscal crisis ensued: the external payments situation deteriorated, and petroleum earnings, constituting 70–75 percent of government revenues, declined. Foreign reserves plummeted, while balance of payments deficits spiraled. External debt obligations totaled $1.3 billion in 1978, $6.5 billion in 1980, $18 billion by 1985, and $27 billion by 1987. Debt service equaled 2 percent of external reserves in 1980, 231 percent four years later. The debt service ratio increased from 1 percent to 30 percent during the same period (World Bank 1981; Central Bank of Nigeria 1987).

As foreign reserves and domestic inventories were drawn down in the early 1980s, and stalemated debt negotiations resulted in a virtual cessation of external credits and capital inflows, the manufacturing and mining sectors declined rapidly. Agriculture, an early and enduring casualty of the oil boom, could not provide a safety valve. The GDP declined by an average of 3.4 percent per annum between 1980 and 1985, and by 3.3 percent in 1986 (*African Business*, April 1988).

Since 1981, a civilian government and two successive military regimes have attempted to cope with increasing economic problems. Prior to 1986, public policies exacerbated the effects of external shocks on the domestic economy. By the beginning of 1986, President Ibrahim Babangida's government showed a greater resolve to alleviate foreign pressures and to promote structural changes in the economy.

Economic Crisis and Public Sector Reform in the 1980s

The downturn in the international oil market began during the presidency of Shehu Shagari, leader of Nigeria's short-lived Second Republic (1979–1983). The multiparty civilian regime was distinguished by its free-wheeling political competition and rampant corruption. Government profligacy and private venality attained unprecedented proportions. Externally induced financial constraints were exacerbated by a virtual hemorrhage of public finances resulting from widespread malfeasance and uncontrolled political disbursements.

President Shagari nevertheless launched some tentative efforts at public sector reform. In 1981 the Presidential Commission on Parastatals (led by Gamaliel Onosode, a prominent private sector figure, and known popularly as the Onosode Commission) was created to conduct a comprehensive inquiry into the organization and operations of the nation's public enterprise sector. Later that year, the president's office commissioned private consultants' studies of thirty-four of the nation's leading public enterprises.[8] The consultants advocated increasing the financial autonomy and accountability of the major public enterprises. Interestingly, the Onosode Commission devoted scant attention to the issue of privatization. Instead it focused on the need to improve management quality and accountability, including a recommendation to remove many public enterprises from civil service salary scales and personnel structures (Federal Government of Nigeria 1981).

President Shagari was unable or unwilling to muster the necessary administrative and financial discipline to effect reform in the public sector; the recommendations of the Onosode Commission and the consultants went largely unresolved. At the end of 1983, plagued by economic decline, political disarray, and growing popular alienation, the Second Republic was terminated by military intervention, bringing to power an eaustere, "corrective" regime led by Major-General Muhammed Buhari.

The new regime ousted the politicians and alleviated some of the more conspicuous, if petty, sources of corruption within the public services. The generals had little to offer in the way of an economic program, however. Their response to increasing economic adversity was a patchwork of continued trade and monetary restrictions, public sector retrenchments, budgetary austerity, and sloganeering.

As with other important elements of economic strategy, the Buhari government stated an intention to achieve public sector reform but failed to articulate a policy program. Nonetheless, adverse petroleum markets and increasing debt pressures compelled the regime to execute extensive cutbacks in public sector personnel and expenditures. In fact, retrenchments in the civil service and the public enterprise sector under Buhari—totaling more than 15,000 jobs—constituted the single largest public staffing cutback in Nigerian history.

The Buhari government made a desultory examination of the possibilities for privatization. By 1984 international financial institutions, led by the World Bank and the International Monetary Fund (IMF), were increasingly advocating privatization as a policy option. Moreover, the British experience with privatization had a deepening impression on important business and government leaders in Nigeria. These converging trends were reflected in public discussion, though not in government policy, during Buhari's rule.

Buhari chose to emphasize commercialization as an instrument of public enterprise reform. That policy conveyed the government's intention to retain control of the nation's major parastatals while introducing management and fiscal reforms to improve enterprise performance. The operational details of commercialization were never elaborated beyond a broad injunction for greater financial self-sufficiency. Many viewed the policy as a concession to northern elites, who wielded a dominant influence in the Buhari government and who strongly opposed the loss of patronage opportunities implied by privatization. In any case, the government never seriously pursued the policy. When economic decline brought an intensification of authoritarian measures, public disaffection and the deepening economic morass prompted elements within the military government to oust Buhari and his close associate, Major-General Tunde Idiagbon. Major-General Ibrahim Babangida assumed power in a bloodless coup in August 1985.

Upon assuming power (and the title of president), Babangida made clear his resolve to scrap the moribund economic policies of his predecessor and to implement serious public sector reform. This policy direction was intimately related to a resumption of Nigerian negotiations with the IMF. Cognizant of the domestic controversy surrounding the negotiations, the president inaugurated a national debate on acceptance of an IMF loan and its attendant conditions. Three months of lively national dialogue conveyed a clear popular consensus against acceptance of the loan. Following official repudiation of the IMF package, the Babangida regime proceeded to implement an economic reform program, dubbed the Structural Adjustment Program (SAP), as an indigenous alternative to an IMF austerity package. The SAP, in all its essentials, met or exceeded IMF stipulations.

Privatization Policy

In his 1986 New Year's Day budget speech, President Babangida announced a halving of nonstatutory allocations to "all economic and quasi-economic parastatals." He also stated the government's intention to divest its holdings in a number of nonstrategic enterprises, including agricultural production companies, hotels, food and beverage manufacturing, breweries, distilleries, distribution companies, electrical and electronic appliances manufacturing. Government holdings in banks and other financial institutions might also be reduced, but "without losing control." The president tried to allay fears of inequitable distribution of these assets by announcing that divestiture would give preference to labor unions, pension funds, universities, social and cultural associations, and local government and state investment companies (Nigeria 1986a: xv).

This brief statement was the first explicit and detailed commitment to privatization by a Nigerian leader. But although it quickly became the benchmark for subsequent national discussions of privatization, it was not backed by a policy or institutional framework for implementation. To begin with, the federal government itself was not fully apprised of its holdings or clear on a definition of what constituted a state-owned enterprise. The situation was even more chaotic at the state level. Consequently, the earliest tasks confronting the government were to compile an accurate inventory of public holdings and to classify enterprises to determine which should be sold and which retained.

In July 1988, after more than two years of confidential discussion and public conjecture, the government issued Decree 25 on Privatization and Commercialization. The decree lists seventy-one federal companies for total divestiture, including hotels, breweries and distilleries, agro-industrial companies, textile mills, flour mills, wood fabrication companies, and insurance companies. The federal government would relinquish controlling interest in twenty-five enterprises, including oil marketing companies, Nigeria Airways, the National Shipping Line, steel rolling mills, and many of the larger industrial enterprises in fertilizers, paper, cement, and sugar processing. The federal government would retain controlling equity in commercial and merchant banks while reducing its shares in development banks from 100 percent to 70 percent. An additional eleven companies would be fully commercialized, that is, restructured to operate without government subsidy, including Nigerian Telecommunications (NITEL), the Nigerian National Petroleum Corporation, the Coal Corporation, the Ports Authority, and three government insurance firms. Nineteen enterprises would be partially commercialized, meaning that government support would be reduced; they included the National Electric Power Authority, the Railway Corporation, the steel mills, all River Basin Development Authorities, the Federal Housing Authority, and the Television Authority (Nigeria 1988). State holdings were not directly affected by the decree.

A significant innovation in the decree was the establishment of a Technical Committee on Privatization and Commercialization (TCPC) with a broad mandate to coordinate the rehabilitation of government companies and to supervise the divestiture of shares. The TCPC represents an unprecedented effort to centralize institutional authority over the SOE sector, and during its first year of activity the committee made significant headway in implementing a divestiture program and promoting reform efforts.

The evolution of Nigerian privatization policy since 1986 has been characterized by a lack of coordination between policy formulation and implementation. The government has devoted considerable energy to identifying the assets, sectors, and companies to be affected by a privatization program, but there has been far less attention to delineating the means and procedures of implementation. The government has been consistently lax in elucidating the question of management transfers and insitutional reform; nor has there been any clarification on the crucial issue of accountability.

Decree 25 itself focuses on questions of share valuation, issuance, and distribution, while making passing mention of managerial reform and institutional change. The edict offers no detailed guidelines for determining

changes in the composition of managing boards, the appointment of executives, or the funding structures of privatized companies. Commercialization also remains a skeletal policy. Aside from relative reductions in government subsidies to the respective enterprises, the fiscal and institutional
arrangements entailed by "full" or "partial" commercialization have not
been elaborated.

Events since the 1986 policy statement offer some significant paradoxes.
In one sense, policy has far outstripped the development of implementation mechanisms; but in another sense "implementation," in terms of divesting public assets, has proceeded in the absence of policy. During the
latter part of 1986 and the whole of 1987, there was little public action on
the promulgation of a privatization policy. During the same period, the
federal government peremptorily liquidated seven agricultural commodity boards and the Nigerian National Supply Company (NNSC); it also
divested the various operations of the Nigerian Livestock Production
Company, a commercial agricultural concern with diverse assets throughout the northern states. A private merchant bank was engaged to evaluate
the assets of three federal government hotels in preparation for possible
divestiture. Moreover, several state governments moved quietly to sell
full or partial equity in industrial, service, and agro-industrial enterprises;
still others foreswore any moves toward privatization, regardless of federal government policy. In late 1988 and 1989, the activities of the TCPC
and complementary efforts from the executive branch showed evidence
of a more comprehensive approach to divestiture and reform, embodying
an institutional focus and a clearer program.

Prospects for Implementation

Nigeria is one of the few countries in sub-saharan Africa that possesses
a formal private capital market. The Securities and Exchange Commission
(SEC) and the Nigerian Stock Exchange, at the behest of the government,
have prepared plans for the implementation of a privatization exercise.
Although they expressed early reservations about the lack of organizational detail in the reform program and misgivings about the economic
viability of most public companies, they have asserted that the necessary
machinery exists for evaluating companies and bringing shares to the
market. Initial efforts at divestiture have met with some success: shares in
four companies were successfully sold during the early months of 1989,
with each issue reportedly oversubscribed.[9]

Federal enterprises affected by Decree 25 are to be privatized through
the institutions of the private capital market; however, if they cannot be
evaluated due to poor financial conditions or inadequate information,
they may be liquidated. In the case of liquidations, the government has

considerable latitude in dispensing with assets. The dismal operational history and weak finances of many companies make liquidation a likely recourse, meaning that substantial assets could fall outside the purview of the regulatory framework established in the decree.

Many companies will present special problems for share valuation, given the poor state of financial records and the frequent undercapitalization that characterize many government enterprises. Moreover, there exists an inherent contradiction between the government's desire to divest certain holdings and the attractiveness of shares on the market. Most public enterprises have displayed continuous financial losses since their inception, a number have been dormant for years, and some never actually began operation. Although the government is naturally anxious to shed its most onerous burdens, it is equally apparent that failing or inactive companies will offer few attractions to private investors. The government has selected relatively appealing enterprises—some of which are already traded on the Stock Exchange—for its initial divestitures.

A further dilemma is presented by the absorptive capacity of the private capital market. Although relatively large in the African context, the Nigerian capital market is thin and rudimentary. A Nigerian banker recently observed that the envisioned privatization exercise, encompassing a potential N2.3 billion in equity, represents 110 percent of the total value of transactions in government securities from 1981 through 1986, which amounted to N2.1 billion (Thompson 1988: 34).

It is reasonable to assume substantial hidden liquidity in the Nigerian economy. Economic life is heavily oriented toward cash transactions, and huge sums have been siphoned abroad or diverted into private domestic accounts during the past fifteen years (Olojede 1986). The propensity for mobilizing these savings, however, will depend on the security and profitability of the proposed investments.

Moreover, liquidity and wealth are inequitably distributed. Economic and political elites have ready access to resources, but previous experience has shown that labor unions, pension funds, and enterprise employees, among those favored as recipients of state assets, lack the resources to purchase shares. As with the indigenization exercise, the government will find it necessary to finance share acquisition for selected groups, and the magnitude of such purchases could mean a significant financial burden that may reduce the net fiscal gains from privatization.[10]

Share allocation is the most emotionally charged issue affecting the implementation of privatization policy in Nigeria. The indigenization exercise left a divisive legacy casting a shadow on current plans for privatization. The domestic private sector is sharply distinguished along lines of national origin, foreign ownership, size, ethnicity, and regional character. A central target of indigenization, particularly with the first decree, was the extensive Asian commercial class—predominantly Lebanese entrepreneurs—as well as European and American multinationals (Biersteker 1987: 91). Suspicion toward these groups has persisted in both the private and the public sector, and there is widespread antipathy against permitting such interests to participate in privatization.[11]

The domestic private sector is divided as well. There is a widespread conviction among non-Yoruba business interests that the indigenization exercise yielded disproportionate benefits for Yoruba business elites. Northern, Ibo, and minority business interests harbor deep-seated resentments from that era, and there is strong pressure on national leaders to ensure geographic equity in the divestiture process. Northern elites, heavily involved in domestic commerce and possessing fewer developed networks with foreign capital than their southern counterparts, are defensive about having to compete in capital markets and productive sectors with Ibos and Yorubas. These latter groups hold a competitive edge by virtue of historical educational advantages and a longer proximity to centers of industrial and financial activity. Northern interests, more so than southern groups, appear to require continued state patronage to maintain their viability.

The scale of capital is also controversial. The indigenous Nigerian private sector remains relatively underdeveloped and fragmented by international standards, oriented toward commerce, transport, services, and small-scale manufacturing. Nonetheless, there exist several large family-run conglomerates that might be expected to have the interest and resources to participate in a privatization program. These groups cannot be compared with the large-scale capitalists of Brazil, India, or Korea, but they represent considerable wealth and influence. There is a strong apprehension among the domestic private sector—preponderantly small- to middle-sized family-run companies—of domination or pre-emption by the larger actors and fear of creating an indigenous industrial "oligarchy" (Odife 1985: 17).

The prevailing political consensus that share ownership should be widely and equitably dispersed may create a basic impediment to policy implementation. The exclusion of foreign capital, non-African nationals, and large-scale private investors from the privatization process considerably narrows the field available for the disposition of assets and the reform of management. The government, recognizing this constraint, released the privatization decree in a broader context of economic liberalization. Changes in the indigenization laws, announced at the beginning of 1989, permit foreign firms to take full equity in large-scale manufacturing, commercial, and service ventures that were previously limited to 40 percent foreign ownership. Private commercial and merchant banks, previously barred from holding equity in domestic firms, were permitted in

1988 to invest in small- and medium-sized agricultural and manufacturing companies.

Divestiture and Reform

Some of the potential hazards of implementation became apparent in the early measures taken with respect to divestiture. Between President Babangida's 1986 statement on privatization and the 1988 privatization decree, the government liquidated several prominent enterprises and attempted to relinquish its holdings in some less productive firms. The most dramatic evidence of the government's commitment was the scrapping of the seven agricultural commodity boards and the liquidation of the National Supply Company and the National Freight Company. Notably, these enterprises were engaged in activities in which indigenous business interests predominate: transport, commerce, and distribution.

The dissolution of the government marketing boards represented part of a broader effort to strengthen market conditions within the agricultural sector, an essential part of structural changes in the economy. The commodity boards, formed in 1977 as successors to the earlier regional marketing boards, were notorious for their financial insolvency and their stifling effects on production. The boards recorded declining purchases and mounting losses during nine years of operation. Early in 1986 the government announced that the boards would be liquidated by year's end. Protests by staff representatives of the boards—representing some 20,000 employees—failed to dissuade the government from implementing the generally popular measure. At the end of 1986 the operations of the boards were concluded, and employees received termination notices. The marketing of major export commodities and food crops became the province of the private trading sector.

The liquidation of the Nigerian National Supply Company (NNSC) represented an equally important measure. Established in 1972 to ensure the distribution of strategic consumer commodities at stabilized prices, the NNSC was viewed as an anti-inflationary mechanism in the period of rapid growth during the oil boom. But a government trading company with control over substantial quantities of consumer staples created a potent mechanism of patronage. During the civilian regime, the NNSC became a virtual adjunct to the political machine operated by the ruling National Party of Nigeria. The company remained a valuable resource for well-placed leaders in succeeding regimes and became for most Nigerians the very embodiment of high-level corruption and mismanagement.

The abrupt liquidation of the NNSC by the Babangida government not only removed a prominent symbol of official malfeasance but also illuminated some of the costs and benefits of government patronage. Popular resentment and economic dislocation caused by the inefficient allocation of goods at inflated prices ultimately outweighed the benefits to be garnered by influential officials and their clients.

Early in 1986 the federal government set out to divest its assets in the Nigerian Livestock Production Company (NLPC), one of several federally owned agricultural production companies selected for privatization. The NLPC was a holding company comprising eighteen separate ventures, including the Nigerian Ranches Company, the Bauchi Abattoir, the Nigerian Dairies Company, and the Madara Dairies. The disposal of these assets revealed gaps in government policies and weaknesses in the institutional machinery governing privatization. The NLPC and Nigerian Ranches were liquidated outright, a move announced by the government after the fact. Some of the assets of the dairy companies were sold to private companies, some to the Plateau and Kaduna state governments, and some to the Nigerian Agricultural Cooperative Bank (NACB). The remaining companies were variously transferred to the NACB, northern river basin authorities, and northern state governments.[12]

The reshuffling of NLPC assets among state governments and federal enterprises hardly conforms to most definitions of privatization and reveals some of the political constraints affecting privatization in Nigeria. Federal authorities were swayed by pressures from northern officials to retain the companies in the public sector; the few actual divestitures were effected through private placements carried out under obscure circumstances. The federal government made one brief announcement in the course of the divestiture exercise, and no further information was offered as to the bidding procedures, criteria for evaluation, or conditions of sale. The public and private receivers were reportedly dissatisfied with the valuation of assets, and the lack of publicity attending the exercise fostered inveterate suspicions of preferential treatment for well-connected buyers (Callaghy and Wilson 1988).

Following the privatization decree, the government made greater headway toward both privatization and commercialization. In addition to the divestitures of 1989, tariffs were raised dramatically for electricity, telecommunications, fuel, natural gas, and rail and air services. More than 12,000 employees were retrenched from major federal corporations, and managerial reorganizations were carried out in more than twenty firms. The strong direction of the TCPC, in conjunction with assertive action from the president's office, were the main sources of these measures.

Politics and Privatization

The social and political constituency for privatization in Nigeria is limited. The initiative for public sector reform has issued from the president and a small coterie of senior technocrats. As might be expected, many strong advocates for privatization can be found among Nigeria's organized private sector. The leaders of important domestic industrial and commercial associations, such as the Manufacturers Association of Nigeria and the Lagos Chamber of Commerce, have spoken in favor of the policy, as have the directors of the Stock Exchange and the major banks. Within the civil service and the public enterprise sector, a narrow but influential stratum of high-level technocrats and professionals supports reform and desires greater efficiency in the public sector. These individuals have exerted a crucial impact on the formulation of policy, though their numbers and authority cannot ensure implementation.

Arrayed against the privatization exercise are numerous groups with limited influence on policy but considerable potential to affect implementation. Opposition to privatization has been vocal. Labor leaders and radical academics have issued the most consistent criticisms of the policy, decrying the relinquishment of government control in crucial sectors of the economy. They maintain that privatization will place the nation's "strategic" assets in the hands of a few wealthy individuals, with adverse consequences for government revenues, employment, prices, and mass welfare (Nigerian Labour Congress 1983). The Senior Staff Association of Statutory Corporations and Government-Owned Companies has also spoken out against the policy, contending that higher levels of funding and less political interference would be sufficient to restore the public enterprises to operational health. Behind the public voices of opposition stand legions public sector employees and managers who oppose efforts to reduce the size of government holdings. Opposition has also issued from members of the military government, notably former Governor Abubaker Umar of Kaduna State, who while in office was a proponent of increased state participation in economic and welfare matters.

The politics of privatization in Nigeria reflect a divergence between Nigerian experience and classic models of state capitalism. State actors clearly do not act as a class or "class fraction" with regard to this issue, though it cuts to the very heart of state power and prerogatives. Public enterprise managers have little stake in their positions, since managerial tenure in the public sector is notoriously unstable and public sector executives typically seek mobility to private opportunities. Moreover, as with other elites in Nigerian society, civil servants and public enterprise staff are divided by diverse social cleavages. Interests also diverge along sectoral lines; the chief executive of a steel rolling mill or a cement factory may have little common cause with managers in the Railway Corporation or the Electric Power Authority.

If the Nigerian state has been susceptible to diverse pressures from societal groups, Nigerian governments, especially military regimes, nonetheless have often been able to exercise autonomy from both public and private sector interest groups on specific policy issues. Summary purges within the civil service and public enterprises have prompted surprisingly little resistance. Labor organization in both the public and the private sector is weak, and labor leaders have acceded, albeit grudgingly and intermittently, to many aspects of President Babangida's economic reforms. Nonetheless, the current regime must act carefully to implement a privatization program without provoking opposition from organized state or private constituencies. Buhari learned the bitter lesson that alienation of these groups is costly. Nationalist elements within the military are suspicious of relinquishing state resources, and the support of northern economic elites has always been highly important to regime stability.

These complex tensions create a volatile political environment for privatization, and the intense controversies inherent in a privatization program could jeopardize movement in other areas of government policy. Moreover, the alienation of strategic constituencies among the state bureaucracy, labor groups, or regional elites could undermine the stability of the current leadership. With these considerations in mind, it is understandable that President Babangida, a skillful political tactician, should have chosen to defer action on privatization. It is also likely that government efforts in this area will remain cautious in the near future.

Future Prospects

The political and economic risks inherent in privatization have been underscored by other challenges confronting Nigeria's current regime. The Babangida government is attempting to implement an ambitious economic reform program while averting widespread popular discontent. The regime has also elaborated a program for a return to civilian rule by 1992. Managing the electoral and institutional reforms in the program will be a delicate and arduous process. Initially, the measures entailed by the SAP, linked to the advantages of rescheduling and implemented by a new and relatively popular government, were introduced with a minimum of public opposition. However, three years of privation and economic deterioration, along with continued intractability in the international economic realm, have soured many on the program.[13] In this context, privatization poses both hazards and opportunities. With little latitude in other areas of domestic economic policy, troubled relations with the IMF and international creditors, and little new money coming in, privatization presents one area where the government has wider options. The state can offer assets to embattled domestic business while pursuing policies attractive to external financial institutions.

Moreover, privatization may be used as a new means of distribution in a context where the rentier state has fewer assets to distribute. This aspect of privatization will become increasingly salient as the transition to civilian rule in 1992 approaches. It can provide an important source of largesse to the new political class and other strategic elites in a situation of economic crisis and political change (Wilson 1988: 28). At the very least, it can be expected that traditional channels and means of state patronage will come into play during the process of divestiture of public assets.

The privatization decree framed a bold and far-reaching program. The government has combined direct efforts at divestiture and reform with an ad hoc process of "privatization on the margins," through which smaller federal and state assets are disposed in piecemeal fashion. In November 1987 the National Council of States, the ruling assembly of military state governors, and leaders of the Armed Forces Ruling Council (AFRC) gave states a green light to proceed with their own privatization efforts. Some states, such as Kaduna and Gongola in the north, have officially disavowed any intention to privatize. On the other hand, the eastern states of Imo and Anambra, the western states of Ondo and Ogun, Bendel in the midwest, and Plateau in the middle belt have already initiated efforts at privatization or commercialization of their enterprises, some of which are fairly advanced (*Newswatch* [Lagos], Nov. 30, 1987: 34).

State governments will probably find willing local buyers for such ventures as hotels, laundry services, smaller agro-industries, and soft drinks, soap, and metal manufacturing. These enterprises are modest in size and could be readily placed with local indigenes, allaying fears of inequitable distribution. In Nigeria's declining economy, where foreign exchange is scarce and expensive, credit is tight, imports have diminished, and state expenditures have receded, the chance to acquire public assets may represent one of the few opportunities for domestic entrepreneurs.

The "margins" of Nigeria's huge and complicated public sector are extensive. Assets exist in many forms, from equity shares to physical plant; there are diverse possibilities for redistributing public holdings. The government confronts a range of options, from the frontal, coordinated strategy of divestiture framed by the privatization decree, to a tactic of piecemeal privatizations and transfers within the public sector. Although the AFRC appears to have introduced an aggressive frontal approach, the ad hoc option remains an attractive default position, given the formidable administrative and political impediments entailed by the program. Privatization at the state level could conveniently divert attention from the reform or divestiture of federal enterprises, thus allowing the AFRC a measure of breathing space in policy implementation.

There is reason to question whether the divestiture of state assets will take place in an evenhanded and consistent fashion and whether the new proprietors will produce the efficiency gains desired by many architects and advocates of privatization policy. Privatization could lead to further concentrations of wealth among influential and well-connected business interests. The perceived inequities of a "rigged" privatization exercise would carry repercussions for the competitive political arena in anticipation of 1992 and would exacerbate resentments over government austerity measures.

Beyond issues of equity, a further question is conspicuous: whether the indigenous private sector possesses the resources, the managerial capabilities, or the incentives to supplant a failing public sector. Information on Nigeria's large and fragmented private sector is sparse; consequently, it is difficult to know where the government will find receivers for public assets and whether the new owners can resuscitate moribund government companies. Privatized firms could further deteriorate under mismanagement or willful plunder by investors seeking quick returns on their outlays. Moreover, the results of the program will depend to an important degree on other economic policies. If the government's economic reforms can restructure incentives and improve business conditions, then the divestiture of state companies might occur in a hospitable environment. If major changes do not occur, then the transfer of assets may simply yield continued stagnation.

The privatization program drafted by the Babangida regime represents the most dramatic scheme of economic reform in Nigeria since the indigenization exercise. Whether the policy will realign public-private sector relations in Nigeria and rehabilitate the economy to any degree or will instead aggravate the tensions of distributive politics and degrade the nation's fragile productive infrastructure is the central issue, and indeed the central choice, in the process.

Notes

1. Biersteker (1987: 266–267) notes that state and federal government holdings constituted only 15 percent of the shares on the Stock Exchange in 1982.

2. Nellis (1986: 5) lists Tanzania with the largest number of SOEs, 400, in sub-Saharan Africa. Zambia appears to have the greatest SOE share in GDP, with a figure of 37.5 percent (Short 1984: 118–119). Statistics on the magnitude of Nigeria's SOE sector are notoriously unreliable, but general figures suggest that Nigeria's SOE sector is the largest among sub-Saharan African countries.

3. Press statement by Commodore Ebitu Ukiwe, Chief of General Staff, Lagos, November 27, 1985.

4. Mary Shirley (1983) has noted sectoral and geographic inequities in the pattern of subsidies to public utilities, large industries, and urban commercial enterprises.

5. Among the most prominent of these were the *Report of the Coker Commission of Inquiry into the Affairs of Certain Statutory Corporations in Western Nigeria*

(Lagos: Ministry of Information, 1962); the Ani Commission, published in the *Report of the Working Party on Statutory Corporations and State-Owned Companies* (Lagos: Ministry of Information, 1967); and the Onosode Commission, published as the *Report of the Presidential Commission on Parastatals* (Lagos: Federal Government Printer, 1982). At least forty other government commissions have conducted inquiries ranging from studies of individual projects and companies to broad investigations of state and federal enterprises.

6. Robert Price (1984) has advanced a similar argument with respect to Ghana. Nigeria differs from Ghana in important respects: the size and complexity of the distributive arena; the mediating structures of federalism; and the palliative effects of petroleum revenues, which have paradoxically fostered greater profligacy and staved off economic decay for a slightly longer period than in Ghana.

7. "Moral economy" describes a system of cultural expectations surrounding economic and political affairs; see Scott (1977) for a fuller treatment. Nigerians do not expect equal apportionment of public power and resources as much as they expect broad opportunities to compete for wealth and influence. As Price observed in Ghana, "Although state largesse was certainly never distributed in an egalitarian manner, few, if any, sizeable groups were excluded from the distributional process" (Price 1984: 189).

8. The consultants included Arthur Anderson, Coopers and Lybrand, and the domestic firms PAI Associates, New Decade, Paul Taiwo and Milestone.

9. The companies were Flour Mills of Nigeria, African Petroleum, National Oil and Chemical Company, and United Nigeria Insurance Company. See *West Africa*, October 2–8, 1989.

10. The northern state governments have sought to establish a merchant bank to facilitate share acquisitions by northern investors in privatized companies. Such support may be viewed as an effort to pre-empt southern, especially Yoruba, acquisitions. Several state governments have also made provision in their 1989 budgets for the purchase of shares "in trust" for local residents. See *West Africa*, May 8, 1988.

11. This was illustrated in 1986, when a senior official in the military government intervened to prevent the government of Imo State from leasing a majority interest in the state's oil palm plantations and processing facilities to an Indian-owned agro-industrial firm. The official, a native of Imo, objected to potential "foreign" domination of the state's strategic oil palm industry. See the *Guardian* (Lagos), April 6, 1986.

12. This labyrinthine process is detailed in Callaghy and Wilson (1988).

13. Increased popular opposition to the Structural Adjustment Program has been evident in the escalating public reaction to sucessive petroleum price increases and in the widespread "SAP riots" that engulfed several Nigerian cities in May and June 1989, leaving at least fifty people dead.

References

Ayida, Allison. 1987. "The War Economy in Perspective." In Ayida, *Reflections on the Nigerian Economy*. Ibadan: Heinemann Educational.

Berry, Sarah. 1984. "Searching for the Evidence: African Agriculture in National and International Perspective." *African Studies Review* 27, no. 2: 61–112.

Berry, Sara, and Carl Liedholm. 1970. "Performance of the Nigerian Economy, 1950–1962." In *Growth and Development of the Nigerian Economy*, ed. Carl K. Eicher and Carl Liedholm, 67–85. East Lansing: Michigan State University Press.

Bienen, Henry, 1985. "Oil Revenues and Policy Choice in Nigeria." In Bienen, *Political Conflict and Economic Change in Nigeria*. London: Frank Cass & Co.

Biersteker, Thomas. 1987. *Multinationals, the State, and Control of the Nigerian Economy*. Princeton: Princeton University Press.

Callaghy, Thomas M. 1988. "The State and the Development of Capitalism in Africa." In *The Precarious Balance: State-Society Relations in Africa*, ed. Donald Rothchild and Naomi Chazan. Boulder: Westview Press.

Callaghy, Thomas M., and Ernest J. Wilson III. 1988. "Africa: Policy, Reality or Ritual?" In *The Promise of Privatization: A Challenge for U.S. Foreign Policy*, ed. Raymond Vernon. New York: Council on Foreign Relations.

Central Bank of Nigeria. 1987. *Annual Report and Statement of Accounts for the Year Ended 31st December, 1986*. Lagos: Central Bank of Nigeria.

FitzGerald, E.V.K. 1979. *The Political Economy of Peru 1956–78*. Cambridge: Cambridge University Press.

Forrest, Tom. 1987. "State Capital, Capitalist Development and Class Formation in Nigeria." In *The African Bourgeoisie*, ed. Paul Lubeck, 307–342. Boulder, Colo.: Lynne Reiner.

Helleiner, Gerald K. 1966. *Peasant Agriculture, Government and Economic Development in Nigeria*. Homewood, Ill.: Richard D. Irwin.

Joseph, Richard A. 1983. "Class, State and Prebendal Politics in Nigeria." *Journal of Commonwealth and Comparative Politics* 21, no. 3: 21–38.

Kilby, Peter. 1969. *Industrialization in an Open Economy: Nigeria 1945–1966*. Cambridge: Cambridge University Press.

Nellis, John. 1986. *Public Enterprises in Africa*. Washington, D.C.: World Bank.

Nigeria, Federal Government of. 1979. *The Constitution of the Federal Republic of Nigeria*. Lagos: Federal Government of Nigeria.

_____ 1981. *Report of the Presidential Commission on Parastatals*. Lagos: Federal Government Printer.

Nigeria, Federal Office of Statistics. 1982. *Nigerian Gross Domestic Product and Allied Macro-Aggregates 1973/74–1981*. Lagos: Federal Office of Statistics.

Nigeria, Federal Republic of. 1970. *Second National Development Plan 1970–74*. Lagos: Federal Government Printer.

———. 1986a. *1986 Approved Budget*. Lagos: Federal Government Printer.

———. 1986b. *Structural Adjustment Program July 1986–June 1988*. Federal Government Information Memorandum. November.

———. 1988. *Decree No. 25—Privatization and Commercialization Decree 1988*. In Federal Republic of Nigeria, *Official Gazette* 75, no. 42: A673–A683.

Nigerian Labour Congress. 1983. *Nigeria: Not for Sale*. Lagos: Nigerian Labour Congress.

Odife, Dennis. 1985. *The Challenge of Privatization*. Lagos: Alkestis.

Okigbo, Pius. 1981. *Nigeria's Financial System*. Harlow, Essex: Longman.

Olojede, Dele. 1986. "The Cash Remains the Best." *Newswatch* (Lagos), October 6: 40–42.

Petras, James. 1977. "State Capitalism and the Third World." *Development and Change* 8: 1–17.

Price, Robert M. 1984. "Neocolonialism and Ghana's Economic Decline: A Critical Reassessment." *Canadian Journal of African Studies* 18, no. 1: 163–193.

Rimmer, Douglas. 1981. "Development in Nigeria." In *The Political Economy of Income Distribution in Nigeria*, ed. Henry Bienen and V. P. Diejomaoh. New York: Holmes and Meier.

Sanda, A. O. 1986. "Systematic Planning in the Public Sector." Reprinted in the *Guardian* (Lagos), August 7.

Schatz, Sayre. 1977. *Nigerian Capitalism*. Berkeley: University of California Press.

Scott, James. 1977. *The Moral Economy of the Peasant*. New Haven: Yale University Press.

Shirley, Mary. 1983. *Managing State-Owned Enterprises*. World Bank Staff Working Paper, 577. Washington, D.C.: World Bank.

Short, R. P. 1984. "The Role of Public Enterprises: An International Statistical Comparison." In Robert H. Floyd, Clive S. Gray, and R. P. Short, *Public Enterprises in Mixed Economies*, 111–194. Washington, D.C.: International Monetary Fund.

Thompson, Jato. 1988. "Preparing for the Sale of Decade." *African Business* (April): 33–34.

Waterbury, John. 1983. *The Egypt of Nasser and Sadat*. Princeton: Princeton University Press.

Wilson, Ernest J. III. 1983. "Public Corporation Expansion in Nigeria: Political Interests, State Structure and Government Policy." In *Transformation and Resiliency in Africa*, ed. Pearl T. Robinson and Elliott P. Skinner. Washington, D.C.: Howard University Press.

———. 1988. "Privatization in Africa: Domestic Origins, Current Status and Future Scenarios." *Issue* 16, no. 2: 24–29.

World Bank. 1981. *Nigeria Country Economic Memorandum*. Washington, D.C.: World Bank.

10

The Politics of
Privatization in Africa

Jeffrey Herbst

Ideas to help promote economic development in Africa tend to burst onto the continent with great brilliance and then quickly fade as the initial enthusiasm for the panacea is replaced by disillusionment in the harsh light of reality. Many strategies that were originally championed because of their economic appeal, including import substitution, regional cooperation, and rapid industrialization, have now been discarded as the obstacles, especially the political impediments, become all too clear. Typically, once disillusionment sets in, the search for an entirely new solution begins, with the result that the potentially helpful aspects of the previous approach are lost.

The latest idea to engender great enthusiasm in Africa is privatization: there is now an emerging consensus that African state-owned enterprises are extremely inefficient and tend to drain even more resources from the state than parastatals in other parts of the world. Unfortunately, the reality that many privatization enthusiasts will soon discover is that, because of the political role these corporations play, African governments will not embrace privatization, no matter what the economic reasoning, and will divest parts of their public sectors only grudgingly if they are so required by external donors. Instead of grand ideas that promise a quick solutions but lead only to disillusionment, a more realistic and lasting solution to the fiscal problems of the African state would be incremental reforms to improve public sector operations, along with very selected divestment.

Public Enterprises in Africa

At independence, most African countries did not inherit large public enterprise sectors. Colonial governments, especially in the years immediately preceding independence, had established economic planning boards, parastatals to operate ports and highways, nascent public enterprises to promote industrial expansion, and agricultural marketing boards (Nellis 1986: 12). Even in relatively large colonies, however, like Kenya, Tanzania, Nigeria, Ghana, and Senegal, state enterprises did not play a significant role in the economy (Ghai 1977: 208; Constantin et al. 1979: 9; Hyden 1983: 97). Only the settler colonies, which needed public enterprises to service the white population and regulate the economy, had a significant number of parastatals. Indeed, in some of the places where whites settled a single person (for example, Leopold II in the Belgian Congo) or a single company (for example, the British South Africa Company in Northern and Southern Rhodesia) actually founded and owned the colony, and it was the owners who were forced to divest so that a government could be formed. Overall, however, the public enterprise sector was not a significant aspect of the economy when most African countries received their independence.

It was after independence that the number of public enterprises in Africa exploded. For instance, in Tanzania, public enterprises went from 80 in 1967 to 400 in 1981 (d'Almeida 1986a: 56). Similarly, public enterprises in Kenya increased from 20 at independence to 60 in 1979, while parastatals went from virtually zero in Ghana to more than 100 in the early 1960s. Other countries, including Zambia, Senegal, Mali, the Ivory Coast, Mauritania, and Madagascar also experienced tremendous growth in their public enterprise sectors (Dutheil de la Rochère 1976: 49–51; Constantin et al. 1979; Hyden 1983: 97; Nellis 1986: 56). Although there are no exact figures, the growth of public enterprises in Africa probably was as fast or faster than that in any other part of the world.

As a result of the expansion of state-owned enterprises over the last two decades, public enterprises are now a pervasive influence in Africa. As Table 1 documents, public enterprises play a more important economic

TABLE 1
Public Sector Employment in Comparative Perspective

	Percentage of Nonagricultural Employment			
	OECD* Countries	*Africa*	*Asia*	*Latin America*
Central government	8.7	30.8	13.9	20.7
State-local government	11.6	2.1	8.0	4.2
Nonfinancial public enterprises	4.1	18.7	15.7	5.5
Total public sector employment	24.2	54.4	36.0	27.4

Source: Heller and Tait 1983: 7.
* Organization for Economic Cooperation and Development.

role in terms of employment in Africa than anywhere else in the world. In fact, the table probably underestimates the economic role of state enterprises in Africa because these tend to be capital intensive due to their concentration in the utilities, mining, and manufacturing sectors. Accordingly, Short's data suggest that the share of public enterprises in the gross domestic product (GDP) of African countries is roughly twice as high as in developing countries generally (17.5 percent compared to 8.6 percent) and that the share of African public enterprises in gross fixed capital formation is roughly 20 percent higher (32.4 percent versus 27.0 percent) than in the average developing country (Short 1984: 118).

Unfortunately, even by African standards, the data on public sector enterprise performance is sparse, lacking in consistent definitions, and somewhat contradictory. What little systematic analysis there is, however, suggests that African state-owned enterprises have performed extremely poorly. For instance, in one study of West African countries, 62 percent of the public enterprises showed net losses, and 36 percent had negative net worth (Nellis 1986: 17). Similarly, a study of state-owned transport enterprises in eighteen francophone countries found that only 20 percent generated enough revenue to cover operating costs and depreciation and finance charges; 20 percent covered operating costs plus depreciation; 40 percent barely covered operating costs; and a final 20 percent were far from covering operating costs. Not surprisingly, in Kenya the average rate of return of public enterprises was 0.2 percent; in Niger the net losses of public enterprises amounted to 4 percent of the country's GDP in 1982; and in Tanzania in the late 1970s one-third of all public enterprises ran losses (Nellis 1986: 20). Other studies indicate that in Benin, Mali, Sudan, Nigeria, Mauritania, Zaire, Sierra Leone, and Senegal public enterprises have accumulated losses that sometimes amount to a significant percentage of the total economy (Nellis 1986: 17–19). John Nellis's overall comments on African public enterprises seem apt:

> The conclusion is that African PE's [public enterprises] present a depressing picture of inefficiency, losses, budgetary burdens, poor products and services, and minimal accomplishment of the non-commercial objectives so frequently used to excuse their poor economic performance. Though every African country has one or more PEs which perform well by the most stringent of standards, on the whole, PE sectors are not fulfilling the goals set for them by African planners and leaders. (Nellis 1986: ix)

The reasons for poor performance in public enterprises in Africa are the same as those found elsewhere. As in the rest of the world, employees in African public enterprises have few incentives to work efficiently or provide high-quality services because operating losses are covered by the government and profits usually have to be returned to the national treasury. The general problems of public enterprises in Africa are aggravated by the fact that a disproportionate number of them are monopolies; they therefore do not operate in a competitive environment. Also, many African public enterprises do not have the same auditing requirements as private firms, and the resulting lax financial controls allow for significant abuses (Olisa 1975).

The performance of state-owned enterprises in Africa also suffers because the political considerations of leaders often prevent public companies from raising prices. For example, the desire of government leaders in Zimbabwe to hold inflation to a minimum has kept many state enterprises from raising prices. As a result, the national airline, Air Zimbabwe, at one time had some of the least expensive international fares in the world (therefore subsidizing international tourists and rich Zimbabweans), a ridiculous position for a poor country to adopt (Commission of Inquiry [Smith Commission] 1986). Unable to raise prices, Zimbabwean state enterprises have had to rely on the treasury to cover their deficits and have become a severe burden on the state. In 1984–1985, for instance, subsidies to the food-marketing parastatals, the National Railways of Zimbabwe, Zimbabwe Iron and Steel Company, and Air Zimbabwe totaled almost Z$300 million—equivalent to 40 percent of the national budget deficit (World Bank 1985: 15, 110).

Interference from government officials has also hindered African parastatals from efficiently conducting normal commercial operations. For instance, in their study of public enterprises in thirteen countries across the world, Mahmood Ali Ayub and Sven Olaf Hegstad argue that Ghanaian parastatals achieved an average return of only 18 percent, while inflation increased at a rate of 96 percent, because managers have little autonomy and are subject to extensive controls on even day-to-day operating decisions. Prices are controlled by the Ministry of Finance and Economic Planning; import licenses for parastatals are allocated by the Ministries of Trade and Finance; letters of credit for imports are approved by the Bank of Ghana; the hiring of non-Ghanians is handled by the Ministry of the Interior; and wage negotiations are conducted by the Price and Incomes Board of the Ministry of Finance. In this bureaucratic maze noncommercial considerations affect every aspect of the business (Ayub and Hegstad 1986: 12, 35–36). Parastatal officials across Africa have little incentive to fight ministerial interference because their remuneration is usually not based on their enterprises' performance and because they can advance far by currying favor with high government officials.

Although the problems of African parastatals are typical of state enterprises found elsewhere in the world, the damage done to the national economies by the commercial problems of state-owned enterprises is greater. First, because public enterprises constitute a relatively large portion of each of the African economies, poor performance by parastatals has greater ramifications for each national economy as a whole. Second, because parastatals often have preferential access to lines of credit, incessant borrowing by public enterprises to cover continual operating losses may severely hinder the capital markets in many African countries (Shirley 1983: 15). Finally, the damage done by African parastatals is relatively greater because poor countries simply have fewer resources to squander if they are to have any chance of development. Africa is therefore the continent most in need of privatization.

Two Perspectives on African State and Public Enterprises

Implicit assumptions about the goals of the state in Africa affect any analysis concerning the public enterprise sector and the prospects for divestiture of state-owned enterprises. An explicit examination of the dynamics of the state and its role in the economy is therefore vital to a proper understanding of privatization and to accurate prediction of what will happen in the future. This is especially true in Africa, where we will never have the luxury of simply waiting to see what the data suggest. Unfortunately, no study of privatization in Africa has put forward a coherent view of the dynamics of the African state that allows all aspects of state-public enterprise relations to be understood. In fact, much of the analysis contains assumptions about the African state that are extremely questionable if examined closely. Therefore, this section will analyze the traditional assumptions concerning the state and parastatals and then develop an alternative explanation that stresses the political role of state enterprises in Africa.

The traditional perspective, heavily influenced by public finance economics, argues that states in Africa and elsewhere in the developing world expand their public sectors because of many of the same concerns that have led developed countries to enlarge state-owned enterprises: market failure, ideology, and a general belief that the state can manage certain sectors better. The general assumption is that African states are oriented toward efficiently providing services, although in the past they may have mistakenly overemphasized the efficacy of public enterprises. For instance, V. V. Ramanadham, perhaps the most prolific writer on public enterprises in the Third World, argues that governments in many developing countries have "accumulated a highly diversified public sector" because

(i) the dearth of private entrepreneurship applied even to medium-sized, light industry. . . . (ii) Where the Socialisation of the means of production was the declared policy of the country, there was no alternative for public enterprise but to cover almost all industrial and commercial activity in the country. . . . (iii) The concept of comparative advantage in public, as against private, enterprise has been too generously interpreted in favour of the former in several countries, by intensifying the weights attached to the social content of the operations—such as model employment, low prices and reduction of regional disparities. This has led governments into sectors that might normally be considered as the preserve of private enterprise. (Ramanadham 1984: 109–110)

After comprehensively reviewing the motivations for expanding state enterprises, Armeane M. Choksi also notes:

Most motives for state intervention arise from a variety of market failure involving imperfections in factor markets, paucity of information, and high risk aversion. Thus, entrepreneurial support and entrepreneurial substitution motives of the state are prevalent in activities in which private profitability is low, but social profitability is high. (Choksi 1979: 7)

Although no scholar in this school asserts that political motives are absent from the desire of African countries to enlarge their public sectors, state expansion is mainly attributed to market failure and ideology.

There is an alternative view of the African state and therefore of privatization. This perspective stresses the need of African leaders, especially given their poor economies and weak administrative structures, to try constantly to expand formal state control over society. As Thomas M. Callaghy notes:

For African ruling groups of all ideological and policy persuasions, the need and desire for greater authority over their societies and territories is a primary concern. State formation efforts and class formation constitute the most salient characteristics of the contemporary African condition. To a large extent, authoritarian forms of rule result not from high levels of power and legitimacy, but from the tenuousness of authority and the search for it. (Callaghy 1984: 32)

Instead of seeing the African state expanding because of market failure and the ideological preferences of leaders, this view stresses the political requirements of all African states to dominate their economies by operating a large public enterprise sector. African leaders lack the alternative that many Western countries have employed—simply regulating the private sector—because administrative weaknesses and underdeveloped bureaucracies prevent them from monitoring many commercial transactions in their own economies. To a very real degree, if African countries do not have significant formal ownership in a sector, they can exercise little control over that part of the economy.

The logic of politics in Africa demands that all leaders try to increase the size of their parastatal sector, for several reasons. First, public enterprises provide a source of power because they give politicians access to the kind of free-floating resources for building client networks that are usually rare in impoverished African countries. Tony Killick, after noting that ideology has often been the rationale for the expansion of state-owned enterprises, argues:

> It would also be a mistake to think of ideology as being the only important way in which politics affects the growth of the public sector. There is another set of political arguments, not at all philosophical and rarely given much public ventilation, which has also been influential. Politicians frequently favor public enterprise because they see it as a source of political power: giving them the ability to place friends and supporters in jobs or to provide them with contracts; giving the appearance of determined action and providing the publicity attached to the opening of a new project; perhaps opening up new illicit sources of income for themselves and their parties. (Killick 1981: 279)

State patronage is especially important in Africa because there are very few means of economic advancement outside of the state. Indeed, as early as 1962 the Coker Commission found that the Action Group in western Nigeria was siphoning off money from parastatals to fund political activities (Commission of Inquiry [Coker Commission] 1962). Similarly, David Fashole Luke explains that the parastatal sector in Sierra Leone expanded after the death of Prime Minister Sir Milton Margai because the new prime minister (his brother, Albert Margai) needed to "consolidate his political base (via the patron-clientelist network of the Sierra Leone People's Party) by opening up new areas for the award of contracts and for appointments to positions in the new or expanded organisations" (Luke 1984: 77). Even advocates of the market failure explanation find that they must resort to analyzing the political imperatives of leaders when explaining the growth of state-owned enterprises in specific countries. For instance, Choksi, after arguing that market failure usually explains the state's expansion of public enterprises, admits that public projects in Ghana tended to be impressive and visible in order to reflect nationalistic aspirations; they were also primarily used to generate mass employment opportunities. This concern with project visibility and employment generation, however, conflicted with the objective of operating a profitable state enterprise. (Choksi 1979: 30)

The desire to use public enterprises for political purposes has undoubtedly increased in recent years as other sources of revenue that African leaders could divert to support cliental networks have dwindled (Kjellstrom 1985–1986: 69).

State-owned enterprises are a particularly attractive source of patronage to both leaders and their clients because parastatals provide numerous relatively discreet ways for leaders to reward followers. Instead of outright cash grants, which would be potentially embarrassing in all but the most corrupt countries, state-owned enterprises offer a wide variety of hidden benefits and subsidies that guarantee substantial rewards to clients without being too ostentatious. For instance, the Mwanakatwe Report noted that "in addition to receiving subsidised housing and furniture," top Zambian parastatal officials enjoy "an entertainment allowance, a free car with petrol provided, water, telephone and electricity bills paid, servants' wages, security guards provided day and night and the benefit of medical aid contributions." Each official also has "generous leave and pension arrangements and may receive a bonus, [and] can be individually supported by his employers to a value greater that that of the annual basic salary he earns" (quoted in Szeftel 1982: 6).

Public enterprises also allow African governments to exert explicit control over spheres of the economy that are otherwise beyond the reach of the state. In developed countries, control can be exercised through a number of regulatory devices, ranging from observation to mandating certain performance standards. In general, however, the regulatory option is not open to African countries because they have extraordinarily weak administrative structures and their statistical infrastructure is underdeveloped. For instance, in studying the indigenization policy in Nigeria, Thomas Biersteker found that the state was consistently unable to monitor efforts by foreign companies to circumvent official degrees or to enforce some aspects of the announced policy because of weak administrative structures. In the end, the government was unable to implement its indigenization program effectively.[1]

Similarly, in Zimbabwe the government believed that it had to create the Minerals Marketing Corporation of Zimbabwe because it did not believe it was capable of regulating multinational companies. The minister of mines, Maurice Nyagumbo, argued in Parliament that *no* form of regulation in the existing free enterprise system could effectively regulate the mining industry:

> Despite the offer by the Chamber of Mines to examine books of its members, I can assure honourable members that no company is prepared to disclose to Government in what manner it is abusing this system. The present system of control depends on the good faith of too many private producers and metal brokers, and offers numerous loopholes for underinvoicing and transfer pricing. (*Hansard*, Jan. 26, 1982: 1382)

In one of the more explicit statements of the desires of an African state, Minister Nyagumbo argued that private enterprise could not continue to dominate the mining sector: "In the main, therefore, the production and disposal of minerals is not within Government's control. This situation is totally unacceptable in our new social order" (*Herald* [Harare], July 25, 1981).

African countries have guaranteed regulatory control over their economies only in areas such as the legal importation of goods, where the physical nature of the activity (for example, bringing goods through one port) allows for observation and therefore control and regulation. As a result, many African governments rely on tariffs rather than market value exchange rates to control imports. Outside these relatively few areas where direct control is possible, African governments have only limited means of controlling their economies.

State-owned enterprises therefore play an important role in all African countries, regardless of ideology. For instance, parastatals are important in both Kenya and Tanzania, a pair usually highlighted for their ideological differences, because of the role these enterprises play in giving the state control over the economy. The Kenyan government, while reviewing the role of parastatals, claimed: "The real significance of these new institutions is as policy instruments" (Kenya 1974: 37). Similarly, in Tanzania the *Presidential Circular on the Rationalization of the Parastatal Organizations* noted: "Broad policy is a matter for the elected TANU Government of Tanzania and the parastatals organizations are instruments of execution—tools which must be used by the policymakers, and which must be at the command of the responsible authorities" (quoted in Nowrojee 1977: 177). Political considerations also were partly responsible for the fact that in nominally capitalist countries such as the Ivory Coast and Nigeria, which were relatively open to foreign investment, "the share of their public sectors in industrial equity capital rose from 10 and 22 percent in the 1960s to 24 and 38 percent, respectively, in 1975" (Steel and Evans 1984: 60). Given the ubiquity of state enterprises, Niles E. Helmboldt and Benjamin H. Hardy correctly conclude:

The first post-independence generation reserved to the state the economic functions that should have been left to the people. Everywhere in independent Africa, governments took on excessive economic responsibilities. . . . State-owned corporations entered every sector of the economy. . . . Ideology actually had very little to do with this; it happened whether the leaders were from the left or the right. (Helmboldt and Hardy 1985: 82–83)

There is nothing peculiarly African about the desire of extremely weak countries to expand their public sectors in order to gain greater control over their domestic economies and minimize the risk of insecurity. Indeed, many have probably underestimated the political role that state-owned enterprises play in developed countries. But because African countries are the poorest in the world, their drive to control as much as possible through the state is stronger than that in countries that are richer and therefore have more buffers against the international economy and greater actual ability to regulate a private sector. In fact, cross-national research finds a reasonably clear inverse correlation between income and size of the public enterprise sector. For instance, Peter S. Heller and Alan A. Tait conclude:

the share of [nonfinancial public] enterprises among the nonagriculturally employed declines hyperbolically as per capita income rises. The effect of this latter relationship is to ensure that the share of public sector employment among the nonagriculturally employed declines with per capita income, with the rate of decline greater among countries at per capita income levels that are above US $600.[2]

Heller and Tait found that, across their sample, 72 percent of the variance in nonfinancial public enterprise employment can be explained by the inverse of per capita income (Heller and Tait 1983: 15).

Given the realities of Africa, the political perspective on state-public enterprise relations offers a better explanation than the classical position on why parastatals have such a pervasive influence in Africa. The political perspective looks to the actual incentives of African leaders, given the administrative and economic realities of their countries, and does not make the common mistake of simply transferring models from Europe to Africa. The evidence, albeit fragmentary, also supports the main assumptions of the political perspective on state-public enterprise relations. This is not to say that the factors identified by the traditional approach, especially ideology, are not at all related to the expansion of public enterprises in Africa. Clearly, ideology does make a difference in the degree to which parastatals are present in any one economy and may explain the differences between African countries; but by itself ideology is not adequate for understanding the much greater role of parastatals in Africa compared to any other group of countries.

It is also true that African private sectors are weak; however, as Nellis notes, the weakness of those sectors "is most often stressed by those who have an ideological or a vested interest in maintaining the power of the public sector" (Nellis 1986: 43). Indeed, it was precisely because the private sector was so strong that the Zimbabwean government felt it necessary to create another parastatal in the mining sector. Market failure is also a legitimate concern in Africa. The new appreciation of privatization among many analysts suggests, however, that the degree of market failure in many African countries is being re-evaluated. Given the poor economic performance of African parastatals over the last few years, it is hard to say that these public enterprises were ever designed to counter market failure.

Perspectives on Privatization

According to those who see primarily market and ideological reasons for state expansion, the move toward privatization in Africa and elsewhere in the developing world is the logical result of the pragmatic realization that state-owned enterprises are significant drains on government budgets and of the waning of the interventionist ideologies that flourished in the 1960s. Thus J. T. Winpenny writes:

> In their approach to privatization, the governments of most developing countries are pragmatic and expedient, rather than ideological. Likewise, despite a widespread belief to the contrary, aid donors are not urging privatization onto reluctant aid recipients. The majority of donors are guided by pragmatism and realism. (Winpenny 1987: 400)

Similarly, Elliot Berg argues that the motivation for public divestiture comes mainly from judgments within Third World countries about the performance of the state-owned sector:

> The dominant perception or sentiment in many LDCs is thus that SOEs [state-owned enterprises] are mostly failures: inefficiently managed, inadequately controlled, deficit-ridden and hence absorbers of development resources, not generators of them. This perception, combined with slower growth and scarcer public revenues in the 1980s, explains the present concern with rehabilitation and reform of public enterprise sectors, as part of overall public sector restructuring. (Berg 1985: 1–2)

The resurgence of a free enterprise ideology under the sponsorship of the Reagan and Thatcher administrations is also stressed as another reason for the current interest in privatization throughout Africa (d'Almeida 1986a: 58–59).

Correspondingly, scholars who base their analysis on the classical position see primarily economic and technical factors standing in the way of state divestiture now that African governments have changed their ideology. For instance, many scholars have identified the lack of a capital market (significant stock markets exist only in Lagos, Abidjan, Harare, and Nairobi) as one of the key barriers to privatization: African states will not be able to adopt the method used by European countries to privatize (Young 1987: 201). Some believe that the capital market issue alone will not only prevent privatization but also cause the public enterprise sector to grow. Jonathan Aylen argues that the "weakness of capital markets in developing countries is a major obstacle to plans for privatization. For this reason alone, public enterprises seem more likely to grow in importance rather than decline." It is "not realistic to suppose that direct [foreign] investment will compensate for failure of domestic equity markets" (Aylen 1987: 23).

Therefore, many scholars who favor privatization argue that important reforms in the economic structure of African countries have to be made before privatization can occur. For instance, Ayité-Fily d'Almeida contends that privatization in Africa depends on the creation of an appropriate institutional and economic setting and the provision of technical advice by international agencies (d'Almeida 1986b: 74). Similarly, Elliot Berg and Mary M. Shirley, in their study of privatization efforts in twenty-four developing countries, conclude that privatization can best be promoted by creating a better policy environment, fostering a special administrative capacity dedicated to divestiture, and providing better technical advice from the IMF and others (Berg and Shirley 1987: 18).

The favorite case study for those who argue that privatization is possible in Africa if the right conditions are met is Togo. There ideology has changed because President Eyadéma has now recognized the virtues of the private sector and has appointed a leading business man to preside over the privatization of a significant number of state enterprises (Winpenny 1987: 399).

Of its seventy state companies, Togo hopes to liquidate eight state enterprises and to privatize eighteen others (Djondo 1988: 16). So far, the major accomplishment of this privatization process has been to lease a state-owned steel mill to an American entrepreneur.

The political perspective on privatization stresses a different motivation for privatization. If public enterprises play the very real political role identified above, it is difficult to believe that African policymakers will suddenly divest them because of new-found concerns about efficiency and a return to neoclassical economics. Indeed, policymakers have long pursued disastrous economic measures because of the logic of the political game in Africa. For instance, many African governments have purposely kept agricultural prices low even though these policies are self-evidently destructive (see Bates 1981). Public enterprises play such an important role in consolidating the political power of leaders that it is unlikely that shifts in ideology alone will cause a significant change in the relationship between the state and the economy in the vast majority of African countries.

The real motivation for divestiture in Africa is not change in ideology or re-evaluation of the commercial benefits of public enterprises but the political power exercised by the World Bank, the IMF, and donor agencies, especially the U.S. Agency for International Development (AID), in convincing African leaders to adjust their economies structurally. If the political perspective is adopted, it makes sense for a country to begin divesting politically beneficial enterprises if there is a significant political disadvantage in keeping them. The holding of public enterprises becomes less advantageous to African leaders when the aid and debt relief they need to survive their current fiscal and economic crises depend on compliance with outside demands for privatization as an integral aspect of structural adjustment. Therefore, by far the best predictor of divestment will be not how effectively African countries can establish a better policy environment or special administrative apparatuses but simply how heavily international financial organizations and aid donors can lean on African countries in order to force them to liquidate or privatize poorly performing state enterprises.

Much of the current interest in privatization in Africa can, in fact, be traced directly to the demands of foreign actors that Third World countries rationalize their public sectors. For instance, the United States increasingly conditions balance of payment assistance to African countries (totaling $240 million in 1985) and project assistance ($70 million in 1985) on the achievement of structural reforms, including privatization (Whitehead 1985: 22). In fact, AID now requires many of its Africa missions to be involved in at least two privatization projects per year (U.S. Agency for International Development 1986: 4). The IMF's new structural adjustment facility also has supported liquidation or privatization in fourteen developing countries, most of them in Africa; given that almost all African countries are eligible for this facility, the IMF will undoubtedly continue to press for liquidation or privatization across the continent in the next few years (Bell and Sheehy 1987: 8–9). Similarly, the World Bank has made liquidation of nonviable public enterprises a condition of structural adjustment lending in Burundi and Malawi and has encouraged divestiture in Togo, the Congo, and several other African countries (Shirley 1988: 43). Increasingly, the structural adjustment demands of these different agencies have been coordinated to make reform, including privatization, more attractive to African countries. In Rwanda, for example, the U.S. policy reform program "carried the policy dialogue beyond the project level and is the leading edge of what will be a major structural reform program by the World Bank" (Whitehead 1985: 42).

Therefore, countries that are suffering the most from economic crisis will be the most likely at least to demonstrate a commitment to privatization because they are most susceptible to external influence. After reviewing the record of the World Bank, Don Babai concluded that "the ability of international institutions to push privatization increases directly with the borrower's level of desperation" (Babai 1988: 269). Therefore, countries in crisis like Togo have shown at least some commitment to privatization, while much richer countries like Kenya and Zimbabwe have been more hesitant. This prediction is in contrast to the analysis of those who argue that capital markets and other technical considerations are the main barriers to privatization because countries in the worst economic positions will have the weakest capital markets and the least amenable economic environments for privatization.

Countries will also be less likely to privatize if the extention of control is such an important aspect of their political projects that placating the IMF and other foreign actors is not considered a significant issue. For instance, in Zimbabwe the idea of extending control is so central to the leadership's political project ten years after independence that no international agency or foreign government even suggests that the government begin divesting public enterprises. The most that foreign actors have done is to try to persuade the national leadership to slow down its expansion of the parastatal sector.

Other than the political pressure brought about by the United States, the World Bank, and the IMF, there are almost no incentives for African countries to divest. Although the worldwide move toward free markets has affected Africa, the significant ideological shifts experienced by other countries have not taken place there. In many countries the state is still seen as playing the primary economic role because of the political incentives that most African leaders face. Even in Togo, uniformly hailed for its privatization efforts, "The presence of the state will be maintained for economic units which have a mission of public service (water, energy, ports), which play a fundamental role in the development of national resources (agriculture, mining, tourism), or which make a substantial contribution to the financial revenues of the state" (*Bulletin de l'Afrique Noire* 1986: 3). After all the contemplated privatizations, the public enterprise sector in Togo will still have an annual turnover of 180 billion CFA Francs, while the assets of the privatized companies are valued at only 4.65 billion (Djondo 1988: 18). Similarly, even in countries that emphasize privatization, such as the Ivory Coast, Ghana, Madagascar, and Senegal, the public sector will continue to control substantial resources for the foreseeable future (Steel 1988: 30). Indeed, if the economic crisis of Africa were to ease, it is likely that many states would try to expand their public enterprise sector again because the fundamental political considerations that leaders face have not changed.

Voluntary privatization is especially unlikely in Africa because leaders will not receive any of the political advantages that governments in other countries have achieved. For instance, African leaders cannot simply sell the shares of their publicly owned companies, as the United Kingdom did, because few state-owned enterprises are commercially viable and because the public at large simply lacks the means of purchase. There is, therefore, no chance to create a climate for "popular capitalism" (assuming African leaders want such an environment). Correspondingly, African countries cannot gain the advantage of deflecting labor movements' protests away from the state when privatizing, as has been the case in Chile, because trade unions are weak in Africa and because most governments have already found adequate ways of stifling worker protests.

In fact, voluntary privatization is extremely unattractive to African countries because state enterprises, if they could be sold, would be purchased by the economically wealthy (Westerners, foreign businessmen such as Indians, or wealthy individuals from certain ethnic groups)—precisely the people to whom African governments do not want to yield control. In Zimbabwe, for instance, only whites or foreigners have sufficient funds to purchase large businesses, and both of these groups are patently unacceptable to the government because it does not want economic power accumulating outside the state. Similarly, in Kenya a task force has been reviewing four hundred state-owned enterprises for three years. Yet in this country with a relatively sophisticated capital market no privatizations have occurred because of government concerns that only foreigners or politically unacceptable local citizens (Indians or Kikuyus) could purchase the companies from the state (Cowan 1987: 15). Only in cases such as the Ivory Coast, where many of the privatized firms have been sold to close allies of the president, will privatization not be politically threatening. It is not that African countries do not have adequate capital markets to privatize at least some companies; rather, what they really lack is politically acceptable capital markets.

Furthermore, privatization that is not encouraged or even forced by foreign actors is unlikely because African countries will not receive the revenue windfalls that have attended the sales of public companies in other countries. Precisely because they were created and expanded for mainly political reasons, many African parastatals will never be viable and therefore need to be liquidated, not privatized. Indeed, some of the privatizations that have occurred in Africa were conducted under terms financially disadvantageous to the state. For instance, the heralded steel mill in Togo was sold because the buyer was given a lease that will cover only 5 percent of the enterprise's annual debt service. The overdue interest and penalties alone will amount to more than the government will probably receive from the entire ten years of the mill's operation. The new owner also enjoys an effective 41 percent protection rate, special privileges to import competing materials, duty-free import of raw materials, and duty-free export of finished goods. Finally, he collects a management fee, receives all profits after taxes, and will get the audited book value of all improvements in the steel mill if the government does not renew the lease (Berg 1985: 9). Berg, falling back on classic protectionist logic, argues that, although "on economic grounds, Togo might have been better off to close the mill and sell the equipment . . . over 150 Togolese have found employment and there are intangible effects whose consequences can't be predicted" (Berg 1985: 9). On the contrary, unless the alternative was for the Togolese to burn the money that is subsidizing the steel mill operator, the country would have been far better off liquidating the plant.

Trends in Privatization

Estimates of the extent of privatization in Africa are extremely poor. There has been no systematic evaluation of divestiture across the continent, and several countries have recently undergone dramatic policy reversals. Berg and Shirley's data, collected in 1985, suggest that liquidations are the most common form of privatization in Africa, with fourteen countries having liquidated a total of 108 enterprises (Berg and Shirley 1987: 21). These same fourteen countries have targeted 306 enterprises for sale, but only 30 have actually been privatized. The enthusiasm for pronouncing ambitious privatization projects but not implementing them is not at all surprising, given the political incentives leaders face. Indeed, leaders have strong motivations to design extensive privatization programs in order to appear to be complying with structural adjustment programs and then to avoid implementing those programs because of their domestic political concerns. Privatizations—or, more likely, liquidations—will therefore be implemented only hesitatingly, as agencies like the IMF begin to evaluate announced structural adjustment programs and seek to force countries to fulfill the ambitious plans they proclaimed.

Although many observers will likely attribute delays in meeting privatization schedules to problems in capital markets or the technical environment, it should be clear that African governments have very real incentives to announce wide-ranging programs but do very little to meet those objectives.

Correspondingly, management and leasing provisions have been more popular in the countries Berg and Shirley surveyed (a total of forty implemented), in part because ceding temporary control of an enterprise to the private sector is more attractive to African leaders than outright privatization (Berg and Shirley 1987: 22–23). With leasing and management agreements, leaders can still hope to influence the operation of the company, and they may believe that they will be able to take over operations again when they are no longer subject to structural adjustment provisions. Although no region needs privatization (including liquidation) more, divestiture will be slowest in Africa.

Conclusions

An unfortunate aspect of much of the current writing on privatization in Africa and elsewhere is the almost exclusive concentration on the process of divestiture. In many works a significant amount of attention is devoted to technical questions, such as the means of financing or establishing a viable macroeconomic climate, while the dynamics of parastatals themselves are ignored (see Hanke 1987). Questions concerning the means of financing privatization are important; but analysis of the privatization process in isolation is premature. To understand the issues raised by divestiture, we must first understand the role of state-owned enterprises in the political economy of the nation. If the political role of private enterprises in Africa is recognized, then certain paradoxes that have emerged as Africa confronts the issue of divestiture can be explained. Given the political perspective developed here, it makes sense why Africa is the continent most in need of privatization but least likely to divest state-owned enterprises; why poor countries experiencing severe economic and fiscal difficulties will be more enthusiastic about privatization than richer countries with developed capital markets; and why many more privatization programs will be announced than will ever be implemented.

Given the political realities, privatization by itself will never be an important element in the battle to promote economic development in Africa because African elites will always have an incentive to maintain a large public sector. There is some room for privatization, but divestment probably will never be a significant aspect of the solution to the fiscal problems of the African state. Instead, reforms of the public sector itself, aimed at allowing state-owned enterprises to operate more effectively, are probably a more productive and lasting approach to some of the problems of African parastatals. Reforms that would bring about better accounting, more efficient management practices, and some isolation of state-owned corporations from the whims of government leaders would address at least some of the problems of the public sector in Africa without requiring leaders to challenge their own political power bases. Such public sector reforms are less spectacular than privatization, but they have a much better chance of succeeding. It is to be hoped that incremental reforms that promote sustained development will capture the imagination of those concerned with Africa's economic health so that we do not continue the search for the chimera of "a solution" to Africa's economic woes while ignoring practical changes that could make a difference.

Notes

Funding for this research was provided by the Pew Foundation Charitable Trust. I am grateful to Mark Gersovitz, John Waterbury, and the participants of the privatization project at Princeton for helpful comments on an earlier version of this chapter.

1. Although Nigeria's indigenization program did place unusually heavy administrative burdens on the state, it is still an instructive case study, because indigenization is one of the few alternatives to public enterprises for an African government concerned about gaining control of its economy. See Biersteker 1987: 292.

2. Heller and Tait 1983: 16. The World Bank estimated in 1983 that 26 of 45 developing countries with per capita incomes of less than US $600 were in Africa (World Bank 1983: 148).

References

d'Almeida, Ayité-Fily. 1986a. "La privatisation des entreprises publiques en Afrique au sud du Sahara—Premiere partie." *Le Mois en Afrique*, no. 245–246: 55–70.

————. 1986b. "La privatisation des enterprises publiques en Afrique au sud du Sahara—Deuxieme partie." *Le Mois en Afrique*, no. 247–248: 67–96.

Aylen, Jonathan. 1987. "Privatization in Developing Countries." *Lloyds Bank Review*, no. 163: 15–30.

Ayub, Mahmood Ali, and Sven Olaf Hegstad. 1986. *Public Industrial Enterprises: Determinants of Performance*. Industry and Finance Series, 17. Washington, D.C.: World Bank.

Babai, Don. 1988. "The World Bank and the IMF: Rolling Back the State or Backing Its Role." In *The Promise of Privatization*, ed. Raymond Vernon. New York: Council on Foreign Relations.

Bates, Robert H. 1981. *Markets and States in Tropical Africa*. Berkeley: University of California Press.

Bell, Michael W., and Robert L. Sheehy. 1987. "Helping Structural Adjustment in Low-Income Countries." *Finance & Development* 24, no. 4: 6–10.

Berg, Elliot. 1985. "Divestiture of State-Owned Enterprises in LDCs." Mimeographed.

Berg, Elliot, and Mary M. Shirley. 1987. *Divestiture in Developing Countries*. World Bank Discussion Paper, 11. Washington, D.C.: World Bank.

Biersteker, Thomas J. 1987. *Multinationals, the State, and Control of the Nigerian Economy*. Princeton: Princeton University Press.

Bulletin de l'Afrique Noire. 1986. "Togo." No. 1322, June 19.

Callaghy, Thomas M. 1984. *The State-Society Struggle: Zaire in Comparative Perspective*. New York: Columbia University Press.

Choksi, Armeane M. 1979. *State Intervention in the Industrialization of Developing Countries: Selected Issues*. World Bank Staff Working Paper, 341. Washington, D.C.: World Bank.

Commission of Inquiry into Parastatals (Smith Commission). 1986. *Air Zimbabwe Corporation*. Harare: Government Printer.

Commission of Inquiry into the Affairs of Certain Statutory Corporations in Western Nigeria (Coker Commission). 1962. *Report of Coker Commission of Inquiry into the Affairs of Certain Statutory Corporations in Western Nigeria*. Volume 1. Lagos: Federal Ministry of Information.

Constantin, F., et al. 1979. *Les enterprises publiques en Afrique Noire*. Volume 1. Paris: Centre d'Étude d'Afrique Noire.

Cowan, L. Gray. 1987. "A Global Overview of Privatization." In Hanke 1987.

Djondo, Koffi. 1988. "Anatomy of a Privatisation Scheme: The Togo Example." *African Business*, no. 114 (February): 16–18.

Dutheil de la Rochère, Jacqueline. 1976. *L'état de la développement économique de la Côte d'Ivoire*. Paris: Centre d'Étude d'Afrique Noire.

Ghai, Yash. 1977. "Law and Public Enterprise in Tanzania." In *Law in the Political Economy of Public Enterprises: African Perspectives*, ed. Yash Ghai. Uppsala: Scandinavian Institute of African Studies.

Hanke, Steve H., ed. 1987. *Privatization and Development*. San Francisco: Institute for Contemporary Studies.

Heller, Peter S., and Alan A. Tait. 1983. *Government Employment and Pay: Some International Comparisons*. Washington, D.C.: International Monetary Fund.

Helmboldt, Niles E., and Benjamin H. Hardy. 1985. "Hope for Africa." In U.S. Congress, Senate Subcommittee on African Affairs, *African Debt Crisis*. 99th Congress, 1st sess., October 24.

Hyden, Goran. 1983. *No Shortcuts to Progress*. Berkeley: University of California Press.

Kenya. 1974. *Development Plan 1974–1978*. Nairobi: Government Printer.

Killick, Tony. 1981. *Policy Economics*. London: Heinemann.

Kjellstrom, Sven B. 1985–1986. "Rationalité économique et impératifs politiques en Afrique au Sud du Sahara." *Le Mois en Afrique*, no. 239–240: 69–96.

Luke, David Fashole. 1984. *Labour and Parastatal Politics in Sierra Leone*. New York: University Press of America.

Nellis, John R. 1986. *Public Enterprises in Sub-Saharan Africa*. World Bank Discussion Paper, 1. Washington, D.C.: World Bank.

Nowrojee, Pheroze. 1974. "Public Enterprises in Kenya." In *Law in the Political Economy of Public Enterprises: African Perspectives*, ed. Yash Ghai. Uppsala: Scandanavian Institute of African Studies.

Olisa, M. S. 1975. "Factors Affecting the Performance of Public Corporations in Nigeria." In *A Decade of Public Administration in Africa*, ed. Anthony H. Rweyemamu and Goran Hyden. Nairobi: East African Literature Bureau.

Ramanadham, V. V. 1984. *The Nature of Public Enterprise*. New York: St. Martin's Press.

Rothchild, Donald. 1987. "Hegemony and State Softness: Some Variations in Elite Responses." In *The African State in Transition*, ed. Zaki Ergas. London: Macmillan.

Shirley, Mary M. 1983. *Managing State-Owned Enterprises*. World Bank Staff Working Paper, 577. Washington, D.C.: World Bank.

———. 1988. "Promoting the Private Sector." *Finance & Development* 25, no. 1: 40–43.

Short, R. P. 1984. "The Role of Public Enterprises: An International Statistical Comparison." In Robert H. Floyd et al., *Public Enterprises in Mixed Economies*. Washington, D.C.: International Monetary Fund.

Steel, William F. 1988. "Adjusting Industrial Policy in Sub-Saharan Africa." *Finance & Development* 25, no. 1: 36–39.

Steel, William F., and Jonathan W. Evans. 1984. *Industrialization in Sub-Saharan Africa*. World Bank Technical Paper, 25. Washington, D.C.: World Bank.

Szeftel, Morris. 1982. "Political Graft and the Spoils System in Zambia—The State as a Resource in Itself." *Review of African Political Economy*, no. 24: 4–21.

U.S. Agency for International Development (AID). 1987. *Policy Determination: Implementing AID Privatization Objectives*. Washington, D.C.: AID. Excerpted in Office of Policy Development and Policy Review, *Privatization: A Technical Assessment*. Washington, D.C.: AID.

Whitehead, John C. 1985. "Statement of John C. Whitehead." U.S. Congress, Senate Subcommittee on Africa, *African Debt Crisis*. 99th Congress, 1st sess., October 24.

Winpenny, J. T. 1987. "The Divestiture of Public Enterprises in Developing Countries." *Development Policy Review* 5, no. 4: 399–406.

World Bank. 1983. *World Development Report 1983*. Washington, D.C.: Oxford University Press.

_____. 1985. *Zimbabwe Country Economic Memorandum*. Washington, D.C.: World Bank.

Young, Peter. 1987. "Privatization around the World." In Hanke 1987.

11

Nicaragua's State Enterprises: Revolutionary Expectations and State Capacity

Forrest D. Colburn

In directing the construction and defense of the Soviet Union at its inception, Lenin argued for nationalization not of the entire economy but of only its most important sectors, what he described as the "commanding heights." This suggestive phrase, and the maxim behind it, is one of Lenin's enduring legacies for leaders of contemporary revolutions. But even when revolutionary elites have not been so inspired by Lenin and the program he articulated to transform Russia—as in Iran—they too have sought to nationalize key sectors of the economy, whether diamond mines or sugar estates. Nationalization is invariably the most consequential economic change in the initial postrevolutionary epoch, and it is held to be instrumental in the transition to some self-defined improved form of government.

This chapter explores the management of Nicaragua's commanding heights by the Sandinista National Liberation Front (FSLN), with emphasis on the critical agrarian sector. Upon ending more than forty years of rule by the Somozas in July 1979, the Sandinistas expropriated the extensive holdings of the family and of individuals intimately linked to the dictatorship. More than two thousand agricultural estates and enterprises were confiscated, ranging from small farms to huge cattle ranches to sugar refineries and representing one-fourth of Nicaragua's land under cultivation and an even higher percentage of the means to process agricultural products. The Somozas' enormous investment—and the Sandinistas' endowment—in agriculture reflects the largely agrarian nature of the Nicaraguan economy. Eighty percent of exports, so necessary to a small state, are derived from agriculture. Despite continual migration to urban areas, the majority of Nicaraguans still earn their living from the land.

Also seized from the Somozas and their associates were 130 industrial or commercial enterprises, ranging from a cement factory to a Mercedes-Benz dealership. Foreign investments were not nationalized, with the exception of a handful of small gold mines owned by two companies, one American and one Canadian. The Sandinistas further enhanced their influence over the Nicaraguan economy by nationalizing the country's banking and insurance systems and by placing all foreign trade under the control of state monopsonies. Finally, they conferred upon themselves broad powers to regulate the private sector.

Private sector control over an estimated 65 percent of the Nicaraguan economy meant that from the beginning of Sandinista rule the outcome of many state initiatives depended on the dialectical performance of the state and countless economic actors. The regime was also constrained by the activities of the defeated "enemies of the revolution," by the vagaries of the international economy, and by international politics—in particular, relations with the "colossus to the north." Still, the consolidation of political power and the nationalization of property enabled the Sandinistas to implement, in diverse settings and locales, their vision of how civil society should be organized. Of significance are not only the intentions of such efforts but also the demonstrated capacity of the state.

The argument I advance here is dyadic: the Sandinista bid to manage enterprises has been economically unsuccessful but politically successful. There are some wrinkles, however. First, while state enterprises are grossly inefficient, they have produced significant results. To use Joseph Schumpter's analogy, economic performance has been like James Watt's first steam engine: it produced power, yet the piston wobbled loosely in the cylinder and hammered and pounded and hissed large quantities of wasted energy into the air. The inefficient management of Nicaragua's state enterprises is troublesome not only because it results in a loss of scarce resources but also because it generates distortions throughout the economy, principally by contributing to the debasement of currency. The inescapable conclusion is that the state sector has been anything but the economic vanguard. Instead, it weakens the economy, exacerbating the exogenous constraints on the possibilities of radical change. Similarly, the poor economic performance of state enterprises exacerbates, rather than alleviates, the structural obstacles to improving popular welfare.

But while state enterprises in Nicaragua are problematic economically, they are useful politically in a number of distinct ways. They serve as a model, if only a preliminary one, of how work should be organized, showing especially how social relations within a firm should be handled in contradistinction to the old order. State enterprises serve as a counterpoint to the private sector; by suggesting an alternative to private management and embodying the threat of nationalization, they can pressure private entrepreneurs and managers into at least superficially meeting state demands. Also, the state's willingness to intercede economically deters intended or unintended sabotage by members of the private sector who drag their feet or abandon their enterprises. More immediately, the enterprises serve as outposts of the state, especially in the case of state farms in isolated areas. As branches of the government, they can facilitate the distribution of a host of services, from providing medical care, to offering transportation to visiting officials, to feeding soldiers. Finally, state enterprises provide patronage-like benefits to the local population, principally employment. At the same time, recipients are a captive audience for government propaganda and directives. Thus, state enterprises provide a host of political advantages or, in other words, political strength to a new regime—a regime that is ambitious but inexperienced and confronted with enemies.

The wrinkle in the political contribution of state enterprises is that their invariable inefficiency, usually manifested through financial losses, can be an embarrassment. The legitimacy of a postrevolutionary regime can be eroded by general economic woes and by specific instances of incompetence. Still, although the loss of legitimacy stemming from economic inefficiency may be significant, it should be emphasized that economic performance is only one of the many factors that influence a regime's legitimacy and that the perceived alternative—the private sector—may for different reasons enjoy even less legitimacy. Equally important, political problems engendered by economic inefficiency are general and dispersed, whereas the political benefits of state enterprises are more immediate and locale-bound.

Establishing State Enterprises

The triumph of the FSLN in ousting Somoza and in subsequently consolidating power led to the strengthening of state authority and the growth of state responsibilities. Existing programs and activities were expanded, most significantly in health and education. Wages, working conditions, and management-labor relations received enhanced attention from a number of government agencies. Defense spending increased substantially. Minor examples of enhanced state activity abound too.

Perhaps more significantly, the state extended its activity into areas previously dominated by private enterprise. One such rubric was the economic "service" sector—a cluster of activities that facilitate or complement production. Banking, insurance, and foreign trade were nationalized. State corporations were established to administer the financial system. Foreign trade became the responsibility of the newly established Ministry of Foreign Trade (MICE) and six exporting enterprises. The state also assumed some responsibility for domestic commerce, exercised by another new ministry, the Ministry of Internal Commerce (MICOIN). A separate agency, the Nicaraguan Enterprise for Basic Food Products (ENABAS), assumed increasing responsibility for the purchase, storage, transportation, and distribution of basic foodstuffs.

Government dominance of the service sector, coupled with traditional monetary and fiscal prerogatives, enabled the state—intentionally or not—to manipulate, through intervention in the market, the fortunes and behavior of specific groups and, more generally, of classes. But results depended on the cooperation, or at least the acquiescence, of private actors. The state could offer incentives and threats, but it alone did not determine outcomes. The widespread nationalization of land and capital, however, enabled the revolutionary regime to engage directly in production and so demonstrate the unbridled potential of the state—and of the revolution it represented.

Nationalized property became the Area of People's Property (APP). Outside of the agrarian sector, the seized entities were diverse and at times eclectic: an ice cream parlor, a discotheque, and a hotel where beds are rented by the hour. Included were a few industrial plants of some importance, producing simple consumer goods like soap. Their diversity creates managerial difficulties for the Ministry of Industry. Of greater economic significance are a handful of national gold mines; although small and backward in technology, they do generate some foreign exchange. (They are managed by an autonomous entity.) The collective economic weight of all of these enterprises, however, cannot begin to measure up to that of the agricultural enterprises nationalized, principally because of Nicaragua's incipient industrialization. These agrarian enterprises are managed by the Ministry of Agricultural Development and Agrarian Reform (MIDINRA).

The decree nationalizing the assets of Somoza and the *somocistas* endowed the APP with about 850,000 hectares of farmland. Initially, it was thought that the confiscated property amounted to half of the country's farmland, but later the acreage proved to be closer to 25 percent. Still, the property nationalized was not only vast but included most of Nicaragua's agro-industrial complexes and about half of the country's large estates. There were also hundreds of small farms, many formerly owned by members of the National Guard.

The first decision made regarding confiscated estates was simply to keep them intact and not to parcel them out to landless or near-landless peasants. But since one of the slogans of the insurrection was "Land to the Peasants," many peasants expected to receive plots from seized estates.

Distribution to peasants did occur, but not for two years and then from land either marginal to the APP or from land confiscated from the private sector. The preferred explanation for state ownership and management was that it would maintain established levels of mechanization and economies of scale and ensure production of export commodities. A confidant of one of the Sandinista commanders asserted, though, that "the state decided to keep the land for political purposes. Consolidation of power would be based on the [Sandinista] army and control of the economy."[1] How much weight to give this political explanation is difficult to evaluate, but it is not only plausible but also complementary to the expressed economic rationale.

Economic Troubles and Political Survival

Exactly what the Sandinista regime wants from its state enterprises has never been made explicit. Perhaps the clearest and most accurate statement comes from an internal MIDINRA document worth quoting at length:

With the consolidation of the agrarian APP, the Revolutionary State has attempted to establish the bases for a new economy (new relations of strength, new social relations and of work in the countryside) and hence has defined as priority objectives in the APP sector:
1. Create autonomous sources of accumulation to diminish the dependence of the country on international capital;
2. Develop new forms of production and of workers' participation;
3. Substantially improve living and working conditions of agricultural laborers;
4. Demonstrate the economic advantages of large-scale state production and of centralized planning;
5. Form entities to assist the production and commercialization of small (peasant) production and show the advantages of integration into superior forms of organization;
6. Try to resolve the "productive backwardness" of peasants through the provision of technical assistance, credit, and state commercialization. (MIDINRA 1982a: 1)

This list of goals is far-ranging and ambitious, but there is no set priority that could guide the decisionmaking of those actually administering the agrarian APP. This ambiguity is evident outside of Managua. A representative view was expressed by two administrators in MIDINRA's Regional IV office (in Estelí): "The enterprises have many objectives. Planning is done with a notion to develop the region."[2]

Despite the plethora of aspirations for the agrarian APP, it has only been the failure of the first of its stated goals—capital accumulation—that has repeatedly brought the agency to the attention of the Sandinista regime at large. Public attention to the APP's financial problems came with the first newspaper headlines dedicated to its performance. The March 7, 1985, issue of *Barricada*, the newspaper of the FSLN, bore the headline: "Every State Enterprise Should Be Profitable." *El Nuevo Diario*, sympathetic to the FSLN, carried a similar headline. The accompanying articles reported on a speech by the minister of MIDINRA, Commander Jaime Wheelock, to four hundred directors of the APP's agrarian and industrial enterprises. He asserted that "state enterprises that this year do not show prospects of profitability will be closed, regardless of what they produce and where they are located. . . . We are going to end this policy of enterprises that are subsidized."[3]

Commander Wheelock's speech was prompted by the accelerated losses of the agrarian APP. The debt of the enterprises as of June 30, 1981, was 1.9 billion córdobas, representing 46 percent of their capital. By March 31, 1984, the debt had risen to 8.8 billion córdobas, a 4.7 increment in three years (MIDINRA 1985c: app. tab. 13). In the interval the real value of the córdoba, always difficult to measure because of government controls, had declined, but not nearly as rapidly as the APP's debt had increased. Another indicator of the enterprises' losses is that in the 1983–1984 agricultural season only 30 percent of the credit extended was repaid (MIDINRA 1984a: 5).

The losses of the agrarian APP have been generalized. In the first six years of postrevolutionary rule, only a handful of enterprises were profitable—two, three, or four in any given year. Among the other enterprises, the magnitude of losses is not explained by their location. Firms in every business and in every part of the country lost money.

Despite Commander Wheelock's admonition, no state enterprises were closed, continued losses notwithstanding. But MIDINRA accelerated ongoing efforts to improve the management of the APP. In addition to such measures as improvements in the annual technical plan and the enrollment of key managers in seminars, an effort has been made to cultivate a new *mentalité*, one that emphasizes efficiency, productivity, and profitability.

Efforts to improve the financial performance of the APP have been overwhelmed by a deterioration in the economic environment in which firms do business. From the beginning, enterprises faced a daunting environment: political tensions, shortages, a trade embargo imposed by the United States, counterrevolution, and an omnipresent uncertainty. In February 1985, though, the government announced a number of new economic measures, including prominently the devaluation of the córdoba and the rescinding of a host of price controls. These corrections contributed to an acceleration of inflation from two-digit figures to three-digit figures in 1986 and four-digit figures in 1987. The government was forced in 1987 to issue larger denominated currency and in early 1988 to reissue currency at a 1 to 1,000 ratio. But inflation only accelerated.

The loss of price stability made evaluation of the financial perfomance of the APP nearly impossible. Most enterprises were suddenly "profitable" because their costs came at the beginning of the year and their revenues at the end. Depreciation became meaningless, as did interest and principle payments. The most profitable enterprises are those that produce for internal demand or are engaged in commercialization. But enterprises that produce export commodities are seemingly less profitable only because state monopsonies have lagged in raising their prices. The combination of inflation and price distortions made calculations of efficiency illusionary.

As articulate Nicaraguan economists have pointed out, the surge in inflation cannot be blamed on the February 1985 reforms but instead must be traced to the accumulated imbalances between supply and demand (see, for example, Medal 1987). The Sandinista regime has pursued expansionary fiscal and monetary policies without a corresponding increase in production. The counterrevolution, with its multifaceted costs, has greatly aggravated the crisis. That the revolutionary state would be wrecked by a counterrevolution was perhaps predicted by the FSLN, as was the foot-dragging of the private sector. From the beginning of its rule, the Sandinista leadership was aware of limits to its autonomy. What is surprising, though, is that even where the Sandinistas had considerable autonomy, prominently in the APP, managerial limitations have made the "state" a serious problem for the FSLN. The nationalized commanding heights have not been the "axis for economic reactivation." Instead, they have had a deleterious effect on an already weak and badgered economy. In short, at stake with the APP is not just Nicaragua's economy but also the Sandinista regime's legitimacy.

Explaining Economic Difficulties

Understanding Nicaragua's postrevolutionary "managerial environment" by disaggregating its dimensions is the best way to explain how and why decisions have been made that—in the end—unknowingly contributed to Nicaragua's economic morass. Consideration of the state administrators' environment begins with the most obvious and immediate feature: the poverty of resources. This poverty, a legacy of the *ancien régime* and the insurrection, has been sorely aggravated in the postrevolutionary epoch by the counterrevolution. But a comprehensive portrait of the state administrators' environment must also include a sketch of the influence of politics.

Political influence on the performance of Nicaragua's state enterprises amounts to more than manipulation of them as political resources and their fulfillment of political tasks in an instrumental fashion. That dimension exists and must be appreciated. But there is another, qualitatively different political import. The revolution brought a change of attitudes, values, and norms—what might be called a new *mentalité*. Perhaps in part because of the heated rhetoric of the revolution, with its debasement of traditional authority, attitudes toward much that the old order held dear, including accounting, profits, banks, and even full days of work, were challenged. The change in attitudes was not complete, evenly shared, necessarily consistent, or enduring. Yet attitudes and values were unmistakably altered in the course of the revolution, with considerable impact on the performance of state enterprises.

The constellation of these three dimensions in the managerial environment explains in large measure the decisions and resulting outcomes for Nicaragua's "Property of the People." Of course, there are individual variations and peculiarities. Nonetheless, the impact of poverty, the pursuit of political as well as financial objectives, and a politically inspired reversal of many values suggest how rational decisions by countless individuals have in the aggregate led to unexpected and undesired results for the Nicaragua revolution. These three dimensions to the administrative environment interact and, more often than not, reinforce one another. As a result, measuring their relative importance is exceedingly difficult, if not impossible. Unsystematic but persuasive evidence suggests, however, that while poverty may be the most immediate constraint, politics is likely to present more enduring obstacles. Despite the acknowledged interplay of the different components of the managerial environment, here they are discussed separately for the purpose of teasing out propositions.

Poverty and Aggression

Many of the day-to-day difficulties that confront administrators of the agrarian APP are simply a result of Nicaragua's poverty. Resources of every type, including administrative skills, are scarce. In addition to the inevitable chaos accompanying the change from private to state ownership, the new-found "enterprises of MIDINRA began to operate without adequate initial capitalization or state support" (MIDINRA 1985c). Once constituted, the enterprises had considerable and continual needs. They employ an intermediate level of farm and agro-industrial technology, necessitating the timely delivery of such inputs as fertilizers and insecticides, machinery, gasoline, spare parts, and the like. The size and geographic dispersion of the enterprises necessitates transportation and, above all, accounting, control, and administrative systems—and the trained personnel to administer them.

Fulfilling these needs has been problematic. The original intention was for MIDINRA's production-oriented enterprises to have their material needs met exclusively by MIDINRA's service enterprises. That mandate proved impossible to attain, and "flexibility was given to enable the agrarian enterprises to contract services from the private sector" (MIDINRA 1982a: 14, 16, 17). But private service firms have suffered from some of the same problems confronting their public counterparts, principally the lack of merchandise owing to the shortage of foreign exchange. There are also problems with the state-controlled storage and distribution of imported goods. And the turn from capitalist countries to socialist ones for farm input and machinery imports makes it difficult to find spare parts for old machinery (such as John Deere tractors) and to use and maintain new, and hence unfamiliar, products. The counterrevolution has exacerbated difficulties because of the deleterious consequences on the balance of payments and the channeling of available imports—most noticeably of gasoline and diesel fuel—to the army.

The consequences for state enterprises are multifaceted but predictable. At times production is delayed or less than optimal because inputs are not available. Sometimes expensive machinery stands idle for lack of spare parts, or even for tires. More commonly, considerable resources, including time, are spent finding—and paying for—goods that should be readily available. Often goods can be found only on Managua's black market, centered in the Eastern Market. At the Julio Buitrago sugar refinery, for example, half of all spare parts are purchased on the black market because state agencies cannot provide them. Prices on the black market are high. As the refinery's administrator put it, "You have to pay what they ask."[4] In addition to high prices, there is also the cost of searching for materials, on the black market or elsewhere. Difficulties in obtaining materials, with the common resort to the black market, may also contribute to petty theft and corruption, as suggested by the oblique Nicaraguan proverb, often quoted in discussions of corruption, "Fishermen profit from tumultuous waters."

Postrevolutionary Nicaragua's poverty is not limited to material resources. The always small pool of experienced managers has shrunk as many have emigrated, either because they were identified with Somoza's regime or because they decided the Nicaraguan revolution was not in their interests. At the same time, the need for managerial talent has mushroomed. In addition to a general increase in the number and size of state bureaucracies, the formation of the APP created a score of enterprises of a size matched in Central America only by the legendary banana plantations of U.S. companies.

Aside from the enormity of the administrative tasks occasioned by the establishment of the APP, difficulties can be traced to the lack of qualified personnel to assume the responsibilities. MIDINRA itself has acknowledged this limitation. An internal ministry document affirmed that "the experience of the cadres that the Ministry has appointed to manage these enterprises is not very great, above all in managing enterprises of the size MIDINRA has, nonetheless, there does not exist in the country cadres who could have done better" (MIDINRA 1984b: 4). Many enterprise directors are agricultural technicians, agronomists, and the like. Lesser-ranking administrators in the enterprises also tend to have limited—or no—managerial experience. For reasons that are not clear, those with some managerial training and experience tend to move from one position to another. Indeed, directors often cite "excessive rotation of personnel" as one of their problems. Administration is also hampered by the functional illiteracy of many laborers, including those expected to collect and monitor assorted kinds of data.

Nicaragua's poverty of resources explains in part the disappointing performance of its state enterprises. Another part of the explanation lies in the pursuit of unattainable economies of scale. Yet these two factors alone do not completely explain why the Sandinistas' bid to manage the commanding heights has gone astray. Not explained is why extant resources have often been poorly employed or diverted to activities that have no relationship to the firms' business.

Political Responsibilities

A revealing description of the function of the agrarian state enterprises was published in a MIDINRA newsletter:

> The agrarian reform enterprises have come to play an important role in sustaining production, considered as an arm of the state in production. . . . They also act as a social and political force in economic and
> - military tasks. (*Informaciones Agropecuarias*, March–April 1987, p. 5)

An integral, if not decisive, explanation for the APP's financial losses can be traced to firms acting as "social and political forces." A searching internal MIDINRA report asserted that the"elevated inefficiency [of state enterprises] is in part due to the economic policies directed towards these enterprises" (MIDINRA 1982b: 2). But economic policies were not found to be formulated and implemented solely on economic criteria:

> If economic policy should establish the correct relation between politics and economics, noticeable imbalances can be observed: while certain policies appear to be directly controlled by political criteria ... others appear to be more tied to economic considerations. ...
>
> The analysis suggests that agricultural policy—an aggregate of different measures—will necessarily be in conflict with "production" tendencies, that favor production as an end in itself, and with "political" tendencies, that favor social organization and its effect over the correlation of forces. ... The complexity of relations ... makes a neat integration impossible. (MIDINRA 1982b: 2, 24)

Politically inspired impositions on state firms have caused them to assume a diverse set of responsibilities at considerable cost.

One of the most common demands upon agrarian enterprises is to provide employment, even when that is not warranted economically. One study suggested that employment on state agrarian enterprises increased 25 percent within two years of their confiscation (IFAD 1980: 88). Demands have included not only an expansion of the total number of laborers but also the provision of continual employment to seasonal workers, especially on coffee and sugar estates. The emergence of labor shortages has moderated demands for employment, but MIDNIRA still points to overstaffing as a contributor to enterprises' financial losses. Yet the preferred rationalization for the continued existence of certain particularly unprofitable enterprises is that they are "the only source of employment in the area."[5] And throughout MIDINRA there is a conviction that redundant workers cannot be dismissed. The motive for providing employment when there is no economic rationale is not only a true concern for the rural poor but also a bid for their allegiance to the revolution, an especially crucial factor in zones of counterrevolutionary activity.

The provision of employment has been accompanied by efforts to improve the often miserable working conditions of rural laborers. An internal MIDINRA document that analyzed enterprises' performance traced part of their initial financial difficulties to the fact that "they had to make extensive investments and social expenditures in housing, kitchens, health centers and schools, etc., with the intent of improving the deploring living conditions inherited from *somocismo*" (MIDINRA n.d.: 142). Although the intent was to provide better conditions for laborers, in practice the benefits provided were often enjoyed by the local community at large. By the third year of postrevolutionary transformation, "social investments" were scaled back. But efforts continue to improve what is sometimes called in Nicaragua "social income." At some enterprises this includes the provision of transportation; at others it means hearty meals. At the Chiltepe dairy farm it amounts to a daily gift of a liter of milk. At other enterprises there is nothing. Benefits have been unevenly distributed, and in many instances mismanagement has diluted the advantages of expensive investments and expenditures.

The imprecision of accounting data makes it impossible to measure the cost of enterprises' social investments and expenditures. Commonly, some investments listed in the balances of enterprises prove to be social expenditures. Acknowledging them as such has negative repercussions for already unfavorable annual income statements. Unsystematic but persuasive evidence suggests that attempts to improve working conditions have entailed considerable cost, although it has been unevenly distributed. Like the provision of employment, efforts to improve working conditions are motivated in part by a heartfelt concern for the poor. And they are in part a response to demands from the poor. But expenditures are also motivated by the desire to win the political allegiance of the rural majority.

Agrarian state enterprises have also contributed directly to defense of the revolution—at considerable cost. Enterprises in border areas station troops and often provide them with food, lodging, and other necessities. Also common is the provision of transportation or the loaning of vehicles. A more widespread burden is the maintenance of militias (sometimes compulsory for employees) and the continuation of salaries for employees called for active duty. The latter often involves not only the direct cost but also an indirect cost of doing without a trained and experienced employee. More immediate, state enterprises within reach of the counterrevolution have been attacked, whether or not they were posting soldiers. Damage to some enterprises has been extensive. Most of MIDINRA's enterprises, however, are in the populous Pacific zone, which has been free of fighting.

As with social investments and expenditures, defense costs have not been adequately recorded. MIDINRA, and other ministries too, regularly ask for information about damage inflicted by the counterrevolution. But those costs are usually not entered into enterprises' accounts. Part of the explanation is that the state enterprises do not regularly prepare balance sheets, which would detail changes in assets and liabilities. The firms only, with difficulty, prepare income statements that highlight financial transactions. Consequently, although the counterrevolution has had an enormous impact on postrevolutionary Nicaragua, it—and defense against it—do not explain the APP's poor financial performance. Still, defense expenditures, indirect and poorly recorded as they are, have been yet another burden.

A different kind of political task performed by state enterprises is price control. The Sandinista regime controls the price of most agricultural products: agro-exports are controlled to "stabilize" earnings of producers, and many food commodities are controlled for the "defense of the consumer." For both kinds of products, state-set prices have been well below those that would prevail in an unfettered market. The depressed prices have undermined incentives to produce in the private sector and have contributed to the financial losses of the APP. The government has publicly acknowledged the problem and periodically raises selling prices with great fanfare. But these price adjustments always lag behind increases in production costs (MIDINRA 1985b: 16–19).

Fulfilling their public service as price regulators has an acknowledged financial cost for state enterprises. An internal MIDINRA report stated:

> The enterprises of the APP confront a different situation than private enterprises concerning commercialization, in that the latter sell their products in the market, free or parallel, in contrast the APP enterprises have to submit their products to state organs, which pay official prices. It can be said that they take advantage of the obligatory position of the enterprises. (MIDINRA 1985c: 7)

The report went on to estimate that prevailing prices for food commodities in the parallel market were higher than state-paid prices by margins ranging from 25 to 300 percent (ibid., 8).

Administrators of state enterprises often argue that their losses are due in large measure to low prices paid by the state. Prices for export crops are regarded as low because the grossly overvalued córdoba undercuts the government's claim that it pays international prices. And throughout MIDINRA it is recognized that prices of food crops are controlled to protect consumers, often explained as a "political reason."

Like costs incurred in supporting the defense of the revolution, the burden of controlled prices is impossible to measure. It certainly is a cost, and as such another explanation for the financial losses of the APP. But price distortions are widespread and uneven; or, as MIDINRA's vice minister of economics bluntly said, *"los precios son una locura"* (prices are crazy).[6] Inputs, including those that are imported, are also priced well below market levels. For example, a gallon of imported gasoline long cost less than two tortillas. Hence, consideration of how state enterprises have been adversely affected by some price distortions should be balanced with an appreciation for how they have benefited from others. State enterprises have been net losers, but not to the extent their administrators claim.

In addition to the fulfillment of these significant tasks, state enterprises have made other contributions to the revolution—or the "process," as it is often referred to by cadres. To assist the agrarian reform, state enterprises have ceded land and capital to cooperatives. Usually the land and capital are not central to the enterprises' activities, but firms commonly retain the debt corresponding to the donated land parcels (MIDINRA n.d.: 143). The Enterprise Commander Marcos Somarriba was asked to host, and underwrite, an expensive vegetable-growing project. Other contributions abound: entertaining visiting dignitaries, ferrying people to demonstrations, even loaning trucks to the local Committee for Sandinista Defense (CDS) to haul away garbage.[7] All these and similar activities have a cost.

Another political use of state enterprises does not inflict a cost upon them. State enterprises serve as a warning—or threat—to the private sector. Any private business that thwarts the revolution can be absorbed by a state enterprise. A much discussed example involved the leader of the principal private sector organization, the Superior Council of Private Enterprise (COSEP). When Enrique Bolaños began to make spirited public pronouncements against the revolution, his cotton estate was confiscated, nominally because of the need to provide land to peasants. But the estate was taken over by the Enterprise Camilo Ortega, and the private sector reached the desired conclusion: engaging in political opposition can lead to the loss of one's assets (*Barricada*, June 25, 1985). More commonly, private enterprises are confiscated because of inactivity or even decapitalization. While retaining a commitment to "national unity," the Sandinista regime has let the private sector know that it will not tolerate vitriolic public criticism and that private capital must be used fully and efficiently. State enterprises help enforce these mandates.

Given the multiple political tasks routinely fulfilled by the agrarian state enterprises, it is not surprising that more than one internal MIDINRA report has complained:

> There is a duality in the treatment of the enterprises, they are viewed as the state in some cases . . . in other cases they are viewed like any other producer. Roles so contradictory and incompatible confound and obscure the fundamental objective of the enterprises, which is to produce at the lowest cost. (MIDINRA 1985c: 9; see also MIDINRA 1984b: 2)

And it is understandable that a ranking Nicaraguan banker who oversees MIDINRA's portfolio laments, "The concept of a firm has been lost."[8]

The ambiguous conception of state enterprises, with the resulting economic repercussions, is not just a result of the firms pursuing political objectives in methodical fashion as ordered by the Sandinista leadership. That is part of the explanation. The conception of the enterprises as the "state" is also based in a new *mentalité* ushered in by the revolution. That *mentalité* has, among other consequences, led to a widespread discarding of the traditional concept of the firm and complicated the management of Nicaragua's commanding heights.

The Revolutionary *Mentalité*

The insurrection that culminated in the ouster of Somoza was accompanied by an unending assault on the values and norms of his regime and on the economic system that underpinned it. Agitation deepened a sense of deprivation and created hope for a better future. The implicit suggestion of revolutionary rhetoric was that a better life was possible for Nicaraguans, but that it had been choked by the rapaciousness of the unjust and exploitative Somoza regime. The triumph of the revolution unleashed a widespread sense of euphoria and a belief that unfulfilled needs would be finally met. Everything associated with the old regime was discredited.

It is difficult to delineate, let alone measure, the impact of this politically charged *mentalité*. But in the aftermath of the revolution there most certainly has been a consequential change in attitudes toward work and authority. On the positive side, the revolutionary *mentalité* has given the Sandinista leadership and its cadres a sense of purpose, a willingness to act, a disregard for risk, and an indifference to personal hardship. Yet the revolutionary *mentalité* has also brought unexpected difficulties that have contributed to postrevolutionary Nicaragua's vexatious managerial environment. These difficulties include an abrupt drop in the productivity of laborers, ambiguity about the objectives of economic entities, a slighting of traditional managerial practices, and disrespect for economic, in contrast to political, locuses of authority. Because these difficulties undermine economic rationality, they have also encouraged the already existing proclivity to use economic entities for political tasks.

Since its ascension to power, the Sandinista leadership has acknowledged that revolutionary aspirations have to be tempered, that certain facile and self-serving interpretations of what the revolution means are misleading. The Sandinistas' own rhetoric has slowly but surely changed—for example, from inciting worker militancy to pleading for labor productivity. But the Sandinistas' enduring convictions, the danger of frustrating the popular aspirations they themselves created, and the presence of counterrevolutionaries prevent the Sandinistas from tackling head on problematic dimensions of the revolutionary *mentalité*. There are gingerly worded admonishments, weak incentives, and no sanctions. With cynics and counterrevolutionaries ever present, even reckless and lax followers must be accommodated. The underlying dilemma is that there is an often ugly trade-off between financial responsibility and political sensitivity. Economic and political logics clash.

Peasants and rural laborers' interpretation of the revolution has been especially problematic, presenting the Sandinista regime with a tumultuous fall in labor productivity. Peasants and rural laborers were most likely to believe that the triumph of the revolution would bring them everything they never had and that they would no longer have to work. It proved impossible for the rural poor "to suddenly have everything," however: there were few liquid assets to seize and redistribute. Rural Nicaragua is poor, and the productive infrastructure that exists cannot be quickly turned into household goods. But while the rural poor were frustrated in their desire to have everything, they proved more successful in achieving the second part of their expectation, "that they no longer have to work."

The state was more affected than the private sector by the labor militancy the FSLN fostered. Hours worked per day on newly established state enterprises fell nearly everywhere. And state enterprises were pressured into increasing employment, usually above what was necessary. An internal MIDINRA report described rural laborers' attitude: "The peasant has come to see the new proprietor as 'state' and not as 'producer' and thus his expectations, rather than of exchanging his efforts with this new producer, are instead to ask and often to demand from it as the state, even before generating some kind of surplus, the social benefits that he had been deprived under the previous form of exploitation" (MIDINRA 1985c: 3). Sandinista-fostered unions are held to have exacerbated the fall in labor productivity. Another internal MIDINRA report complained: "the union organization in the countryside is strongest in state enterprises and has not reached the level of maturity that the workers potentially have and to the contrary has caused a fall in the productivity of labor and a decline in labor discipline" (MIDINRA 1984b: 3). Many administrators of state enterprises maintain that their most difficult and intractable problem is labor indiscipline.

The difficulties that rural laborers present to the revolutionary regime are openly acknowledged and regularly reported, for example, in *Barricada*, the state newspaper. Commander Wheelock summarized the problem:

> Since the triumph of the Revolution we have observed in the countryside that contracts made by labor organizations with the Ministry of Labor, and in general with productive enterprises, have presented a tendency to set lower norms for work than existed previously. In sugar, the fall has equaled 40% of the historic norm, in rice 25%, in coffee 60%, this is to say, a very steep fall in the productivity of labor. What has happened as a consequence of this? Now we need two workers to do what before one did. (Wheelock 1984: 110)

The problem of low productivity is augmented by "a lack of discipline," which "complicates the management of state enterprises." Workers plant demands, and "if expectations are not meet they feel frustrated and cynical."[9]

In an effort to reverse the decline in labor productivity, MIDINRA began a campaign during the 1984–1985 agricultural season to provide monetary incentives for laborers to work for piece rate earnings instead of daily wages (MIDINRA 1985a). The approach, called *normalización* (the setting of work norms), was copied from Cuba, where it has proven effective in increasing worker productivity (Central Junta of Planning 1981: 123–135). Despite the gains in productivity, more of which are expected, the legacy of labor indiscipline suggests that the very set of values that revolutionaries preach—and that are instrumental in their seizure of power—subsequently erode state capacity to manage the commanding heights of the economy.

The revolutionary *mentalité* of administrators also contributes to the financial woes of the agrarian APP, although less visibly. Administrators have not interpreted the revolution as meaning the end of toil. On the contrary, they tend to be hardworking. But they concentrate their efforts on producing goods and services without much, if any, care for cost or the net economic consequences of their activities. This indifference is due in part to the fact that many administrators are agricultural technicians by training and find the day-to-day obstacles in the field or shop floor daunting. But the indifference to financial details can also be traced to the common attitude among administrators that they are working in the service of the revolution. Whatever they do, other than self-aggrandizement, which is rare, is justified and deserving of cooperation. "Control" is not necessary because they are the state, the revolution.

The dominant set of values held by state administrators leads them, as a whole, to be lax not only in controlling costs and revenues but also in meeting their financial obligations. The latter engenders conflict, often pitting the state against the state. Enterprises are delinquent on their utilities, write checks without funds to cover them, and even fail to pay their bills to one another. Most noticeably, MIDINRA's commercial enterprises routinely delay—for months—paying MIDINRA's production enterprises for the goods they purchase (MIDINRA 1985d). In contrast, MIDINRA's commercial entities pay private enterprises promptly.

Conflict is most evident and consequential within the nationalized banking system. The attitude of many administrators toward the bank was summed up by one enterprise director who called it a "monster."[10] The underlying perception regards the bank, at worst, as an ugly capitalist legacy and, at best, as a bureaucracy insensitive to the needs of the revolution. Conflict abounds, but the enterprises prevail. As one administrator said, "It is always possible to receive more money from the bank, claiming that if additional funds are not received production will be disrupted."[11] But negotiations are a "game." Persuasive final arguments for unpaid bankers to loan more money include, "It will not be possible to pay the workers and then there will be a political problem."[12]

Responsibility for the prevailing managerial environment, in which it is rational for an administrator to slight economic criteria, should be traced to Nicaragua's leadership. In a revealing passage, Commander Wheelock, writing more as a member of the ruling FSLN National Directorate than as minister of MIDINRA, suggests the origins of Nicaragua's managerial *mentalité*. He acknowledges that the regime has overburdened itself economically and then asks himself: "Why? for the morale of the revolutionary to do everything. . . . It is a revolutionary attitude to defy aspects of everyday life and some economic realities." His following sentence is equally suggestive: "Of course, after a while the Central Bank began to complain of monetary emissions" (Wheelock 1984: 74). Economic realities cannot be defied for long, particularly in a small developing country.

Illusions of Reform

The financial losses of state enterprises have prompted a search for reform. But impulses for reform are circumscribed by the same forces that necessitate reform. First, the resources to contemplate and experiment with reforms are often lacking. Second, the employment of economic entities for the fulfillment of political tasks often generates a constituency, and the advantages afforded this constituency are not easily withdrawn. Usually there is a trade-off between economic costs and political benefits. Third, the continued necessity of appearing "revolutionary," of distancing oneself from the *ancien régime* and the counterrevolution, constrains the possibilities of reform, including the idea of jettisoning state enterprises altogether.

These constraints mean that reform is limited to discussions of petty details. Excluded are consequential issues such as a clear definition of the objectives of enterprises and of their relationship to party, bureaucracy, and citizen. These more fundamental issues have been either ignored or, more commonly, ambiguously treated. For example, less than three months after Commander Wheelock publicly proclaimed that all of Nicaragua's state enterprises must be profitable or they would be shut down, he told a group of enterprise directors completing a seminar on administration, "The technical study of administration is important, but it is necessary to have revolutionary solutions to the problems of the enterprises." The APP has to have "historical content."[13]

The difficulties of extracting state enterprises from their inevitable financial losses suggests a questioning of the conviction among revolutionaries, and their sympathizers, of the desirability of nationalization and ensuing state management of dominant economic entities. The need for this reassessment is augmented by the erosion of regime legitimacy that can accompany continued inefficiency in state enterprises. Aspirations for social change, and distaste for private property and initiative, need to be paired with a sober calculation of state capacity.

Notes

1. He spoke on the condition of anonymity, June 1985.

2. Interview with Manuel Castro and Fidel Olivas, Estelí, January 1985.

3. *Barricada*, March 7, 1985; *El Nuevo Diario*, March 7, 1985. The text of the speech was printed in *Informaciones Agropecuarias*, March–April 1985.

4. Interview with Alberto Gallo, Masachapa, January 1985.

5. Interview with Mario Alemán, administrator, MIDINRA Central, Managua, Janurary 1985.

6. Meeting with Silvio Lanuza, Vice Minister of Economics, MIDINRA, Managua, May 1985.

7. Interview with Roger Fonseca, manager of the UPE Tierras Blancas, the Enterprise Oscar Benavides, Chagüitillo Sébaco, May 1985.

8. Interview with Antonio Medrano, administrator, Bank of America, Managua, February 1985.

9. Interview with Manuel Castro and Fidel Olivas, administrators in the MIDINRA Region IV office, Estelí, January 1985.

10. Interview with Manuel Duarte, director, the Enterprise Adolfo García Barberena, El Crucero, January 1985.

11. Interview with Alberto Gallo, administrator, the Enterprise Julio Buitrago, Masachapa, January 1985.

12. Interview with Iván Zelaya, economics director for Region V, Matagalpa, January 1985.

13. Speech by Commander Jaime Wheelock, Minister of Agricultural Development and Agrarian Reform, Managua, May 1985.

References

Central Junta of Planning. 1981. *El Sistema de Dirección y Planificación de la Economía en las Empresas*. Havana: Editorial de las Ciencias Sociales.

IFAD (International Fund for Agricultural Development). 1980. "Informe de la Misión Especial de Programación a Nicaragua." Rome. Mimeographed.

Medal, José Luis. 1987. "Políticas de Establización y Ajuste Estructural en Nicaragua (1980–1986)." San Jose. Mimeographed.

MIDINRA (Ministry of Agricultural Development and Agrarian Reform). 1982a. "La Política para el APP." Managua. Mimeographed.

———. 1982b. "Los Problemas de Fondo en el Manejo Reciente de la Política Agropecuaria." Managua. Mimeographed.

———. 1984a. "Evalución Financiera de las Empresas de Reforma Agraria Ciclo 1983–84." Managua. Mimeographed.

————. 1984b. "Sistema de Dirección de Empresas." Managua. Mimeographed.

————. 1985a. *La Normación del Trabajo*. Managua: MIDINRA.

————. 1985b. *Plan de Trabajo 1985*. Managua: MIDINRA.

————. 1985c. "Problemática de las Empresas del Sector Agropecuario Adscritas al MIDINRA." Managua. Mimeographed.

————. 1985d. "Relaciones Comerciales entre las Empresas Agropecuarias Adscritas a MIDINRA y a las Empresas Comercializadoras." Managua. Mimeographed.

————. N.d. "Revisión Integral de las Empressas Estatales Agropecuarias y Fortalecimiento de sus Sistemas de Dirección y Gestión." Managua. Mimeographed.

Wheelock, Jaime. 1984. *Entre la Crisis y la Agresión*. Managua: MIDINRA.

12

China and Privatization

David Bachman

Prior to June 4, 1989, when the Chinese military brutally crushed a broad-based mass movement demanding political pluralization, China's economic reforms captured world attention and were regarded as an example of the wave of privatization that is emerging around the world.[1] Privatization of the Chinese economy, however, followed a path very different from that taken in the non–Marxist-Leninist developing world and in developed capitalist economies. Among the major differences between the Chinese experience and that of other states, we can note that China's privatization focused on "control" property rights (rights concerning control over the disposition of the products of enterprises), not ownership property rights (Pryor 1973: chap. 1, app. A–1); the size and extent of state ownership and control in China was much larger than in other cases; large-scale state-owned industry and financial enterprises and organizations were not the principal objects of privatization; and China's privatization took place in an environment in which a true national market did not exist, where many prices were set administratively, where the legal system was not institutionalized, where a complex political environment affecting managers undermined their ability to maximize economic gains, and where the single channel of upward mobility in the society was controlled by the Communist party.

It is wise to remember that the reforms China had accomplished in individual economic sectors prior to June 4, 1989, were not unprecedented in the Communist world. Arguably, the rural economies of Poland and Yugoslavia were more privatized than the Chinese agricultural economy. A number of Eastern European economies had joint ventures with Western nations, and international trade and financial flows had a greater effect on these countries than was the case in China. Even in the industrial sector, certainly in Yugoslavia and probably in the case of Hungary, privatization had proceeded further than in China (Sacks 1973; Horvat 1976; Tyson 1980; Hare, Radice, and Swain 1981; Burkett 1983; Hare 1983; Kornai 1986: 81–123). Even the Soviet Union had more developed labor markets than does China (Malle 1987). Moreover, Poland is preparing a radical privatization of its economy, as the Solidarity government moves rapidly away from a Stalinist economic system, and Hungary appears poised to do the same. (On international strategies and more general comparisons, see Knight 1983; Nove 1983; Comisso and Tyson 1986.)

What, then, justifies all the attention given to the Chinese reforms? Why is China seen as such an important example of privatization? A number of factors lie behind this emphasis. First, China is a large economy, easily within the top ten in the world and, depending how one estimates China's gross national product (GNP), possibly the fourth largest. Second, its economy has been growing rapidly for more than a decade. In the 1980s, only South Korea rivaled China's rate of economic advance. Some projections suggest that China's GNP will be larger than the Soviet Union's by the year 2000 (*New York Times*, Mar. 28, 1988). Third, despite the purge of General Secretary Zhao Ziyang and other prominent reformers, further reform remains on the political agenda, at least rhetorically. More thorough reforms were under active consideration prior to Zhao's removal (Gaige 1986; Delfs 1988). China's reforms have not enjoyed smooth sailing; but even though the system remains in flux, and despite recent retrogression, continued reform seems inevitable.

Chinese leaders talk about reform frequently, referring to change to a more efficient system or policy. Seldom do they use the word *privatization*, and they deny that they are privatizing the economy. Indeed, one of Zhao's "crimes" was his willingness to embrace the idea of privatization. Reforms can be restorationist—that is, they can rehabilitate procedures that were common in the past but came under a cloud during the Cultural Revolution—incremental, or fundamental. These varieties of reforms are not all equivalent to privatization, meaning here, "policies designed to stimulate the substitution of private for public provision" (Hemming and Mansoor 1987: 1; Starr 1987). Reform policies are designed to make the economy work better; they do not presume that the private sector is the only way to do this. Many reform policies are aimed at improving and/or rationalizing state control through such mechanisms as improving managerial skills, insulating the economic from the political realm, and refining the tools of (state) macro-economic control. In other cases, the relationship between reform and privatization is unclear. Consider the case of expanded managerial autonomy. The appointment of managers to important state-owned enterprises remains under the control of the Chinese Communist party's (CCP) version of its *nomenklatura*, the Party's list of positions and potential job candidates. In fact, even after substantial reforms of the personnel system, the party secretaries and managers of twenty-four enterprises remain on the Central Committee's *nomenklatura* (Burns 1987: 44). The state still owns these enterprises and controls appointments of their leading personnel, not just their managers. But at the same time, the state is telling these people to act autonomously and giving them greater prerogatives in determining the economic activities of enterprises, including some degree of control over assets. This policy is clearly designed as a reform. But is it a case of privatization?

China has adopted hundreds of policies designed to change the nature of the economic and political systems that existed during late Maoism. Many of these policies have had only limited success at best, and some have been rejected after a brief period of implementation. Results have been mixed. Overall output figures have been positive, but measures of productivity and other indications of qualitative change have not satisfied China's leaders and outside observers (Gaige 1986; *Beijing Review*, Nov. 9–15, 1987; Tidrick and Chen 1987). Technical levels and innovation have not increased rapidly or widely. Yet, the less than fully satisfactory results have not meant, as they did in the Soviet Union and Eastern Europe, that reform had to stop and the basic Stalinist system was restored. Rather, problems have generally spurred the leadership into adopting more reforms. Results, even after further reforms, remain less than ideal, but the process seems to hold out hope for the future, even after Tiananmen Square (Harding 1987; *FBIS*, Jan. 25 and Mar. 28, 1988).

Chinese Reform/Privatization in Comparative Perspective

Size and Extent of the State Economy

The object of reform and privatization is much larger in China than in any other case of public sector reform. China's GNP exceeded 1 trillion *yuan* in 1987, or about $300 billion. In 1985 China ranked sixth in crude oil and sugar, fifth in electricity and chemical fibers, fourth in world steel production, third in sulfuric acid and chemical fertilizer, second in coal and televisions, and first in cement and cotton cloth. Since 1980 China has vied with the United States for the top position in world grain production and ranks second in world pork, beef, and mutton (taken together) production. In most other crops indigenous to China, China ranks among the world's top four producers. In short, China is among the world's largest economies (SSB 1986: 719–720, 724; *Beijing Review*, Mar. 7–13, 1988).

In 1976 the state dominated, if not totally controlled, all aspects of the economy. The reforms of recent years have made it impossible to determine just how much autonomy enterprises have gained from state intervention and determination of production, marketing, and investment. All enterprises have been subject to some of the winds of reform. Given China's population and number of economic enterprises (more than thirty-five million firms of all kinds), reform affects more enterprises than in any other case of reform/privatization.

In 1985 there were 463,000 urban industrial enterprises in the Peoples Republic. Of these, 7,900 were classified as large- and medium-sized state-owned enterprises, some of which are as large as any in the world—the true commanding heights of Chinese industry. Altogether, there were about 94,000 state-owned factories and 368,000 "collective enterprises." In addition, there were 1,570,000 rural collective industrial enterprises and more than 10,000,000 private rural enterprises (this last figure is not limited to industrial activities). Furthermore, there are more than 25,000,000 commercial enterprises, with state enterprises accounting for more than 4,000,000 of this total, collective enterprises about 9,000,000, and individual enterprises more than 12,000,000 (SSB 1986: 189, 177, 414; Wong 1988).[2] All of these enterprises are the objects—and many are the products—of reform. In contrast, the Hungarian economic reforms, perhaps the most extensive in the Soviet sphere of influence, involved only about 700 enterprises (Hare 1983). The point of this comparison is not to denigrate the magnitude or significance of other cases. Rather it is to suggest how difficult it is for anyone to monitor reform in China effectively.

There is no clear relationship among type of ownership, degree of planning, and degree of state intervention in economic activity except in the crudest and most unsatisfactory way (one useful attempt is Wong 1986). True, the very large state-owned enterprises are more likely to be subject to planning and state intervention. For individual and private enterprises, the degree of planning is very small; but many of these endeavors are dependent on the good will of the state, or at least local cadres, and cadre intervention is quite extensive, with both positive and negative effects. Most of these enterprises are integrated into the pattern of patron-client relations that characterizes Chinese society, so they are between plan and market (Wong 1985; Oi 1986; Walder, 1986b; Wong 1987).

The universe of enterprises—their differences in scale, variety, ownership patterns, and so on—is so large and the interactions among them are so complex that we can make only general assessments about the status of reform. This inability to aggregate the results of reform at the enterprise level is compounded by China's weak and biased statistical system and the continuing horatory role of the media in the propagation of models for emulation (Travers 1982; World Bank 1983: 1:223–243).

Control versus Ownership Property Right Reforms

Discussions of privatization have focused on selling off state-owned assets, of turning activities under state control over to the private sector (see, for example, Hanke 1987). In other words, ownership rights are being transferred. In China, too, there have been changes in the structure of ownership since 1976. But while the relegitimation of private enterprises, the encouragement of collective enterprises, the formation of joint ventures, and even the existence of 100 percent wholly owned foreign subsidiaries have been important developments, all but collective enterprises have failed to affect industrial production significantly (and collective and private enterprises are currently under political clouds). Moreover, privatization is not the goal for large state-owned enterprises. State-owned enterprises produce about two-thirds of all industrial output, and the proportion is even higher in high-technology and capital-intensive sectors. Although some experiments with shareholding and other aspects of ownership changes have been discussed, no top leader is on record as supporting ownership reform for the state-owned industrial sector (a number of reform-minded economists, with access to the very top, are; see Gaige 1986).

Instead of concentrating on ownership questions, Chinese enterprise reform policies in the last few years have concerned the separation of ownership and management. State ownership remains a largely unquestioned parameter of the industrial economy, but since 1978 efforts have been under way to expand enterprise autonomy and, more recently, to increase managerial autonomy. Particularly since 1986, the Factory Manager Responsibility System has been the most important reform in industry, and it is likely to receive further attention with the adoption (after years of debate) of the State Enterprise Law in April 1988 (Naughton 1985; *China New Analysis* 1344 [Oct. 1, 1987]; *FBIS*, Jan. 20, 1988).

The managerial responsibility system, in theory, is supposed to do exactly what its name implies, that is, make managers responsible for the economic activity of their enterprises, to give them much broader powers within the enterprise, and to reduce the role of enterprise party committees (read: the enterprise party secretary) in the governing and administration of the enterprise. Today, again in theory, managers have much greater power to decide on such things as how large the work force should be, what is to be produced, how it is to be marketed, where raw and semifinished materials are to come from, who will occupy mid-level management positions, and so on. Coupled with the manager responsibility system has been a change in state-enterprise financial relations. Managers and the state arrive at an agreement as to how much profit and tax the enterprise is to turn over to the state treasury. The enterprise is allowed to keep either all above-contract profits or an increasing rate of the above-quota profits.

For smaller state-owned enterprises, several proposals to "lease" management rights have been reported. Potential managers are supposed to bid on state enterprises, promising to deliver to the state a set amount of money over a fixed period. The successful bidder and his guarantors are allowed to retain all earnings after paying the contracted amount. If the enterprise fails to produce the required amount, the manager and his guarantors are responsible for making up the difference. A more extensive version of this system applies not only to profit contracting or leasing but also to assets within the enterprise (*New York Times*, July 7, 1987; *Newsweek*, July 20, 1987; *China New Analysis* 1344 [Oct. 1, 1987]; *New York Times*, Feb. 10, 1988).

These proposals and policies are reasonable good faith efforts on the part of the central leadership to improve enterprise management and to promote commodity production. Yet, they are doomed to yield less than satisfactory results because they ignore the basic political-social-economic network within which an enterprise of any sort operates (to be discussed below). Of somewhat less importance is the failure to consider intra-enterprise authority relations, which also sharply constrain the ability of managers to be risk takers.

Chinese industrial reforms in recent years have focused on increasing the control property rights of enterprise managers. Expanded shareholding has been considered and tried in a number of cases, but the apparent rights of stockholders are more akin to those in Japan than in the United States (Ignatius 1987; *New York Times*, Apr. 27 and Nov. 11, 1987). Consequently, stock and share ownership essentially has been a way of mobilizing capital rather than a means of influencing managerial behavior. But expanded, even greatly expanded, managerial control rights will not fundamentally transform China's political economy; nor will they likely have a major impact on productivity, profitability, and technological innovation. China's managers have limited skills and are not terribly open to new ideas, but this is of relatively minor importance to the success of enterprise reforms at this time (Fischer 1986; *Newsweek*, Apr. 18, 1988). In an economy characterized by chronic shortage (Kornai 1980), where prices bear only a limited relationship to costs, where the legal system is not institutionalized,[3] and where the power of Party officials is still so closely linked with economic performance in the locality they supervise, meaningful public sector reform of any sort is unlikely. The question then becomes: Can these constraints on reform be lessened and ultimately eliminated?

The Lack of a Privatization Infrastructure

The National Market

Markets have been restored in China under the reforms, and commodity circulation has expanded dramatically. But this does not mean that a national, unified market exists, that the resulting fragmented markets are impersonal, and that market allocation is viewed as wholly legitimate.

Perhaps the biggest constraint on the formation of a true national market in China is the country's deficient infrastructure (Lyons 1987; Salem 1987). Yet, since the obstacle to be overcome here is straightforward, it is also the easiest to handle, although building China's infrastructure will be a long, expensive process. In part, there is no unified national market because China's transportation and communications systems are so overloaded that they cannot ensure adequate distribution of products. The result is a fragmented, regionally based series of markets. Moreover, the lack of a national market and the deficiencies of the distribution system affect large, bulky products more than they do smaller products. To a certain extent, this means that heavy industry under state ownership is less subject to market regulation than is light industry. Again, this situation reinforces the lack of reform in what is already the least reformed element of the economy.

But the infrastructural difficulties can at least be ameliorated through allocation of resources. The other two factors that constrain markets in China may be less tractable. First, the markets are not impersonal. Chinese society, local mercantilism, the state personnel system, and the limited transportation capacity all contribute to markets colored by personalistic and other relationships.

Chinese society is noted for the extent to which *guanxi*—the usual English translation, "connections," only loosely captures the flavor and power of the concept—dominates interpersonal relations. Mutual exchange of favors (though not implying strict reciprocity, especially in cases of superior-subordinate relations) is commonplace. Even in rural areas, where local industrialization has made remarkable progress, cadres have at their disposal a great deal of information and power that is decisive for the success of these enterprises. Entrepreneurs make special deals for their friends and relatives, and obviously for cadres who can make or break them, and charge higher prices to outsiders. Enterprises prefer building long-term, stable relationships that minimize risk rather than subjecting themselves to the full effects of the market. Transportation bottlenecks practically ensure that local enterprises cater only to local markets, making it increasingly likely that buyers and sellers are familiar with each other and establish *guanxi* ties. Finally, while cadre control over rural enterprises and peasants has diminished somewhat, cadres retain important sources of power and still have a strong interest in the activities of rural enterprises. All this means that markets, even in what is the most reformed sector of the economy, are colored by personalistic and other ties. How markets can be made more impersonal is not at all clear (Gold 1985; Oi 1986).

Finally, markets have much less legitimacy in China than they do in developed capitalist economies. In the West, at least some sort of explanation must be supplied when governments intervene in markets, be it for reasons of natural monopolies, externalities, vertical mergers, "unearned income," or the like.[4] In capitalist economies, the superior efficiency of market allocation, compared to all other mechanisms of resource allocation, is a matter of almost theocratic belief. But this is hardly the case in socialist economies. Even when markets have been allowed to exist in China, they have not been sacrosanct. Policies and cadres have constantly interfered with their operation. Many CCP members and not a few members of the population see markets generating gross inequality. Markets as institutions and as allocation mechanisms remain under an ideological cloud, which the best efforts of radical reformers have been unable to dissipate. Consequently, cadres and policymakers are not subject to serious sanction when they interfere in the workings of markets. Again, it is not at all obvious how the market mechanism can gain the legitimacy that would force the state to at least justify its interference in market operations (Hsu 1985).

The Price System

Another critical shortcoming in China's reform efforts is the lack of a price system that reflects true costs of production. Indeed, most people see the lack of real prices as the most serious obstacle to reform in socialist economies. Although I believe that the state personnel system is the single most important factor explaining the limits of reform in socialist systems (as discussed below), I agree that the influence of defective prices is also very strong.

Chinese reformers are well aware of problems with their price system and have tried to introduce more realistic cost elements. As a result, there are now at least five different kinds of prices in China: state-fixed prices (they do not fluctuate); state-guided prices (set by the state, but they can fluctuate within a state-determined maximum and minimum—much like an international currency "snake"); market-regulated prices (reflecting supply and demand); floating prices (set by the market, but with maximum and minimum rates of fluctuation set by the state); and local temporary prices (in the event of difficulties, local authorities can set prices for short periods). Consequently, at least a dual-track pricing system has emerged. But while this may at least promote more realistic accounting measures, it may also compound other problems (*China New Analysis* 1329 [Feb. 15, 1987]).

First, it is in everyone's interest to receive raw materials and energy at the lowest price (state-set prices) but to sell at the most flexible—that is, the highest—price. This reinforces the bargaining nature of the economy, as enterprises plead with the state for special pricing deals. Second, state-owned enterprises—the most technically advanced and capital inten-sive—usually have less latitude to change prices than do collective or private enterprises. This means that state-owned coal mines almost uni-formly operate at a loss, while small collective collieries reap windfall profits as a result of China's energy shortage. This imbalance certainly does not encourage them to become more efficient, to introduce econo-mies of scale, and so on. The same pattern is replicated in many areas, and it means that local industry obtains an unfair advantage compared with state industry, with obvious efficiency losses to the economy. Finally, the five types of pricing are complex and difficult to administer, and they only encourage cadre intervention in market operation (Naughton, 1986; Walder 1987; Wong 1987).

Thorough price reform seems to be the only way out of the morass. But the inflationary and budgetary implications of such a policy have made it impossible for the state to undertake this. Instead, gradual expansion of the number of products subject to some element of market activity seems to be the only way that price reform can or will be implemented. But this policy reinforces the pattern of bargaining over prices, and the ability of local enterprises and cadres to co-opt price reform to their advantage can-not be underestimated.

Many of the guiding lights of the reform effort have been advocates of price reform. Yet, the political leadership has found itself unable to sup-port major, rapid price reform (and a 30 percent inflation rate and wide-spread social dissatisfaction in 1988 reinforce this view). As a result of the deadlock on price reform, or at least its slow-motion implementation, some younger Chinese economists are arguing for radical privatization of the Chinese economy. They have not won the academic debate even within the circle of Chinese economists, much less converted prominent political leaders to their views (Delfs 1988).

The Legal System

From a very low base in 1976, China has made extensive progress in codifying laws, increasing the number of trained legal personnel, and building legal institutions. But although legal construction has been ex-tensive and in many ways a very positive development, the law has yet to be invested with much authority. It does not seriously constrain the be-havior of cadres or enterprise managers, or many others for that matter.[5]

Several factors account for this lack of institutionalization. One is sim-ply time. Legal developments have come so rapidly that, with so few qualified personnel capable of understanding and acting on them, the law has not had a chance to sink in, to become familiar, much less accepted. But while this reason should not be denied, it is not the most salient problem confronting the legal system. More fundamentally, legal officials and judges are state personnel, under the control of the Party personnel system. The Party can, and frequently does, intervene in legal proceedings. As a result, only a very brave or a very stupid judge would find against the state if a manager filed a breach of contract suit against the local administrative body responsible for industrial contracts. Moreover, few sanctions could be taken against the state organ, and the judge's ruling could not or would not be enforced. In such circumstances, managers are unlikely to take cases of contract breach to court. In addition, a number of critical issues remain unresolved under the law, such as whether managers have the right to use enterprise assets owned by the state for loan collateral issued by state banks or, more broadly, what rights managers have over the disposal of state-owned factory assets. A more serious problem is that Chinese contracts may not be voluntary agreements freely entered in to by both parties, as is required in American law. Managers may have very little choice in choosing their counterparts in contracts and little say in setting terms.

The Party and the leaders of the legal system are well aware of the problems of Party interference in legal administration. The Party has established its own Discipline Inspection Commission to handle cases of Party members who violate Party principles. The State Auditing Commission and a recently re-established Ministry of Supervision, designed to uncover bureaucratic abuses, all symbolize the Party's commitment to greater regularity and the creation of stable expectations. But the effect of this multiplication of quasi-judicial organs often works against the goals these institutions are designed to achieve: organizations compete for scarce personnel and fight over bureaucratic turf. Moreover, the Party's Discipline Inspection Commission often prevents legal organs from handling cases involving Party cadres who have violated the law, thus undermining respect for the legal system. As yet, judicial and prosecutorial independence remain the aspiration of a number of legal personnel, but one that rank-and-file Party members are highly suspicious of, if not actively hostile to. Breaking down these attitudes is a long-term, difficult process.

The Political Environment

Stated simply, managers may be responsible for the economic performance of their enterprises, but many aspects of the economic situation are beyond their control (Jiang 1984; Naughton 1986; Walder 1986b; *China New Analysis* 1344 [Oct. 1, 1987]). China's economy is characterized by shortages, particularly of energy resources and raw materials, which means that the state plan cannot fulfill demands. The state has thus been forced to authorize markets for producers goods. Because of the shortage of these materials, market prices have been 100–300 percent higher than plan prices. Enterprises must necessarily enter into close relations with administrative bodies to ensure steady supply of needed inputs, which compose about 75 percent of production costs. If the administrative bodies are unable to supply all the planned materials, enterprises must make use of the market. Enterprises have limited control over the sale price of what they produce, however. If they must rely on the market for inputs but cannot pass the increased cost of production to end users, it is very likely that enterprises will suffer losses, which managers, no matter how well qualified, would find difficult to avoid.

This results in a situation where managers enter into protracted bargaining relationships with administrative bodies and other enterprises in efforts to minimize risk. They do what they can to lower targets and quotas, to receive tax exemptions, to change prices, to hoard raw materials, to be allocated as much as possible through state planning and distribution systems, and so on. In these efforts, bribery, corruption, thievery, flattery, foot-dragging, brinkmanship, and other strategies are employed. Thus, the fundamental relationship an enterprise has with its external environment is a political one, characterized by bargaining and not oriented toward the market. The factory manager responsibility system is not going to make a dent in this political bargaining relationship (Lampton 1987).

One might wonder what local administrative (and Party) officials get out of their relationships with enterprises. Although conclusive evidence is lacking, it appears that enterprises under local supervision are key determinants of local power and chances for promotion. First, local enterprises provide officials with chances to exercise patronage and increase the material well-being, if not of themselves directly, then of relatives, patrons, and/or clients. Second, local budgetary revenues come from the profits and taxes of local industry. This does not mean that local officials force managers to be profit maximizers; rather, officials use their extensive discretionary powers in economic and financial affairs to make it easy for enterprises to make profits, by adjusting quotas, taxes, prices, and so on. Third, China and the CCP still emphasize substantive, as opposed to procedural, rationality. Although the precise criteria for promotion in China remain unclear, it seems a high rate of local economic growth is essential for a leader to be considered seriously for advancement. Without doubt, many other factors are considered as well; but if a local leader's region does not show rapid economic growth, he has few chances to advance. Fourth, it follows that local officials behave in what might be called a mercantilist way. They do what they can to promote production within their regions in order to look good. If "exporting" to other areas helps to spur local production, so much the better. But it is also in their interests to exclude the "importing" of finished products from other areas because this may undermine "domestic" industries. A relationship of mutual dependence between local enterprises and local leaders therefore develops (Jowitt 1983; Rigby 1983; Lyons 1987; Wong 1987).

Large state-owned enterprises are likely to be under the direct supervision of the central government, more specifically, the functional ministry charged with responsibility in each field. Almost by definition, large enterprises are so important to the national economy that the ministry or even the central government does what is necessary to keep these enterprises producing, even if this is unprofitable. Thus, despite many years' worth of effort to improve the efficiency of state-owned industrial enterprises, no appreciable increases in profitability have appeared. In 1985 the losses of urban industrial enterprises increased by 16.2 percent over the previous year; in 1986 they increased by 65 percent over 1985; and in 1987, by over 14 percent over 1986 (*FBIS*, Jan. 25, 1988). These figures may simply indicate that poorly managed enterprises are doing worse than they were before and that profit increases in other enterprises compensate for these declines. Nonetheless, many enterprises have not improved their performance.

Within enterprises, managers also confront a complicated social environment, one that only reinforces the factory-locality bargaining relationship. Wage funds have risen more rapidly than productivity. Only in 1984 did workers' real wages in state industry surpass 1956 levels. Although many of the problems within enterprises are the legacy of Maoist policies, workers have seen increasing wages as their right and not as part of an implicit contract of increasing productivity and work effort in exchange for improved wages. When managers have attempted to raise norms, workers have responded with slowdowns and other forms of resistance. Managers still have great difficulty firing workers, though this may be changing gradually.[6] Moreover, since enterprise performance largely depends on raw material and energy inputs, which are in short supply, it makes little sense for managers to concentrate on coercing higher productivity from workers. Rather, a live-and-let-live tacit agreement emerges between management and labor, and management devotes its efforts to cultivating administrative and other external agents who have power over the enterprise. Recent efforts to institute a contract work system to replace the system of de facto worker tenure has not had an appreciable effect on worker-management relations in the state sector (Walder 1986a; Walder 1987; White 1987).

Party Control over Mobility

As mentioned, I believe that the Party's control over the personnel system and social mobility is the most serious obstacle to reform in China. Prior to 1976, the Party controlled all aspects of mobility and life chances. Since the beginning of reform, it has had less say over life chances, and prosperity for some is possible without active involvement with or intervention by the CCP. But ability to move (particularly from one urban area to another), to change jobs, and to rise to a position of power and authority are still firmly under the control of the Party (Davis Friedman 1985; Manion 1985; Oi 1986; Walder 1986a; Burns 1987). Someone who wants to advance, move, or change jobs is thus reduced to a supplicant dependent on the Party to bestow its blessings. Needless to say, this gives the Party members who control personnel evaluations vast amounts of informal power. Local Party secretaries use this power to coerce managers, regardless of whether their desires conform with central policy. Moreover, there is only limited vertical and horizontal social mobility in China, with two consequences. First, promotion possibilities are limited, with many people competing for advancement. This situation enhances the patronage powers of local leaders (to say nothing of the potential for bribery, corruption, and the like). Second, one is likely to spend one's whole career in a single factory or organization. If one alienates one's superiors, retribution may extend throughout one's entire working life. Superiors control not only advancement opportunities but also many other aspects of working conditions and the provision of social benefits. It does not take much effort for superiors to inflict hardship on subordinates.

Some changes that have taken place within the personnel system marginally improve the situation. A clear message is being passed down the Party and state hierarchies: younger, more educated people are supposed to advance more rapidly. Commitment to Party ideology or service to the Party is much less likely to improve one's chance for advancement. But some changes may increase, rather than decrease, workers' dependence on the Party *nomenklatura*. The reach of the central *nomenklatura* has been reduced, but with the effect of heightening the power of local organizations in determining chances for promotion. Moreover, despite changes in the personnel system, the Party Organization Department (along with the Propaganda Department) is among the most conservative organs in China. Usually only long-time Party stalwarts head organization bureaus, and they are unlikely to be impressed by better educated, seemingly pampered young people. All this means that people impatient to bring about fundamental changes rapidly are unlikely to be promoted; and even if they did advance up the hierarchy, they would likely be co-opted or coerced into following the demands, suggestions, orders, and requests of Party and state superiors. Objective indicators of performance, to the extent they exist, are much less important than political relationships. So long as the Party rules China and upholds Party leadership as one of the four cardinal principles, this underlying reality will sharply constrain reform efforts.

Conclusions and Prospects

In the long term, the lack of a privatization infrastructure—no unified national market, an irrational price system, the lack of an institutionalized legal system, the overall political environment in which enterprises exist, and Party control over mobility—all make the prospects for successful privatization in China problematic. In the short run, the lack of political will to privatize and a related ideological antipathy to privatization are the biggest obstacles to policy development in this area. Even Zhao Ziyang's critics concede that he did not expressly favor privatization but that he supported it indirectly by encouraging the private and collective sector to grow more rapidly than the state sector. It was economists close to Zhao who articulated demands for a radical privatization of the Chinese economy (*FBIS*, July 21, Aug. 10, 31, and Sept. 22, 1989). As a result of the Tiananmen Sqaure massacre and the subsequent retreat from reform, concerns about excessive income inequalities have resurfaced, and private, or individual, enterprises and collectives are under attack. While the leadership continues to see a role for individual enterprises, it has created incentives for local cadres to attack them by suggesting that most individual enterprises evade taxes and engage in corrupt business practices (*FBIS*, July 12 and Aug. 31, 1989).

China's political future is murky at best. Scenarios of a complete breakdown of the Chinese state or a return to a Stalinist model of development are not far-fetched. Nonetheless, certain economic and social imperatives will continue to keep private and collective enterprises alive, and the failure to improve the economic performance of state-owned industry will force the issue of privatization on the political agenda in the future. In 1982, at the time of the Third National Population Census, almost 46 percent of the Chinese population was under 20 years of age (SSB 1986: 80); and after coming down in the early 1980s, the birth rate is now again on the rise. As a result, the Chinese state will face a continuing problem of finding jobs for its people for a prolonged period. The more the state limits private enterprise, the more the state must bear the burden of employing people itself—and simply put, the state sector is incapable of absorbing the huge cohort of youths seeking their first job every year. Private and collective enterprises must continue to expand, or the state will face huge social problems. The continued existence and growth of the private ownership will resuscitate the idea of private sector solutions to state problems.

The Chinese leadership has been complaining about the inefficiency of the state industrial sector for at least ten years. In that time, no fundamental change for the better has occurred; in many respects, the situation may have worsened. The current leadership has blamed collective and private enterprises (and Zhao's lack of attention to state enterprises) as the causes of this inefficiency. But the problems of China's state enterprises involve structure and system, not particular policies. Without greater incentives and pressures to produce efficiently (that is, to subject production to the test of the market), it is highly doubtful that basic changes in enterprise efficiency will occur. Even conservative leaders will face the question of what is to be done after the failure of more traditional planning methods becomes evident. Although they probably will not opt for privatization and marketization, these issues will certainly reappear among the choices available to them, albeit in muted form.

Thus the issue of privatization, and the economic and social forces that give rise to it, will be reproduced in the Chinese political economy no matter what the current hardline leaders may think. They can criticize the idea—quite effectively, given their perspective (*FBIS*, July 21 and Aug. 31, 1989)—and arrest, persecute, or drive into exile its champions, but the policy problems of employment and efficiency that privatization addresses will not be solved.

Notes

Funding for this paper was made possible by a grant from the Pew Charitable Trusts and the Center for International Studies, Princeton University. I wish to thank Yu Xiaowei for research assistance and John Waterbury and Gregory Chow for comments on earlier drafts of this chapter.

1. This chapter was originally written prior to the Tiananmen Square (or Beijing) Massacre and has been only partially revised. Despite the immediate, highly negative retrogression in Chinese policymaking, long-term trends continue to favor reform and privatization in China, as will be discussed in the conclusion.

2. The juridical status of these enterprises is uncertain. In recent years, the state has guaranteed the sanctity of private property and private enterprises in general. Local cadres, however, often interfere in the operation of these endeavors, and every individual entrepreneur is of course aware that in the past the state has expropriated, closed, and/or merged almost all private economic enterprises. See the section on the legal system below; Wong 1986; and Wong 1988.

3. Indeed, it is hard to imagine a factory manager suing the state or a local administrative department if the latter unilaterally altered the enterprise profit contract. It is even more difficult to conceive of a Chinese court supporting the manager.

4. Various hypotheses for public ownership are surveyed in Pryor 1973: chap. 2.

5. This section draws on Lubman 1982 and Baum 1986.

6. A survey of ninety-four factories where the enterprise law was implemented in a trial found that 69.5 percent of managers said they would make major changes in personnel when the law took effect. Yet, once the law was implemented in these test points, only 6.6 percent actually made major personnel changes; 69.1 percent made minor changes; and 24.3 percent made no change at all (Salem 1988).

References

Baum, Richard. 1986. "Modernization and Legal Reform in Post-Mao China." *Studies in Comparative Communism* 19, no. 2: 69–104.

Burkett, John P. 1983. *The Effects of Economic Reform in Yugoslavia*. Institute of International Studies Research Series no. 55. Berkeley: Institute of International Studies Research.

Burns, John P. 1987. "China's *Nomenklatura* System." *Problems of Communism* 26, 5: 36–51.

Comisso, Ellen, and Laura D'Andrea Tyson, eds. 1986. *Power, Purpose, and Collective Choice*. Ithaca, N.Y.: Cornell University Press.

Davis Friedman, Deborah. 1985. "Intergenerational Inequalities and the Chinese Revolution." *Modern China* 11, no. 2: 177–202.

Delfs, Robert. 1988. "Property to the People!" *Far Eastern Economic Review*, December 22, pp. 12–13.

FBIS. *Foreign Broadcast Information Service, Daily Report, China*. Various dates.

Fischer, William A. 1986. "Chinese Industrial Management." In JEC 1986, vol. 1.

Gaige. 1986. Zhongguo Jingji Tizhi Gaige Yanjiusuo Zonghe Diaochazu, eds. *Gaige: Women Mianlinde Tianzhan yu Xuanze* [Reform: the challenges before us and our choices]. Beijing: Zhongguo Jingji Chubanshe.

Gold, Thomas B. 1985. "After Comradeship." *China Quarterly* 104: 657–675.

Hanke, Steven H., ed. 1987. *Privatization and Development*. San Francisco: Institute for Contemporary Studies.

Harding, Harry. 1987. *China's Second Revolution*. Washington, D.C.: Brookings Institution.

Hare, Paul G. 1983. "The Beginnings of Institutional Reform in Hungary." *Soviet Studies* 35, no. 3: 313–330.

Hare, Paul, Hugo Radice, and Nigel Swain, eds. 1981. *Hungary: A Decade of Economic Reform*. London: George Allen and Unwin.

Hemming, Richard, and Ali M. Mansoor. 1987. *Privatization and Public Enterprises*. International Monetary Fund Working Paper. Washington, D.C.: International Monetary Fund.

Horvat, Branko. 1976. *The Yugoslav Economic System*. White Plains, N.Y.: M. E. Sharpe.

Hsu, Robert C. 1985. "Conceptions of the Market in Post-Mao China." *Modern China* 11, no. 4: 436–460.

Ignatius, Adi. 1987. "Socialist Inhibitions about Speculation Put Damper on Stock Trading in China." *Wall Street Journal*, August 18.

JEC (U.S. Congress, Joint Economic Committee). 1982. *China under the Four Modernizations*. 2 vols. Washington, D.C.: Government Printing Office.

_____. 1986. *China's Economy Looks toward the Year 2000*. 2 vols. Washington, D.C.: Government Printing Office.

Jiang Zilong. 1984. *All the Colours of the Rainbow*. Beijing: Panda Books.

Jowitt, Ken. 1983. "Soviet Neo-Traditionalism." *Soviet Studies* 35, no. 3: 257–297.

Knight, Peter T. 1983. *Economic Reform in Socialist Countries*. World Bank Staff Working Paper no. 579. Washington, D.C.: World Bank.

Kornai, Janos. 1980. *The Economics of Shortage*. Amsterdam: North-Holland.

_____. 1986. *Dilemmas and Contradictions*. Cambridge, Mass.: M.I.T. Press.

Lampton, David M. 1987. "Chinese Politics: The Bargaining Treadmill." *Issues and Studies* 23, no. 3: 11–41.

Lubman, Stanley B. 1982. "Emerging Functions of Formal Legal Institutions in China's Modernization." In JEC 1982, vol. 2.

Lyons, Thomas P. 1987. *Economic Integration and Planning in Maoist China*. New York: Columbia University Press.

Malle, Silvana. 1987. "Planned and Unplanned Mobility of Labor in the Soviet Union under the Threat of Labor Shortage." *Soviet Studies* 39, no. 3: 357–387.

Manion, Melanie. 1985. "The Cadre Management System Post-Mao." *China Quarterly* 102 (June): 203–233.

Naughton, Barry. 1985. "False Starts and Second Wind." In Perry and Wong 1985.

_____. 1986. "Finance and Planning Reforms." In JEC 1986, vol. 1.

Nove, Alec. 1983. *The Economics of Feasible Socialism*. London: George Allen & Unwin.

Oi, Jean C. 1986. "Commercializing China's Rural Cadres." *Problems of Communism* 35, no. 5: 1–15.

Perry, Elizabeth J., and Christine Wong, eds. 1985. *The Political Economy of Reform in Post-Mao China*. Harvard Contemporary China Series no. 2. Cambridge, Mass.: Harvard University Press.

Pryor, Frederick L. 1973. *Property and Industrial Organization in Communist and Capitalist Nations*. Bloomington: University of Indiana Press.

Rigby, T. H. 1983. "A Conceptual Approach to Authority, Power, and Policy in the Soviet Union." In *Authority, Power, and Policy in the USSR*, ed. T. H. Rigby et al. London: Macmillan.

Sacks, Stephen R. 1973. *Entry of New Competitors in Yugoslav Market Socialism*. Institute of International Studies Research Series no. 19. Berkeley: Institute of International Studies.

Salem, Ellen. 1987. "China's Funds at Low Tide." *Far Eastern Economic Review*, November 19, pp. 96–97.

————. 1988. "More Cracks in the Iron Rice Bowl." *Far Eastern Economic Review*, March 24, p. 89.

SSB (State Statistical Bureau), comp. 1986. *Statistical Yearbook of China 1986*. Oxford: Oxford University Press.

Starr, Paul. 1987. "The Limits of Privatization." In *Prospects for Privatization*, ed. Steve H. Hanke. New York: Academy of Political Science.

Teiwes, Frederick C. 1984. *Leadership, Legitimacy, and Conflict in China*. Armonk, N.Y.: M. E. Sharpe.

Tidrick, Gene, and Chen Jiyuan, eds. 1987. *China's Industrial Reforms*. New York: Oxford University Press for the World Bank.

Travers, S. Lee. 1982. "Bias in Chinese Economic Statistics." *China Quarterly* 91 (September): 478–485.

Tyson, Laura D'Andrea. 1980. *The Yugoslav Economic System and Its Performance in the 1970s*. Institute of International Studies Research Series no. 44. Berkeley: Institute of International Studies.

Walder, Andrew G. 1986a. *Communist Neotraditionalism*. Berkeley: University of California Press.

Walder, Andrew G. 1986b. "The Informal Dimension of Enterprise Financial Reform." In JEC 1986, vol. 1.

Walder, Andrew G. 1987. "Wage Reform and the Web of Factory Interests." *China Quarterly* 109 (March): 22–41.

White, Gordon. 1987. "The Politics of Reform in Chinese Industry." *China Quarterly* 111 (September): 365–385.

Wong, Christine. 1985. "Material Allocation and Decentralization." In Perry and Wong 1985.

Wong, Christine. 1986. "Ownership and Control in Chinese Industry." In JEC 1986, vol. 1.

Wong, Christine. 1987. "Between the Plan and the Market." *Journal of Comparative Economics* 11, no. 3: 385–399.

————. 1988. "Interpreting Rural Industrial Growth in the Post-Mao Period." *Modern China* 14, no. 1: 255–283.

World Bank. 1983. *China: Socialist Economic Development*. Washington, D.C.: World Bank.

13

The Political Context of Public Sector Reform and Privatization in Egypt, India, Mexico, and Turkey

John Waterbury

The four countries under consideration here are all large, highly diversified LDC economies that share several specific characteristics. First, until the last five years or so, they have all followed development strategies based on import-substituting industrialization (ISI), in which state enterprise has played the leading role. India has only marginally modified that strategy in recent years; Egypt has talked a great deal about a major strategy overhaul, but so far has done little to implement it; Mexico has begun a process of austerity and the promotion of exports; and Turkey has been one of the star performers among those LDCs recently converted to an export-led growth strategy.

The state enterprise sectors of all four are relatively old: in the case of Turkey, the public sector enterpises (PSEs) date from the late 1920s and the 1930s; in Mexico, from the 1930s; in India, from the late 1940s and 1950s; and in Egypt from about 1954 on. Thus these countries offer the maximum possibility for the formation of coherent managerial elites in the public sector, for the development of dependent, privileged labor organizations, and for enterprise longevity and tradition that we are likely to find in noncommunist LDCs. We may hypothesize that in these countries the defense of the public sector is likely to be the strongest, the resistance to reform the most pronounced, and the range of vested interests affected by reform and privatization the broadest.

Moreover, the state in each of these countries has been interventionist along a broad front. There have been attempts at comprehensive planning, far-reaching regulation of all economic activity, administered pricing, guidance of market forces, quantitative trade restrictions, and substantial if not total control of banking and other financial institutions by the public sector. All four still maintain plan organizations, draw up four- or five-year plans, and see the state as coordinator of all major economic activity.

The private sector of each of the four varies in strength, but all share at least two features. First, existing private sectors were depicted with the familiar epithets "comprador," "parasitic," and the like. They were to be regulated and carefully monitored so that they would no longer take advantage of the masses. Indeed, much of the rationale for heavy state intervention in the economy was to protect the poor from private greed and to undertake projects that shortsighted, unskilled, and undercapitalized private actors could not. At the same time, each radical ideology held out the prospect that some day a truly nationalist, enlightened, farsighted entrepreneurial bourgeoisie might emerge—one, however, that would always play a subordinate role to state enterprise.

The second factor in common is that the policymakers and leaders of all four countries have in the last decade or so expressed profound disappointment with the way in which ISI has proceeded and in the performance of PSEs. The pathology of statism is familiar: chronic loss-making PSEs, privileged labor aristocracies, burgeoning domestic deficits, accelerating inflation, and mounting external debt. Something approaching crisis, especially in external accounts, was manifest by the mid-1970s, to some extent driven if not caused by the external oil shocks. What we saw, I argue, was an attempt to streamline and "rationalize" the statist experiments. This period witnessed the emergence of statists of the right, but statists nonetheless. Their goal was to replace redistributive state socialism with cost-effective state capitalism. Turgut Özal of Turkey and Salinas de Gortari of Mexico, however, have shown their determination to reduce the economic size of the state significantly.

The four countries differ in the course of adjustment after the first attempt to deal with the crisis of the mid-1970s. Mexico and Egypt, increasingly fat with oil and external rents (workers' remittances, tourism), abandoned the stabilization-cum-structural adjustment programs with which they briefly flirted in 1976 and 1977. The Egyptian regime faced cost-of-living riots in January 1977, when the government tried to reduce consumer subsidies. India never really succumbed to crisis. Supplemented by the discipline of the emergency period 1974–1977, it managed through careful fiscal and trade policy to protect its fundamental ISI and statist strategy. Turkey, on the other hand, dealt with its severe domestic and external accounts crisis of 1978–1979 through a military takeover and the authoritarian implementation of a structural adjustment program and a shift to export-led growth.

Relative Sizes of the Public Sector

The size of the public enterprise sector in each of these four countries differs markedly. Egypt's is by far the largest and, in relation to gross domestic product (GDP), proportion of total employment, value of fixed assets, share of investment, and contribution to value-added, yields an image similar to those of Eastern European economies. Turkey, Mexico, and India tend to cluster in most respects. In India, for example, total sales turnover in 1983–1984 represented about 28 percent of GDP, value-added about 6 percent, and the wage bill about 11 percent for the 214 union- or federal-level PSEs. Over a twenty-four-year period their average rate of profit on sales was only 0.5 percent. Throughout the 1970s the public sector's share in gross domestic fixed capital formation grew steadily from 38 percent in 1970–1971 to 52 percent in 1982–1983 (Ahluwalia 1986: 946). The PSEs employ about 2.2 million people out of a total public workforce of 16.8 million at the state and union level and out of a total organized workforce in the nonagricultural economy (establishments with 10 or more employess) of 24.1 million. In 1988 the share value of all Indian PSEs was about $22 billion, while that of the private corporate sector was $6.7 billion (*India Today*, May 31, 1988; see also CMIE 1983). These various indicators constitute a great deal of economic and social leverage. State-level public enterprise, it is important to note, by all estimates employs more people than the union enterprises and controls assets worth more than the union's.

Mexico's public enterprise sector may be, relative to the Mexican economy, the smallest of those under consideration, even though Mexico is the only major oil exporter among them and the Mexican oil company (PEMEX) is the single most important enterprise in the Mexican state sector. In 1982 public outlays on PSEs amounted to 26 percent of GDP, and in 1980 their sales represented 17.2 percent of GDP (led by PEMEX), up from 12 percent in 1970. In the early 1980s the PSEs employed nearly 900,000 people, or close to 5 percent of the total active population. One observer put total public employment, presumably including state-level civil servants, at 4.5 million in 1985 (Castañeda 1987: 99). When taking into consideration all government outlays, we find that public expenditures as a proportion of GDP rose from 32 percent in 1978 to 42 percent in 1983 (in general, see Castro and Ramirez 1983; Hill 1984; Zedillo 1986; Cuadernos 1988).

As of 1984, the public enterprise sector in Turkey comprised 74 major companies distributed among 33 holding companies, such as the venerable ETIBANK with 14 mines, 7 factories, and nearly 26,000 employees. In 1982 the PSEs accounted for 33 percent of total and 54 percent of public investments, 25 percent of total value-added (down from 34 percent in 1979), and 11 percent of GDP (down from 13 percent in 1978: Karataş

1986). Although various austerity measures were undertaken after 1979 as part of Turkey's structural adjustment program, employment in PSEs rose from 550,000 in 1980 to 722,000 in 1986, before falling to 683,000 in 1987. The latter figure represents about 15 percent of the total *employed* nonagricultural workforce in that year.

Finally we come to the giant in this group, the Egyptian public sector. It has its origins in the nationalizations that followed the Suez War of 1956. At that time British and French assets in Egypt were taken over by the state. But even prior to this, the Egyptian state had begun the creation of public sector enterprise in the iron, steel, and fertilizer industries and in its plan to construct the High Aswan Dam. Over the ensuing twenty years the public sector grew prodigiously. Its center of gravity came to lie in heavy industry, but the state also acquired a dominant position in banking, insurance, and foreign trade. The entire public sector in 1984–1985 employed 1.35 million persons—more than 10 percent of the entire work force and about a quarter of the nonagricultural workforce. We may add to this figure 2.8 million civil servants, which means that about two-thirds of the nonagricultural workforce is on the state payroll. These gross figures do not include the armed forces (about 400,000) or the police (about 150,000).

Despite the disparity in size between Egypt and the other three countries, all show the extent to which PSEs are relatively dominant in their respective economies. They are the single most important source of nonagricultural employment, control the most capital-intensive industries, usually absorb a third or more of public investment, and in all four enjoy a dominant position in banking and financial intermediation. With the exception of the petroleum sector and PSEs enjoying monopoly positions, they have tended to show a very modest rate of profit, while in each country there are several chronic loss-makers that contribute significantly to both the public domestic deficit and to the external debt. At the same time they generally borrow at preferential interest rates from public banks, enjoy lower corporate tax rates, and are allowed to run up large cumulative debts through unsecured borrowing.

Even loss-making PSEs may be a significant source of revenue to government treasuries, and the public enterprise sector in general may be seen as a captive source of public revenue. The Egyptian example is illustrative: PSEs pay the government 35 percent of all profits before distribution; they pay corporate profits tax at around 40 percent after distribution; they pay 5 percent of net profits into statutory reserves; and with another 5 percent of net profits they purchase government bonds. As employers, they automatically pay in the bulk of all social security and accident and health insurance payments for their 1.3 million employees. From 1980 to 1985 aggregate PSE transfers rose in nominal terms from £E 2.6 billion to

£E 4 billion and averaged about two-thirds of total gross government revenues (Ahmed 1984: 69; World Bank 1986:100).

Issues of Political Management

The political and macro-economic challenges facing these countries are such that reform and privatization will figure low on the policy agenda. In all four countries, but to a much greater extent in Turkey and Mexico than in India and Egypt, austerity, reduced public outlays, and structural adjustment have taken a heavy social toll, with absolute declines in the standard of living for large segments of the population and with rising rates of unemployment (15–20 percent of the active populations of Mexico and Turkey). Not surprisingly, the adjustment process has produced fissures in dominant coalitions. A military takeover ended the civilian regime in Turkey in September 1980, and the new civilian regime that took power through elections in 1983 must constantly look over its shoulder at its military overseers. In Mexico, the dominant Institutionalized Revolutionary Party (PRI) claimed a narrow victory in the July 1988 elections after the defection of left-center interests led by Cuahtemoc Cárdenas and the alienation of important segments of organized labor. From outside the PRI, the rightist probusiness Partido de Acción Nacional (PAN) made a strong electoral showing.

Political leadership in these and other LDCs may believe that the economic payoffs of privatization will not cover the social costs of diverting scarce technical human resources to the complicated task of preparing companies for transfer and stimulating capital markets or the political costs of trying to package and sell the policy to reluctant members of incumbent coalitions. But privatization on a limited scale may present fewer difficulties in political management than public sector reform. The easiest shifts in assets may come through outright liquidations. The question is not so much one of social equity—the adjustment process has already caused more havoc than would reform or privatization—but rather of a thoroughgoing revamping of operational, technological, and managerial aspects of PSEs. The latter, during or after a process of shedding through privatization and liquidation, will inevitably be the large, so-called "strategic" behemoths of the heyday of ISI. They will be the least susceptible to internal reform, although, as Turkey has shown, granting them greater autonomy from supervising ministries and allowing them to set their own output prices can lead to superficial improvement in their financial performance (Mertoğlu 1987). By contrast, because the issues of unemployment and inflation generated through the macro-adjustment process are the focus of national debates over distribution and equity, the sale or closing of a few PSEs may produce little political heat.

In all four countries "social pacts" have come under severe strain or have been broken. No leader can afford to aknowledge that fact, and the process has gone much further in Turkey and Mexico than in Egypt and India. In Egypt the package of social welfare benefits, the use of the civil service and public sector as the employer of last resort, and the scale of the consumer subsisdy system are much more extensive than in any of the other three countries. There is much more to undo in Egypt's social pact than in India's. Indeed, India's economic performance throughout the 1970s and early 1980s has been such that it has not had to reduce existing commitments to social welfare. The country has not yet experienced the crises of the other three in its external accounts: its debt has been manageable, its exchange rate properly valued, and its domestic inflation remarkably low.

Egypt and Mexico (until very recently) have both enjoyed single party-dominant regimes, whereas Turkey in the 1970s engaged in turbulent multiparty politics yielding fragile coalition governments. Competition for votes led to costly pork-barrel politics. Wages in the public and union-ized sector of the economy grew far more rapidly than GDP, as did public employment in general. Liberalized trade and foreign exchange regulations allowed expansion of private sector activity based on an import surge. Coalition members outbid one another in backing public sector projects in key constituent districts. Only the steady flow of worker remittances postponed the day of reckoning. Ironically, it was the newly installed left-of-center government of Bülent Ecevit (Republican People's Party) in March 1978 that had to pay the bill: it entered into negotiations with the International Monetary Fund (IMF) for a standby based on devaluation, deficit reduction, and export promotion. Aside from devaluation, Ecevit was unable to implement the agreement. He had to honor the labor and middle-income groups that had elected him, and large wage settlements and other heavy public outlays maintained the deficit at high levels. This, however, did not prevent him from losing the next by-elections to the right-of-center Suleiman Demirel (Justice Party) in November 1979. Demirel undertook the stand-by himself and put implementation in the hands of his undersecretary for planning, Turgut Özal. All this was carried out in a state of growing urban terrorism and labor agitation, which was either the cause of or the pretext for the most senior officers to intervene and, under authoritarian rule, implement the stand-by agreement. After the September 1980 coup, the military kept Özal on as the chief architect of adjustment and of a concerted shift to export-led growth. Up to this point, and indeed until 1984, privatization was not explicitly part of the adjustment process.

The Egyptian case is considerably different. In the spring of 1976 negotiations began with the IMF for a stand-by agreement with all the familiar components. The formal signing was postponed until after parliamentary elections in November. In late January 1977, the minister of economy presented part of the package to parliament, announcing major cuts in consumer subsidies, nominally offset by some public sector wage increases and by pledges to increase taxes on private wealth. Riots broke out the next day up and down the Nile Valley; they required military intervention, caused as many as eight hundred deaths, and shook the regime to its foundations. The reform package was abandoned entirely. Sadat went to Jerusalem, and in March 1979, two years after the riots, the Camp David accords were signed. In the meantime, Egypt began to collect external rents from worker remittances, Suez Canal tolls, and tourism. With the signing of the Camp David accords, the already substantial strategic rents paid to Egypt by the United States mushroomed, and a surge in Egyptian oil production, coupled with the second surge in oil prices, generated $3–4 billion annually in new revenue. All incentive for reform and adjustment was lost. The basic structure of the Egyptian economy, with the exception of the external rents, has changed remarkably little since 1975–1976 (Waterbury 1983); and now that revenues from remittances and especially from petroleum have fallen off sharply, Egypt is left to face the same structural problems it confronted decade ago, only with ten million more people to support.

The Mexican scenario has been somewhat similiar to Egypt's, minus war and strategic rents. The Echeverría sexenio, 1970–1976, coming on the heels of the riots and violence of 1968, witnessed a great expansion in state-led growth. At the same time, Echeverría tried to promote exports without any devaluation of the peso. Although growth remained high, the deficit, inflation, and debt grew apace. A process that Zedillo has called "import de-substitution" took place, accompanied in 1975–1976 by massive capital flight and culminating at the end of the sexenio in devaluation of the peso. Devaluation was followed in the Lopez Portillo sexenio by cutbacks in investment. But these first steps toward adjustment were soon abandoned (Zedillo 1986: 975).

The reason was the oil rents of the late 1970s, with which Lopez Portillo sponsored an expansion of PSE investment in petrochemcials, steel, and electricity. At the same time, he liberalized foreign trade and talked of bringing Mexico within the General Agreement on Trade and Tariffs (GATT). By 1979, private sector imports were running at $14 billion, well in excess of public sector imports. Simultaneously, capital flight took on dramatic proportions, rising from about $4 billion in 1981 to more than $10 billion in 1982 and thereafter.

The beginning of the de la Madrid sexenio reflected no crisis of confidance in state-led growth. He contributed to the Plan Global de Desarrollo of 1980–1982, which aimed to "fortify the state in order to satisfy the demands of a society in full growth," and in 1981 he invoked all the statist symbols of several decades, referring to the public sector as the vanguard of national development and to the PSEs as major levers of the state to be used in cognizance of the popular will as expressed in the social and constitutional pact (see Castro and Ramirez 1983: 25). It was this statist of the right who had to begin to deal with postponed problems of adjustment when petroleum prices began to plummet. The size of the debt on the one hand, and the fact that it was and is commercial debt, and the absence of strategic rents on the other meant that Mexico could not afford to adopt Egypt's glacial response to adjustment. Privatization, "desincorporación," liquidation, and debt-for-equity swaps were on the Mexican agenda by 1984.

As these four countries move toward adjustment, dominant coalitions have to be reconstituted. This typically entails the promotion of a new breed of technocrat, expert in business and financial management, to positions of real power. Thus we have seen Rajiv Gandhi surrounded by his "whiz kids," the ascendancy of Salinas de Gortari in Mexico, and Özal conferring with his U.S.-educated "Princes" (as they are called in the Turkish press). Old allies who managed labor–white-collar alliances, ran the party—whether the Congress, or the PRI, or even the now-defunct Justice Party through whose auspices Özal first rose to prominence—are shunted aside but left in a position to snipe at and obstruct the new leadership. The public sector workforce and managerial corps represent a bird in hand, one that cannot be released before allies in the private sector grow in strength and confidence and are brought into the alliance. In none of these countries has that fully occurred, although in Turkey and Mexico the process has begun, and no one is predicting that private sector confidance is on the horizon or that the private sector will soon be ready to shoulder a major part of national economic activity and lead the export drive.

For and Against Public Sector Reform and Privatization

Politicos, Bureaucrats, and Managers

Those who undertook the economic management and political ward-heeling of the ISI phase continue to represent powerful, vested interests. They may be in eclipse, faced with the ascendancy of the new breed of business school graduates and technical economists, but they are the ones with the experience to keep those PSEs functioning that are not going to disappear and to hold together political alliances that have, in all four countries, yielded decades of relative political stability. In Mexico, under

Salinas, the balance of forces may have tipped decisively in favor of the technocrats and the neoclassical economists, but the political and economic logic of maintaining a strong state presence in the economy remains compelling.

Early in his incumbency (which ended in electoral defeat in late 1989), Rajiv Gandhi assailed the Congress party leadership at all levels for corruption, complacency, and organizational sclerosis. Several of his mother's loyalists during the emergency were particularly offended and either quit the party or went into a kind internal dissidence. There was a widespread journalistic image of Rajiv running the affairs of state on the strength of advice from a handful of young, politically inexperienced technocrats who merely manipulated computer models of the economy (see Jain 1986). As one disgruntled state-level (UP) Congress ward heeler is alleged to have remarked when cumputers rejected the siting of a big industrial project in his state, "Let the computer fetch the votes."

Turgut Özal in Turkey stands astride several cleavages that divide the political establishment of his country. He has brought into key positions of economic management a group of young technocrats, the magnitude of whose analytic expertise is matched only by their lack of political experience in Turkey. At the same time, Özal represents what might be called the provincial middle and entrepreneurial classes. They are inward looking, worried about future membership in the European Economic Community (EEC), and suspicious of the big private enterprises in Istanbul and Izmir. But it is precisely the latter that have and must continue to take the lead in Turkey's export drive, so that Özal must court them as well. Finally, senior bureaucrats and military officers (not to mention the peak trade union) still adhere in part to the statist legacy of Atatürk and of the 1960s. Turkey's is still very much a contingent civilian regime. Özal has proven himself skilled at balancing these various constituencies; but as his export-led growth strategy evolves, not all of them can be equally protected.

In terms of reconstituting the dominant coalition, Egypt's has changed the least. The shift to right statism under Sadat in the early 1970s has not been significantly modified by Muhammad Hosni Mubarrak. He is still a military man, and the military is still an integral part of the regime. The dominant National Democratic party has been filled with retreaded politicos from the defunct Arab Socialist Union. As in Mexico, they have allies in organized labor and the intelligentsia. The major policy figures in recent years, whether in or out of the current government, are all comfortable with a high degree of state intervention.

Because economic adjustment and liberalization have advanced the least in Egypt and India, the reconstitution of political coalitions is also the least advanced. In Mexico and Turkey, where the process is well and painfully under way, the political management challenges are commensurately greater.

It has often been hypothesized that the managers of PSEs would likely oppose any efforts at substantial reform of their sectors and, above all, any efforts to sell majority interests to the private sector or to liquidate public enterprises. My own research of the last three years has led me to believe that the hypothesis is not very useful. Top-level public sector managers rarely constitute a coherent, organized lobby or interest group, and they are unlikely to devise shared strategies to defend their patrimony.

Sometimes managers are political hacks, paid off without regard to their skills or preparation for their state jobs. Appointment as chief executive officer of a PSE may be a fairly harmless way of disposing of retired military officers or, as was the case early in the statist period in Mexico, of paying off labor leaders and active military officers. In India, the use of PSEs for political payoffs at the state level is common. Generally, however, political loyalty is combined with managerial competence and professionalism (Grindle 1977 has made a convincing case for this in Mexico's giant food corporation, CONASUPO). We must be clear about the scope of the phenomenon: we may be talking of no more than internal shifts within governments, in which a new minister may juggle company heads within his sector in order to assure himself of maximum loyalty and compliance among a set of clients. By and large, we know from the literature on PSEs throughout the world, but especially in Eastern Europe and in the LDCs, that managers must become skilled politicians in manipulating vertical linkages with ministries and ministers that control the flow of raw materials, set industrial prices, provide foreign exchange, and advance credits. The skilled manager does not answer to the shareholders, nor does he have much control over the variables that determine his profits and losses (the gross deficit on the operations of Turkish PSEs was wiped out in one year after the government of Turkey allowed most PSEs to set their own prices for goods and services). Rather, he learns to coax from his supervisory bureaucracies (probably his tutelary ministry, the treasury, and the plan organization) the resources and protection that will enhance his performance. He may pursue his strategy at the expense of other PSEs, like some Indian steel manufacturers in the public sector who would like to be able to import higher-grade coking coal rather than use that provided by the public coal sector. In short, horizontal relations among managers develop, if at all, in the same sector, but even then rapid turnover in managers and intersectoral shifts place a premium on individual survival strategies.

One should not minimize the periodic, albeit rare, moments in which real politicization pervades the selection of managers. Electoral politics in

Turkey in the 1950s, late 1960s, and 1970s led to some bald allotments of management positions to political allies. After Sadat purged the Egyptian political establishment of "leftist" elements in 1971, it is said that their clients among public sector managers went with them. Sexenios in Mexico see a thousand or so top-level officials shuffled; but while some may fall on hard times, most have strong chances of resurfacing (Wilkie 1968; Smith 1979). The Janata victory in India in 1977 represented the first time since 1947 that Congress was defeated in national elections; but, due perhaps to the scruples of Prime Minister Morarji Desai, Janata did not seize the opportunity to pack the union PSEs with its cronies.

Top-level managers have a range of options open to them that few other civil servants enjoy and that may tend to dilute their loyalty to their enterprise or to the public sector as a whole. For many, there is the option of exit to the private sector, where they can cash in on their technical and managerial skills or their ability to bring private interests into contact with appropriate government interests.

Public sector management may present only a minor challenge to privatization. At the firm level, however, top management may have little incentive to undertake serious internal reform and restructuring. As they near the end of their careers, it is unlikely that managers will begin the necessarily painful restructuring of their enterprises, the fruits of which will not become apparent until after they retire and for which they will receive little credit. As a group, they have become increasingly professional over the decades, and their careers have seldom been troubled by major political purges; but stability and professionalism have not outweighed the structural impact on managerial behavior that dictates constant attention to the bureaucratic and political determinants of supply, pricing, and finance.

In contrast to the state managers, the top-ranking and middle-level civil servants may in fact pose a far more serious obstacle to public sector reform and privatization, albeit one that manifests itself more in fragmented obstructionism than in formal organizational confrontation. This phenomenon is most pronounced in India. First, specialized bureaucracies and agencies have developed in order to monitor, audit, and finance public sector activity. As the latter shrinks or gains more autonomy at the firm level, the need for the supervisory bureaucrats diminishes accordingly. PSEs provide bureaucratic agencies not only their raison d'être but also various kinds of side payments and rents generated by the regulatory and financing process itself.

Second, many of the middle- and upper-level bureaucrats may not enjoy the same alternative career opportunities open to public sector managers, and they risk finding themselves in dead-end jobs in functionally irrelevant agencies. And in the process of adjustment, civil servants are fired. De la Madrid, for example, laid off thirty thousand of them in a matter of months. The more senior or important will probably receive a golden handshake of some kind, but that can hardly compensate for the loss of a bureaucratic empire.

Labor

In contrast to senior bureaucrats, unionized labor in the public sector is likely to offer organizational resistance to reform and privatization, although its efforts may not be as effective as the individualistic foot-dragging of civil servants. Turkey, Egypt, Mexico, and, to a lesser extent, India have all relied on peak labor confederations, the bulk of whose membership is on public payroll. It is within these quasi-corporatist arrangements that the major elements of the social pact have been worked out. The implicit bargain has generally been a high level of union discipline in exchange for favorable wage and benefit packages and job security. In all four countries, the image of a labor "aristocracy" is not inaccurate (Turkey's three million unemployed in 1985 exceeded the number of unionized workers: see Kopits 1987: table 10): the tradeoff has been a beneficial one from labor's standpoint. But will the state's efforts to cut back welfare programs, reduce employment, link wages to productivity, and close down PSEs provoke strikes and other forms of disruption on the part of organized labor?

Mexico can be used to demonstrate some general points. The peak organization, the Confederación de los Trabajadores Méxicanos (CTM), was created in 1938 and became one of the pillars of the PRI. From its inception, it declared the goal of Mexican labor to be to join the battle of production. Since the 1940s it has been led by Fidel Velasquez, a key figure in maintaining the pact between organized labor and the state. In the late 1970s the CTM had more than 730,000 individual members, but most of its member unions were small. The major union within it, and the real guts of the CTM, is the Federación de los Trabajadores del Distrito Federal with 300,000 members (Prevot-Shapira 1983: 95). Alongside the CTM, but even larger than it, is the Federación de Sindicatos al Servicio del Estado. About 50 percent of Mexico's nonagricultural workers are union members, and the CTM, with other PRI labor affiliates, controls about 70 percent of the unionized workforce.

The right to strike is protected in Mexico, but most wage-benefit packages are drawn up through mandatory collective bargaining in which the union with the most members at the firm or industry level represents all the workers. Thus, while there are several unions of both left and right lying outside the corporatist frame, leadership in crucial bargaining situations will fall to the co-opted. Not surprisingly, unions have broken away from the mother confederation, the rank-and-file have challenged leadership, and all have looked with disquiet at the rise of the financial technocracy that guides the adjustment process. Although strike activity has been on the rise throughout the last decade, it has been contained with remarkable ease. Minipacts are maintained with key unions, such as that between PEMEX and the petroleum workers' union, STPRM. It, like many other unions, essentially controls the distribution of wage-benefit packages, the hiring of contract labor, and, of course, access to union membership itself. Some parts of the public enterprise sector routinely draw on labor leaders for executive personnel (see Carr 1983: 97).

Unions that cooperate with the government of Mexico are rewarded with benefits packages that protect their income against the inflation that has slashed real wages across the entire Mexican workforce by at least 40 percent in real terms over the last seven years. But even unionized labor has suffered. Barry Carr estimates that between 1981 and 1983 more than 70,000 unionized laborers in the textile, metal, and automotive industries were laid off, while PEMEX fired 40,000 "temporary" workers. Over the same period more than 1.5 million nonagricultural jobs were lost in the Mexican economy (Carr 1983: 104).

The social pact with labor has held remarkably well, but it is under strain. Fidel Velasquez must be nearing the end of his tenure, so that Salinas or the next president of the republic may have to help negotiate a difficult transition. Moreover, Velasquez, the CTM, and nearly all labor unions were unhappy with the choice of Salinas to succeed de la Madrid. As budget minister, Salinas had won a reputation for being particularly tough on all public sector wage increases. The economic crisis of the fall of 1987, brought on by a collapse of the Mexican stock exchange and a huge outflow of private capital, led to the elaboration of a new pact among labor, the government, and the private sector in which the government attacked inflation through price controls and easy importation of non-essential consumer goods while at the same time indexing wages to prices as calculated on a monthly basis. Neither orthodox nor heterodox, the deal is known as the *plan de choquecito*. In a major move at the beginning of his sexenio, Salinas arrested the former head of the STPRM and the de facto "king" of the union's vast portfolio, signaling a major modification in existing corporatist arrangements.

Neither Egypt nor India has yet to undo its economic experiments and attendant social pacts, so that relations between the government and the peak organization have not become as strained as in Turkey and Mexico. In at least two instances, organized labor in Egypt and India has been able to block in whole or or in part moves to privatize state-owned enterprises: in Egypt, a joint venture between Nasr Automotive and General Motors was vetoed; in India, labor stymied the privatization of Scooters India. In

Turkey and Mexico, where painful adjustment has already resulted in high rates of unemployment and real declines in wages for most workers, organized labor has not yet been able to impede the process. Like the politicians themselves, labor may feel that it has bigger battles to fight than privatization, and confrontation may more likely occur over policies of deficit reduction, hiring and wage freezes, and devaluation.

The Private Sector

The two oldest and most diversified private sectors in these four countries are those of Mexico and India. Most observers argue that while private actors have been conceded part of the economic kingdom, the various regimes have so far denied them the political kingdom. All but Turkey have legislation on the books that restricts major sectors of the economy to public enterprise, and Turkey's numerous state monopolies have served the same purpose. All four countries have reserved the right to license and regulate all private enterprises. Official programs and pronouncements still treat entrepreneurs with suspicion and opprobrium, as a kind of necessary evil whose energies must be carefully channeled by the state in order to minimize exploitation and speculation.

It is true that Mexican business interests, especially those from the northern part of the country, have come to dominate PAN, which can mobilize at least 15 percent of the vote even in rigged elections. But that party by no means speaks for all the Mexican private sector (Cornelius 1987; Maxfield and Anzaldua 1987). Part of big business has always felt more comfortable in close collaboration with the state rather than in opposition to it. Moreover, a large sector that grew up supplying protected domestic markets and drew some of its management and ownership from former state officials looks to the state to shield it from the big private groups and, above all, from foreign private capital. These kinds of cleavages are already well known in Turkey and India and will become increasingly salient in Egypt if that country further liberalizes its trade regime.

In all four countries public authorities have called upon the private sector to play a more dynamic role in national growth. The appeal may not be at all tempting. Bank nationalizations in India in 1969 and in Mexico in 1982 are only the most heavy-handed among recent assaults on private interests. It will take a great deal more deregulation, nonpunitive taxation, and relaxation of state competition for credit before private sectors will be anything more than what their enemies assume them to be—timid, out for a quick profit, and ready to move their capital abroad at a moment's notice. Where adjustment has proceeded the furthest, and where private sector initiative is the most needed, private entrepreneurs may find themselves in the most precarious position.

In India, the private and public sectors share the huge domestic market, and private investment as a share of total investment has been rising. At the same time, the large established houses, along with several newcomers, have been doing very well. In this preadjustment era, Indian public and private enterprises enjoy a variable sum game. So too in Egypt. But there the game will be much more difficult to sustain. The collapse of oil prices has already put a severe strain on Egyptian public finances, and the announcement in 1987 that the private sector would be "allowed" to mobilize £E 18 billion of total investments of £E 40 billion in the coming five-year plan was disingenuous to say the least. The case remains, however, that private investment is growing relative to public in the two countries where adjustment has made the least progress.

In a general way, the state is trying to minimize its role vis-à-vis the private sector as the risk absorber of last resort. Even though these four ISI experiments subordinated their private sectors to state plans, regulated their activities, and denied them political legitimacy, they simultaneously assured them protected domestic markets, cheap credits for priority investments, cheap raw materials from public sector suppliers, huge contracts for supply to public sector customers, guaranties for foreign loans, and, especially in India and Mexico, nationalization and takeover when private enterprises "went sick." It is not hard to imagine that the private sector would like to see less regulation, easier access to credit and foreign exchange, and the freedom to set prices; but it is difficult to imagine why it would welcome the cutting of symbiotic ties to the state that a "lean and mean" state might entail. Those ties displaced much business risk onto the shoulders of the state and put considerable profits into private pockets.

Public Sector Reform

Reform of the manner in which the public sector operates came onto the policy agendas of all four countries long before issues of structural adjustment arose but at a time when the ISI strategy was being judged, both internally and externally, as deficient. The hard look began in India after the death of Nehru in 1964; in Egypt, in 1965–1966, when Nasser himself exhorted managers to take efficiency and productivity seriously; in Mexico, perhaps not until de la Madrid's sexenio; and in Turkey, in the mid-1960s as well. Each country contemplated two main types of reform. One is to change the context in which the PSEs operate, that is, the formal relations of control between supervising ministries and companies, the structure of sectoral groupings, the instruments of PSE finance, the criteria for assessing performance, and the regulatory regime, especially the pricing policy of both inputs and products or services. The second type involves reform within enterprises themselves, that is, promoting new management practices, technological transformation, attention to quality control and marketing, careful cost accounting, inventory management, financial planning, and an end to redundant labor and managerial overstaffing. The first type of reform, has been tried extensively but has not improved economic and financial efficiency in PSE operations. The second has been tried only in isolated instances. It may well be the more difficult to implement precisely because it may be the more significant in improving performance. Put another way, more is at stake for management and labor in enterprise reform than in contextual reform.

Egypt's public sector grew rapidly in the 1950s, predominantly through nationalization of foreign interests and secondarily through the creation of new state enterprises. The Egyptian companies were organized into three holding companies that had diversified interests and were supposed to compete with one another. Then, after the sweeping nationalizations of 1961, the GOE opted for grouping PSEs by sector—textiles, petrochemicals, banks, insurance, trade, and so on—with each sector closely supervised by a "general organization" that reported to the tutleary ministry, which in turn reported to the Ministries of Plan and Finance and to the cabinet. In 1975 the general organizations were abruptly abolished. They were judged to have interfered too closely in the day-to-day operations of the firms and to have constituted feifdoms that controlled financing, foreign exchange, and patronage throughout extensive sectors (Waterbury 1983). As a result of this reform, however, issues of supervision were shoved onto the desks of the relevant ministers. Instead of company CEOs accepting greater autonomy and responsability, the whole gamut of decisions previously handled at the general organization level was simply passed upstream. As a result, in 1983 something like the old general organizations were re-established, albeit under a different name.

The interrelated issues of supervision, administrative and political interference, degree of firm autonomy, and individual managers' responsibility for the performance of their firms arise everywhere and seem to defy satisfactory resolution. Sectoral holding companies seem to offer some magical appeal. In Turkey, for instance, performance and organization of PSEs were scrutinized by a select committee over a four-year period beginning in 1964, but with few results. As Turkey entered its crisis in the late 1970s, a four-year plan was drawn up (1979–1983), but never applied, that presaged the application of what I would call the Nasserist model (Erkzen 1981). All PSEs were to be put under sectoral general directorates, which would set targets for production and investment and determine marketing strategy. The public enterprise sector as a whole would enjoy a uniform legal status, and would be subject to a rational sectoral division of labor. Equity would be owned by the state, with the exception of joint ventures with foreign capital; each sector would have its own specialized bank; there would be uniform employment regulations and wage scales for all PSE personnel; and the State Investment Bank and the State Planning Organization would oversee the whole operation.

After the 1980 military takeover, the Ulusu government in 1982 enacted Law 2929, which established thirty-one sectoral holding companies, with each sector to report to the High Board of Auditors and to the Grand National Assembly. However, after Özal became prime minister, he abolished Law 2929 and replaced it with Decree Law 233, which ended the sectoral holding companies and, as in Egypt in 1975, brought ministers back into direct involvement in the management issues of individual firms (Karataş 1986).

The new legislation introduced a number of other reforms. PSEs were divided into two categories: those delivering basic goods and services, which would not operate according to commercial criteria; and all the rest, which would be able to determine their own prices but would no longer enjoy tax or credit privileges that would give them an edge in competiton with the private sector. Nominally, management is to be selected and retained on the basis of performance according to the judgment of the boards of the PSEs themselves. Labor and management are to be hired on a contract basis (Kopits 1987: 14). Such personnel does not fall under the regulations of civil service employment and is denied the right to organize or unionize.

In India, in September 1984, Arjun Sen Gupta, special secretary to the prime minister, was appointed to head a committee to study ways to improve public sector organization and performance on the eve of the Seventh Plan. The so-called Sen Gupta report was never officially released, but there has been considerable public comment on it (see, for example, Trivedi 1987). It recommended that the GOI maintain control over strategic planning but leave day-to-day operations of the PSEs to managers at the firm level, and it proposed the formation of holding companies to shield the firms from interference from the center. The report endorsed an arrangement that has been most extensively tried in France, that of the *contrat plan*. This letter or memorandum of understanding between either a sectoral holding company or the firm itself with the relevant ministry fixes, over a specified time period the targets of the firm and the specific commitments of the ministry to arrange financing, provide inputs, and set appropriate prices so that the target can be met.

In the last decade, Mexico has experimented with both sectoral regrouping and performance agreements. Early in its tenure the Echeverría administration created the Commission of Coordination and Control of Public Expenditure to try to check the accumulating deficits of the PSEs. Different agencies were in charge of planning, control, and investment for PSEs. Then in 1977 Lopez-Portillo launched an administrative reform program that created a new entity, the Secretariat for Budget and Investment, out of which both de la Madrid and Salinas de Gortari emerged (see Castro and Ramirez 1983). The major innovation has been the introduction in 1985 of Conventions of Rehabilitation, as well as Conventions of Deficit/ Surplus, between the major financial ministries and several parastatal firms (Cuadernos 1988: 98–108).

In all four countries, whatever the fate of privatization, there will long remain a large and probably inefficient public sector. It will consist of lumpy sunk investments, very likely outmoded or lacking any comparative advantage, which employ hundreds of thousands, produce inferior goods and services, and draw heavily on public finance. It will be harder to reform this sector than to liquidate or privatize parts of it.

Top-level managers by and large will not want responsibility thrust upon them as a result of contextual reform, especially in an environment that has become much more competitive. Nor will they have much incentive to undertake reforms within their firms, reforms that would require new modes of behavior on their part and elicit the animosity of a workforce that may have to work harder all the while it is being trimmed. Managers in Egypt and India told the author that any initiatives in firm-level reform would have to be undertaken solely on the basis of a manager's own sense of pride and determination. There was no set of rewards or incentives yet in place that could compensate for the hardship that such reforms would entail. There were, by contrast, many disincentives: rapid turnover of managers, morale problems in the workforce, the foot-dragging of middle management, the political pressures to hire unneeded labor or management, and the sense that those who urge reform will in fact give only lukewarm support to it.

New management techniques will have to be learned at a time when public authorities routinely criticize the sloppiness and costliness of public sector undertakings and compare them with the cost-effectiveness of the private sector. Twenty years ago the PSEs were the most exciting game in town, leading their societies into the industrial age, in control of the commanding heights. Now, when the greatest effort at internal reform is required, they are a kind of public laughingstock. It is hard to imagine why senior managers would make much of an effort under these circumstances. It is easy to imagine that they will assume that the state, in most instances, will continue to bail out chronic losers and that their best strategy is to wait out their time to retirement.

Privatization

Privatization has been undertaken in a serious way in Turkey and Mexico but not yet in Egypt or India. Even in the former two, it is still very much in the beginning stages. In all four, advocates of privatization see its advantages as lying primarily in deficit reduction and only secondarily in generating new income for the state.

Mexico and Turkey began almost simultaneously to draw up plans for privatization in 1983 and 1984. From the outset, the then prime minister, Özal, talked a much tougher game than President de la Madrid. Özal announced that loss-making PSEs would be either liquidated or sold. He further proclaimed that the state would give up its presence in nonstrategic sectors and sell off its minority holdings in some thirty-six companies. More than forty PSEs were tentatively targeted for privatization as early as 1984, but the overall structural adjustment process consumed most of the attention of Özal's economic advisors. It was not until after the legislative elections of 1987 that Özal felt he had the mandate and the compliant parliament that would allow him to move ahead with a transfer of state-owned equity to private hands.

In the meantime, he experimented with two interdependent instruments that have served his political objectives well. In late 1984 the government of Turkey issued the first in an ongoing series of revenue-sharing certificates (sometimes referred to as quasi-equity) in the electrical power station of the Kerban Dam and in the first Bosphorous bridge. These certificates in essence bore a guaranteed rate of return in excess of the rate of domestic inflation. They were heavily oversubscribed, and certificates in other public utilities have been issued continuously since 1984 with equal success. The issues were made under the auspices of various newly created public funds, the most important of which are the Mass Housing and Public Participation Fund and the Defence Fund (see Coşan and Ersel 1986; Leeds 1988). Now worth between 3 and 5 billion dollars, the funds remain off the national budget and present accounts annually to the Grand National Assembly. They are non–interest bearing, a fact that is advertised to the many Turks attracted by Islamic banking principles; and the placement of fund revenues in housing, roads, and other infrastructure can be (and has been) politically targeted. Özal has touted the revenue-sharing formula as a form of popular capitalism, one that protects the average Turk against inflation. The funds receive revenues from other sources as well, including taxes on alcohol, exit taxes, and the like. The Mass Housing and Public Participation Fund will receive about 15 percent of the proceeds of any equity sales of PSEs, and it will be the agency that supervises the sales.

In 1986 the Morgan Bank undertook a privatization master plan for Turkey, identifying the best prospects for privatization and setting a tentative time table. In the first group were to be Turkish Airlines; four cement plants owned by the PSE Çitosan; hotels owned by Turban and the Turizm Bank; USAŞ, a catering service in Turkey's airports, and two telephone and switchboard equipment manufacturers belonging to the Ministry of Post, Telephone, and Telegraph, Netaş and Teletaş. In a later phase, the holdings of Sümerbank and Etibank were slated for privatization.

By late 1987, with a new parliament dominated by his Motherland party, Turgut Özal was ready to move. Using some five thousand bank branches, and after a publicity blitz, 22 percent of Teletaş's equity, worth about 12 billion lira (approximately $1 million), was put on sale at TL 5,000 per share. More than 41,000 citizens made requests worth TL 34 billion for the offering, and in March the Mass Housing and Public Partcipation Fund approved a select list of new stockholders, favoring the smaller investors. The initial subscription went well, but the new issue, quoted on the Istanbul exchange, collapsed when the first buyers collected dividends and took profits. A second offering in Teletaş has been delayed. This disappointing outcome ironically involved a company that was already private and in which the state was selling part of a minority holding.

Future offerings will confront the obstacle of the country's embryonic capital market. The GOT will probably have to follow the French example and persuade some of the big private groups in Turkey to hold a large enough stake in the privatized firms to protect the market value of their shares. Recent surveys indicate very little interest in stock offerings as an investment (TÜSIAD 1987). By contrast, the privatization of some of Çitosan's cement plants is being carried out through direct sale to a French conglomerate.

Mexico, like Turkey, is still in the preparatory phase of privatization, but since 1988 it has been pushing ahead rapidly. About half of all PSEs are to be "disincorporated," merged, sold, or liquidated. The assets thus slated produce a modest 2.1 percent of total public sector production, although in the industrial and mining sectors, exclusive of PEMEX, the proportions would be 30 and 32 percent (Pichardo 1988: 28–29). As Salinas de Gortari began his incumbency, fifty PSEs worth some $300 million had been identified for immediate sale (*Latin America Minitor*, Nov. 1988, p. 596). The question is: Who is likely to buy them? The Mexican private sector is still reeling from the bank nationalizations of 1982, the collapse of the Alfa Group, the credit squeeze, and the stock market crash of October 1987. One way out may be debt-equity swaps. These were tried in 1985 and, over a year and a half, amounted $1.4 billion. The major foreign interests were large automotive multinationals (Nissan, Volkswagen, Chrysler, and Ford). The swaps were suspended in 1988 because of their possible inflationary impact.

Under the pressure of dealing with the debt crisis and structural adjustment, the de la Madrid government announced in January 1985 its intention to sell or liquidate 236 PSEs. By early 1986 it had begun the process of "rationalizing" the big steel holding company, SIDERMEX, and in May of that year it closed down the steel plant Fundidora of Monterrey, which had employed seven thousand workers.

In both Turkey and Mexico, the governments rest on fragile coalitions and narrow parliamentary majorities. Both are subject to challenges from the left and the right. In Turkey, Özal changed the law to make it possible to create or liquidate PSEs by ministerial decree, subject to parliamentary review; in Mexico, creation or dissolution of a PSE requires an act of parliament. In either case, the possibility of obstructionism is real, and how much political capital Özal or Salinas will want to spend on privatization is moot.

Privatization has scarcely become part of Indian policy vocabulary, but some intermediate steps have been taken. Faced in the Seventh Plan with having to raise much of their own investment, the more successful Indian PSEs, like Bharat Heavy Electricals, Hindustan Machine Tools, and Maruti Udyog, have resorted to issuing debentures to the public and, in some instances, to seeking foreign shareholders among firms with which they have collaborated. Some debenture issues were quite successful, but response was poor to bonds offered by the Rural Electrification Corporation and the National Thermal Power Corporation.

There has also been talk of selling shares to the workers in PSEs and in private sector firms. But inasmuch as this idea has come up in the context of salavaging "sick industries," of which there were an estimated ninety thousand in 1986, the workers might not leap at the opportunity were it to come their way (*The Hindu*, May 1, 1986).

In India we may see increased leasing out of public facilities and contracts awarded to private suppliers in such sensitive areas as defense and telecommunications. Some states in the federation have begun to privatize some of their assets, but at the federal level privatization is not yet on track.

Nor is it yet moving in Egypt, but the country seems to be nearing a moment of truth. The early 1970s saw the beginning of a movement toward privatization. In 1973 the Budget and Finance Committee of the People's Assembly issued a severe report on PSE performance and hinted that selling off loss-making units might be in order. Law 43 of 1974, regulating foreign and Arab investment, stipulated that any joint venture between a PSE and a foreign investor would automatically be considered part of the private sector and would come under the 1954 Companies Act. Joint ventures were set up mainly in banking but also in manufacturing. In 1977 a team of economic advisors assembled by the Ford Foundation and working in what is now the Ministry of Foreign Cooperation identified about a dozen companies that could make credible share offerings on the tiny Cairo exchange. No action was taken on the team's recommendation.

Hesitation probably stemmed from the extreme "thinness" of the country's capital market, the adverse effect of the earlier parliamentary report, and the sharp reaction that some joint ventures had provoked from the workers involved. The major case was that of the PSE Chloride Battery Company, which was for all intents and purposes totally taken over by Union Carbide. It was at about this time that the Egyptian Confederation of Trade Unions developed its veto power on joint ventures mentioned above.

That power and the sudden devaluation of the Egyptian pound in the spring of 1987 led to the suspension of a deal between NASCO, Egypt's PSE for the manufacture of passenger cars (under license from FIAT), and General Motors. To get around the foreign equity issue, it was agreed that GM would lease facilities and hire about 1,500 workers from NASCO's passenger car division. About 9,000 workers would be left behind in the mother PSE. The new entity, the General Misr Car Company, would become the sole manufacturer of passenger cars in Egypt, using the Opel, Ascona, and Corsa models, and a 180 percent tarriff would be maintained on imported passenger cars. Components manufactured in Egypt would be exported to GM subsidiaries in Europe, and GM promised to invest $160 million in developing local feeder industries. Labor and public sector management did not like the deal, which in 1986 was valued at $300 million (see *Business Monthly*, American Chamber of Commerce, Cairo, May 12, 1986). But the 1987 devaluation so changed the cost of imported components that GM proposed manufacture of an older, less sophisticated model. The Egyptians refused, and there matters lie. The company still exists but is involved only in truck assembly.

One of the initiators of the project was Fu'ad Sultan, who had been head of a joint venture bank, the Misr-Iran Development Bank, that has taken part of the equity in the new company. Sultan is the most outspoken advocate of privatization in Egyptian policy circles. He was made minister of tourism in 1985 with the clear mandate to reform a tourism sector dominated by public sector hotels and the national airline. He has launched an ambitious leasing plan whereby reputable foreign hotel chains, like Club Med, lease hotels on a long-term basis and manage them according to their own standards. The program has apparently born fruit, and Sultan has argued that the method should be extended to other parts of the public sector. The dominant party has criticized his ideas, but the Wafd has joined him in advocating privatization in the real sense of the word.

It may be that in the future, and with coaxing from the U.S. Agency for International Development, the Egyptian government will pursue employee stock option programs (ESOPs) as a means to dilute public ownership and placate organized labor. Such a move has been undertaken with the founding of a joint venture between a public sector tire company and Pirelli of Italy.

Egypt's economic crisis is such that structural adjustment can no longer be postponed. There has not been sufficient improvement in public sector performance after decades of contextual tinkering to divert the public gaze from continuing losses and cumulative deficit. It seems only a matter little time before a credible lobby for privatization will make itself felt in Egypt.

Conclusion

The political leaders in charge of the adjustment process, whether or not it includes privatization, will be torn, whatever their ideological predilections, between two conflicting sets of goals (see the Introduction to this volume). On the one hand, effective adjustment will require policies of liberalization, deregulation, and privatization that, as Deepak Lal (1987) has argued, should not be seen so much as the state beating a strategic retreat as the state trying to strengthen itself by putting within fiscal reach a whole set of economic activities that had been regulated into the gray or black market. But the same policies entail stripping the state of important patronage and pre-emptive control levers that can neutralize opponents, keep labor docile, win elections, and punish the disloyal. Prior to the 1984 elections in India, Indira Gandhi nationalized thirteen "sick" textile mills, gave a 25 percent pay hike to 500,000 coal miners, and, through public sector banks, sponsored loan fairs for the poor and lower-income strata nationwide. It would take monumental economic crisis to induce a leader to give up that kind of control.

Yet there is evidence in these last years of structural crises in the developing world that state leaders want to remove some of the major distributional issues in their societies from the shoulders of their public sectors and administrations. It may be convenient to shift some of this burden onto the private sector that has undeniably grown in resources and skills in the last twenty to thirty years. The state may step back on a selective basis and call for private entrepreneurs to come forward and make a profit; at the same time, as social pacts are gradually abandoned by the state, it can shift the blame for the growing inequities onto private actors who cannot defend themselves politically. The state, then, would arbitrate social conflict but also retain control over sufficient economic resources to prevent the private sector from becoming truly autonomous and able to dominate political life.

Private sector actors are being asked to reinvigorate economies—or at least their export sectors—at a time when they cannot fully protect themselves against arbitrary state action and when the international environment is not conducive to sustained success in the export domain. Stories like those of the Alfa Group in Mexico, Banker Kastelli in Turkey, or private sector importers in Egypt who owe about $3 billion in bad debts are likely to proliferate. Moreover, successful private entrepreneurs will find that their taxes and profits may be siphoned off to cover the losses of the remaining PSEs that employ too many people to liquidate but are too debt-ridden or obsolete to be sold.

Thus, while it is undeniable that public sector reform and privatization are the order of the day in many LDCs, and while even India may find itself compelled to undertake them, there is good reason to expect that the process will not be linear and certainly not smooth. Rather, we should expect reversals, partial retreats or returns to ISI, and the periodic expansion of state enterprise as the private sector goes through yet another painful learning experience.

References

Adiseshiah, Malcolm, ed. 1985. *The Why, the What and the Whither of the Public Sector Enterprise.* New Delhi: Lancer International.

Ahluwalia, Montek. 1986. "Balance-of-Payments Adjustment in India, 1970–71 to 1983–84." *World Development* 14, no. 8: 937–962.

Ahmed, Sadiq. 1984. *Public Finance in Egypt: Its Structure and Trends.* World Bank Staff Working Paper no. 639. Washington, D.C.: World Bank.

Aksoy, Ataman. 1980. "Wages, Relative Shares and Unionization in Turkish Manufacturing." In *The Political Economy of Income Distribution in Turkey,* ed. E. Özbudun and A. Ulusan. New York: Holmes and Meier.

Aysan, Mustafa. 1980. "State Economic Enterprises and Inflation in Turkey." *İşletme Fakultesi Dergisi* 9, no. 2.

Başbakanlik, T. C. 1987. Yüksek Denetleme Kurulu, *Kamu Iktisadi Teşebbüsleri, Yili Genel Raporu.* Ankara.

Bianchi, Robert. 1986. "The Corporatization of the Egyptian Labor Movement." *Middle East Journal* 40, no. 3: 429–444.

Bilgiç, Mehmet. 1987. "Privatization: The Case of Turkey." In *Privatization and Development,* ed. Steve Hanke. San Francisco: ICS Press.

Carr, Barry. 1983. "The Mexican Debacle and the Labor Movement." In *Mexico's Economic Crisis: Challenges and Opportunities,* ed. D. L. Wyman. University of California, San Diego, Center for U.S.-Mexican Studies, Monograph Series, 7.

Castañeda, Jorge. 1987. *México: el Futuro en Juego.* Mexico City: Joaquín Mortiz Planeta.

Castro, Alejandro Carrillo, and Sergio Garcia Ramirez. 1983. *Las Empresas Publicas en México*. Mexico City: Miguel Angel Porría.

Celasun, Merih, 1983. *Sources of Industrial Growth and Structural Change: The Case of Turkey*. World Bank Staff Working Paper no. 641. Washington, D.C.: World Bank.

CMIE (Centre for Monitoring the Indian Economy). 1983. *Public Sector in the Indian Economy*. Bombay: CMIE.

Cornelius, Wayne A. 1987. "Political Reform vs. Economic Liberalization in Mexico under de la Madrid." Paper presented at a seminar convened by the Latin American Centre, St. Antony's College, Oxford University, June 2.

Coşan, F., and Ersel, H. 1986. "Turkish Financial System: Its Evolution and Performance 1980–1986." *Capital Market Board Publications*, no. 7: 27–88. Ankara.

Cuadernos de Renovacion Nacional. 1988. *Reestructuracion del Sector Paraestatal*. Mexico City: Cuadernos de Renovacion Nacional.

Erkzen, Aykut. 1981. "Approaches to the Reorganization of the State Economic Enterprises and the Policies of the Fourth Plan." In *METU Studies in Development*, special issue: "Two Decades of Planned Development in Turkey." Ankara.

Far Eastern Economic Review. 1988. "Why India's Public Sector Does Not Work." January 14, pp. 56–61.

Fortune India. 1986. "Public Sector Enterprises: Leave 'em alone." March, pp. 10–18.

Grindle, Merilee. 1977. *Bureaucrats, Politicians and Peasants in Mexico*. Berkeley: University of California Press.

Hill, Raymond. 1984. "State Enterprise and Income Distribution in Mexico." In *The Political Economy of Income Distribution in Mexico*, ed. P. Aspe and P. Sigmund. New York: Holmes and Meier.

Handoussa, Heba, 1986. *Images of the Public Industrial Sector in the Five Year Plan, 1987/88–1991/92*. 11th Annual Conference of Egyptian Economists. Cairo. (In Arabic.)

India Today. 1988. "After the Binge, the Bill." February 29, pp. 52–56.

Israfil, Cengiz. 1987. *The Privatization Program in Turkey*. Istanbul.

Jain, Girilal. 1986. "Politics of Rajiv Gandhi." *Mainstream*, March 1, pp. 11–14.

Jones, L. P., and E. S. Mason. 1982. "Why Public Enterprise?" In *Public Enterprise in Less-Developed Countries*, ed. Jones and Mason. Cambridge: Cambridge University Press.

Karataş, Cevat. 1986. "Public Enterprise in Turkey: Reform Proposals, Pricing and Investment Policies." *METU Studies in Development* 13, no. 1–2: 135–169.

Kopits, George. 1987. "Structural Reform, Stabilization and Growth in Turkey." IMF Occasional Paper, no. 52.

Lal, Deepak. 1987. "The Political Economy of Economic Liberalization." *World Bank Economic Review* 1, no. 2: 273–300.

Leeds, Roger S. 1988. "Turkey: Rhetoric and Reality." In *Promise of Privatization*, ed. Raymond Vernon. New York: Council on Foreign Relations.

Maxfield, Sylvia, and Anzaldua, Ricardo, eds. 1987. *Government and Private Sector in Contemporary Mexico*. University of California, San Diego, Center for U.S.-Mexican Studies, Monograph Series, 20.

Mertoğlu, Huseyin. 1987. "Increasing Indebtedness and Decreasing Investment in SEE Balances Expected." *Yapi Kredi Economic Review*, 1, no. 2: 43–47.

Pichardo, Pagaza Ignacio. 1988. *El Proceso de Desincorporación de Entidades Paraestatales: el Caso de México*. Mexico City: Colegio Nácional de Economistas.

Prevot-Shapira, M-F. 1983. "L'évolution de l'organisation syndicale Méxicaine." *Problèmes d'Amérique Latine*, no. 69 (September): 79–121.

Rudolph, Lloyd, and Susanne Rudolph. 1987. *In Pursuit of Lakshmi: The Political Economy of the Indian State*. Chicago: University of Chicago Press.

Sankar, T. L., and J. S. Sarma. 1986. "An Analysis of the State Level Public Enterprise Performance and Perspectives." In *Management and Role of Public Enterprises: Indo-French Experiences*, ed. S. B. Jain, vol. 2. New Delhi: BPE-SCOPE.

Sharif, Khalid. 1987. "The Experience of Developing Countries in Liquidating Loss-making Public Sector Companies." *Al-Ahram al-Iqtisadi*, November 24, p. 29.

Smith, Peter. 1979. *Labyrinths of Power: Political Recruitment in Twentieth-Century Mexico*. Princeton: Princeton University Press.

State Planning Organization (Turkey)/The Morgan Bank. 1986. *Privatization Master Plan*. New York.

Tamayo López Portillo, J. J. 1963. "El papel del sector publico en el proceso de acumulación de capital en una economia de menor desarrollo." *Revista Investigación Economica* 23, no. 92.

Trivedi, Prajapati. 1987. "Sen Gupta Report on Public Enterprises: Eloquent Fuzziness at Its Best." *Economic and Political Weekly*, May 30, pp. 55–66.

TÜSIAD (Turkish Businessmen's Association). 1987. *The Socio-Economic Situation and Outlook of the Turkish Household*. Istanbul: TÜSIAD.

Walstedt, Bertil. 1980. *State Manufacturing Enterprise in a Mixed Economy: The Turkish Case*. Baltimore: Johns Hopkins University Press for the World Bank.

Waterbury, John. 1983. *The Egypt of Nasser and Sadat: The Political Economy of Two Regimes*. Princeton: Princeton University Press.

Wilkie, James W. 1968. *The Mexican Revolution: Federal Espenditure and Social Change since 1910*. Berkeley: University of California Press.

World Bank. 1986. *Arab Republic of Egypt: Current Economic Situation and Economic Reform Program*. Washington, D.C.: World Bank.

Zedillo, Ernesto De Leon. 1986. "Mexico's Recent Balance-of-Payments Experience and Prospects for Growth." *World Development* 14, no. 8: 963–991.

14

The Politics of Privatization in Brazil and Mexico: Variations on a Statist Theme

Ben Ross Schneider

By the early 1980s Brazil and Mexico had hefty state sectors with hundreds of state enterprises. The 1970s had witnessed rapid expansion, but that period also marked the beginning of widespread disenchantment with such growth. "Bloated," "corrupt," "chaotic," and "uncontrollable" were adjectives increasingly applied to these state enterprises, and throughout the 1980s pressures built on nearly all sides to do something about them. The governments ran out of money to finance them. Conservative leaders in industrial countries began exporting their views on the merits of free enterprise. International development agencies started urging and funding programs to reform the public sector. Private businessmen renewed their demands for state retrenchment. Less restricted presses uncovered more and more irregularities and abuses in state firms. And citizens of both countries, now empowered by votes that meant something, grew less and less tolerant of these abuses. Given all these pressures, why, as of mid-1989, had privatization programs in both countries amounted to little more than state housekeeping?

Understanding the politics of privatization—the selling or otherwise divesting of state enterprises—requires some appreciation of how state firms fit into broader political economies.[1] The strategy of state-led development adopted in both Mexico and Brazil was quite successful in promoting industrialization (though not equitable distribution) and generating some of the highest growth rates in the world. Over the course of four decades the strategy, in which state enterprises figured prominently, also fostered deep-seated expectations and vested interests: the state was responsible for steering and guaranteeing growth.

Real privatization would require reassigning the state's developmental role or convincing officials that they could achieve development with less state intervention. So long as state actors feel that their popularity and legitimacy depend on their success at promoting development, they will have little incentive to relinquish the instruments they use to foster growth. And, so long as they distrust the private sector, they are unlikely to leave their political futures up to private performance. Thoroughgoing privatization depends on a shift in public attitudes and political discourse to the view that the state is not responsible for development, to a recognition by state actors that less intervention can achieve more, and to a new faith in a more dynamic, unbound bourgeoisie.

Such sea changes in attitudes were not the driving force behind the modest privatization programs in Mexico and Brazil in the 1980s. Rather, pragmatic officials, many of whom favored a continued strategy of state-led development, have pushed privatization in order to rationalize state intervention and streamline government administration. The overall similarities in the marginal impact of privatization programs in both countries reveal how difficult it is to dislodge strategies of state-led development. Although the comparison documents continuing similarity, the analysis can also delve into telling differences that help explain the remaining variations in privatization policies, especially why they have proceeded further in Mexico than in Brazil. The contrasts highlight peculiarities often neglected in case studies, such as the stronger partisan and pragmatic incentives in Mexico, the higher political costs of privatization in Brazil, and the deceptively large numbers bandied about in Mexico.

The Expansion of State Intervention and Enterprise

Overall the Brazilian and Mexican states held roughly similar positions at the beginning of the 1980s. Both controlled the critical flows of resources—trade, foreign capital (equity and debt), credit—as well as managed the usual fiscal and monetary controls. Quantitative levels of state spending, investment, and production in the 1970s and 1980s were similar in the two countries, though they began to diverge in the 1980s (see Tables 1 and 2).[2]

The origins and distribution of the core of state enterprise were also similar. Nationalist, developmentalist leaders created state firms beginning in the 1930s and 1940s in capital-intensive industries such as steel, transport, oil (and later petrochemicals), mining, electricity, and telecommunications. Both states became heavily involved in finance, and both created development banks that were strategic promoters of postwar industrialization. The number of Brazilian and Mexican state enterprises and the scope of their activities expanded at an increasing rate into the

TABLE 1

Public Spending and Investment in Brazil and Mexico, 1945–1980

	Government Spending (percent of GNP)		Government Investment (percent of total investment)	
	Mexico	Brazil	Mexico	Brazil
1945	7.7	18.4 (1947)	40.0 (1939–1950)	
1950	8.2	20.3		
1955	9.9	20.0	39.0 (1950–1959)	
1960	12.6	25.7		
1965	23.9	28.0		38.1
1970	24.6	25.7	34.4	38.8
1975	36.4	34.6	42.5	42.0
1980	41.6	27.6	42.8	43.7 (1979)

Sources: For Mexico, spending (Ayala 1988: 60), investment (Story 1986: 68); for Brazil, spending 1945–1965 (Guimarães et al. 1979: 137), spending 1970–1980 (Longo 1982: 129), investment (Reichstul and Coutinho 1983: 45).

TABLE 2

Production and Investment of State Enterprises in Brazil and Mexico, 1960–1984

	Parastatal Production (percent of GDP)		Parastatal Investment (percent of gross fixed capital formation)	
	Mexico	Brazil	Mexico	Brazil
1965	15.7			13.3
1970	14.1	16.2	11.1	20.3
1975	15.6	25.2	21.0	25.1
1980	22.4	18.3	21.0	22.7
1984	31.0		17.3	

Sources: For Mexico, production (Casar and Peres 1988: 44), investment (Ruiz Dueñas 1988: 481–482, largest firms only, excludes financial firms); for Brazil, production (Longo 1982: 129), investment (Reichstul and Coutinho 1983: 45).

Note: These figures are presented to give rough estimates of trends in aggregate impact. The numbers come from authors who sometimes use different criteria for defining state enterprises. The data for Mexico are particularly troublesome: calculations vary between sources (and sometimes within the same book) by as much 100 percent. My major criterion for selecting the data in Tables 1 and 2 was to get the maximum historical coverage from a single source.

1970s (Figure 1), and then their number doubled. In both Brazil and Mexico production and investment doubled between 1960 and 1980, though the timing of the surge varied (see Table 2). By the late 1970s state enterprises accounted for about one-fifth of total production and investment. These proportions are relatively low by international standards (World Bank 1988: 169), but they afford developmentalists in the government plenty of leverage to steer overall industrialization.

Although both states have hundreds of enterprises, only a handful are responsible for the bulk of state production. In the early 1980s the six largest state firms in Brazil accounted for 81 percent of sales of all enterprises, 69 percent of spending (Brazil 1983: 62–63), four-fifths of investment, and virtually all state enterprise debt (Frieden 1987: 105). In Mexico, PEMEX alone recorded nearly three-quarters of the total production of state enterprises (Pichardo 1988: 26). Both Brazil and Mexico could sell all but a dozen or so enterprises without reducing the state enterprise share of gross domestic product (GDP) and investment by more than about 20 percent.

Noticeable differences, potentially relevant for the analysis of privatization, emerge in a comparison of the number of firms, their political reputations, and the patterns of investment financing. The acceleration in the creation of firms was more pronounced in Mexico, which helps explain why the Mexican government was able to shed more firms (mostly of recent vintage). The more firms you have, the more you can sell off.

Firms like the oil monopolies PEMEX and Petrobrás have long histories and are associated with popular mobilization against foreign companies. Other firms are more closely identified with presidential whim and controversial policies. In Mexico, Echeverría was notorious for his expansion of state enterprises, especially firms that could promote national control, employment, or redistribution. His successor, José López Portillo, and his strategy of bonanza development were closely associated with state petroleum and petrochemical firms, and later bank nationalizations in 1982. To the extent that leaders can discredit previous presidents and their programs, they can also go after the enterprises they created. Both Presidents Miguel de la Madrid and Carlos Salinas de Gortari have been able to play on opposition to their predecessors to generate support for privatizing firms created in the 1970s.

In Brazil, in contrast, the military rulers created most of the state firms. But proponents of privatization have rarely linked their proposals to a repudiation of authoritarian rule, in part because so many of the military's collaborators, including President José Sarney, are still in positions of power (Schneider 1987: 612–22). Moreover, statizing leaders, such as ex-President Ernesto Geisel (1974–1979), and their policies still enjoy prestige

FIGURE 1
Number of State Enterprises in Brazil and Mexico, 1930–1990

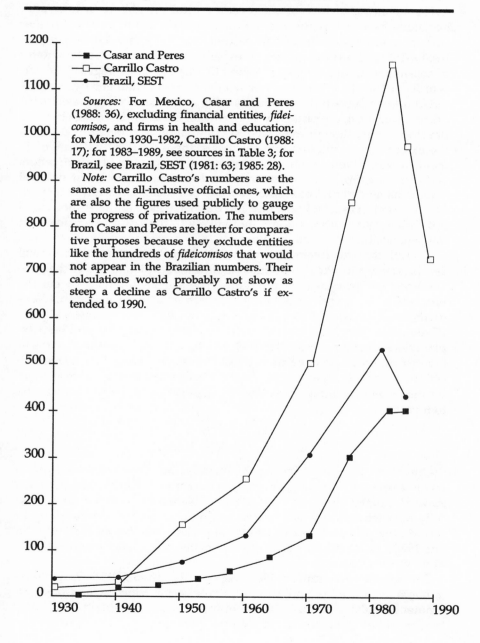

—■— Casar and Peres
—□— Carrillo Castro
—●— Brazil, SEST

Sources: For Mexico, Casar and Peres (1988: 36), excluding financial entities, *fideicomisos*, and firms in health and education; for Mexico 1930–1982, Carrillo Castro (1988: 17); for 1983–1989, see sources in Table 3; for Brazil, see Brazil, SEST (1981: 63; 1985: 28).

Note: Carrillo Castro's numbers are the same as the all-inclusive official ones, which are also the figures used publicly to gauge the progress of privatization. The numbers from Casar and Peres are better for comparative purposes because they exclude entities like the hundreds of *fideicomisos* that would not appear in the Brazilian numbers. Their calculations would probably not show as steep a decline as Carrillo Castro's if extended to 1990.

and support. Hence the controversial reputations of many state firms in Mexico favor privatizers more so than in Brazil.

The financing of investment reveals critical differences in how policymakers have used enterprises. Brazilian firms historically had higher rates of internal financing, 40–60 percent over the period 1966–1975 (Trebat 1981: 53). Consumers financed expansion in these core sectors. Rates of self-financing in Mexico (excluding CONASUPO) averaged 3–17 percent from 1972 to 1978).[3] In other words, Mexican state enterprises provided a huge subsidy to consumers who, in the case of steel, electricity, oil, and transport, are primarily large private firms. Both strategies can be developmental, though they favor accumulation in different sectors. To the extent they continued into the 1980s, these different patterns of finance would have an ambivalent impact on the politics of privatization. Self-financing firms are more attractive to private buyers, but political leaders have fewer financial incentives to sell them, especially if they invest at a high rate as in Brazil (see Table 2). They have stronger motives to sell deficit-ridden firms but are more likely to meet stiff resistance from the beneficiaries of their subsidies.

Overall, the size, diversity, and evolution of state enterprises in Brazil and Mexico up to 1980 were similar and cannot explain much of the variation in their privatization programs. The salient differences were the numbers of firms and the patterns of investment. To the extent that hundreds of minor firms in Mexico are associated with the controversial presidents who created them, they are likely easier to privatize and help explain the higher numbers of firms eliminated. In principle, the patterns of investment financing have an equivocal impact, but they should give officials in Mexico stronger incentives to use privatization to ease pressure on the deficit and encourage Brazilian officials to hang on to firms with funds to invest.

Desestatização in Brazil

One of the first rifts between the Brazilian military regime and previously supportive industrialists came in the campaign in 1974 for *desestatização* ("destatization"; see Cruz 1984). President Geisel tried unsuccessfully to patch up these differences, less by privatizing than by trying to include the private sector in new state projects (see Evans 1982). By the late 1970s, however, opposition to the regime overshadowed dissatisfaction with the state.

Through the government of João Baptista Figueiredo (1979–1985), *desestatização* resurfaced periodically in private sector criticism, and the government regularly renewed its commitment to privatization.[4] In the end, the Figueiredo government reduced the number of state enterprises from

530 in 1981 to 420 in 1984 but mostly through accounting legerdemain and without putting a dent in total state production and investment. Of the 110 firms eliminated, officials sold 17 (including a publisher, a paper company, a palm oil processor, and the equipment of several firms), incorporated 16 into regular government agencies, liquidated 9, and fused, reclassified, or transferred (for example, to local government) the remaining 68 (Brazil 1985: 28–35).

When José Sarney took office in early 1985 (in place of the mortally ill president-elect, Tancredo Neves), he inherited Tancredo's promises of privatization and public sector reform. But after two years it was clear that Sarney had no particular program for or commitment to privatization. The major sale was the Hotel Blumenau. Meanwhile, the Sarney government expanded state intervention into sectors like microcomputers and software, created new ministries, and extended wage and price controls in successive attempts to stabilize the economy.

Sarney also maintained the tradition of trying to use the developmental state to generate popular support. Sarney's best-known project was the North-South railroad, which attracted controversy from the beginning because it ends up coincidentally in Sarney's home state of Maranhão. Irregularities in the awarding of private contracts further mired the project in scandal in 1987, but Sarney refused to abandon it. In January 1988, in a five-minute television spot produced by the government, he announced that construction would begin on the $2.4 billion railroad. The project moved slowly for lack of investment funds, but Sarney did get to inaugurate the first completed stretch in mid-1989.

Beyond fumbling developmentalism, the state has done double political duty for Sarney in his attempts to shore up his support coalition and to secure the fifth year of his term. Sarney never enjoyed stable majority support in Congress.[5] His political position was doubly insecure because the length of his term was unclear. The military's constitution stipulated five years, but Tancredo had promised four, a term favored by many in the Congress. Sarney wanted five and made the fifth year his top political priority.

Sarney systematically applied the state's resources to these political ends. He traded appointments for support and allowed his supporters to do the same throughout the lower reaches of the state hierarchy.[6] For instance, steel plants are often important to regional elites who attempt to nominate plant managers. By 1987 the situation had gotten so out of hand that the president of the Siderbrás (a state holding company) resigned, claiming he could no longer supervise the operating firms because he had no say in the appointment of their managers (see *Jornal da Tarde*, Apr. 18, 1988). Sarney had few incentives to privatize the appointments and resources that aided his political program.

From 1981 through 1987, the government sold a total of thirty-five small firms, at least half of those before Sarney took office (*Exame*, Aug. 24, 1988). The prospects for further privatization were dim at the beginning of 1988, when David Moreira, the executive secretary of the new Interministerial Council on Privatization, resigned because, he claimed, the government lacked the political will to sell the sixty-seven firms the council had targeted (*Gazeta Mercantil*, Jan. 28, 1988).

The push to privatize seemed to pick up steam over the course of 1988. In March the Sarney government revived the Council on Privatization as the Federal Council for Destatization.[7] By June, after Congress voted a fifth year for Sarney's term, privatization was back near the top of the policy agenda, as one of several short-lived proposals to promote market-oriented reform. Sarney even committed himself to selling a firm a month (*Latin American Weekly Report*, June 2, 1988). In August he decreed the creation of yet another new Federal Council on Privatization and announced a list of seventy firms (expanded to one hundred in October) to be privatized. This list included several enormous and old state enterprises, such as Caraíba (copper), the railroads, and Usiminas (steel). The program was not so ambitious or new, however. Most of the firms had appeared on earlier lists (several on lists from the Figueiredo government); some no longer even belonged to the state; and some were very recent entrants into the state sector.

In the end, 1988 turned out to be a good year for more than lists, decrees, and administrative bustle. The Council on Privatization reported that it sold six firms, fifteen radio stations, and miscellaneous minority shares for a total of $479 million, more than twenty times the value of the five firms sold in 1987 (Brazil 1989: 2). The major firms included Aracruz (cellulose, $156 million), Celpag (cellulose, $73 million), Caraíba Metais (copper, $90 million), and Cimetal (steel, $59 million). These results, however, had little to do with the council and Sarney's fanfare. Nearly all the firms (which generated virtually all the revenues) belonged to the National Bank for Economic and Social Development (BNDES) (see BNDESPAR 1989). Its subsidiary, BNDESPAR, had been preparing to sell these firms long before 1988. Their activities, though independent in operation, became part of Sarney's umbrella program.

BNDES managers have long pressed for privatization to rid the bank of private firms (mostly its troubled debtors) that it had come to own in order to keep them from going under.[8] The *Financial Times* (Oct. 26, 1988) claimed it was "the only government agency committed to privatisation." Since its establishment in the 1950s, BNDES has stood apart from the usually disorganized and politicized economic bureaucracy (see Martins 1985 and Willis 1986). It is more favorably disposed to the private sector than most state agencies and in recent years has become increasingly market

oriented. Several factors have reinforced a pro–private sector, proprivatization orientation during the Sarney government. Many BNDES pragmatists favor privatization in order to enhance the bank's developmental
intervention.[9] They want to use their meager investment capital strategically on firms on the cutting edge of development rather than on liabilities
that politics willed to them.

In addition, BNDES has been going through a generational change. The
old guard of development economists that was with the bank in the 1950s
and 1960s, when it was the primary financial agent for expanding state
firms, is retiring. The Young Turks who are replacing them are more
likely to be trained in finance and business administration and are more
concerned about things like solvency.[10] Lastly, the generational change
coincides with the arrival of a different sort of BNDES president. Unlike
most previous presidents, Márcio Fortes was a private businessman and
has been vocal in his support for free enterprise.

Federal policymakers have also recognized that the state lacks the resources to invest. In 1985, according to Paulo Galletta, the executive secretary of the new Federal Council on Privatization, the government as a
whole had to pay out over half its tax receipts just in interest, and in 1987
state enterprises devoted in aggregate about half their revenues to debt
service (Galletta 1988a: 1). The state has nothing left to invest. Hence, privatization can both ease financial constraints on the state and promote
investment in capital-starved ex-state firms. In other words, marginal
state firms are a drag on development; selling them can enhance state
capacity by allowing managers to reorient their attention and other resources strategically. In Galletta's words, "privatization is one of the only
instruments capable of promoting growth" (*Exame*, Aug. 24, 1988).

Privatizers at the federal level had less success than their counterparts
in BNDES. The obstacles were more numerous: lack of staff (the Council
on Privatization had thirteen professionals in 1989), weak and changing
jurisdiction (the supervising ministries were still responsible for finding
among their wards new firms to sell), a weak president (Sarney), a reinvigorated Congress with many veto points, vociferous unions in major
state firms, and a suspicious press.[11] In addition the staff of the Council on
Privatization did not know how Sarney was using state enterprises to
maintain political support. They could only publicize potential candidates
for sale and wait for the political fallout to see how significant the firms,
or their appointed managers, were.

In sum, the primary motivation for privatization during the Sarney
government came from mid-level officials trying to rationalize the developmental state. Sarney had no ideological commitment to privatization,
but he appeared willing to endorse privatization when officials could convince him that the financial crisis of the state was more pressing than his

political agenda. The private sector has not had much influence. Publicly, businessmen professed their support for privatization; but privately, firms that depend on particular state enterprises have lobbied to block their sales.[12] Privatization has not affected the Brazilian political economy much.

What is surprising is that the privatization program went as far as it did. The government sold only a few dozen firms, but their value and the revenues collected by the government were substantial and, through mid-1989, matched the figures for the seemingly more extensive Mexican program. The explanation is that the firms sold were among the easiest to unload in terms of political cost. They were private firms that had recently fallen into the hands of BNDES, which had been working to sell them for years. Moreover, the firms were not key pawns in Sarney's political maneuvers, and BNDES managers were partially insulated against interference from the rest of the Sarney government.

But the numbers need to be put in context. Through mid-1989 the government, almost exclusively BNDES, had raised about $500 million on firms that in 1988 had somewhat over $1.2 billion in turnover (BNDESPAR 1988). But while BNDESPAR was selling firms, the rest of the government was creating firms and investing in old ones, so that the net increase in state assets was probably positive over this period.[13]

Observers use many different measures to gauge the extent of privatization. The easiest, most common, but least useful indicator is the number of firms. The designation "firm" is arbitrary: any single firm could be fused with others or subdivided into numerous separate firms. Numbers of firms are particularly misleading in comparative analysis. Through mid-1989 Mexico and Brazil had sold enterprises of roughly the same total value, but in Mexico the firms numbered in the hundreds, in Brazil in the dozens. So the value of assets or production stripped from the state is a better, though still imperfect, measure.

To get at the impact of privatization on the political and developmental role of the state, I would propose a more complex measure of privatization: take the total investment of the firms privatized multiplied by the number of years the firms have been in the state sector, and divide it by the investment of the firms that remain in the state sector multiplied by their combined ages as state firms.

$$\frac{\text{Average investment} \times \text{age (years public) for privatized firms}}{\text{Average investment} \times \text{age for remaining state firms}}$$

Average investment is a better measure of a firm's political and developmental potential. Managers and politicians both seek control of firms that invest a lot. The age of a firm is a proxy for how deeply political and bureaucratic interests are entrenched in and around a particular firm. Petrobrás emerged out of massive political mobilization in the 1950s, continues to receive support from powerful allies, and now has an investment budget almost on par with that of the federal government. No one is discussing privatization. Nova América, a recently privatized textile firm, has a tiny investment budget (in fact, it just started making a profit in 1987), and became a state ward after going bankrupt in 1985. It was politically simple to privatize.

I do not have the figures to calculate the index for Sarney's privatization program, but my estimate would be close to zero. The BNDES firms were all once private and fell into BNDES hands in the 1970s and 1980s when they could no longer repay their loans to the bank. Some of the firms were profitable when resold, but their average investment was modest at best. In the meantime, few of the oldest and largest firms (including BNDES, which now has more resources to invest) were threatened with privatization in the Sarney government.

Desincorporación in Mexico

Under President de la Madrid, the Mexican government proceeded further than Brazil in market-oriented reform, including reduction of the number of state enterprises. Reforms like deregulation and trade liberalization may fundamentally alter Mexico's political economy, but privatization was mostly a matter of state housekeeping and a gesture to restore business confidence.

De la Madrid made it clear from the beginning that the state was to retain its developmental role—the *rectoría* or guidance—of the economy:

> To direct the process of development is the fundamental responsibility of the Mexican State. Its obligations in this regard cannot be renounced and are necessary to fulfill the constitutional project of nationalism, plural democracy, and mixed economy. (de la Madrid 1982)

Privatization was not central to de la Madrid's early economic plan, though his administration adopted a modest program in 1983.

Desincorporación (which includes liquidation, extinction, and transfer, as well as sale) got off to a slow start but grew quickly after 1985 (see Table 3). The government divested only twenty-three firms in 1983–1984 (compared with thirty in 1981 [Vera 1988: 20–21]). In February 1985 de la Madrid announced a new economic package that included an expanded divestment program targeting 236 government entities (of which only 52 were operating enterprises; see Vera 1988: 23). The government again extended the program in 1987–1988.

TABLE 3
Evolution of the Parastatal Sector in Mexico, 1982–1989

	State Enterprises	Firms in Process of Disincorporation	Total
1982	1,039	116	1,155
1983	1,003	83	1,086
1984	989	72	1,061
1985	824	159	983
1986	660	219	879
1987	562	242	804
1988	460	273	733
1989	403	326	729
(as of 15 June)			

Sources: For 1982–1988, Mexico, *Las Razones* (1989: 6:478); for 1989, CEESP (1989: cuadro 5). The universe for these two studies differs slightly.

Since 1985, various government agencies have regularly published conflicting updates on the number of firms divested. In mid-1988 the Contraloría put out the most comprehensive report.[14] To the 1,155 entities inherited by the incoming administration in 1982, including 759 majority-owned firms, 75 minority-owned firms, 103 decentralized organs, and 223 *fideicomisos* (special earmarked funds or trusts), the de la Madrid government added 59 new firms, mostly as fusions of old ones, for a total of 1,214. Through June 1988 the government had slated 765 for *desincorporación*: 218 to be sold, 28 transferred, 78 fused (mostly financial and movie-related firms), 135 extinguished (mostly *fideicomisos*), and 258 liquidated. Calculations made by the Center for Economic Studies of the Private Sector (CEESP), based on slightly different data, show that the governments of de la Madrid and Salinas had authorized the disincorporation of 804 of the 1,222 enterprises existing in December 1982 and had completed the process for 478 firms as of June 1989 (CEESP 1989: cuadro 3).

By the numbers, Mexico is a world leader in privatization; it sold over a fifth of an estimated 1,000 firms privatized in the whole Third World (Nellis and Kikeri 1988: 27). *Desincorporación*, however, has not greatly reduced the state's economic weight. All the 765 firms *authorized* for *desincorporación* through 1988 (many of which had not yet been divested) accounted for merely 3 percent of state enterprise production in 1983 (or 15 percent, excluding PEMEX and the financial sector).[15]

Desincorporación has also had a minor impact on revenues and deficits. All 765 targeted firms accounted for only 10 percent of budgeted expenses for the state sector in 1983. The 116 firms sold through mid-1988 netted nearly a trillion 1988 pesos, or about $422 million. Even this cumulative sum would do little to reduce the budget deficit, which in 1987 alone was thirty times larger. Officials hastily sold off another twenty-one firms in the last months of the de la Madrid sexenio (six-year term) for another $612 million (Aeroméxico alone raised $330 million).[16] Even if we put the total at a little over $1 billion, the state sector probably grew in aggregate under de la Madrid in that it invested and thereby created more assets than the government sold. Calculating the measure described above would probably also yield an index close to zero, though larger than the index for Brazil.

The motives for *desincorporación* vary across firms and over time. The official directive to cabinet secretaries was to find firms that were no longer "strategic or priority." Article 28 of the Mexican constitution (as amended in 1983) defines the following sectors or activities as strategic and hence the exclusive reserve of the state: national mint, post office, telecommunications, central banking, petroleum, basic petrochemicals, radioactive minerals and nuclear energy, electricity, railroads, and the "public service of banking and credit" (Pichardo 1988: 15). Priority sectors are those where the state can enter from time to time, but neither the directive nor the constitution includes specific means for determining if a firm is priority or not. The decision to divest still leaves wide margin for discretion.

Government pragmatists were largely concerned about deficits, administrative costs, and coherence. The overall impact on the total government deficit was minor, but nonstrategic deficitary firms like Fundidora Monterrey (steel) and DINA (diesel engines) probably caught privatizers' eyes (see Mexico, *Las Razones*, 1987: 282). In the hundreds of smaller firms divested the concerns were largely administrative: reduce the number of firms and thereby the supervisory cost to the state (see Mexico, Hacienda 1988: 61). Among other things, officials wanted to get out of nonpriority and nonstrategic activities like movie theaters, hotels, cashmere, porcelain, bicycles, and carbonated beverages (Mexico, *Las Razones*, 1989: 477). "Priority" has numerous definitions, but many recent acquisitions had little or no justification for entering the state in the first place. For example, many of the first firms divested had been inadvertently nationalized when López Portillo took over the banks in 1982 and discovered they controlled many productive firms.

Beyond these issues of internal state management, top political leaders can use privatization to pursue such goals as courting the private sector and disciplining labor, though they rarely admit to such aims publicly. As in Brazil, business dissatisfaction with state expansion predates current reforms. President Echeverría is the main protagonist in private sector accounts of state profligacy and betrayal. Among other policies antagonistic to private sector interests, Echeverría created hundreds of new state firms, increased spending, extended regulation, confiscated land, and drove the peso to its first devaluation in decades. López Portillo attempted reconciliation but never fully recovered business confidence. Then, the economic crisis of 1981–1982, and especially López Portillo's precipitous nationalization of the banking sector in September 1982, really poisoned relations.

But if privatization was designed to placate business, how would capitalists really benefit from *desincorporación*? Liquidation, extinction, and transfer often have no direct impact on the private sector. Sales of firms at discounted prices would please buyers; but buyers are few, and other businesses might resent the subsidy in the sale that could only aggravate the general fiscal disequilibrium. Moreover, the pragmatic goal of deficit reduction could clash with business interests. To the extent that artificially low prices rather than poor management generate the losses, it is usually business consumers who reap the subsidy and who would therefore stand to lose by privatization.[17]

The privatization program in Mexico was more gratifying to the private sector as a signal of the government's orientation than as a means for direct gain. It first reversed the statizing and threatening policies of de la Madrid's two predecessors. Private sector associations constantly raise the totem of privatization and rail in principle against state intervention (see Casar and Peres 1988: 110–115). But privatization was not a specific government response to these demands of business lobbies. The private sector had little say (and apparently was not particularly interested) in which firms the government sloughed off. *Desincorporación* was not the result of the vectors of interest-group pressures in pluralist politics.

Rather, government officials latched on to privatization as one of the few measures that could improve the investment climate. For officials, the economy required investment, any investment, to grow; and in 1982 and for the near future the government had little to invest and depended heavily on private investment just to stave off massive depression. Industrial growth in Mexico always depended on private investment (see Story 1986), but before 1982 policymakers could usually count on private investment to follow public investment. By 1982 rising international interest rates and falling oil prices (and hence tax revenues) compressed the government's resources: public investment fell by 43 percent from 1981 to 1983 (Mexico, INEGI, 1988: 829).

Officials had little choice but to turn to the private sector. Although private investment dropped in 1982 and 1983 by about 20 percent a year and stayed low (Mexico, Instituto 1988: 829), government officials and business representatives agree that private investment would have dropped further without the privatization program.[18] In fact, an astonishing 81 percent of business leaders surveyed at the end of 1988 claimed that privatization stimulated private investment in general.[19]

Another probusiness signal is also an antiunion signal. The de la Madrid administration has used *desincorporación* to resolve intractable labor disputes. The most controversial liquidations of Fundidora Monterrey and Aeroméxico cost more than twenty thousand workers their jobs.[20] According to government officials, both firms lost a lot of money in excessive labor costs. When, in the course of contract negotiations, the unions struck, the government declared their firms bankrupt (and subject to liquidation), which canceled existing labor contracts. In each case options existed to restructure and/or privatize, but de la Madrid preferred to liquidate.

The liquidations sent a clear message to labor—and to private employers—concerning the limits of government willingness to negotiate. In steel, Fundidora Monterrey has become management's shorthand for what happens if labor resists modernization. In May 1989 workers struck another government steel plant, Altos Hornos de México, in opposition to a modernization program that included reducing the workforce by more than a fifth. In July the company spokesman said that either Altos Hornos "modernizes for the good of its own workers or else it will die, like Fundidora" (*Proceso*, no. 661, July 3, 1989).

The benefit to the private sector is indirect. Government labor contracts are usually more generous than those in private companies, and the government usually takes the lead in setting the parameters for collective bargaining. If the government sets a less generous precedent, the private sector can be expected to follow and gain from it. If government unions moderate their demands, as they did after Fundidora Monterrey, then so too would unions in the private sector.[21]

According to Jesús Silva Herzog, finance minister from 1982 to 1986, the predominant motive within the government for pursuing privatization varied over the course of the sexenio (interview, July 3, 1989). In the early years the primary goal was to restore business confidence and investment. After the fiscal crisis in 1985 (and after business-government relations had improved), the focus shifted to reducing the deficit and administrative chaos. Then, in 1988, attention focused on elections and defeating the National Action party (PAN), which has campaigned for years on a promarket, pro–free enterprise platform and which until 1988 mounted the most serious challenge to the Institutionalized Revolutionary Party (PRI). After the elections, the motive for continued privatization seems to have been de la Madrid's desire to leave his mark on the state (see Mexico, Hacienda 1988: 5) and to help his successor by "disincorporating" firms that would be politically costly for Salinas to get rid of early in his term.

Reducing the number of state enterprises simplified supervision and control. The previous overextension contributed to dissipating officials' attention and fragmenting policymaking (see Rueschemeyer and Evans

1985). A leaner state sector is a more effective instrument of state policy. In some instances organized labor posed a challenge to the state's control of its firms. *Desincorporación* has disabused unions of their hopes that the government would be an accommodating bargainer.

Lastly, as part of a successful overture to the private sector, privatization has helped restore the "alliance for profits," thereby strengthening the state and the PRI. To be effective, developmental states require minimal cooperation from capitalists, and such cooperation was increasingly reluctant in Mexico in the late 1970s and early 1980s. Renewed business confidence at the end of de la Madrid's term no doubt contributed to a willingness to participate in the successful stabilization pact. Also, to the extent that business opposition fueled rising support for the PAN, privatization may have contributed to stemming that party's gains in 1988 to the PRI's advantage.

De la Madrid entered office an avowed statist. He maintained this approach throughout and pragmatically adjusted policy to enhance the state's *rectoría*. The goal of making the state more effective, rather than ideology, foreign encouragement, or partisan gain, primarily inspired Mexican privatization. Ignacio Pichardo, a member of de la Madrid's cabinet, concluded that, in the wake of *desincorporación*, remaining "paraestatal entities will be in a better position to fulfill their historic role as motors of national development, thus contributing to strengthening and consolidating the principle of state *rectoría* consecrated in our Constitution" (Pichardo 1988: 38).

Strategies and Coalitions for Privatization

The primary motives of state elites that drive privatization elsewhere fall into three analytic categories: ideological, partisan, and pragmatic. Ideologues are liberals who favor privatization in any guise at any time and often at any cost: the more market, the better. Partisans use privatization to create new party stalwarts and to undermine their opponents. For example, spreading the shares of ex-state enterprises as widely as possible—people's capitalism—can curry short-term favor (depending on the deepness of the discount) and create new groups that are structurally more receptive to the message of the party of privatization. Or, partisans can use privatization to attack their opponents, such as organized labor, directly. Privatizing pragmatists are officials concerned with reducing unnecessary administrative and financial drain on the government. Their concern is policy effectiveness rather than ideals and political gain, and they focus attention selectively on superfluous activities, uncontrollable spenders, and overly politicized agencies. For the most part though, the pragmatists are politically anemic in the big battles of privatization.

So far, pragmatists have been the major force behind the still marginal privatization in Brazil and Mexico. Where are the ideologues and partisans with whom to ally to extend privatization?

Ideologues

Prevailing ideological tendencies in Brazil and Mexico have not favored privatization. First, ideology has historically been a weak force in the manipulative electoral politics of both countries. In Brazil, the ideological positions of parties and politicians have not been critical in electoral outcomes, and these positions are almost always negotiable. In Mexico, the official ideology of the revolution is pervasive but not determinant in elections or power struggles within the PRI. Second, the opening of both political systems in the late 1980s reinvigorated ideological debate, but privatization was only one of many points of contention. Issues of social justice, civil rights, government ethics, and debt repayment were usually more hotly debated than state enterprise. By the end of the decade, however, the issue of appropriate state intervention was increasingly prominent in ideological discussion, particularly in the Brazilian elections. Third, the widespread ideological commitment to state-led industrialization has a long history and works against more ambitious privatization programs (see Bielschowsky 1988 on Brazil).

Support for privatization might have come from excluded political movements, which tend to be more ideological and programmatic (Shefter 1976). Of the opposition parties in Mexico, the PAN is the oldest, most ideological, and most likely to advocate privatization. The PAN platform generally praises free enterprise, but liberalization is officially only one of many objectives. In the 1988 presidential campaign, the PAN's forty-page platform devoted only half a page to the role of the state in the economy. The document argues for restricting the state to its essential functions, but these include planning and the *rectoría* of the economy (PAN 1988: 13). The left eclipsed the PAN as the major electoral challenge to the PRI in 1988, but it remains too fragmented to discuss one ideological core. Most positions favor state control of many sectors of the economy, however, and the left's presidential candidate, Cuauhtémoc Cárdenas, favors national control through state regulation.

Parties and ideologies in Brazilian politics have always been fluid and accommodating. They are even more so during the protracted transition from authoritarian to democratic rule. The majority Party of the Brazilian Democratic Movement (PMDB) is generally considered centrist, but in ideological terms it is more catholic than zealously centrist. As for its position on privatization, the PMDB's ideological stance has been impossible to identify.[22] The Brazilian Social Democratic party (PSDB), founded in

1987, seemed to follow the recent agnosticism of European socialist parties: members were not keen on nationalization of industry but still defended effective state intervention. Further to the left, the Workers' party (PT) has adopted a fairly traditional socialist platform and a nationalist ideology that favors state over foreign control.

Brazil lacks a strong, unabashed, right-wing party. Initially the Liberal Front party (PFL) seemed a likely candidate for this role and even chose the label "liberal" to hark back to earlier defenders of the market. But since its creation in 1985, the PFL has suffered deep internal divisions, and some prominent members, such as Aureliano Chaves, are staunch defenders of state enterprise and intervention. Further to the right, the Democratic Social party (PDS), the party that supported military rule, is still struggling to restore its image. While nominally in favor of privatization (especially the outspoken Senator Roberto Campos), the party has been too weak and disoriented to affect the debate much. A new but still small Liberal party seems to take its label more to heart. Its presidential candidate, Afif Domingues, made privatization a major campaign theme.

In sum, ideologues and programmatic parties have not accelerated privatization in Brazil or Mexico. Either the party or the ideological commitment to privatization is weak.

Partisans

Single-minded partisans favor privatization to the extent it will increase support for them or their party and/or decrease support for their opponents.[23] When, as in Brazil and Mexico, cheap shares in state firms are not offered to the general public, the opportunities for generating net electoral support are limited because material benefits cannot be widely distributed. Any single privatization proposal may provide one buyer a large benefit (and give an indirect and invisible tax break to a large dispersed constituency) but will impose a heavy sacrifice on many workers, managers, consumers, and suppliers. The losers are usually more numerous and vocal than the potential winners.

Why have officials in charge of selling state enterprises in Brazil and Mexico not used the stock market to raise more capital and engender greater electoral sympathy? The obstacles seem to be mainly logistical. The stock markets in both countries are shallow, highly volatile, and dominated by large investors and speculators. Brazil and Mexico in fact have very few "public" corporations in the sense of companies where most shares are traded and no single shareholder owns a majority. Privatizers in both countries would like to rely more on the stock market, but for now such a strategy is too time-consuming and risky while the benefits are uncertain. People's capitalism seems to work best politically when it is part of an overall partisan and ideological battle for free enterprise as in Great Britain and Chile.

Opposition groups may force government leaders to adopt a partisan program of privatization. The success of the PAN gave de la Madrid partisan incentives to sell off enterprises, while the rise of the antiprivatization left in 1988 may encourage Salinas to slow further *desincorporación*. The motives are still partisan but negative: deflate the opposition.

In other countries a salient element in the calculus of partisan privatization is union strength. If unions are strong, militant, in the opposition, and able to stymie the state by striking the public sector, politicians have a strong incentive to privatize. Thatcher, Chirac, Alfonsín (and perhaps even Menem), and to an extreme degree Pinochet have all used privatization both to undermine powerful opposition unions and to enhance their ability to govern. In the language of recent state theory, state actors trade a loss in capacity for enhanced autonomy (see Rueschemeyer and Evans 1985).

Mexican privatization has weakened unions but paradoxically the very unions that have helped sustain the PRI in power for so long. If anything, the apparent partisan motives would recommend avoiding confrontational privatization (and such motives may have restrained more radical proposals). But privatization addresses partisan concerns *within* the PRI, where de la Madrid and Salinas head a more technocratic, modernizing wing against traditional politicians and sectoral organizations such as the labor unions.

Pragmatists

Given their limited power, pragmatists in both Mexico and Brazil have pushed privatization surprisingly far. Two additional groups of pragmatists could propel further privatization in the near future: politicians and managers of state enterprises. Although these two groups are usually considered major obstacles to privatization programs, the continuing fiscal crisis of the state and the extensive use of appointments for political purposes have already convinced some politicians and managers, especially in Brazil, that they might be better off if the firms they rely on or work for are transferred to private owners.

For political pragmatists, the issue has been how to use the state to fulfill development expectations and to build support coalitions within the political elite. Until the debt crisis, extensive state intervention worked in Mexico and Brazil in promoting industrialization, and clientelism usually proved to be adequate political currency to maintain minimum support. Expanding resources allowed leaders to promote industrialization *and* distribute patronage. Scarcer resources may make the trade-off zero-

or even negative-sum, where trading appointments for support no longer meets the expectations of supporters but at the same time paralyzes the developmental state: a "web of compromise" that fails even to deliver political support (Schwartzman 1982). This negative-sum possibility would throw the political economy into systemic crisis, which could propel political pragmatists into a stronger and more antistate coalition.

The Brazilian steel industry, in which state enterprises produce all flat rolled steel, offers an interesting case of pragmatic pressures for state managers to privatize. By the close of the 1980s, state mills were operating at capacity, and new investment was urgently needed. State managers saw three major obstacles to sufficient and effective investment: government (and state enterprise) debt, price controls, and politicians.[24] Neither the government nor its holding company, Siderbrás, had access to investment financing. The government's anti-inflation policies maintained very low steel prices, which kept the operating firms from breaking even, let alone from generating profits that could be reinvested. And Sarney's weak position encouraged him to trade appointments in steel for political support. Politicians have always been involved in managing steel firms, but many managers think the practice has gone too far. Privatization would solve all these problems and at the same time make selling firms attractive even to strong statists. The private sector is flush with resources, the government cannot keep prices as low for private firms, and politicians cannot appoint allies to manage privatized firms.

Conclusion

One thrust of the comparison between Brazil and Mexico has been to highlight the similarities in contrast to other political economies, especially those where privatization and liberalization have proceeded further. Despite the intense pressures of the debt crisis—fiscal entropy and demands from international lenders—neither Brazil nor Mexico has dug into the core of state enterprise. The trend may be towards increasing market-oriented reform, but in the 1980s privatization programs in Brazil and Mexico were variations on a statist theme.

The Sarney government tampered little with Brazil's form of state-led industrialization based on import substitution. Mexican leaders embarked on a new development strategy, but state guidance was still at the heart of the strategy (for example, state officials decided that Mexican firms would compete without tariff protection) and prominent in official documents, including the constitution. In the absence of stronger ideological and partisan incentives to deepen privatization, Mexican and Brazilian pragmatists have taken their programs about as far as they can alone.

Of course, the two countries differ in fundamental ways that help explain why privatization proceeded somewhat further in Mexico. The PAN presented an ideological and partisan challenge absent in Brazil, to which the PRI responded with partisan policies, including at times privatization, designed to undermine the PAN's appeal. The PRI represents the critical difference between the two political economies. It provided Mexican officials with a more solid base of support and greater policy freedom. The "captive" support or quiescence of unions, peasant associations, and regional political machines allowed the technocratic, bureaucratic faction within the PRI to dominate and pursue policies that would be suicidal for most elected governments in Latin America. In the case of privatization, this support (or lack of opposition) gave bureaucratic pragmatists greater leeway.

In Brazil, the leeway that the PRI provided technocrats through incorporation and co-optation, the military provided through repression, at least through 1979. Since then, weak and unelected presidents have relied on manipulating government agencies in the distribution of spending and jobs to maintain minimum coalitions, which greatly increases the political costs of privatization. A government with strong electoral support, even leftist or populist (à la Menem), might well have greater opportunities to privatize, especially if, like the Spanish socialists, they link state enterprises to the authoritarian regime.

Politics in the 1990s could bring renewed pressures and rewards for privatization in both countries. Nearly all the candidates for the presidential elections in Brazil in November 1989 supported some kind of reduction in state intervention, so the consensus among politicians was that privatization could bear electoral fruit (*Brazil Watch*, July 24–Aug. 7, 1989). Even the candidate of the Brazilian Communist party declared his support for privatizing firms with no social function (*Jornal do Brasil*, June 10, 1989). The consensus owed something to the meteoric rise of Fernando Collor de Mello, who led all early polls by a commanding margin. Collor's platform was vague but promarket, and his early popularity derived largely from his moralistic attacks on bureaucrats and politicians. Collor in fact ran against political parties and against the state. It is unclear how the moral attacks will translate into policies: lower salaries, privatization, or a crackdown on corruption? Nonetheless, general moral opposition to the state appealed to Brazilian voters.

The Salinas presidency so far portends continuity in economic policy. He has continued de la Madrid's policies in stabilizing, deregulating, and opening up the economy, and in processing firms already targeted for *desincorporación*. As of mid-1989, however, Salinas had not yet moved to expand the program (though officials were looking with increasing interest at possible means for deregulating and privatizing telecommunications). In part, this hesitation may reflect the fact that de la Madrid got rid of the simple cases. The pause may also reflect his priorities: first renegotiate the debt and stabilize prices. If and when he succeeds on these fronts, he may well proceed with further state shrinking, though he will have to resist the temptation to increase government investment to jump-start growth once pressures on the deficit ease.

Notes

I am grateful to Carlos Bazdresch, John Waterbury, Kathleen Thelen, Denise Dresser, María Amparo Casar, Juan Ricardo Pérez, José Carlos Braga, and Van Whiting for comments on earlier drafts, and to the Pew Charitable Trusts, the Program in Latin American Studies and the Center for International Studies at Princeton University for research support. I am responsible for the final product. Parts of this essay originally appeared in Schneider (1989).

1. Space limitations preclude a full contextual analysis here. See Schneider (1989), where I develop a conceptual framework of the bureaucratic political economy for analyzing the obstacles to economic and political reform in Brazil and Mexico. Here I focus more on the empirical story of privatization.

2. Government expenditure and production by state enterprises rise sharply from 1975 to 1980 in Mexico, well beyond the levels in Brazil. The figures are in some respects abnormal. The oil boom in 1979–1982 vastly increased the receipts of PEMEX, without any change in state activity. Longo (1982) also suspects that the Brazilian government expenditures that he reports may have been understated for 1980.

3. Over the same period PEMEX financed 23–70 percent of its investment from internal sources (Trebat 1981: 55). Excluding PEMEX would drop the ratio for the remaining firms.

4. For the recent history of privatization in Brazil see Abranches (1984), Kapstein (1988), and Werneck (1988 and 1989).

5. Sarney actively supported the military regime, and in 1985 he was the president of the pro-regime Social Democracy Party (PDS). He split with his party in June 1985 and led a dissident faction to support Tancredo, who was elected by a coalition dominated by the Party of the Brazilian Democratic Movement (PMDB). Though nominally a member of the PMDB, which won big in the 1986 elections for the Constituent Assembly and Congress, he never gained reliable support within a naturally suspicious PMDB.

6. The distribution of broadcasting licenses, mining concessions, and other discretionary funds has reportedly conformed to Sarney's strategy, particularly the quest for the fifth year. See *Senhor*, Jan. 26, 1988.

7. The Council for Destatization and its executive secretariat were subordi-

nate to the Secretariat of Planning (Seplan) and included as voting members the ministers of Seplan, Finance, Industry and Commerce, and Labor. In addition, the president appointed one representative from business and one from labor. Decreto 95.886.

8. In fact an ex-president of BNDES, Marcos Vianna, proposed privatizing many state firms as early as 1976. In a confidential memo to Planning Minister Reis Velloso (which later appeared in the *Jornal de Brasília*, May 26, 1976), Vianna argued for reducing the state's role in the economy and listed sector by sector where the state should remain and where it should withdraw. The proposal did not go anywhere in the Geisel government.

9. See, for example, the pragmatic approach advocated by Guilherme Gomes Dias, head of planning of BNDES, in his article in the *Gazeta Mercantil*, Aug. 22, 1989.

10. Interview with Sérgio Zendron, director of BNDESPAR, June 8, 1989.

11. Interviews with Paulo Galletta (June 12, 1989) and David Moreira (June 5, 1989), former heads of the federal privatization programs. Galletta provides a candid assessment of the political obstacles, as compared to more successful programs, such as those of the Thatcher government (Galletta 1988b).

12. Private firms blocked the extinction of the Instituto Brasileiro do Café (see *Veja*, Oct. 30, 1985, and Dec. 23, 1987) and delayed the sale of Caraíba.

13. Emilio Ocampo, ex-president of a major state enterprise in Mexico, recommended using this measure of *net* privatization: assets sold minus assets created (interview, June 30, 1989).

14. Pichardo (1988). Unless otherwise specified, all figures on privatization come from this report.

15. In some sectors the impact was greater. Excluding PEMEX, the reductions are significant in mining (30 percent) and manufacturing (32 percent). And the state will cease to produce consumer durables.

16. Mexico, Hacienda (1988: 71) and *Latin American Monitor*, November 1988, p. 596. Mexicana del Cobre was the largest firm sold, for $1.4 billion in Mexican debt paper (*Latin American Monitor*, November 1988, p. 596). The government never disclosed the actual sale price (including the discount on the paper debt used by the buyers), but it must have been in the hundreds of millions. This firm, however, had been a "state" enterprise for only a matter of months because it defaulted on some government loans earlier in the year.

17. The implementation of privatization programs often reveals the contradictory preferences of capitalists and state pragmatists, who both favor the policy in principle. Officials are likely to want to sell loss makers first. But capitalists may thwart the sale, either because the firm's losses are their gains or because they have no interest in a state lemon. On the other side, state officials are unlikely to want to sell profitable firms. Not only do they generate

scarce revenue, but the potential broader political gain from privatization is diminished in cases of perceived give-aways to a small number of private buyers.

18. Interviews with Jesús Silva Herzog (ex-minister of finance), Carlos Abedrop (ex-president of the bankers' association), and Agustín Legoretta (ex-president of the Business Coordinating Council [CCE]), July 1989.

19. N = 190. Another 18 percent responded that privatization encouraged investment only in specific sectors. Only 1 percent thought it had no effect, and no one thought it discouraged investment (Alduncin 1989: 42).

20. The resurrected Aeroméxico rehired some of the fired workers. For detailed official accounts of these liquidations, see Mexico, *Las Razones* (1987: 4:362–368, on Fundidora Monterrey, and 1989: 6:463–476, on Aeroméxico).

21. Interview with Carlos Abedrop, ex-president of the bankers' association, July 7, 1989.

22. Even those who ran the privatization program of the Sarney government could not isolate the PMDB position (interviews with David Moreira and Paulo Galleta, June 1989).

23. Ideological and partisan motives usually coincide and may be difficult to distinguish in particular cases. They are analytically distinct, however, and do not necessarily coincide. Moreover, even apparent ideologues, if they have been astute enough to attain the power to execute their programs, are likely to assess strictly partisan considerations before privatizing.

24. See *Gazeta Mercantil*, June 1, 1989, and *Brasil Mineral*, August 1988, for assessments by Siderbrás managers and statements in favor of privatization. The president in 1989, Moacélio Mendes, was pushing to extend the privatization program (interview, June 13, 1989).

References

Abranches, Sergio H. 1984. "State Enterprise and Modes of Privatization: A Critical View Based on Brazilian Examples." Serie Estudos no. 27, Instituto Universitário de Pesquisa do Rio de Janeiro.

Alduncin Abitia, Enrique. 1989. *Expectativas Económicas de los Líderes Empresariales, Determinantes de la Inversión Privada, Posición Competitiva Internacional de las Empresas Líderes de México*. México: Banco Nacional de México.

Ayala Espino, José. 1988. *Estado y Desarrollo: La Formación de la Economía Mixta Mexicana (1920–1982)*. México: Fondo de Cultura Económica.

Bielschowsky, Ricardo. 1988. *Pensamento Econômico Brasileiro: O Ciclo Ideológico do Desenvolvimentismo*. Rio de Janeiro: Instituto de Pesquisa Econômica Aplicada.

BNDESPAR (Banco Nacional de Desenvolvimento Econômico e Social—Participações). 1988. "Privatizations after Decree no. 91.991."

————. 1989. "Destatizações Realizadas após o Decreto no. 91.991 de novembro 1985."

Brazil, Conselho Federal de Privatização. 1989. "O Programa Federal de Desestatização em 1988." Mimeograph.

Brazil, Secretaria de Controle de Empresas Estatais (SEST). 1981. *State Enterprises in Brazil and the Control of SEST: Background and 1980 Results.* Brasília.

————. 1983. *Relatório SEST 1982.* Brasília.

————. 1985. *Sinopse da Atuação da SEST no Período 1980–84.* Brasília.

Casar, María Amparo, and Wilson Peres. 1988. *El Estado Empresario en México: Agotamiento o Renovación?* México: Siglo XXI.

Carrillo Castro, Alejandro. 1988. *The Empresa Pública y la Reforma Administrativa en Empresas Públicas.* Mexico: Presidencia de la República.

Carrillo Castro, Alejandro, and Sergio Garcia Ramírez. 1983. *Las empresas públicas en México.* Mexico: Porrúa.

CEESP (Centro de Estudios Económicos del Sector Privado). 1989. "Seguimiento de Desincorporación de Entidades Paraestatales, 1982–1989." June.

Cruz, Sebastião Carlos Velasco e. 1984. "Empresários e o Regime no Brasil: A Campanha contra a Estatização." Ph.D. dissertation, University of São Paulo.

de la Madrid H., Miguel. 1982. *Cien Tesis sobre México.* Mexico: Grijalbo.

Evans, Peter. 1982. "Reinventing the Bourgeoisie: State Entrepreneurship and Class Formation in Dependent Capitalist Development." *American Journal of Sociology* 88, special supplement, pp. 210–247.

Frieden, Jeffry A. 1987. "The Brazilian Borrowing Experience: From Miracle to Debacle and Back." *Latin American Research Review* 22, no. 1: 95–131.

Galletta, Paulo. 1988a. "A Exaustão do Setor Público e a Desestatização." *Economia em Perspectiva,* no. 50 (September): 1–3.

————. 1988b. "Condicionantes da Privatização." Paper presented to the Italy–Latin America Coloquium, Rome, December.

Guimarães, César, Maria Lúcia Teixeira Werneck Vianna, and Sebastião Carlos Velasco e Cruz. 1979. "Expansão do Estado e Intermediação de Interesses no Brasil." 2 vols. Rio de Janeiro: Instituto Universitário de Pesquisa do Rio de Janeiro.

Kapstein, Ethan B. 1988. "Brazil: Continued State Dominance." In *The Promise of Privatization,* ed. Raymond Vernon. New York: Council on Foreign Relations.

Longo, Carlos Alberto. 1982. "Uma Quantificaão do Setor Público." In Paulo Rabello de Castro et al., *A Crise do 'Bom Patrão.'* Rio de Janeiro: CEDES/APEC.

Martins, Luciano. 1985. *Estado Capitalista e Burocracia no Brasil Pós 64.* Rio de Janeiro: Paz e Terra.

Mexico, INEGI (Instituto Nacional de Estadística, Geografía e Informática). 1988. *Anuario Estadístico de los Estados Unidos Mexicanos 1987.* Mexico, D.F.

Mexico. 1987 and 1989. *Las Razones y las Obras. Gobierno de Miguel de la Madrid. Crónica del Sexenio 1982–1988.* México: Presidencia de la República y Fondo de Cultura.

Mexico, Secretaría de la Contraloría. 1988. *Reestructuración del Sector Paraestatal.* Mexico: Cuadernos de Renovación Nacional.

Mexico, Secretaría de la Hacienda. 1988. "La Venta de Empresas del Sector Público: Fundamentos, Procedimientos y Resultados, 1983–1988." October.

Nellis, John, and Sunita Kikeri. 1988. "The Privatization of Public Enterprises." Public Sector Management/Private Sector Development Division, World Bank.

PAN (Partido Acción Nacional). 1988(?). "Plataforma Política del Partido Acción Nacional, 1988–1994."

Pichardo Pagazo, Ignacio. 1988. "El Proceso de Desincorporación de Entidades Paraestatales: El Caso de México." Mexico: Secretaría de la Contraloría.

Reichstul, Henri, and Luciano Coutinho. 1983. "Investimento Estatal 1974–1980: Ciclo e Crise." In *Desenvolvimento Capitalista no Brasil,* ed. Luiz Gonzaga Belluzo and Renata Coutinho. São Paulo: Brasilense.

Rueschemeyer, Dietrich, and Peter B. Evans. 1985. "The State and Economic Transformation: Toward an Analysis of the Conditions Underlying Effective Intervention." In Peter Evans, Dietrich Rueschemeyer, and Theda Skocpol, *Bringing the State Back In.* New York: Cambridge University Press.

Ruiz Dueñas, Jorge, 1988. *Empresa Pública: Elementos para el Examen Comparado.* México: Fondo de Cultura Económica.

Schneider, Ben Ross. 1987. "Politics within the State: Elite Bureaucrats and Industrial Policy in Authoritarian Brazil." Ph.D. dissertation, University of California, Berkeley.

———. 1989. "Partly for Sale: Privatization and State Strength in Brazil and Mexico." *Journal of Interamerican Studies and World Affairs* 30, no. 4: 89–116.

Schwartzman, Simon. 1982. *As Bases do Autoritarismo Brasileiro.* Rio de Janeiro: Editora Campus.

Shefter, Martin. 1976. "Patronage and Its Opponents: A Theory and Some European Cases." Paper presented at the Conference of Western European Area Studies, University of Wisconsin, Madison.

Story, Dale. 1986. *Industry, the State and Public Policy in Mexico.* Austin: University of Texas Press.

Trebat, Thomas J. 1981. "Public Enterprise in Brazil and Mexico: A Comparison of Origins and Performance." In *Authoritarian Capitalism,* ed. Thomas C. Bruneau and Philippe Faucher. Boulder, Colo.: Westview.

Trebat, Thomas J. (1983). *Brazil's State-Owned Enterprises: A Case Study of the State as Entrepreneur.* Cambridge: Cambridge University Press.

Vera, Oscar. 1988. "The Political Economy of Privatization in Mexico." Paper presented at a conference on the Privatization of Public Enterprises in Latin America, University of San Diego, California, May.

Werneck, Rogério L. Furquim. 1988. "The Uneasy Steps of Privatization in Brazil." Paper presented at a conference on the Privatization of Public Enterprises in Latin America, University of San Diego, California, May.

———. 1989. "Aspectos Macroeconômicos da Privatização no Brasil." Departamento de Economia, Pontífica Universidade Católica do Rio de Janeiro, abril.

Willis, Eliza Jane. 1986. "The State as Banker: The Expansion of the Public Sector in Brazil." Ph.D. dissertation, University of Texas, Austin.

World Bank. 1988. "Strengthening Public Finance through Reform of State-owned Enterprises." In *World Development Report 1988*. New York: Oxford University Press.

15

Chile: Privatization, Reprivatization, Hyperprivatization

Paul E. Sigmund

In no country in the world, not even Margaret Thatcher's Britain, has privatization been carried as far as it has in contemporary Chile. Not only has the public sector been drastically reduced, but many of the social services that in most Western countries—including Chile itself—have long been considered government responsibilities have been in whole or in part turned over to the private sector. This is true in education, health, housing, and especially social security—an area in which regulated private pension funds have almost completely replaced the government-operated social security system that has been in place since the 1920s. It is also true of state-owned enterprises, which have been sold to private investors, workers, and foreign banks and multinationals at a rapid rate. Such a complete transformation is possible because in Chile in the 1980s there has been a rare combination of ideological motivation, political strategy, and concentration of power in the hands of one of the few remaining military dictators in Latin America, Augusto Pinochet.

The ideological commitment has come from the small group of economists known—from the university at which many did graduate work—as the "Chicago boys," who are convinced that the most efficient and just economic system is one in which market forces are dominant and the state plays a subsidiary role. The political determination to privatize was motivated by fear that when Chile democratized it would return to state control of the economy unless drastic steps were taken to make that impossible. The political power to make the necessary changes came from General Pinochet, who ruled Chile from the 1973 coup that overthrew the elected Marxist-dominated government of Salvador Allende until 1990.

Since the coup, there have been three stages of privatization in Chile. The first took place between 1973 and 1978, when the military government returned more than 250 firms that had been seized by the Allende government to their original owners. It also sold off another 200 state-owned firms and banks, some of which had been bought out by the government recently and others of which had long been owned by the state. The second wave of privatizations took place between 1979 and 1983 and involved housing, education, health services, and social security, as well as the decentralization of labor organization. The third stage, which began in 1985, involved a drastic sell-off of nearly all remaining state-owned enterprises for ideological and political rather than economic reasons. (The state-owned copper mines were exempted.)

The headlong rush to privatization in Chile was all the more surprising because it is a country with a long statist tradition. Even in the nineteenth century the revenues from the extraction of nitrate and, later, copper made it possible to build a relatively large state bureaucracy and centralized state. Social security programs were initiated beginning in the 1920s, family allowances were established in 1934, the state development corporation (CORFO) was created in 1939, and a comprehensive government health system (really several different systems) was put in place in the early 1950s. Under the Christian Democratic government of Eduardo Frei (1964–1970) majority control of the American-owned copper mines was purchased by the government as part of the so-called "Chileanization" program, and similar programs were initiated to assure majority ownership by the state of electricity and steel production. Under the Popular Unity government of Salvador Allende, more than five hundred companies were taken over, either by nationalization (the major copper mines) and purchase (some banks, automobile assembly, electronics) or by "temporary" seizure ("intervention" or "requisition") using legal loopholes in existing legislation. Legal loopholes were also used to accelerate the process of expropriation of farmland under the 1967 agrarian reform law, so that by 1973 35 percent of Chilean agriculture was under state control (Sigmund 1977: 190). By the time of Allende's overthrow on September 11, 1973, the government share of the gross domestic product (GDP) had grown from 15 percent to 40 percent (part of that increase was due to a rise in government spending rather than state takeovers), and subsidies to state enterprises and the "reformed" sector of agriculture amounted to 55 percent of public expenditure (Sigmund 1977: 280; U.S. Embassy, Santiago, 1985b).

Postcoup Privatizations

Following the coup, the military turned to a well-trained group of economists from the Catholic University who had studied with Milton Friedman and Arnold Harberger at the University of Chicago. After overcoming some resistance on the part of nationalist-corporatist elements within and outside of the military, the Chicago boys proceeded to implement a free market model in an economy that by 1973 had become overwhelmingly statist. In a shotgun wedding between what had earlier been two antagonistic traditions, free market economic liberalism and social welfare-oriented Catholic social thought, the new regime published a Declaration of Principles that argued that the free market was an example of the principle of "subsidiarity"—the allocation, wherever possible, of social and economic functions to lower associations rather than to the state—which had been advocated by Pope Pius XI in his 1931 encyclical *Quadragesimo Anno*. In 1973 and 1974, 259 intervened and requisitioned enterprises were returned to their owners, and more than 200 state-owned firms and banks were sold to private investors in the 1970s, often at prices well below book value (Edwards and Edwards 1987: 97; Mönckeberg 1988: 20). Because the country was in deep economic crisis and its capital market limited, only a few conglomerates (*los grupos*) with access to foreign capital could afford to purchase the companies and banks, and this produced a considerable concentration of economic power in a few corporate interlocking directorates. Limits on bank stock purchases were systematically eluded so that *los grupos* acquired control of both the financial and the industrial sectors.

The Chicago boys established a system in which market-determined prices replaced the price controls of the Allende period, a realistic exchange rate was implemented, and tariff protection was drastically reduced from an average rate of nearly 100 percent—in some cases, much higher—to a uniform 10 percent. The Chicago boys argued that Chile could be transformed into a Latin American Hong Kong, with highly competitive exports based on its comparative advantage and the low wages that resulted from the banning of left-dominated unions after the coup. The runaway inflation of the Allende period (estimated at 700 percent in 1973) was brought under control, the economy went into deep recession ("the shock treatment"), and then bounced back between 1977 and 1981, experiencing a boom that the *Wall Street Journal* described as "the Chilean economic miracle."

Although the government-controlled sector of the economy had been reduced, it still amounted to 25 percent of GDP, and the state owned six of the ten largest enterprises and ten of the top twenty-five, dominating such important areas of the economy as communications, petroleum refining, electric power generation, and copper mining and refining. There was strong resistance on strategic grounds to proposals to denationalize copper and petroleum. Copper had a special importance for the military not only because it was the principal source of foreign exchange (export diversification and low international prices reduced its share from 70 percent to 40 percent in the Pinochet years) but also because an unpublished law allocated 10 percent of the dollar value of copper sales in foreign exchange to the military. Following the first wave of privatizations, the remaining thirty-five or so state enterprises were "rationalized" along free market lines with a view both to reducing their subsidies from the state and to increasing their saleability in the event of privatization. Prices for public services were raised, "featherbedding" was eliminated by reductions in the number of public employees from 161,000 to 89,000 (the firings also provided an opportunity to get rid of those whose loyalties, whether to the left or to the centrist Christian Democrats, were suspect), saleable holdings of state enterprises such as real estate were sold off, and in many cases companies were reorganized so that they could be publicly traded on the stock market. A majority of the remaining state enterprises were held by CORFO, but utilities, transport, communication, and copper and petroleum production and refining were separate state enterprises created by specific laws. CORFO had a military man at its head for all but six months after the 1973 coup, and military men were in key management positions in nearly all the state enterprises.

Modernization and Privatization of Social Services

By 1980 the Chicago boys' policy seemed to have achieved astounding success. The economy was growing at 5–8 percent a year. Pinochet was able to win a (possibly fraudulently inflated) 66 percent majority in a snap plebiscite on a hastily written constitution that gave him continuing dictatorial powers until 1989. Foreign investors were finally beginning to look seriously at Chile. Defenders of the regime began to argue that the continuing economic prosperity would establish the underpinning for a decentralized libertarian market-oriented society that, after the transitional period provided for in the constitution, could lead to one of the most open societies in the contemporary world.

To carry out their program of "utopian libertarianism" (Sigmund 1981) the members of the economic policy team now turned to what they saw as an overextended, inefficient, and politicized set of government social services. Led by a brilliant Harvard-trained economist, José Piñera, they proposed a series of "modernizations," drastic reorganizations of social services that extended market criteria and the private sector to areas that had previously been under government control. Under Piñera's Labor Plan (*Plan Laboral*), the right to strike was permitted, but only after a majority vote of the workers who had affiliated individually (no closed shop) with unions that were limited to a given factory or enterprise. (Labor leaders were also forbidden to organize nationally or to involve themselves in politics.) In housing, continuing a policy of targeting areas of extreme poverty that had been initiated in the mid-1970s, government subsidies (amounting to 75 percent of cost and a low-interest loan for the rest) were aimed at the very poor, and housing was to be built by private firms on a competitive basis with special emphasis on the erection of the *caseta sanitaria*—a core consisting of kitchen and bath with sewage and electricity—around which the rest of the house could be built by its inhabitants (*autoconstrucción*). As in the past, the lower middle class could also get some subsidized loans for strictly prescribed, but privately built housing (U.S. Embassy, Santiago, 1987a). The most important changes, however, were in the areas of education, health care, and social security.

In education, the government announced a long-range program to turn over control of the primary schools to the local governments. Subsidies based on average income and the number of enrolled students would be provided for the poorer areas from a Common Fund for Municipalities, but decisions about curriculum, hiring and firing, and the allocation of funds between public and private nonprofit schools would be left to the local governing bodies. Income from licenses and real estate taxes that formerly went to the central government was to remain with the municipality. Private nonprofit corporations under contract with the municipality were authorized to run the schools.

There were a number of problems with the plan. It was immediately protested by the national teachers union, since under the new system teachers would lose their pension and job rights and were to be treated as private sector employees subject to dismissal at any time. In addition, there had been no local elections since the coup, so that local governments were under the control of Pinochet-appointed mayors and, where they existed, corporatist advisory Communal Development Councils (CODECOS), again largely Pinochetista in character. The program was implemented only gradually, but by 1987 most primary education was under local control. Eight thousand teachers had been fired, and under the Labor Plan the others could not, as in the past, go out on strike except on the local level—in which case substitutes could be hired after sixty days (Hevia 1984; U.S. Embassy, Santiago, 1987a).

While the "modernization" of primary education involved municipalization more than it did privatization in the traditional sense, on the university level the privatizing impulse was applied more thoroughly. The state university system formerly dominated by the University of Chile and its branches was broken up into regions. Subsidies to existing universities (the Catholic universities in Santiago and Valparaiso, as well as the public universities) were drastically cut back and replaced by two new funding sources. First, tuition was sharply raised, to be financed by low-interest loans (1 percent plus indexing for inflation) that became immediately payable if a student failed or was expelled for political or other misconduct. Second, research funds were made available on the basis of the number of the top-ranking students (in a national academic aptitude test) who chose a given university, thus promoting competition among the universities for good students. (In fact, very little research money was made available.) In addition, new private universities were encouraged, although at the outset they were to be under the tutelage of existing universities to ensure quality control. The professional programs that were the subject of university programs were restricted to a specific list; other areas were left to professional institutes, most of them organized under private auspices.

In practice, the new system led to a sharp reduction of government funding for higher education. Between 1980 and 1988 the amount going directly to the universities, including the research funds based on the number of top students, dropped from 19 billion to 12.5 billion 1983 pesos (Thorud 1983: 155). As of 1986, twenty private professional institutes had been recognized, with enrollments totaling 18,000 students, and three private universities had been established with a total enrollment of 6,000 students. This compared with a total of 132,000 students in publicly supported higher education. The private institutions in most cases did not charge significantly higher tuition than those supported by public funds, since their faculty was almost entirely part-time and they were in areas like architecture, social science, education, and business administration, which do not require substantial outlays for overhead. More private universities were planned, but expansion in this area was slowed by the economic depression between 1981 and 1985 (Orellano 1987).

In the area of health, a large, complicated, and inefficient public health care system was reorganized in 1980 to allow the upper and middle classes to opt out of the public health care system. Previously, all employees were required to contribute to the state health service even when, as was the case for the upper middle and upper classes, they did not use its facilities, preferring the better service and higher quality of private clinics and doctors. As of the early 1980s, those who chose to do so could direct their medical withholding payments to a recognized government-supervised private health care plan (Instituto de Salud Previsional, or ISAPRE). Those contributions amounted to 4 percent of salary (after 1983, 6 percent up to an indexed ceiling), and additional charges could be imposed by the private health provider. The armed forces continued to have a separate and heavily subsidized health care program.

About 12 percent of the workforce has opted for the private ISAPREs. Public health care has been decentralized into twenty-seven regional sectors. The central government provides support to the regional and municipal programs on a per visit and contractual basis. There is considerable variation in government expenditure for health care, however, since municipalities can also subsidize health programs from their own funds, and one estimate places the differential between high- and low-income areas of Santiago in per capita expenditure on health at 1300 percent. As in the case of primary education, local clinics for primary care are rapidly being municipalized, and health workers in them have lost job security rights and have seen their rights to strike limited (Contreras 1986).

Critics of the new system argue that it has led to a deterioration in health care for the majority of Chileans while benefiting the upper income groups (Scarpaci 1988). In addition, the ISAPREs have been criticized for limiting enrollments and canceling the contracts of those with serious illnesses. Chile has been proud of its record in the area of health care, particularly in the reduction in infant and child mortality from 65 per 1000 in 1973 to 19 per 1000 in 1986 (Chile, Secretaria de Desarrollo, 1987)—the result of prenatal and preschool health programs of this and earlier governments. But since 1980 public expenditure for health has dropped from 5 billion to 3.8 billion 1977 pesos, and health as a percentage of government spending has dropped from 14 to 7 percent (U.S. Embassy, Santiago, 1987a; Scherman 1986).

The most controversial, far-reaching, and, in this writer's view, successful of the modernizations was the privatization of social security. Beginning in 1981, the Chilean government in effect phased out the previous social security system, comprising about fifty widely varied programs covering 75 percent of the workforce. (A minimum safety-net pension for the unemployed and infirm remained as a government responsibility.) Arguing that the current pay-as-you-go system was bankrupt and inequitable (93 percent of retirees received a minimum pension, 70 percent of which had been eroded by inflation), Piñera proposed that future social security deductions go to private pension fund administrators (Administradoras de Fondos de Pensiones, or AFP), which would be subject to government regulation as to the soundness of their investments but which would compete with one another for individual compulsory retirement payments. Employees would receive a retirement bankbook and could shift their funds as they wished. The vested pension rights from the old system were transformed into bonds that were cashable at the time of retirement. Employees could opt to remain under the old system, but the deduction for the AFP system (10 percent), plus the premium for accident and disability insurance, was substantially less than under the government system (13.5 percent versus 17 percent). The reform was made attractive to employers because the compulsory employer contribution was abolished, thus lowering future labor costs, although all employees received a one-time 18 percent raise (Ortuzar 1987).

In effect, the government had made the employers and employees an offer that they could not refuse. Except for those very near to retirement, there was a massive emigration from the public social security system (90 percent of those eligible are in the new system; Piñera 1988: 8). The financial pressure on that system was also lightened by establishing a uniform and less generous retirement age (60 for women, 65 for men), but payments for earlier pension obligations now constitute about 25 percent of the Chilean government budget, since it has lost the pay-as-you-go income that was supposed to finance the old system. A total of twelve AFPs began to compete with one another, using salesmen and modern advertising techniques. Although the timing of the new system seemed bad, since it was initiated just before a massive recession in the Chilean economy, the restrictions on AFP investments, mostly placed in government obligations, prevented them from incurring losses beyond the initially high start-up and advertising costs.

Critics (Arellano 1985; Baeza 1986) argued that the old system could have been rescued by raising the retirement age and that the new system appears more successful because the government has accepted the burden of paying the earlier obligations. Some cases were cited of excessive management fees, but defenders argued that competition and freedom to change AFPs would prevent such abuses. The program developed considerable support, as each month Chileans saw their retirement savings grow before their eyes in their AFP bankbooks. In addition, the administrative service provided by the AFP was far better than that of the former social security bureaucracy. The program began to get international attention, with articles in the *Wall Street Journal* and favorable comments by William F. Buckley in the *National Review*. The joint opposition program of six centrist parties, issued in January 1988, committed a democratic government to re-examining the AFP system. On October 5, 1988, President Pinochet was defeated in a plebiscite on his re-election, but a return to the old social security system seems unlikely, if only because the real average annual returns to the individual accounts from June 1981 to December 1987, despite the massive contraction of the economy (-14 percent GDP) in 1982, has averaged from 8 to 11 percent a year (Cheyre 1988).

In time, the amount of capital invested in the AFPs made them one of the major possible sources of investment funds. In 1985 the regulations concerning investment instruments were changed to permit up to 30 percent of AFP funds to be invested in stocks, with a limit of 5 percent in any given company. This change was made just at the time that the government was embarking on a new privatization effort, and the AFPs became major purchasers of shares in privatized state enterprises. The AFPs also attracted the attention of foreign financial institutions, and the larger AFPs now have substantial foreign ownership. The largest, Pro Vida, is 40 percent owned by Bankers Trust, and the second largest, Santa Maria, is 57 percent owned by Aetna Insurance Company. American International Insurance owns 93 percent of a smaller fund, and Japanese banks own 52 percent of another. One observer estimates that two-thirds of the pension fund assets are controlled by foreigners (Errazuriz 1987).

In early 1982, Chile entered a deep recession. The relative importance of international and domestic factors in provoking the collapse can be argued, but there is no doubt that the policies of Sergio de Castro, finance minister since 1976—involving a fixed exchange rate, banking deregulation, excessively low tariffs, no limits on private foreign borrowing, and overconfidence in "automatic adjustment" by the market—were all contributory elements (Edwards and Edwards 1987: chap. 8). Beginning with the collapse of a large sugar company, a wave of bankruptcies swept through the economy, resulting in a massive increase in unemployment—reaching at one point about a third of the workforce, if government make-work programs are included—and the beginnings of mass protests against the Pinochet regime. Bank failures due to bad loans to finance speculation by *los grupos* forced the government to take over the largest private financial institutions and associated enterprises, including the Bank of Chile, which had successfully resisted Allende's efforts to take it over in the early 1970s, leading some observers to comment on the emergence of "the Chicago way [*via chicagoiana*] to socialism." Gross national product (GNP) dropped by 14 percent in 1982. Chile's debt reached $20 billion, much of it incurred by the private groups, but now the government was compelled to violate its free market principles and guarantee the foreign private debt in order to maintain its standing in debt renegotiations. De Castro was fired, the peso was devalued, some of *los grupos* were dissolved, and it appeared that the experiment in free market economics had ended in failure.

The Clearance Sale on State Enterprises (1985–1987)

Despite the 1982 debacle, the Chicago boys remained in key positions. The tariff rate was increased to 20 percent, and a sizable devaluation led exports to rebound. After a brief experiment with non-Chicago finance ministers from the traditional right, Hernan Büchi, one of de Castro's longtime protégés, began a successful stint as finance minister in February 1985. Büchi immediately began to reactivate a program of further privatization of state enterprises that had been proposed in the early 1980s but placed on the shelf because of the economic crisis. Originally announced as a program to sell a 30 percent interest in twenty-three companies, by 1989 it involved full privatization of thirty-three state enterprises (Marcel 1989b: 6, 31).

Before he became director of the planning office in 1983, Büchi had been on the board of directors of the state-owned telephone company, vice president of the state steel company, and vice president and later president of the state electric company. In the case of the electric company, he had presided over the division of the company into a number of generation and distribution companies so that they could be sold to the private sector (Mönckeberg 1988).

With a view to avoiding the mistakes of the post-1973 privatizations and to changing the whole structure of ownership in Chile so as to make it impossible to re-establish the state domination of the precoup period, Büchi and his associates used several innovative and controversial mechanisms. The first step was to reprivatize the banks that had been taken over in the post-1982 period after the crash. Here, as part of the "popular capitalism" program, special borrowing facilities were made available that allowed potential investors to buy up to $32,000 in shares by paying 5 percent down and the remaining 95 percent with an interest-free fifteen-year loan, payments on which were tax deductible. With such advantageous facilities, it is no wonder that the Bank of Chile and the Bank of Santiago were reprivatized by 1986, three years before the original target date (U.S. Embassy, Santiago, 1987b; Rosende and Reinstein 1986).

A second step involved the establishment of norms for debt-for-equity swaps, allowing foreign investors to use dollars to purchase Chilean foreign debt instruments at a discount from foreign holders of Chile's debt and to convert them into domestic assets in Chile. In 1985 the Central Bank published Chapter 19 of the Foreign Exchange Regulations, outlining how such transactions were to be carried out. In 1986 a total of $300 million of the $20 billion Chilean foreign debt was converted into equity, and in 1987 the amount rose to $675 million. Another $694 million was exchanged in the first five months of 1988. This was in addition to $1.2 billion in foreign dollar holdings that had been exchanged for discounted Chilean pesos by Chilean citizens under Chapter 18 of the Foreign Exchange Regulations, which was designed to attract flight capital back to Chile. Another $450 million in Chapter 18 transactions was exchanged in the first five months of 1988. Between 1985 and 1988, Chapter 18 and 19 transactions resulted in a reduction of the Chilean debt of $4.19 billion (Livingstone 1987; *Chile Economic Report* [New York], July and August 1988; Fontaine 1988).

Much of the Chapter 19 operation was directed to the purchase of shares in state enterprises participating in the privatization program, as well as shares in Chilean banks and pension funds. New foreign investment in Chile came from Australia and New Zealand, with $400 million from New Zealand coming in as investment in forestry, fishing, and dairy products, and the direct sale of 30 percent of the Chilean Telephone Company's (CTC) government-owned stock to the Bond Corporation of Australia for $280 million along with another 15 percent in share capital as compensation for new technology and expanded service (Christian 1988).

Other sales to foreigners included 77 percent of the state explosives company (ENAEX) to the Austin Powder Company for $8.5 million and the electricity generating plant of Pilmaiquen to Bankers Trust Company for $20.8 million, estimated to be half its replacement value (Mönckeberg 1988). The debt-for-equity swaps were regulated by the Central Bank, and certain very attractive investments in natural resources, such as the Escondida copper mining operation being developed by Broken Hill of Australia, were limited as to debt-equity financing (10 percent).

A third method used to sell off state enterprises was the sale of a given percentage of shares to workers. In the case of the accelerated privatization of the state-owned Pacific Steel Company (CAP), its workers and executives bought 41 percent of its shares under a program that made purchases highly attractive by offering special prices and low-interest loans, which were to be canceled in case of death of the borrower. In the steel and the telephone and electricity companies, workers were allowed to draw up to 50 percent of the company reserves for their severance pay, 10 percent in cash and the rest in shares that would be repurchased at an indexed price at the time of retirement. The state nitrate company even distributed shares to its workers directly without any charge. In two cases, a computer company and one of the electricity companies, 100 percent of equity is now owned by the workers under a government-financed, long-term, low-interest loan scheme. (It is ironic that a military government would achieve what social theorists of the left wing of the Christian Democratic party had urged for twenty-five years: worker-owned firms.) In the other cases, workers and employees own a minority share, sometimes with (for example, Endesa, the electric company), but usually without, the right to elect one or more members of the board of directors. In the case of the government-owned sugar company, worker shares of 5 percent converted the state share into a minority and thus satisfied one of the requirements of the international agencies involved in debt refinancing (Errazuriz and Weinstein 1986; *El Mercurio*, Feb. 12, 1988).

By 1988, 170,000 workers owned about 14 percent of the state enterprises that were in the process of being privatized (Marcel 1989a)—and since the stock market had been rising since 1985, they were happy with the scheme. Major Chilean and foreign investors also supported the special arrangements for worker ownership, which they viewed as a kind of risk premium insurance against nationalization.

The fourth way in which privatization was promoted was the decision by the Council of the Chilean Development Corporation (CORFO), which owned many of the state enterprises, to authorize the sale to the AFP pension funds of shares of certain state enterprises, including electricity, communications, steel, telephones, explosives, and drug laboratories. The decision, after it was approved by the AFP Risk Evaluation Committee, fundamentally altered the portfolios of the pension funds.

In order to avoid any investor having a controlling interest in the privatized firms, the AFPs were not allowed to own more than 5 percent of the shares in a single firm. Once again, the attempt was made to diversify ownership among the Chilean population and limit the possibility of a return of the privatized firms to the public sector.

There is now an increasing awareness in Chile that the pension funds are becoming the major potential source of investment capital outside of the state. A total of $3 billion, or 15 percent of the GNP of Chile, was in the AFPs by 1987, and it is estimated that by 1990 they will have accumulated $4.3 billion in their accounts (Perez 1987; Piñera 1988), 30 percent of which now can be invested in shares. There is pressure for the Risk Evaluation Committee to raise the limits on the amount the funds can invest and to expand the range of permissible investments. The permission to buy shares in privatized firms was the first break in what had generally been a conservative investment strategy, limited almost exclusively to government bonds and safe mortgage instruments. Some further liberalization of permitted investment in stocks is likely in the future (U.S. Embassy, Santiago, 1987a).

The potential for further privatization is limited. The 1980 constitution forbids the privatization of the existing state-owned copper mines. The Chilean State airline (LAN), a consistent money loser has been reorganized and its shares offered to international bidding, and various methods have been used to sell off the state-owned coal mines. Two military-controlled state enterprises involving shipbuilding and armaments seem unlikely candidates for privatization. This leaves the new Santiago subway system and two water companies as possibilities for the future. The government has also changed the law to allow the establishment of privately owned television stations.

Much depends on future political developments in Chile. General Pinochet's defeat in the 1988 plebiscite on a second eight-year term as president means that the competitive elections for the two houses of Congress scheduled for December 14, 1989, will also include a competitive election for the presidency. If the pro-Pinochet government candidate loses, or even if he wins and a hostile majority is elected in the 1989 congressional elections, it is not likely that the privatization program will be continued. The opposition is committed to modification of the labor legislation, a "restudy" of the pension system, and a "review" of the Chapter 19 debt-equity procedure (*El Mercurio*, Jan. 28, 1988).

The privatization debate was carried out in the opposition magazines and newspapers. The rapid privatization of the Pacific Steel Company produced a particularly hostile reaction because the company had been created by the government and public money had subsidized it for many years. Raúl Saez, a former finance minister under the Christian Democrats and one of the "nine wise men" of the Alliance for Progress, was particularly incensed by the CAP privatization and helped to form the Committee for the Defense of the National Patrimony in late 1986 to oppose the privatization programs (Saez 1987). Particular criticism has been directed at the sale of "the national patrimony," at what appears to be an artificially low price per share, and, in the case of foreign investors, at a 33 percent debt-equity discount.

A second criticism focuses on the fact that there were no strong economic reasons to privatize the firms, since the massive government subsidies of the Allende period had already been eliminated before the enterprises had been privatized and the process of reorganization and rationalization of prices and employment policies (*saneamiento* or "cleansing") had produced an efficient state sector that did not require subsidies except for the four money losers: the airline, the coal company, and the two military suppliers. Thus, it is argued, future profits that could have been available to the state were being turned over to the private sector or to foreigners.

A third problem was the price at which the companies were sold. Because of the boom-and-bust character of the Chilean economy, it was possible to make widely divergent calculations of the value of the enterprises, if based on estimates of future earnings. If the stock market was used, many shares offered in a short time on the Chilean exchange could saturate what was a small market and depress prices. Another method was to compare the compensation paid by the government at the time of nationalization of the electric company in 1970 or the purchase of the telephone company from ITT in 1974. A further approach was to calculate replacement value, and here it was argued that the sale price was often only about 25 percent of replacement cost. Book value, often established during the boom years, was sometimes far in excess of purchase price. In the case of the steel company, 1985 book value per share was $4.39, its shares were being sold at $0.41 from a low of $0.11 earlier in the year, and the sale price set by the government was $0.25 a share (Errazuriz and Tironi 1986). By one computation, the implicit subsidy in the 1986–1987 sales ranged from 27 percent to 69 percent, depending on the method of evaluation (Marcel 1989a: annex; 1989b: 39–44).

Finally, the critics were particularly concerned over the role of the pension funds, especially since the major AFPs have substantial foreign ownership. They argued that the net effect of the privatization program was to turn over the savings and investment capital of the nation to a small group of Chilean and foreign investors, leaving the state to subsidize the old pension system and to support a few inefficient state enterprises that no one cared to buy.

The reply of the proponents of the program was that the excesses of the earlier privatization efforts after the 1973 coup had been avoided under the new scheme. No single investor or group of investors could purchase more than 20 percent of the shares of the privatized firms. There was widespread stockholding by the workers and the middle class. And if profits were made, they were due to the greater efficiency and competitiveness of private enterprise.

As far as foreigners were concerned, the debt-equity scheme reduced the foreign debt by $2.4 billion dollars in two and a half years, releasing the funds that would have gone out of the country for interest ($300 million a year) and amortization for internal development, and bringing in foreign know-how and markets. It was also noted that important foreign investments had not used the debt-equity mechanism; Bond International Company of Australia, for example, purchased a 45 percent interest in the Chilean telephone company without using Chapter 19 and agreed to expand the number of telephones in Chile from 7 per 100 inhabitants in 1988 to 11 per 100 in 1992. Proponents also argued that the general boom fostered by the debt-equity scheme would lead to a spillover in other areas and an expansion of the economy that would benefit the whole society.

Critics replied that the debt-equity scheme allowed repatriation of profits after four years and of capital in ten years, which would postpone but not eliminate the drain on foreign exchange. They argued that interest saved by debt prepayment was less than the direct investment lost by the scheme, and they quoted Harold Macmillan's description of the Thatcher privatization program as "selling off the family silver to meet current expenses." An opposition economist estimated that only about half of the proceeds of the privatizations was used for investment or debt reduction, with the rest spent on current expenses (Marcel 1989a: 72).

An overall judgment on the controversy depends on one's general attitude toward foreign investment and toward the tradeoff between reduced debt and increased foreign ownership. More generally, an estimate is needed of the efficiency and productivity of the newly privatized firms compared with their earlier performance as public enterprises.

The Lessons of Chile

In many ways, the Chilean experience of privatization is unique. Absolute control by a military dictator was combined with a single-minded commitment to the free market by his civilian economic advisors for most of the period between 1975 and the present. Privatization was not carried out because of a need to relieve the burden of state enterprise deficits; that problem was resolved relatively quickly after the 1973 coup. Rather, the Chicago boys were committed to a vision of a decentralized and privatized economy as morally, politically, and economically superior to the long Chilean tradition of state intervention. The willingness to involve foreign investors in the privatization program also was related to the policymakers' belief that integration of Chile into the world economy was superior to the autarchic import-substitution, welfare-state approach of the 1960s.

The first privatizations were carried out too rapidly and, owing to the lack of a capital market, resulted in a concentration of economic power in a few conglomerates that combined holdings in both industry and finance. This contributed to overextension of credit and excessive indebtedness, which led to the collapse of the economy in 1982. Thus the lesson of the first phase of privatization was to avoid overborrowing internationally and interlocking directorates domestically. Privatization helped to produce both a boom and a bust in the late 1970s and early 1980s.

The second stage of privatization involved the reorganization of social services, notably health care, education, and social security. The evaluation of the modernization program in each case must be different. The health reform diminished government assistance to the majority of the Chilean population while removing from the top 12 percent the burden of contributing to a public health service they did not use. Funds for higher education were decreased and a greater burden was placed on student loans rather than a straight government subsidy to higher education. On equity grounds, since the percentage of the population that attends university is low and the economic advantages of higher education are considerable, this would seem to be an improvement. But the use of the loan system for political purposes to discourage student protest and possibly to penalize opponents of the regime were negative aspects of the university reform.

A judgment of the program to encourage the establishment of private institutions and universities must depend on whether quality standards have been maintained at the same time that fees do not restrict access of qualified lower-income groups. So far, this seems to be the case, although the benefits of the system are restricted geographically to the large urban centers. (The poor had not been able to attend Chilean universities even when they had low or no tuition.) The loan requirement probably constitutes an additional obstacle—but this should be balanced against the increase in the number of places available under the new system.

The reform of social security seems on the whole to have been a positive step. Although there have been criticisms of advertising costs and of foreign ownership of many of the pension funds, the system seems to have combined efficiency with returns on savings. The question for the future is whether the increasing amounts available in the pension funds will lead to more risky investments and possibly to politically motivated government requirements concerning the direction of their investments. Already there is a proposal that pension fund investments be used to promote low-income housing (Tomic and de la Maza 1987). Their use as a mortgage guarantee by the potential homeowner might be desirable; a more general diversion on social grounds in a democratized Chile would be politically tempting but economically dangerous.

An additional problem with the privatization of education in Chile was its use to conduct political purges. Once the civil service–type guarantees that had protected state employees were removed, it was possible for the privatized and decentralized systems to cite efficiency reasons for what were in reality partisan firing decisions.

The third wave of privatization took place after the 1982 collapse led to government takeovers of important banks and financial conglomerates. Learning from the earlier experience (and from the example of the privatization of Volkswagen in Germany in the 1950s), policymakers devised new schemes involving special arrangements to encourage "popular capitalism," including loans to small investors and inducements to workers to use their severance pay reserves. There has been substantial worker participation in the new programs. Yet workers have little or no say in electing members of the boards of directors, and when shares rise in value, they are tempted to sell them, essentially getting an advance on severance pay. It is doubtful whether the program will have a significant redistributive effect, but politically it has created a new group that is likely to oppose future nationalizations.

A further problem with the new privatizations was the substantial increase in foreign ownership, both directly through the debt-equity swaps and indirectly through foreign participation in the pension funds that are now permitted to buy shares in the privatized companies. Will this lead to a nationalist reaction after Chile returns to democratic politics in 1990? In the case of the steel industry, the most controversial privatization, will one see a pattern of alternating nationalization and denationalization such as took place in Britain?

Finally the privatization of electricity and telephones also raises the question of how to treat the so-called natural monopolies. The breakup of the electric company is supposed to promote competition, and regulatory procedures have been established, but past Latin American experience has tended to be either too permissive or excessively restrictive on rate increases.

The sell-off of the state enterprises and the privatizations of social services in Chile are designed to alter both outlook and conduct in ways that will make the changes irreversible regardless of what government follows that of Pinochet. There is no doubt that both worldwide trends and their own adverse experience with statism have led many Chileans, including a significant element on the left, to appreciate the value of market forces and private initiative. On the other hand, there has always been a strong commitment to social justice in Chile, which often takes the form of welfare legislation and government action. There has also been a strong tradition of economic nationalism in Chile that is hostile to foreign ownership. How to achieve a balance between economic efficiency, national autonomy, and social equity is a problem for all modern governments. The Chilean reforms, with their strong emphasis on competition and market allocation, provide a useful and controversial laboratory for the continuing debate about privatization.

References

Arellano, José Pablo. 1985. *Politicas Sociales y Desarrollo, Chile, 1924–1984*. Santiago: CIEPLAN, 1985.

Baeza, Sergio, ed. 1986. *Analisis de la Prevision en Chile*. Santiago: Centro de Estudios Publicos. (See especially articles by J. P. Arellano and A. Mujica.)

Cheyre Valenzuela, Hernan. 1988. *La Prevision en Chile Ayer y Hoy*. Santiago: Centro de Estudios Publicos.

Chile, Secretaria de Desarrollo y Asistencia Social. 1987. "Evolucion de la Extrema Pobreza en Chile." Santiago.

Christian, Shirley. 1988. "Chile's Growing Transpacific Ties." *New York Times*, March 28.

Contreras, Rodrigo, et al. 1986. *Salud Publica, Privada y Solidaria en Chile Actual*. Program de Economia del Trabajo, Academia de Humanismo Cristiano, Document no. 44 (July). Santiago.

Edwards, Sebastian, and Alejandra Cox Edwards, 1987. *Monetarism and Liberalization: The Chilean Experiment*. Cambridge, Mass.: Ballinger.

Errazuriz, Enrique. 1987. *Capitalización de la Deuda Externa y Desnacionalización de la Economia Chilena*. Program de Economia del Trabajo, Academia de Humanismo Cristiano, Document no. 57 (August). Santiago.

Errazuriz, Enrique, and Ernesto Tironi. 1986. "Perdidas al Vender Empresas Publicas." Memorandum, Comité de Defensa del Patrimonio Nacional, November 19.

Errazuriz, Enrique, and Jacqueline Weinstein. 1986. *Capitalismo Popular y Privatización de Empresas Publicas*. Program de Economia del Trabajo, Academia de Humanismo Cristiano, Document no. 53 (September). Santiago.

Fontaine Talavera, Juan Andrés. 1988. "Los Mecanismos de Conversion de Deuda en Chile." *Estudios Publicos* (Santiago) no. 30 (Autumn): 137–157.

Hevia, Ricardo. 1984. "El Mecanismo de la Municipalizacion Educacional en Chile." In *La Regionalización Educacional en Chile*, ed. Ernesto Schiefelbein. Santiago: Corporación de Promoción Universitaria.

Jiménez de la Jara, Jorge. 1985. *Politica y Sistemas de Salud*. Santiago: Corporación de Promoción Universitaria, 1985

Livingstone, James M. 1987. "Chile and the Debt to Equity Conversion Option." Paper presented at the Hoover Institution Conference on Foreign Debt, September 17–19.

Marcel, Mario. 1989a. "Las Privatizaciones de Empresas Publicas en Chile, 1985–1988." *CIEPLAN, Notas Tecnicas*, no. 125 (January).

———. 1989b. "Privatizaciones y Finanzas Publicas." *Colección Estudios CIEPLAN*, no. 26 (June).

Mönckeberg, Maria Olivia. 1988. "Un País en Liquidación." *APSI* (Santiago), no. 234 (January 11–17).

Orellano, Mario. 1987. *Las Funciones Academicas en la Educación Superior Privada*. Document no. 15/87 (July). Santiago: Corporación de Promoción Universitaria.

Ortuzar, Pablo. 1987. "La Reforma Previsional de 1980." *Estudios Publicos* (Santiago) no. 25 (Summer): 17–75.

Perez, Francisco 1987. "Las AFP: Motor del Nuevo Mercado de Capitales." *Economia y Sociedad* (Santiago) no. 66 (November–December): 16–27.

Piñera, José. 1988. "Chile and a Novel Approach to Social Security." *Firing Line*, April 28. Transcript.

Rosende, Francisco, and Andres Reinstein. 1986. "Estado de Avance del Programa de Reprivatización en Chile." *Estudios Publicos* (Santiago) no. 23 (Winter): 251–274.

Saez, Raúl. 1987. Letters to *El Mercurio*, January 9 and 13.

Scarpaci, Joseph. 1988. *Primary Medical Care in Chile: Accessibility under Military Rule*. Pittsburgh: University of Pittsburgh Press.

Scherman, Jorge. 1986. *Las Politicas de Salud y su Impacto en Los Sectores Populares: Chile 1974–1986*. Program de Economia del Trabajo, Academia de Humanismo Cristiano, Document no. 54 (October). Santiago.

Sigmund, Paul E. 1977. *The Overthrow of Allende and the Politics of Chile, 1964–1976*. Pittsburgh: University of Pittsburgh Press.

———. 1981. "Chile: Market Fascism or Utopian Libertarianism?" *Worldview* (New York) 24, no. 10: 4–6.

Thorud, Carlos Franz. 1983. *Teoria y Practica del Financiamento Universitario, 1965–1983*. Santiago: Corporación de Promoción Universitaria.

Tomic Errazuriz, Francisco, and Francisco de la Maza Chadwick. 1987. "Ahorro Previsional y Vivienda: Un Nuevo Mecanismo Financiero." Draft proposal.

U.S. Embassy, Santiago, Economic Section. 1985a. *The Pension Funds—A Growing Financial Power*. January 11. Airgram.

———. 1985b. *State Enterprises: Backbone of the Chilean Free Market Economy*. July 18. Airgram.

———. 1987a. *Social Programs in Chile*. January 14. Airgram.

———. 1987b. *Privatization of State Enterprises in Chile*. March 27. Airgram.

16

The Politics of Economic
Liberalization in India

Atul Kohli

The capacity of different types of governments for facilitating economic change in the Third World has been a subject of enduring interest in comparative development studies. During the 1950s and 1960s, this interest was evident in the debates over the developmental capacities of communist versus noncommunist political systems. More recently, the impressive economic performance of the newly industrializing countries (NICs), mainly of East Asia but also of Latin America, has given rise to a challenging new idea: state-induced market-like competitiveness may be the secret for facilitating rapid economic growth. While the economists continue to analyze the economic components of this proposition, political analysts need to investigate the issue of the political prerequisites of economic policy choices. Thus, an important question for research is: What types of regimes are most likely to choose and successfully pursue efficiency-oriented, "liberal" pattern of economic development?

The existing debates on this issue tend toward one of two positions. A number of analysts have proposed that the observed association between the well-organized, technically competent authoritarian regimes and the pursuit of a market-oriented development strategy is more than a mere association, that authoritarianism of a specific type may well be necessary for adopting a development strategy that strives to promote both domestic and international economic competition.[1] The logic of this proposition often rests in part on the need to contain political pressures generated by those who lose out in a market-oriented model of development and in part on the need to provide political stability so as to attract investment. Conversely, other analysts have challenged this emphasis on structural constraints by highlighting various dimensions on which policy choice

exists: ideology of the leaders rather than the nature of regime organization, it has been proposed, is a key determinant of economic policy choice;
winners and losers of a market-oriented readjustment are difficult to pre-
dict and to identify; authoritarianism hardly guarantees political stability;
and leaders with will and skill can push an economic program of their
choice quite far.[2]

This chapter analyzes some empirical materials from India that shed
light on the broader question of how much room for economic policy
choice a developing country leader has, especially in a democratic setting.
Over the last decade, India's leaders have sought to liberalize that country's relatively controlled and import-substitution model of development.
Initial steps in this direction were taken both by the Janata government
(1977–1980) and by Indira Gandhi from 1980 to 1984. Since coming to
power in late 1984, Rajiv Gandhi has made the liberalization of the economy a priority. Significant changes in the domestic political economy and
some changes that alter India's links with the world economy have recently been introduced. These include easing of state control on such activities of national firms as entry into production, production decisions,
and expansion in size; lowering of corporate and personal income taxes;
a long-term fiscal policy that substitutes tariffs for import restrictions and
assures business groups of future patterns of taxation; some devaluation;
and lowering of import barriers on selected items.

These changes do not as yet add up to a dramatic reform. A "liberal"
model of development has not replaced the "mixed economy" model
premised on state controls and import substitution. The legal and bureaucratic framework of a highly interventionist state remains intact, as do the
numerous public sector activities and governmental restrictions on private economic activity. Nevertheless, policy reforms have been aimed at
enhancing competitiveness and at broadening the scope of individual and
corporate initiative within the old framework.

The purpose of this chapter is not to assess the merits of these policy
reforms. Serious debates on the issue of whether "liberalization" is the
way for India to go or not have been under way for some time;[3] such
discussions are also best carried out by policy oriented economists. The
purpose of the present essay rather is to analyze the political underpinnings of these economic policy changes.

I shall argue that the immediate and most sustained push for liberalization has come from a group of technocratically inclined leaders who have
come to control the levers of India's economic policymaking. Business
groups have, on balance, supported the government's attempts to liberalize the domestic economy. They have opposed any serious attempt at
international opening, however. For reasons to be specified, professional
and other groups within India's urban middle class also supported the

government's early policy reforms. Conversely, concerted and direct opposition to the reforms has come from three quarters: the rank and file of the ruling party, the Congress; the left intelligentsia; and the organized working class in the public sector. Diffuse but numerically significant opposition has also been expressed by such rural groups as the "middle peasants" and the landless poor. ·

The growing opposition to reforms has not forced the government to reverse its economic agenda. On the contrary, both Indira Gandhi and Rajiv Gandhi succeeded in implementing some significant policy reforms. These policy initiatives highlight how and why leaders indeed have some room for policy choice. At the same time, however, the need to build political support has pushed Rajiv Gandhi to slow down his liberalization program. Although liberalization has not come to a grinding halt, a more populist economic program has been simultaneously readopted. This policy behavior, in turn, gives credence to those who would maintain that a major shift in development strategy from a state-controlled economy to a more liberal one is not easy within the framework of a democratic regime.

Some Preliminaries

Prior to presenting a political analysis of India's changing economic policies, I shall provide three pieces of important preliminary information. First, the term *economic liberalization* is no more than a grab bag for numerous policy measures that governments may undertake selectively. In the Indian case, as will become clear, it does not really refer to opening of the economy to the outside world in terms of freer movement of capital, goods, or money. Privatization of the domestic public sector is also not a policy priority in India. What liberalization really refers to, therefore, is a set of policy measures aimed at loosening governmental controls on the functioning of the private economy. Even within this limited scope, it is important to recognize further that the attempted decontrols influence only the industrial and the service sectors directly and the agricultural sector indirectly.

A second caveat concerns the fact that this chapter focuses strictly on the policy process. Therefore, when I analyze the forces that have propelled the move within India toward economic liberalization, there is an overemphasis on the proximate causes—such as the role of the elite—and a tendency to neglect the distant or "structural" changes in the environment of the elites that are clearly also significant. I will mention only a few of these structural changes in both the international and the national context. Careful elaborations of these distant, causal factors would require studies in their own right.

Within India's international context, a number of factors loom large that have inclined its leaders toward liberalizing the controlled economy. The success of the NICs, especially of Asian countries like South Korea, has created a sharp sense of having been left behind. Whereas in the past this position was often blamed on colonialism, a new generation of leaders is now forced to ask whether the country's emphasis on "socialism" and "import substitution" was mistaken to begin with. Additionally, the fact that major communist countries like the Soviet Union and China seem to want to embrace the market is of considerable significance. For the present there are few exemplary models left in the world that could help sustain antimarket arguments. And finally, there has been an important change in the nature of external forces that help legitimize Indian technocrats as skilled in their fields. Instead of the left-leaning economists of an earlier generation, who were often trained in England, those deemed as really competent by Indian leaders now generally receive their education in American universities and some of their practical training in such international development institutions as the World Bank. A fair degree of "consensus" prevails in these legitimizing institutions on the issue of what is an appropriate development strategy. This consensus, in turn, becomes a significant force propelling policy movement toward liberalization.

Within India's national context there have also been changes that are important "background variables," although these will not be discussed in any detail below. For example, it is widely acknowledged within India that the public sector is grossly inefficient. Along with this perception, virtually no one would disagree that India's redistributive efforts like land reforms have not been successful. This sense of the "failure" of "socialism" provides a major opening for a "new beginning." Of course, as we shall see, there are major disagreements concerning the appropriate future direction—toward more or less "socialism." A sense of the past failure of socialism, however, is part of contemporary India's political consciousness. Additionally, over time, the force of anticolonial and nationalist sentiments has declined. While again there is no consensus on this issue, many of India's new leaders are more willing to open the economy to and to learn from the West than the leaders of the postindependence generation. This general decline in a commitment to socialism and nationalism has, in turn, created new political and economic possibilities.

Last in this list of preliminary information, it is important to point out briefly the economic background of the more recent governmental efforts toward economic liberalization. While India's economy continued to grow at its steady but sluggish pace of 3 to 4 percent per annum through the period 1950–1980, the country's industrial growth slowed from about 7 to 8 percent before the mid-1960s to about 5 percent per annum over the last two decades (Ahluwalia 1985). The overall growth rate has picked up in the 1980s, but it remains unclear whether this acceleration will prove to be self-sustaining. The sluggish industrial growth generated an excited debate, especially because India's savings rate over the last several decades has continued to climb from under 10 percent of gross national product (GNP) to over 20 percent in the early 1980s.[4]

The competing explanations that have been proposed for India's relatively slow industrial growth can be grouped around three alternative hypotheses: that the inefficiencies generated by a closed and state-controlled economy are the root cause of slow growth (Bhagwati and Srinivasan 1975; Ahluwalia 1985); that the sluggishness reflects low aggregate demand;[5] or that the deceleration is associated with declining public investments and the related infrastructural bottlenecks.[6] These hypotheses, and especially the policy implications that flow from them, do not have to exclude one another. Nevertheless, each argument is distinct and leads to a different policy emphasis.

These debates demonstrate that there is little agreement as to the appropriate direction of change. The policy changes that the Indian government has undertaken over the last several years are thus not "objective" responses to an objective situation. That an objective situation exists, namely, an economy whose industrial sector is not the most impressive, is clear; the need for change, therefore, may be said to be rooted in the economic situation. There is also a broad agreement among economists that many of the governmental controls have outlived their utility in India. The responses to this situation, however, are political choices. Specialists who study the "objective economic situation" do not agree that there is a single, clear way to solve the problem. These disagreements among specialists only add contentiousness to what are already difficult political questions: Who has the power to push through their preferred policies and why? Who benefits from these policies and why?

Liberalization under Indira Gandhi

The trend toward liberalization of the Indian economy was initiated not by Rajiv Gandhi but by his mother, Indira. This fact has not received as much attention as it deserves. An understanding of why Indira Gandhi initiated such policies after coming back to power in 1980 helps to put into perspective what was really new under Rajiv Gandhi. This background is also important for understanding why Rajiv's attempts at liberalization provoked considerable reaction, including negative political reaction, whereas Indira Gandhi's went relatively unnoticed.

The Indira Gandhi who returned to power in 1980—after the brief Janata interlude of about three years—was not the firebrand of *garibi hatao* (alleviate poverty) vintage. Whereas the antipoverty rhetoric was seldom translated into real policy even before or during the Emergency (1975–1977), now even the rhetoric was altered. Critical observers have suggested that after 1980 Indira Gandhi moved "rightwards" (Manor 1988), whereas her own former advisors have noted that during this phase she was more "pragmatic"[7] or, by implication, less "ideological."

The changing political orientation was evident in a number of policy areas. Communal themes, for example, especially themes of Hindu hegemony that appeal to India's Hindi heartland, gained currency in Indira's political speeches (Manor 1988). Under her son Sanjay's influence, militant thugs were inducted into the ruling party as a source of mobilization for both mass rallies and elections. Although the rhetoric of both socialism and nationalism was maintained, antipoverty programs were put on the back burner. There was also a change of attitude toward such international institutions as the International Monetary Fund (IMF); negotiations for the largest loan ever granted by the IMF were completed during this phase. And finally, many of the new economic policies tended to move in the liberalizing direction.

After completing the loan agreement of 5 billion in Special Drawing Rights (SDRs) with the IMF, Indira Gandhi made some important economic policy decisions during 1981–1982: steel and cement prices were decontrolled; manufactured imports were liberalized; and controls on both entry and expansion by national firms were relaxed. During 1981 the government sanctioned four times as many applications for expansion and new undertakings as in any of the five preceding years (P. S. Jha 1982). Over the next two years, as the "perspective" on the seventh plan developed, it became clear that the new "emphasis" would be on "efficiency of investment" and that this would be accompanied by a general move "away from administrative to financial controls" (see, for example, P. S. Jha 1984). Soon thereafter, following the recommendations of the L. K. Jha Commission on Economic and Administrative Reforms, the government placed twenty important industries under "automatic licensing" (*Economic Times*, Sept. 1, 1984). In practice, this policy meant virtual decontrol of expansion and new production in these industries.[8]

Why did Indira Gandhi adopt these policy changes, and with what political consequences? First, the new economic direction has to be seen as part and parcel of the overall political shift that Indira Gandhi adopted. This involved a move away from India's "left" or "populist" values of "secularism" and "socialism" and toward the package hitherto offered primarily by the "right" parties, namely, "Hindu chauvinsim and a pro-business orientation." It is important to underline that there is no inherent reason why Hindu chauvinism has to go hand in hand with a preference for business or why liberalizing policies aimed at enhancing market competitiveness should be pro-business policies. In India's political culture, however, the two packages of "secularism and socialism" and "Hindu chauvinism and a pro-business orientation" have tended to offer two alternative "legitimacy formulas" for mobilizing political support. The logic underlying these value packages seems to be something as follows.

Secularism in India has often meant eschewing appeals to caste, religion, and community as a tool of political mobilization. Although practice often deviated from principles, India's founding fathers understood that national integration in a multinational and multiethnic polity like India could be facilitated only by avoiding the politicization of deep-rooted "primordial loyalties." For the task of political mobilization, therefore, Nehru favored appeals along economic lines—the need to uplift the poor, the downtrodden, the poor peasants, and so on. Socialism was related to this political logic. Whatever socialism has meant in practice—in India it has never meant anticapitalism, but rather state-guided capitalism, involving planning, public sector emphasis, state-controlled economy, and a few antipoverty programs like land reforms—its electoral significance was always closely associated with a preference for secular over communal appeals.

In contrast, those who wanted to argue for business interests faced a dilemma: in a poor democracy like India, how does one mobilize the support of the majority, who are after all very poor? One solution to this puzzle was to cut the majority-minority pie at a different angle. If the poor were the majority by the criteria of wealth, Hindus were the religious majority. Appeals to the majority religious community against minority communities, then, can be an alternative strategy for seeking electoral majorities by downplaying class issues in favor of communal ones. Whereas the Congress party traditionally stood for the secularism and socialism package, parties like the Jan Sangh (the present Bhartiya Janata party, or BJP) have advocated Hindu nationalism and a probusiness attitude.

When Indira Gandhi returned to power in 1980, several things must have been clear to her. In the entire Hindi heartland Congress had been routed by the Janata party in the 1977 elections. Even though she had won the 1980 election, primarily due to factionalism and incompetence within the Janata, her support base in the Hindi heartland was, at best, soft. She had to build up this support and fast.[9] The full force that business communities had thrown behind Morarji Desai's government must have also left Indira Gandhi peculiarly vulnerable, especially for the future of electoral finances. It appears that after 1980 Gandhi sought to build her support in the Hindi heartland and with business communities by shifting away from the formula of secularism and socialism and toward Hindu chauvinism and a pro-business orientation. The new political posture had two ingredients: an emphasis on communalism that has great appeal in the

Hindi heartland; and a more "pragmatic" attitude aimed at building up her support with industrial and commercial groups.

It must also have been clear to Indira Gandhi that her "socialism" was not working. Antipoverty programs had simply not been very successful (Kohli 1987). The support she was getting from the poor, therefore, was based not so much on concrete rewards but primarily on her ideological and rhetorical appeal. This rhetoric she knew she could maintain, while watering down the overall socialist program. Further socialist rhetoric would not have brought her much more political capital in any case; the limits of rhetorical socialism had been reached. A movement toward liberalizing the economy, while maintaining some rhetoric of socialism and some of the antipoverty programs, she must have calculated, was likely to strengthen her politically.

Besides such overtly political considerations, other factors probably played some part in pushing India toward economic liberalization. The extent to which the conditions imposed by the IMF influenced policy changes is hard to judge. The World Bank has also periodically kept up the pressure on India's government to decontrol and open up the economy. In a large and relatively well-established polity like India, however—"well-established" in the sense of being staffed by competent bureaucrats—the influence of organizations such as the IMF and the World Bank can never be decisive. Even the decision to enter an agreement with the IMF, and all that such an agreement involves in terms of policy changes, must be viewed as a prior political decision by the Indian government. Once the government chose to enter this arrangement with the IMF, however, it is clear that pressure built to "get the prices right" in the economy.

Within the government, since the 1970s, report after report put together by bureaucrats and specialists had been recommending liberalization of one aspect of the economy or another.[10] The decision to set up commissions, however, is a political one. Commission members are appointed by leaders, and the policy preferences of these members are generally well known. And most important, whether the government chooses to act on a report or not is a political decision. For every report that recommends liberalization of the economy, there are literally dozens of others gathering dust, waiting for some action on their recommendations concerning how to improve the conditions of small farmers or of scheduled tribes or how to desilt India's rivers.

Another factor that is worth considering here is the changing economic situation itself. As noted above, industrial growth had been sluggish for much of the 1970s, and 1979 had been a particularly bad year. The Janata government took some economic measures around that time that could be interpreted as "liberalizing" (P. S. Jha 1982). Industrial growth jumped back to over 8 percent in 1980. The extent to which this "success" created a momentum for further liberalization is hard to judge; the timing for the adoption of a new political program seems, however, to have been more than just a coincidence.

Some policy alternatives clearly suited Indira Gandhi's political design better than others. To attack "demand constraints" would have meant, among other measures, shifting resources toward agriculture—thus alienating urban industrialists and middle classes—as well as attempting what had not worked before, that is, land reforms and other income-generating projects for the poor. To increase public investments was also not easy. If P. Bardhan's (1984) analysis is right, this would have meant "rationalizing" the patronage network that holds India's dominant classes in a delicate alliance with one another and in support of the state.[11] Her credentials with the poor were, in any case, well established. Since these were based primarily on ideological appeals, she was not about to lose this support over the short run. Given political difficulties elsewhere, she must have decided that communal appeals to the dominant Hindu community and economic measures supporting the business and industrial groups were her best bets.

Yet it was not at all self-evident that the so-called liberalization measures would be welcomed by business groups. Import liberalization has been seriously resisted by India's well-established, indigenous capitalists. So, to put the general political decision of wooing business support into practice, Indira Gandhi must have asked one or more of her senior advisors, perhaps L. K. Jha, what was wrong with Indian industry and what did businessmen really want.

Jha had long worked with both businessmen and the government. Although he had never favored rapid opening of the economy to external forces, he had argued for removing restrictions on both entry and expansion of firms and for reducting direct and indirect taxes.[12] These measures are supported by most business groups: big businesses favor removal of constraints on expansion of capacity; although small businesses often fear this, freedom of entry raises even their prospects for competing in some hitherto unexplored areas. The message to the business community must have been clear: socialism was being put on the back burner, and a new policy regime that might work to their benefit was being initiated.

The economic policy shift under Indira Gandhi is thus best understood as an integral aspect of her overall political strategy. This, in turn, was aimed at strengthening the "soft" areas of her support. Why did these policy shifts go relatively unnoticed? Given her "socialist" commitments, why did a policy trend toward the liberalization of the economy never become a political liability for her? An important part of the answer is fairly simple: the extent of change was not significant enough to raise too many political eyebrows. And yet, this answer in turn raises a thorny question of political management: When can changes be made to look "marginal" and when do they appear "significant," deserving political response from all those who may wish to oppose them?

Indira Gandhi was a master political artist. As noted above, she understood well that her popular image was one of a leader on the left. She had built up these credentials not by careful implementation of socialist policies but by undertaking highly visible acts, such as nationalizating the banks, pursuing antimonopoly legislation, and adopting poverty alleviation as the central platform of her party and government. It is a well-established political adage that leaders of the left can more easily take selected rightist decisions without invoking the wrath of the left—or vice versa. When leaders are judged by their citizens, what they seem to stand for turns out to be as important over the short run as the substance of the policies they pursue. Indira Gandhi benefited from this general political trust that groups in the popular sector bestowed on her.

She further gained from both the circumstances and the effective stage management she provided for the policy changes. India's political attention increasingly focused on such regional issues as Assam and Punjab, rather than on economic policies. Indira herself downplayed the significance of the economy and of economic achievements as tools of legitimacy. When attention did turn to the economy, the picture presented for popular consumption showed more continuity than change. The rhetoric of socialism, though toned down, was maintained; so were most of the antipoverty programs. Left-of-center economic advisors, including K. N. Raj and Sukhamoy Chakrovarty, were retained in visible, but largely ceremonial, positions in the Economic Advisory Council. The policy changes, however, were influenced by such advisors in the background as K. C. Alexander, L. K. Jha and Arjun Sengupta. The changes themselves appeared largely "technical": a lowering of a limit here, an expansion of a restriction there. The attempt, it seems, was to depoliticize economic decisions as far as possible.[13]

Indira Gandhi's attempts to liberalize the economy did not draw sharp political reaction, for a number of reasons: the scale of change; the conscious attempt to maintain an image of continuity as well as to depoliticize economic decisions; and, of course, other pressing political circumstances that drew attention away from the economy. During Indira Gandhi's last few years, the tension between the pursuit of "economic rationality" and the "rationality of democracy" was kept within manageable bounds. It is hard to know how far she intended to push liberalization and how far she would have succeeded.

Liberalization under Rajiv Gandhi

During Rajiv Gandhi's five years in power (1984–1989), economic policy went through three phases. During the first six months of his rule, there was a genuine attempt at a new beginning, a decisive shift from the state-controlled and import-substitution model to a liberal model of development. As this effort ran into political obstacles, the pace of change slowed. The next two years are best characterized as "two steps forward" toward the defined agenda and "one step backward." As Rajiv's political popularity continued to decline, the loss of Haryana elections in May 1987 marked the beginning of the third phase. This was the return to India's "muddle through" model of economic policymaking. Although leaders remained committed to economic liberalization, and the general trend continued in this direction, political considerations necessitated the renewal of populism. The sense that there was to be a new economic beginning in India was thus quickly lost.

Rajiv's rise to power was largely circumstantial. There is no doubt that during his mother's administration he had begun to be groomed as heir apparent. His training, however, was no more than two to three years in process when Indira Gandhi's assassination suddenly brought him to power. He was a natural heir in the sense that Indira herself had placed him in that role, and he was more or less accepted as such by her loyal second tier. These political minions did not enjoy any independent political support. They must have calculated that their own and the Congress party's best chance to maintain power was to select Indira's son; he was likely to inherit a fair amount of Indira's popularity and to gain new support as Indians sympathized with him over her assassination.[14] Rajiv's initial power and legitimacy were thus based on factors that had little to do with his own preferred economic policies. Only a handful of Indians must have known, and the rest probably did not care to know in the postassassination mood of trauma and crisis, what type of economic policies the new government would pursue.

During the very brief period of his rise and consolidation, Rajiv Gandhi and his advisors must have made a crucial decision: the new regime was going to stress a "new beginning" rather than continuity with the past. Shortly after winning a massive electoral victory, Rajiv summed up his government's economic approach as advocating a "judicious combination of deregulation, import liberalization and easier access to foreign technology" (*Times of India*, Jan. 6, 1986). That this involved a sharp break from Nehru and Indira Gandhi's rhetorical emphasis on "socialism, planning, and self-reliance" should be self-evident.

As if to underline the break from the past, Rajiv Gandhi surrounded himself with a new breed of politicians and advisors. Consider some of those who appeared influential, at least in 1985–1986. Confidants like Arun Nehru and Arun Singh had backgrounds as executives of multi-national corporations. Economic advisors included Montek Ahluwalia, Abid Hussain, Bimal Jalan, and Manmohan Singh. Individuals like L. K. Jha were considered to have direct access to the prime minister. While clearly competent managers, economists, and bureaucrats, they were all marked by a "technocratic" rather than a "political" image. Some of them had World Bank backgrounds; most of them were known for their decon-trol and proliberalization proclivities.

It is important to note here that this issue of the nature of economic policymakers is as much or more a matter of image than of substance. For example, if one focuses primarily on the economic advisors of an earlier generation—Pitambar Pant, I. G. Patel, Bootlingam, Vishnu Sahay, Tarlok Singh, Ashok Mehta, V. T. Krishnamachari—there is probably more conti-nuity than change between this group and Rajiv Gandhi's advisors in terms of both technical skills and preferred policies.[15] What has changed, however, is both the nature of the political leadership and the sense of who—the leaders or the advisors—is really in charge of economic policy-making. Since Rajiv and his crucial political aides had a "managerial" and "technocratic" image, there was a sense that the political leaders and their technical advisors were cut from the same cloth. Additionally, Rajiv's rel-ative inexperience created a popular impression that policymaking was increasingly in the hands of bureaucrats and experts. Such considerations added up to an image of a sharp break in the nature of India's economic policymakers.

The queston, then, is: What explains the government's emphasis on change over continuity? The question is especially salient because the eco-nomic changes that Indira Gandhi had already introduced and those that Rajiv's government eventually pursued could have easily been accommo-dated within an image of continuity.

Rajiv and his advisors initially intended the changes to go much further than they actually did. This ambition must have seemed feasible due to Rajiv's unusual rise to power. His electoral victory had been based on sympathy and fear on part of the electorate. This victory freed Rajiv Gandhi—if only momentarily and artificially—from coalition entangle-ments and interest-group pressures. This freedom from "politics as usual" must have heightened the illusion that a new beginning was possi-ble, even in a polity like that of India.

The considerable sense of power, and the hurry in which power had been acquired, must have created the sensation among the new rulers that they had hijacked the state. The state suddenly stood autonomous, seemingly free of societal constraints, ready to be used as a tool for impos-ing economic rationality upon the society. Situations of state autonomy like this always encourage the powerful to pursue their ideological whims.[16]

The illusion of autonomy and, with it, the euphoria of a new beginning lasted about six months. The first major product of this new beginning was the 1985–1986 budget, presented by the government in March 1985, less than three months after coming to power. The budget created many ripples. The word "socialism" was not mentioned even once in the budget speech.[17] Substantial tax concessions were offered to both the corporate and the urban upper-middle classes. Imports were liberalized in certain sectors, especially in the one favored by Rajiv Gandhi himself, namely, electronics. And most important, licensing regulations for domestic industries were relaxed drastically, and the limit on the size of a firm that qualifies it as a "monopoly" were raised substantially.

The reaction of both business and upper-middle groups was euphoric. India's leading news magazine, *India Today*, ran such cover lines as "The Economy: Buoyant Mood" and "We are Gearing for Take-Off" (Mar. 15 and Apr. 15, 1985). Other commentators enthusiastically welcomed "the most important budget in thirty years" (Nani Palkhiwala, *Times of India*, Apr. 2, 1985). Since the parliament was totally dominated by individuals beholden to Rajiv Gandhi for their positions, there was no question at this early date of substantial opposition from that quarter. The left and other opposition parties reacted sharply; they characterized both the new government and its budget as "pro-rich." In the middle of 1985, however, these were voices in the wilderness.

The opposition that began to simmer at the grass roots, however, did not take long to boil over. It was first expressed on a significant scale— much to the surprise of the new leadership—within the ruling party. The occasion was an attempt by Rajiv Gandhi and his cronies to have the Congress party ratify an economic resolution that would bring the party formally behind the new economic beginning that he had already begun with the budget. The resolution that was eventually ratified, however, recommitted Rajiv and the Congress party to socialism.[18]

The significance of this event should not be underestimated. Many people in India are so jaded with Congress's "socialism" that any talk of it is deadening to sensibilities; it simply evokes no response or, worse, a very cynical one. Even the head of India's leading chamber of commerce dismissed Congress's recommitment to socialism as "mere rhetoric."[19] But rhetoric though it may well have been, its significance was considerable. A recommitment to socialism underlined clearly and starkly that the government's economic policies would maintain continuity with the past, that socialism would define the limits within which new policies would have to fit. Such limits are very flexible, of course; the economic resolution, while reaffirming socialism, also accepted all of the policy changes

Rajiv's government had introduced so far.[20] Nevertheless, a tolerance for what many observers would consider gross inconsistencies is a very different political picture from wholehearted support of liberalization of the economy. Rajiv's first major encounter with his own party thus immediately set limits on how far he could carry economic policy changes.

That confrontation marks the beginning of the second phase of Rajiv Gandhi's economic policymaking. Over the next two years or so, his government continued to promote piecemeal liberalizing reforms, while re-emphasizing its commitment to socialism. In spite of the constraints, the government succeeded in pushing through some important reforms; other proposals, however, had to be modified or reversed to fit the socialist commitment.

Increasingly, the rhetoric on economic policy became confusing. While celebrating Congress's centenary the day after the confrontation with the working committee over the economic resolution, Rajiv reaffirmed that Congress's goal, now as ever, was socialism (*Deccan Herald*, May 7, 1985). Over the next few months economic policy changes involved several liberalizing measures. When presenting the Seventh Plan to the National Development Council in November, however, Rajiv Gandhi once again argued that the "industrial policy remains unchanged" (*Statesman*, Nov. 19, 1985). Around the same time, Rajiv argued that, when and where "import substitutes are not cost-effective," there India should opt for "imports, especially of technology" (*Statesman*, Nov. 14, 1985). This statement was followed by the release of a government report that emphasized the need for "boosting exports" and for an "outward-looking" industrialization strategy.[21] Lest observers nail down the government's real policy, two days later government spokesmen reiterated that, whatever liberalization may take place, the public sector would continue to maintain the "commanding heights" of the economy (*Indian Express*, Nov. 20, 1985). The prime minister himself went on to argue for "top priority" for the public sector and to re-emphasize that there was "no shift from socialism" (*Hindusthan Times*, Dec. 6, 1985). The main thrusts of the Seventh Plan, it was further suggested, would be "eradication of poverty, self-reliance, and growth with social justice" (*Indian Express*, Dec. 19, 1985). Finally, several months later, the government let it be known that privatization of the public sector was not on the agenda, that the "mixed economy" model would stay (*Economic Times*, Sept. 14, 1986).

If the rhetoric was confusing, and probably purposely so, some pattern is more discernible in the actual policy changes. Shortly after the Congress party made Rajiv recommit himself to continuity with the past, a new textile policy was quietly passed. Without too much discussion or debate, this policy removed the restrictions on the capacity of the mill sector. Though seemingly a minor, technical change, it struck at the heart of some of old Congress's nationalist values. The removal of restrictions, it could be argued, would assure that both the power loom and the hand loom sectors would go into a long-term decline as the more "efficient" mill sector took over. While clearly "rational," such a change would have been abhorrent to the first-generation nationalists. The British dumping of the more "efficient" textiles had been understood by the nationalists to have caused the destruction of the Indian textile industry in the nineteenth century and thus of nascent Indian capitalism. Now, a generation later, Indian leaders were themselves promulgating similar policies.

Other important policy changes followed. The role of the Planning Commission was decisively diminished, again without any pronouncements, by the creation of a new Ministry of Programme Implementation. Significantly, the "new fiscal policy" announced in November 1985 replaced import quotas with tariffs and laid out long-term patterns of taxation, assuring the corporate sector that no negative surprises were looming over the horizon (*Hindusthan Times*, Dec. 12, 1985). In spite of the worsening balance of payments, the government did not reverse the liberalized import policy, even in the capital goods sector that had been hurt quite badly. Companies restricted under the "monopoly" act were, moreover, given further concessions (*Indian Express*, Jan. 23, 1986), and the budget of 1986–1987 brought some further excise and customs relief to national firms (editorial in *Economic and Political Weekly*, Mar. 1, 1986).

A number of factors help to explain the minimal opposition that these policies aroused in the popular sectors. As in the case of the textile policy, these changes generally affected one specific segment of the society more than others. Also, the values violated—in this case, themes from the anticolonial heritage—are no longer felt as deeply as before. Since neither the values nor the interests of the society at large were hurt, political opposition was minimal. Other policy changes that went unopposed, at least over the short run, shared another set of traits: more often than not, they supported powerful business interests; and they were brought about quietly, without much fanfare, as seemingly technical changes in a piecemeal fashion. Very few political groups in India have the resources required to monitor economic policy changes of this minute nature. Opposition groups, therefore, generally concentrate their political energies on policies that are highly visible and that influence widely shared interests and values in the society.

If these policies went largely unopposed, another set evoked considerable response. Policies that had to be modified or reversed show one of two characteristics: they were opposed by powerful groups like businessmen; or they created diffuse but real disenchantment among the popular sectors. A number of examples will support these generalizations, as well as highlight the policy fluctuations and reversals that have occurred due to the growing opposition.

The Seventh Plan came under attack from within the ruling party itself. Although the details are not known, it is clear that several groups from within the Congress approached Rajiv to register their protest, namely, that the plan did not assign enough resources to antipoverty programs. The plan was changed to accommodate this political opposition, even though the planners knew and argued that resources devoted to such programs in the past had not been used effectively.[22]

A different type of policy fluctuation characterized the approach the government adopted toward industries that import goods and thus directly affect the balance of payments. A good example here is the automobile industry. During 1985 the government let it be known that it would look kindly on expansion of automobile production, including further foreign collaboration and especially with Japanese manufacturers. After numerous expansion plans got under way, the government in early February 1986 changed its mind; the implementation of the new automobile policy was postponed indefinitely. Among the reasons cited were the need to conserve petroleum and the worsening balance of payments situation (*Economic Times*, Feb. 2, 1986). There is also indication, however, that pressure was brought on the government by established automobile manufacturers who feared a glut of overproduction and competition from new and probably better products (*Economic Times*, Feb. 2, 1986). What adds credibility to this interpretation is the fact that the policy was not reconsidered, even when petroleum prices dropped on the world market in July 1986 and India's balance of payments situation improved considerably. Instead, the government used the occasion of a shift on the anticipated automobile policy to make a more general statement that marked an important policy change: "[The] pace of domestic liberalization has not been slackened . . . external liberalization (however) was not really an objective of the (overall) policy" (*Economic Times*, Feb. 24, 1986).

The more serious opposition, because it was at the popular level, came over the issue of price hikes in February 1986. Within a few days of announced increases in the price of petroleum and other related products, every opposition party in the country had presented plans for strikes and the closing down of one city or another. Congress politicians themselves had argued against these increases, fearing a popular backlash. Before the strikes materialized, the government reversed its decision (editorial in *Telegraph*, Feb. 7, 1986).

Rajiv Gandhi's overall political popularity went into a sharp decline in late 1986. He lost virtually every state election after the assembly elections in March 1985 and was eventually defeated in the national elections in November 1989. The loss in Haryana in May 1987 was especially devastating because it is in the area that until then had been Congress's power base, the Hindi heartland. This defeat has two important implications for understanding economic policy fluctuations. First, the image of Rajiv and his government as "pro-rich" stuck. This image was related both to the style of political management and to the substance of the economic policies adopted; it also contributed to Rajiv's loss of electoral popularity. Second, irrespective of how damaging these economic policies proved to be politically, one possible way to recover sagging political fortunes in India is clearly to adopt populist economic policies.

It is this last set of considerations that came to influence economic policymaking during 1987–1989. Throughout the second phase, the pace of economic policy changes slowed from what was probably intended to be a major departure from India's mixed-economy model of development. Socialism was re-established as the framework. In spite of this rhetorical reversal, as well as the change of pace and some important setbacks, the overall thrust was to continue to push ahead toward lifting governmental controls and restrictions on the Indian economy. With the electoral debacle in Haryana, however, the future of economic policy became unclear; India returned to its usual pattern of muddling through.

There was a growing sense in the aftermath of the Haryana elections that a major policy reversal might be in the making. This did not come to pass. It is fair to suggest that Rajiv Gandhi and his key advisors remained committed to liberalizing India's economic policy regime. The opportunities to do so, however, had narrowed. As Rajiv's popularity declined, the opposition criticized him for neglect of the farmers and the poor. This challenge, led by V. P. Singh in the Hindi heartland, by Jyoti Basu of the Communist Party of India, Marxist (CPM) in West Bengal, and by Devi Lal in Haryana, exposed Rajiv's electoral vulnerability in the popular sectors. The BJP's harping on themes of economic nationalism also took an antiliberal direction. As these challenges grew, the thrust toward economic liberalization slowed. The angry conclusion of a prominent Indian journalist on this score appears to be only a slight exaggeration: "While no one can doubt that Gandhi was sincere in his desire to liberalize the economy, it is equally beyond doubt that he has failed" (P. S. Jha 1987).

The increased allocations for farmer aid and antipoverty programs in the proposed budget for 1988–1989 only highlight that electoral pressures nearly pushed issues of liberalizing the economy to the sidelines. Some important liberalizing measures were pursued during 1988 and 1989, and they may also be put back on the agenda by the new government under V. P. Singh. Early statements, however, promise greater budgetary allocations to the agricultural sector, suggesting that the economic priorities of the new government will continue to be influenced by electoral considerations.

In less than five years, Rajiv and his advisors dissipated the enormous political capital that they had acquired almost accidentally. A sense of power and autonomy during 1985 had encouraged new leaders to try to impose their own "rationality" on the society. The society hit back, and the state lost the temporary autonomy it had gained.[23] The loss of this power is now likely to lead to policies that make more sense from the point of view of winning elections and thus of democratic power than of "economic rationality."

Conclusion

Over the last decade the leaders of India have sought to liberalize the country's relatively controlled and closed economy. Whereas such actions are probably necessary for boosting India's relatively slow economic growth, the focus of this analysis has been on the political roots and consequences of economic policy change.

Indira Gandhi in her last four years quietly initiated some important liberalizing economic initiatives with minimal political opposition. She could do so because the changes were on the margin and because they were undertaken piecemeal and without political fanfare. Moreover, Indira Gandhi was perceived as a well-established socialist leader. Her attempts to initiate liberalization, unlike her son's, did not evoke a sense that cherished nationalist values of sovereignty and a concern for the poor were about to be replaced by an open embrace of the rich—both Indian and foreign.

Rajiv Gandhi attempted to push liberalization further and in a shorter time. Major policy initiatives were taken in this direction. Over time, however, the pace of change slowed down. After some initial successes, there were important setbacks, and the reforms generated considerable political opposition, eventually contributing to Rajiv's electoral defeat.

The reforms were pushed by a technocratic leadership that appeared to believe firmly in the economic merits of liberalization. Major support—at least for domestic, as distinct from international, liberalization—came from industrial and commercial groups. The urban middle classes also appreciated the tax reforms and the availability of consumer goods.

The extent to which the reforms have succeeded is thus best explained with reference to the ideology of the new rulers. These rulers emerged for reasons that had little to do with their positions on economic policy. Over the short run, they used their considerable autonomous power to push through a few reforms. It is also important to recognize that these reforms were supported by powerful and vocal urban groups. Those specific reforms that met resistance from powerful business groups—like the attempts to liberalize the automobile manufacturing policy—were put off. Additionally, the reforms that were successfully implemented tended to exhibit two characteristics: their negative impact was limited to a small,

specific group (as, for example, the reforms in the textile industry); and/
or they were pushed through as technical changes without political fanfare. A temporary condition of state autonomy, the ideology of the rulers,
the support of powerful socioeconomic groups, and the capacity to depoliticize some of the economic issues thus appear to be the main factors that
help to explain a partial success in liberalizing India's economy.

Conversely, what looms larger than these partial successes is the rapidity with which the constraints on government initiatives came into play.
Many political and social groups reacted negatively to government's attempts at economic reforms. Their opposition was not based on economic
issues alone, nor was it always expressed in a coherent and direct fashion.
For some, like the Congress rank and file, opposition was probably
mainly opportunistic; but it was also based in part on ideology and in part
on fear of the electoral implications of the new policies. The left intelligentsia seemed genuinely to believe that the new policies would have
disastrous consequences. According to them, higher growth is not assured by the new economic policies; moreover, national sovereignty and
a redistributive orientation might be sacrificed. Labor groups in the public
sector feared erosion of employment security. The political reaction of
rural groups was less direct, but even they seemed to communicate to the
government that its pro-people image was suspect.

As all these groups reacted negatively, the fear of losing electoral support forced Rajiv Gandhi's government to slow down the pace of economic change. It is only with some exaggeration, therefore, that one is led
to conclude that attempts within India to implement policies that leaders ·
consider to be economically rational came into confrontation with the
rationality of democracy. Since an internal, demand-led, redistributive
growth model is even less politically feasible in contemporary India,
chances are that the new government in India also has few options for
stimulating growth and liberalizing the economy. The analysis here suggests that such a policy trajectory may cost the Indian government popular political support.

Finally, these empirical materials from India have a bearing on an enduring debate within comparative development studies, with which this
chapter began. This debate posits links between specific regime types and
development strategies. Some arguments in Latin American studies have
suggested that the numerous bureaucratic-authoritarian regimes during
the 1960s had their origins in the exhaustion of the import-substitution
model of development. The implication was clear: moderate regimes may
find it difficult to implement policies that, by prevailing economic logic,
are deemed to be rational and necessary. The success of Southeast Asian
NICs has often been attributed to the role of certain types of market policies pursued by authoritarian states. As East Asian and Latin American

NICs redemocratize, the issue of their capacities to impose economic rationality has also once again become an open question. The issue of the fit between regime type and development strategy is thus likely to continue to be debated.

The Indian case suggests that it is indeed difficult for a democratic regime to undertake a major shift in development strategy. It has been evident throughout the discussion above that some economic reforms were possible all along. It would thus be absurd to deny that powerful leaders like Indira Gandhi or Rajiv Gandhi can initiate and implement some policy changes that they and their advisors deem necessary. There are, however, fairly tight limits on how far and how fast a liberalization program can be implemented in a democracy.

The counter argument, that nondemocratic cases have also faced obstacles in liberalizing their economies, is simply no argument. It simply says that liberalization measures can provoke opposition in numerous settings and that many nondemocratic regimes are not capable or willing to run roughshod over such opposition. An analysis of a democratic case at least enables one to specify the nature and the mechanics of political opposition.

The conclusions are disturbing. In social settings where "cultures of efficiency" are not well established, calls for efficiency and competitiveness do not buy broad political support. This creates real problems for Third World democratic states that are not products of capitalism but that seek to promote efficient capitalist development. The need to build broad coalitions pulls these fragile democratic governments in policy directions other than those that may best promote an efficient and competitive economy. These issues of political rationality ought to complement those concerning economic rationality when policymakers and observers analyze, judge, or advise what developing country governments should or should not do.

Notes

This chapter is part of a larger research project on "India's Growing Problems of Governability." Research for this project has been supported by the Ford Foundation and by Princeton University, especially its Center for International Studies. An earlier version of this chapter was presented at the annual meetings of the American Political Science Association (Chicago, September 3–6, 1987). Another version appeared in *World Development* (March 1989). I would like to thank the following for their helpful comments on the first draft: Jagdish Bhagwati, Donald Crone, Jyotirindra Dasgupta, John Echeverri-Gent, Stephen Haggard, Robert Kaufman, John P. Lewis, Guillermo O'Donnell, Ashutosh Varshney, John Waterbury, and Myron Weiner.

1. A wide variety of literature in different contexts tends to argue this position. Only a selected sample of this literature is cited here. First, some scholars have traced the roots of Latin American authoritarianism in the 1960s to the need to "deepen" industrialization. Implicit in this claim was the argument that moderate regimes find it difficult to adopt a pattern of development that some would consider to be "rational" and necessary. See, for example, O'Donnell 1973. For debates around this hypothesis, see Collier 1979. Second, and related to this, numerous scholars of Brazil have argued that the economic adjustments and the high rates of growth that Brazil achieved during the period 1964–1974 would not have been possible without the military regime. For specific empirical materials, see the essays by Thomas Skidmore and Fernando Cardoso in Stepan 1973; more broadly, see Evans 1979. Third, the success of market-oriented industrialization in select East Asian countries like South Korea has been associated with the role of an authoritarian state. See, for example, Jones and Sakong 1980 and the essays in Deyo 1987. And finally, some development economists, who generally favor a "liberal" model of development, have also wondered whether it is possible to pursue such a model without an authoritarian regime. See, for example, Bhagwati 1986.

2. This literature emphasizing the role of leadership and the "room for choice" has in recent years developed around the issue of implementing the International Monetary Fund's "stability" program. See, for example, Nelson 1984; Bienen and Gersovitz 1985; and Haggard 1985.

3. Academic works that would broadly support the liberalization policy prescription include Bhagwati and Srinivisan 1975 and Ahluwalia 1985. For a brief but succinct statement on the need for liberalization by a policymaker, see L. K. Jha 1986. For a sampling of the critical views, see Datta 1985; Paranjape 1985; Raj 1985 (pts. 1 and 2); and Patnaik 1986. Two essays that, like this one, focus on political issues are Rubin 1985 and Kochanek 1986.

4. A good review of this and other debates surrounding India's slow industrial growth is Varshney 1984.

5. For a statement linking limited aggregate demand to slow industrial growth, see Chakravarty 1984. This thesis also crops up in several criticisms of the "new economic policy" cited in note 3. Moreover, a "statement" by twenty-nine Indian economists, criticizing government's emphasis on liberalization, suggested that one important component of any new development strategy should be "expansion of home market." This statement is further discussed below. It was published in *Mainstream*, Oct. 26, 1985, pp. 24–25, and discussed in many newspapers and magazines, including *Economic and Political Weekly*, Oct. 26, 1985, pp. 1813–1816.

6. This thesis was first put forward by Srinivasan and Narayana 1977. Since then it has been argued by quite a few observers, but especially by Bardhan 1984.

7. Interview with Arjun K. Sengupta, Washington, D.C., June 28, 1985.

8. Most close observers of Indian economic policy agree with this conclusion. See, for example, the editorial in *Economic and Political Weekly*, Dec. 1, 1984. Also confirming my impression were discussions with T. N. Ninan, former senior editor (now executive editor), *India Today* (New Delhi), Dec. 11, 1985, and with N. S. Jagannathan, editor, *Financial Express* (New Delhi), Dec. 14, 1985.

9. Jim Manor (1988) emphasizes this as a cause of the more "communal" Indira Gandhi of the 1980s.

10. Since many of these reports are not public documents, complete citations cannot be provided. Their contents are generally made known via newspapers. Four of the important relevant documents of the last decade were the reports of the Alexander Commission, the Dagli Commission, the Arjun Sengupta Commission, and the L. K. Jha Commission.

11. An interesting essay that discusses these issues in detail is Rubin 1985.

12. Interview with L. K. Jha, New Delhi, Dec. 16, 1985.

13. Interview with Arjun Sengupta, Washington, D.C., June 28, 1985, and with L. K. Jha, New Delhi, Dec. 16, 1985.

14. For a detailed discussion of how leaders in India get into power, see Hart 1988.

15. I am indebted to John P. Lewis for bringing this point to my attention.

16. It is reported that a senior World Bank official flew into India at this time and advised the new government to dismantle the structures of economic control "all at once." It is not clear as to how many of the advisors of the Indian government with World Bank connections were sympathetic to this approach. L. K. Jha in an interview (New Delhi, Dec. 16, 1985) suggested that he reacted "very negatively to such suggestions." Given the opposition that even piecemeal liberalization has provoked within India, one wonders about the political sensibilities of both those in power and those who provide "rational" economic advice around the globe. Do ends justify all means? Does it matter whether the political system can withstand such sharp economic changes or not? Or is it that, given "rational economic policies," and thus a "rationalized economy," all else will work itself out in good time? More sober observers, even economists who favor liberalization of the Indian economy, have openly worried about the capacity of Rajiv Gandhi and his advisors to appreciate the serious political obstacles that such an effort will create. For an extremely well-balanced and sensible essay along these lines, see Datta Chaudhry 1985. Other economists like Jagdish Bhagwati have also, in a more general context, recognized these obstacles; see Bhagwati 1986.

17. For a summary and a discussion of the 1985–86 budget, see *Times of India*, Mar. 21, 1985.

18. These events received considerable attention in the press. For example, see *Times of India*, May 7, 1985; *Statesman*, May 7 and 9, 1985; and *Telegraph*, May 14, 1985. 19. Interview with D. H. Pi Panandiker, secretary general, Fed-

eration of Indian Chambers of Commerce and Industry, New Delhi, Dec. 12, 1985.

20. See *Times of India*, May 7, 1985. Also see All India National Congress (I), *Economic Resolution*, adopted by the All India Congress (I) Committee, New Delhi, May 6, 1985.

21. The Abid Hussain report was released in mid-November 1985. For an abbreviated discussion, see *Economic Times*, Nov. 18, 1985. The report itself is now a public document; see India, Commerce, 1985.

22. Interview with Raja Chelliah, member of the Planning Commission, New Delhi, Dec. 13, 1985.

23. For reasons of space, I have eliminated from this chapter detailed discussion of the groups that supported or opposed the new policies. See Kohli 1989: 316–322.

References

Ahluwalia, I. J. 1985. *Industrial Growth in India: Stagnation Since the Mid-Sixties.* New Delhi: Oxford University Press.

Bardhan, P. 1984. *The Political Economy of Development in India.* Oxford: Basil Blackwell.

Bhagwati, J. 1986. "Rethinking Trade Strategy." In *Development Strategies Reconsidered,* ed. John P. Lewis and Valeriana Kallab. New Brunswick, N.J.: Transaction.

Bhagwati, J., and T. N. Srinivasan. 1975. *Foreign Trade Regimes and Economic Development: India.* New York: Columbia University Press.

Bienen, H. S., and M. Gersovitz. 1985. "Economic Stabilization, Conditionality and Political Stability." *International Organization* 39, no. 4: 729–754.

Cardoso, F. 1973. "Associated-Dependent Development: Theoretical and Practical Implications." In *Authoritarian Brazil,* ed. Alfred Stepan. New Haven: Yale University Press.

Chakravarty, S. 1984. "India's Development Strategy for the 1980s." *Economic and Political Weekly,* May 26.

Collier, D., ed. 1979. *The New Authoritarianism in Latin America.* Princeton: Princeton University Press.

Datta, B. 1985. "The Central Budget and The New Economic Policy." *Economic and Political Weekly,* April 10, pp. 693–698.

Datta Chaudhury, M. 1985. "The New Policy." Seminar, December, pp. 18–22.

Deyo, F. C., ed. 1987. *The Political Economy of the New Asian Industrialism.* Ithaca, N.Y.: Cornell University Press.

Evans, P. 1979. *Dependent Development: The Alliance of Multinational, State, and Local Capital in Brazil.* Princeton: Princeton University Press.

Haggard, S. 1985. "The Politics of Adjustment: Lessons from the IMF's Extended Fund Facility." *International Organization* 38 (Summer): 503–534.

Hart, H. 1988. "Political Leadership in India: Dimensions and Limits." In *India's Democracy: An Analysis of Changing State-Society Reltions*, ed. Atul Kohli. Princeton: Princeton University Press.

India, Ministry of Commerce. 1985. *Report of the Committee on Trade Policies.* New Delhi. December.

Jha, L. K. 1986. "In Search of a New Economic Order." *The Illustrated Weekly of India*, April 6, pp. 20–23.

Jha, P. S. 1982. "The End of the Tunnel: Return to Sanity in Economic Policy," *Times of India*, April 9.

———. 1984. "Seventh Plan Perspectives: A New Direction for Industry." *Times of India*, August 13.

———. 1987. "Economic Expansion Ensnared in Red Tape." *India Abroad*, December 11.

Jones, L. P., and I. Sakong. 1980. *Government, Business and Entrepreneurship in Economic Development: The Korean Case.* Cambridge, Mass.: Harvard University Press.

Kochanek, S. A. 1974. *Business and Politics in India.* Berkeley: University of California Press.

———. (1986), "Regulation and Liberalization Theology in India." *Asian Survey* 26, no. 12: 1284–1308.

Kohli, A. 1987. *The State and Poverty in India: The Politics of Reform.* Cambridge University Press.

———. 1989. "Politics of Economic Liberalization in India." *World Development* 17, no. 3: 305–328.

Manor, J. 1988. "Parties and the Party System." In *India's Democracy: An Analysis of Changing State-Society Relations*, ed. Atul Kohli. Princeton: Princeton University Press.

Nelson, J. 1984. "The Politics of Stabilization." In *Adjustment Crisis in the Third World*, ed. Richard E. Feinberg and Vallerina Kallab. New Brunswick, N.J.: Transaction.

O'Donnell, G. 1973. *Modernization and Bureaucratic Authoritarianism: Studies in South American Politics.* Berkeley: University of California Press.

Paranjape, H. K. 1985. "New Lamps for Old! A Critique of the New Economic Policy." *Economic and Political Weekly*, September 4, pp. 1513–1522.

Patnaik, P. 1986. "New Turn in Economic Policy: Context and Prospects." *Economic and Political Weekly*, June 7, pp. 1014–1019.

Raj, K. N. 1985. "New Economic Policy." *Mainstream*, December 14 and 21.

Rubin, B. R. 1985. "Economic Liberalization and the Indian State." *Third World Quarterly* 7, no. 4: 942–957.

Skidmore, T. 1973. "Politics and Economic Policy Making in Authoritarian Brazil, 1937–1971." In *Authoritarian Brazil*, ed. Alfred Stepan. New Haven: Yale University Press.

Srinivasan, T. N., and N.S.L. Narayana. 1977. "Economic Performance Since the Third Plan and Its Implications for Policy." *Economic and Political Weekly*, annual number, February.

Stepan, A. 1973. *Authoritarian Brazil*. New Haven: Yale University Press.

Varshney, A. 1984. "Political Economy of Slow Economic Growth in India." *Economic and Political Weekly*, September 1, pp. 1511–1517.